Henry Grimes recorded .... some of the most imaginative American jazz musicians including Sonny Rollins, Cecil Taylor, and Albert Ayler. This book examines his long and eventful musical career, recounting his continuously creative artistic life as musician and poet.

Henry Grimes and Barbara Frenz, New York City, December 2009
(© Thomas Rösch).

Barbara Ina Frenz, born in 1961 in Zurich, Switzerland, is a German historian, author and copywriter living in Frankfurt am Main. Frenz grew up in a jazz-loving family, studied history, philosophy, and art history in Frankfurt, and gained her PhD with a study on equality in the Middle Ages. She was a research associate at the Universities of Frankfurt and Würzburg from 1989 to '99, undertaking historical studies sponsored by various foundations. Since 2001, after further education in creative writing, she has worked as a concept developer and copywriter in advertising and as a writer of poetry, texts in history and culture, and contributions to the German jazz magazine *Jazz Podium*.

In the last decade, she has focused her studies on the history of jazz music and the life journeys of jazz musicians. She became very interested in Henry Grimes through listening to live recordings of him playing in the late 1950s and early '60s, and started researching this biography.

Translated from German by J. Bradford Robinson, an American musicologist whose research focuses on the music of the Weimar Republic. Among his publications are translations of two books by the German historian Carl Dahlhaus and a biography of Mozart by Georg Knepler. He served as a principal adviser on jazz for *The New Grove Dictionary of American Music* (1986), to which he also contributed many jazz articles.

MUSIC TO SILENCE

TO MUSIC

A BIOGRAPHY OF

HENRY GRIMES

Barbara Frenz

northway publications

Published in 2015.
Northway Publications
39 Tytherton Road, London N19 4PZ, UK.
www.northwaybooks.com

Published in the United States in 2015 by
Northway / Parkwest, Miami, Florida, 33231
Library of Congress Control Number: 2015940220

Edited by Ann Cotterrell, Northway Publications.

The publishers acknowledge with thanks the kind permission of copyright owners to reprint the photographs used in this book. Permissions
have been sought in all cases where the identity of the copyright
holders is known.

Front cover photo of Henry Grimes in Harlem, New York City, 2014,
by Hollis King, © Hollis King.

Cover design by Adam Yeldham of Raven Design.

ISBN 978 0992822279

Reprinted 2020, 2022

Printed and bound in Great Britain by TJ Books Limited, Padstow,
PL28 8RW

Contents

Henry Grimes and Sonny Rollins backstage after Sonny's concert at the Tarrytown Music Hall, Tarrytown, NY, December 6, 2009 (© www.johnabbottphoto.com).

Foreword

When I first met the subject of this book, I was working with the Max Roach–Clifford Brown band. We were playing an engagement in Philadelphia, Pennsylvania – a great music town that harbored world-class players like Coltrane, the Heath Brothers, Benny Golson, Sun Ra, McCoy Tyner, Jimmy Garrison, Rashied Ali, Lee Morgan, Bobby Timmons, John Gilmore, Archie Shepp, Ted Curson, Reggie Workman, Hank Mobley, and Kenny Barron, among many others.

Our band often had open stage sets in which musicians were invited up to play. On one such night, an intense young bassist took his turn. I was struck by his determined manner of playing. He seemed to hear and immediately respond to his muse in an unbroken circuit between muse and man. His style could be described as both traditional and beyond tradition – at the same time.

It was always inspiring playing with Henry. I felt that I could play anything with him and it would work and fit. We became friends and, sometime later, when I started my own group, I invited him to play with me. The years I worked with Henry were some of the most exhilarating of my musical life. We worked in small groups, often piano-less, with such people as Billy Higgins and Don Cherry and with pianist Paul Bley and drummer Roy McCurdy. Henry was also on my *Big Brass* album, arranged by Ernie Wilkins, and on my *Sonny Meets Hawk* album, with the illustrious Coleman Hawkins.

Henry's music, the music of the man, has been such an immense gift to me in my own career. It's something for which I will always be grateful.

Put another way, I was celestially blessed when I heard and met Mr. Grimes that night in Philadelphia.

Sonny Rollins
January 2015

Introduction

Some readers of this book will probably already be familiar with the outline of Henry Grimes' life. His moving story has been recounted again and again in music journals and arts pages since 2003.[1] In the meantime, this 'lost and found' narrative has become a bit tired. The purpose of this biography is not only to revitalize that narrative, but also to shed greater light on Henry Grimes' productivity and his unceasing engagement with art, extending beyond music. The main focus is on his evolution as a seminal jazz musician from the late 1950s to the present day. The initial inspiration for the book came from his powerful and imaginative playing on live recordings from his 1963 European tour with the Sonny Rollins Quartet.

The book documents Henry Grimes' life-path as a musician, which he continued to be, in a different way, even during his more than three decades in downtown Los Angeles when he didn't own a bass and was unable to play music professionally for even a single day. Instead, he worked hard at bone-grinding jobs until well beyond retirement age while teaching himself literature and writing poetry.[2] This biography describes his artistic career, using a wide range of sources. It depicts him as a constantly changing historical figure who lives – and has to live – in a society built on social exclusion and primarily aligned with material gain.

Musicological discussions are avoided unless they come from Grimes himself or from others who chose this way to speak of him or the music of which he is an important part. In a few passages, I convey my own personal impressions of his bass and violin playing. These impressions are deliberately subjective and follow no musicological criteria. To the present day, Henry Grimes' playing of the bass, and, since 2005, the violin, has held me spellbound, whether recorded or in live appearances. Because of my enthusiasm for his art of improvisation, I was not always able to maintain the cool detachment expected of a biographer.

Documents on Henry Grimes are numerous, widely dispersed, and, for the early years, mostly random. Interviews were a primary source for this biography. I conducted several long interviews with

xii MUSIC TO SILENCE TO MUSIC

Grimes in New York City in 2006–07 and 2009–10. I was also able to talk at length with Sonny Rollins and Andrew Cyrille about their close collaborations with him. Further, I conducted a three-hour interview with the drummer Clarence Becton, who toured with Grimes in 1967 and drove with him to the West Coast.[3] Finally, I analyzed other people's interviews with Grimes or musicians who worked with him. In this way I was able to add ever-new details from his life, and occasionally to discover contradictory facts or memories.

The remarkable thing about Henry Grimes' memories is that primarily they have to do with music. By his own admission, he can recall some recording sessions note for note, while remembering nothing at all about their external circumstances. Grimes is not a storyteller (to the chagrin of many a journalist). When he does speak, he prefers to present thoughts on music, other art forms, or philosophy, usually discreetly sidestepping conversations about people and events, neither of which he describes anecdotally.

This biography is not constructed continuously in linear fashion. Occasionally it departs from chronological order, especially in the chapter on Henry Grimes' musical activities between 1960 and 1966. Here I chose thematic points of emphasis, which resulted in small chronological leaps forwards and backwards. The first chapter, too, represents a leap in time. It leads directly to Grimes' violin playing and so to his musical beginnings, starting with the violin in 1947. A key aesthetic experience that drew him ineluctably into the world of music at about the age of twelve places the focus on Grimes' own perspective. The chronological depiction begins largely in chapter 2, with an important role being given to Henry Grimes' vantage point and those of his musical companions. Their accounts and thoughts form the lifeblood of the biography.

The book was written in German and completed by December 2012. After that time there followed two intense working phases in 2013 and 2014–15: that of the English translation and that of editing. Only in exceptional cases were later events or publications by or about Henry Grimes taken into account. It is hoped that any important documents or writings that could not be included in the biography will stimulate further studies.

At this point I wish to express my gratitude to all those who so greatly contributed to the success of the book. Henry Grimes deserves my thanks for his magnificent concerts, which I have been able to experience in person, and for the blend of memories and reflections that he shared with me in many hours of conversation. His sublime humor gave these interviews an additional surprise touch. I thank Margaret Davis Grimes for her many important suggestions on the subject and for her critical reading of the manuscript, which she carried out with great care and acumen. I thank both of them for their generous hospitality on my many research trips to New York, during which we became friends. I thank the tenor giant and master improviser Sonny Rollins, whose wonderful friendship I have experienced since about 2005 and who wrote the foreword to this book, for his exceptional spirit and generosity. In a long telephone interview, he spoke vividly and in great depth about his work with Henry Grimes in 1959 and 1963, contributing key ideas on Henry's musical personality. I also thank the outstanding drummer and percussionist Andrew Cyrille, whom I hold in high esteem as well, for his remarkable generosity: in two interviews, he shared his detailed memories of the time he and Henry spent with Cecil Taylor and also shared his refreshingly demystifying views on Grimes' life after 1967. In addition I wish to thank the far too little-known drummer Clarence Becton for his warmhearted hospitality and great willingness to communicate: during my visit to his Amsterdam apartment, he spoke for a good three hours in great detail about his 1967 tour with Henry Grimes in Jon Hendricks' band and gave me important thoughts on Henry and his music.

Equally deserving of thanks is the Darmstadt Jazz Institute in Germany, whose staff members always lent a willing ear to my concerns during many research visits and generously offered their help. I'm especially grateful to Dr. Wolfram Knauer, the head of the Institute, for his sound and friendly advice. Dr. Patrick Simek earned my cordial thanks for critically reading large sections of the book and offering valuable suggestions. I also thank Joe Dimech for helping out with some extra research on press mentions of Henry Grimes – besides his dissertation on bassist Steve Davis, and I thank master designer Hollis King for his artistic spirit that is present in the cover photo he made of Henry, as well as Selcuk Kunt for his advice as a designer. Dr. J. Bradford Robinson, who translated the text from German into idiomatic American English, was an invariably helpful collaborator. I am equally grateful to Ann Cotterrell of Northway Books for incorporating the Henry Grimes biography in their list, and for her great cooperation. Finally, I wish to thank my husband, Dr. Thomas Rösch, for his courage, patience, and ongoing dialogue on the subject.

One thought was constantly on my mind while working on this book, and was further nourished by the reflections that Henry Grimes formulated in his interviews: words on music and musicians can generate a spark; however, it will only catch fire beyond the words themselves in direct contact with the music, thereby becoming an aesthetic experience that opens the mind and makes it amenable to insight.

Barbara Frenz
summer 2015

1

'I just wanted to play the violin, and it happened'

Henry Grimes' Solo, an album released in 2009,[1] has its origins in the historic depths of African-American and European music, as well as in the past and present personal experience of the performer. Henry Grimes' violin playing, captured on several recent albums,[2] is music from life. It holds the listener spellbound with its orchestral wealth of colors, its idiomatic swing, its delicate, baroque fissures, its propulsive quest and its urgency. It liberates the mind.

It must have been around 1948. Henry Grimes was about twelve years old and sat in the audience during the high school graduation ceremony of his sister Yvonne, about six years his senior. The girls' school orchestra played, and Henry was overwhelmed by their violin playing. After that, he wanted nothing more badly than to play the instrument himself. He probably expressed his wish clearly at home – soon the search began for a nearby violin teacher. Grimes still recalls it today. 'It was like music was mine,' he told Marc Medwin in a 2010 interview about his earliest musical experiences. 'It was all about invention for me.'[3] His mother especially supported his musical development, he recalls, mentioning the high costs it must have involved.[4] Carl Whitman – that was the name of his first violin teacher – came to his home and brought him a 'banged-up fiddle', the only one he owned until 2004. He took lessons from Whitman until he was about sixteen, when he switched to a Hungarian teacher. In junior high school he only played the violin, 'but it wasn't jazz, it was classical.'[5] It was not until 1952, at the Juilliard School in New York, that he turned completely to the double bass. There, too, he dealt exclusively with European music from the classical-romantic period and earlier.[6]

Once he was asked whether the violin was ultimately not his instrument after all. Probably pressured by his lack of an instrument at the time, he replied: 'I liked it, but there just was something that I didn't like about it. Maybe it is just that I am not a violin player. I'm a bass player, so that must be what it is.'[7] When he enrolled at Juilliard, he took up bass and stopped playing the violin. In 2004 the violin came back to him – his wife presented him with one for his sixty-ninth birthday[8] – 'and now I'm playing free-style violin.'[9] Asked how he came to music at all, he answered promptly: 'Well, I just wanted to play the violin first and it happened. I played the violin from elementary school through high school. By the time I went through high school I had added about four more instruments to that, which was part of the music training in Philadelphia.'[10]

That training was not in jazz,[11] but in European music in the broadest sense. In those days, jazz music was not an established part of a general education, neither at public schools nor at conservatories. It was learned and mastered outside educational institutions, where white Eurocentric value systems prevailed. The learner chose her or his musical mentors right off the street, so to speak. Max Roach, eleven years older than Henry Grimes, put it this way for his generation: 'We weren't allowed to go to schools and conservatories, so we had to found our own conservatory. We called it the "conservatory of the street". Minton's Playhouse, bars, street corners: those were the places where we learned. Same with black theaters, where we heard Duke Ellington's music and took recordings home to analyze them. We learned from that, too.'[12] Amiri Baraka put it like this: 'Jazz is essentially a city music, a music sophisticated in its inclusion of broad urban influences that are international in depth. It is populist in its open expression of mass language and progressive by that fact and its openness. It could not begin in the conservatories and concert halls. It was banned from these. It was the music of the slaves, newly "freed" and newly re-enslaved under different terminology.'[13] By the time Grimes started to study music, African-Americans were allowed to attend conservatories, even though neither there nor in high schools were the music and culture of jazz on the curriculum.

Playing the violin was already so important to young Henry that he neglected his social contacts. 'Playing the violin kept me away from cliques. From a certain point I moved more and more toward music while the others got together in cliques.'[4] The trumpeter Wilmer Wise, himself from Philadelphia, remembered Henry Grimes as a violin player: 'The first band I played in was a band called the Barsity Boys, like "varsity" but spelled with a B – why? I don't know.... a fellow named Edward Gregg played on my trumpet case, Henry, I think played the violin. He was a violinist when I first met him. And Leon (Henry's twin brother) played clarinet. And it must have been a godawful sounding group.'[15] The music of the Barsity Boys survives only in these words, so there is no way to check this derogatory verdict. But even then Henry must have stood out with his above-average musical abilities, for he began to play violin in the school orchestra while still at Barrett Junior High School in South Philadelphia. He also played in bands outside the school. It was around this time that he met Albert 'Tootie' Heath, Bobby Timmons, and Ted Curson – they all attended the same school and would soon make names for themselves on drums, piano, and trumpet, respectively.[16]

Asked in 2003 what actually attracted him to music, Grimes answered that for him music is 'just the idea of what makes you want to play. You know, what you feel.... And music is a good association. To feel music going through you and you going through it [...]. You know, I can't explain it but music takes you through a whole lotta things through life, understanding it. That's what I felt about it, and it became my life. A lot of natural fires were happening along with it, and I stayed with it.'[17]

Henry stayed with it, though he didn't even hold an instrument in his hands from roughly 1969 to December 16, 2002. In his long years of isolation, music was both there and not there: 'I wasn't thinking about music at all. I was thinking about it, but not in a sense of creating some new music. So I'd say about thirty years I've been under that kind of a cloud.'[18]

Behind Grimes' 'reticence' and 'introversion',[19] ('a very quiet person. You would have to engage him in conversation'),[20] is a constant and complex interaction with music and art. From 1969, when he no longer owned an instrument, he began to teach himself the history and theory of literature and to write lyric poetry and prose reflections.[21] Even today, besides playing bass and violin, he continues to write poetry.

2

Early Years in Philadelphia (1935–56)

Swing, Bebop, and a Precarious Existence – Family Life

Henry Alonzo Grimes was born on November 3, 1935, in
Philadelphia, at that time a bustling metropolis with an outstanding
musical community that would also give rise to Philly Joe Jones,
Jimmy Garrison,[1] the brothers Jimmy and Albert 'Tootie' Heath,
Lee Morgan, Archie Shepp,[2] McCoy Tyner and Reggie Workman.
John Coltrane moved there with his mother at the age of seventeen
and began his professional career, at first on the alto saxophone.[3]
Henry Grimes grew up in the southern part of the city, in the block
bounded by 17th and Fitzwater, Christian and Carpenter Streets.
South Philadelphia was 'an integrated environment of Italians,
Blacks, and Jews'.[4] It was 'the original Negro settlement, but the
flux had been to the north'.[5] Henry describes this working-class district as 'semi-rough',[6] and recalls that his family moved several
times in South Philadelphia. First they lived in a house that he
remembers loving, and that had a piano. He was seven or eight at
the time and played on this piano. 'I'd say I played fluently; others
would say I did free improvisation.'[7] The period, while the young
Henry Grimes was taking a serious musical interest, was a time of
turmoil in jazz music. There were still many swing bands organized
in segregated unions for black and white musicians, with bebop
beginning to draw growing numbers of excited listeners.[8]

At some point the house that the Grimes family lived in became
too expensive, and they moved to an apartment with an adjoining
church office. As the new apartment was much smaller than the
house, some pieces of furniture had to be left behind, presumably
including the piano, for Grimes remembers it only in connection
with the house. Ever since his childhood, he had experienced and
learned how to do without familiar objects from one day to the

next, and to make ends meet with very few resources. His early familiarization with hardship as a little boy probably helped him to become resilient and immune to frustration in his later years in Los Angeles.

In South Philadelphia, Grimes first attended Arthur Elementary School at the corner of Catharine and South 20th Street. He then went to Barrett Junior High School on the corner of 16th and Wharton Street, and finally Mastbaum Technical High School in the northern part of the city, a sort of 'elite training academy' for modern jazz music. There will be more to say about this school later.[9]

Henry's parents both had musical backgrounds and played instruments before their three children were born. His mother, Georgia Elzie Grimes, played the piano, and his father, Leon James Grimes Sr., whose family came from Florida,[10] played the trumpet. Grimes surmises that both probably worked as professional musicians before stopping at some point. 'They played a sort of gospel music.'[11] They never explained their reasons for abandoning music.[12] Whatever the case, when Henry was a child, they earned their living by working at Horn & Hardart, a coin-operated chain restaurant somewhere between 9th and 15th Street. 'It's the place you put a coin in and then you get out a piece of pie or whatever you want. They did not both work in the same one: my mother worked in one, my father worked in another one.'[13] His father was a cook, his mother a cleaner.[14] It would have been nearly impossible for them as musicians to feed a family of five. Nevertheless, or perhaps for this very reason, music played an important role in the Grimes household. Henry recalls his parents listening with great pleasure to big band programs on radio: Tommy Dorsey, Jimmy Dorsey, Stan Kenton. At first the above-mentioned piano was still in their home. Besides Henry, it was also played by the then very young Hasaan Ibn Ali, later known as 'The Legendary Hasaan' who went from house to house, playing for those who had a piano. On June 1, 2003, Grimes dedicated a bass solo to him at the Henry Grimes Festival sponsored by radio station WKCR.[15]

The Grimes household also had something very special: a record player. It belonged to Henry's sister Yvonne, and it was mainly she, rather than their parents (who probably lacked the time), who used it. A record player in a black working-class family of the 1940s and 1950s was not to be taken for granted, and people from the neighborhood regularly met at the Grimes' home to listen to records. The trumpeter Wilmer Wise especially recalls the bebop recordings he heard there.[16] Yvonne Grimes, a music lover who later became an office worker,[17] favored Billie Holiday; she also played Charlie Parker, Dizzy Gillespie, and Clifford Brown. Grimes remembers hearing Coleman Hawkins' famous 1939 version of 'Body and Soul' on it and, as a child, he loved the swing music of Jimmy and Tommy Dorsey.[18] When he went to high school, he heard 'jazz on the radio every day, all kinds of style that existed then'.[19] He especially liked Django Reinhardt, to whom he dedicated a composition on his album *The Call* in 1965. 'Later on, it was Charlie Parker, Miles Davis, and all the quality musicians of those schools. I knew them for years and just trying to contemplate what they were playing just led me where I am.'[20]

There was another musician in Henry's family besides himself: his twin brother Leon. Leon played clarinet and tenor saxophone from his youth. 'He got a saxophone, played with a lot of musicians,' Grimes remembers, 'but he stopped that.'[21] Andrew Cyrille commented in an interview: 'He [Henry] had a brother also. He played saxophone. Both of them learned.'[22] The poet, playwright, essayist, and activist Amiri Baraka, still known as LeRoi Jones at the time, wrote in 1965: 'He [Archie Shepp] had known a tenor player named Lee Grimes in Philadelphia, and Grimes, an extraordinary tenorist, according to Shepp, was influenced by 'Trane when it wasn't fashionable. "Lee was the first person I heard playing harmonics. Because I was raving about Lee, someone said I ought to hear Coltrane."'[23] It is not unlikely that Archie Shepp, when asked about the Philly scene, mentioned Leon Grimes, remembering his first name incorrectly as 'Lee' (he also spoke of Lee Morgan in the same interview). Unfortunately it is not known whether Leon Grimes and John Coltrane ever met. Whatever the case, Leon's musical career was already over by the time of Archie Shepp's interview. He 'had problems with other individuals', as his twin brother puts it. 'Not so much of conflicts, but not favoring ... relationships with people.'[24] The last time Henry Grimes saw his twin brother was, he says, in 1955, when they were about nineteen. He knows nothing about his later life.

2037-2043 [East] Clearfield Street, back view of Mastbaum Technical High School in North Philadelphia, 1951. Grimes graduated from Mastbaum in 1952 (photo courtesy of PhillyHistory.org, a project of the Philadelphia Department of Records).

Five Instruments and a Comic Strip – Mastbaum Technical High School (1949–1952)

After finishing junior high, Grimes' twin brother Leon and trumpeter Wilmer Wise went to Bok Technical High School in South Philadelphia, while Henry, Ted Curson, Lee Morgan, and Archie Shepp went to Mastbaum Technical High School at the corner of Frankford and East Allegheny Avenue in the north-east part of the city.[25] At that time, Mastbaum Tech, like Cass Tech in Detroit and DuSable in Chicago, was a genuine breeding ground for future greats of jazz music, even if its curriculum only offered classical music:[26] 'I went to a public high school called a trade school, where I received an excellent musical education, while other students there were taught to be auto mechanics or secretaries. The music students had to master five instruments in order to graduate.'[27]

Archie Shepp elaborates: '[...] there were some guys playing at the high school I went to. [...] Mastbaum was the school – though ...that's where there were a whole lot of cats playing...that's north

Philly. Most of the cats lived further south in north Philly. Everybody was trying to get that Early Jazz Messenger sound then. Lee Morgan and an alto player named Kenny Rogers really got me started playing jazz.'[28] Today Mastbaum Technical High School, judging from its home page, no longer seems to appreciate its musical tradition.[29]

Grimes' fellow high-school student, trumpeter Ted Curson, remembers – as per Michael Fitzgerald's report – that Henry had artistic skills that went far beyond music and made him a popular figure at school. 'He wasn't a really talkative guy. I don't remember him maybe saying a hundred words. But even through school, he did something that no one else did. He had a comic strip. He was a great artist and had a good sense of humor. He had all of us in this comic strip. And we'd be waiting for the end of the week for it to come out. He had us like hanging by our fingernails waiting to see what he was.... Henry definitely had this comic strip all through Mastbaum and it was wild! A lot of stuff you agreed with, a lot of this stuff made you angry. But that's the way it was! He was the only one I knew that had something like that. He'd draw the pictures of you and put all the text in and it would be passed all around school.'[30] Grimes himself refers to these artistic activities as 'sporadic'. Unfortunately his comics are no longer extant. Most of them, he says, were like film scripts. He often watched horror movies and then put the people he knew in his comics, presenting one of his teachers as Dracula. He remembers doing these things for fun, simply setting out to write and draw as if he were improvising music. The name of his high school comic was 'Son of Alf Alfa', probably taken from the 1930s cartoon figure Farmer Alfalfa (also known as Al Falfa). Later he named a piece on his album *The Call* after this high school comic.[31]

In Grimes' day, the curriculum at Mastbaum High was roughly at the level of college programs, and thus very demanding. The students received ear training and lessons in harmony, voice, and orchestration. '[...] in High School I started playing bass. It was a vocational type of school and you had to take up about 5 instruments. I played drums, English horn, tuba and bass'[32] – plus the violin.[33] 'It was a spectacular education, really deep into mystical elements of music.'[34] The bass quickly became his instrument of choice. In no time at all Grimes was a first-class bass player and was summoned to the city orchestra to play difficult symphonic music.[35] Besides his experience with rhythm and blues bands, it was probably his steady orchestral training from high school that gave rise to the unusually 'heavy bass sound' and orchestral style that many fellow musicians admire in his music.[36]

'My contact to music was very alive [...] I learned everything to get into a professional life [...] Before my professional playing [...] I would be studying a lot of professional standpoints in High School.'[37] When he left school he knew he 'wanted to be a bass player.'[38] Around 1953 he started playing in Philadelphia. 'I started thinking about how to make money. I figured out that playing the bass was the best [...]. Somebody would call me up to work with him in a band and make some money.' He added that his years at Juilliard from 1952 were especially important for attaining the necessary self-confidence on the bass.[39]

'Philly Jazz'

'Philly, at that period, was a bastion for the music.'[40] Thus Fred Jung, speaking to Henry Grimes in 2003. Grimes himself sees the Philadelphia of the 1940s and 1950s mainly as a good breeding ground for aspiring musicians, and less as a hub of musical activity where one could earn good money as a freely evolving musician. Of course, he adds, big names such as John Coltrane, Jimmy Garrison, Miles Davis, and Charlie Parker moved or played there and were familiar with the city.[41] 'Philadelphia had good bands, good groups, hard-working, gifted musicians,' he remembers. 'I didn't get to work with all of them, but I did get some good training and inspiration from the musicians all around me.'[42]

'Philly Jazz' unquestionably had a very strong attraction in the early 1950s when Grimes was a teenager and young man. There were many jazz clubs in the city: Pep's, the Showboat (where Grimes first met Sonny Rollins), the Blue Note (corner of 15th and Ridge), the Oasis, the Aqua Lounge in the western part of the city, and other social clubs and bars that offered live music. The club owners and managers, Reggie Workman recalls, were so closely involved with the music that they allowed underage musicians to hold jam sessions and play till the early hours of the morning, although they were not allowed to be where alcohol was served.[43] Wilmer Wise, too, had a lively, almost idyllic inner picture of the Philly scene: 'I remember churches and bars, all having a good time. Philly was a safe place, no drugs.' Wise played there with Ted Curson, Don Cherry, and Lee Morgan, 'who was a cocky guy from the North Side. He was classically trained also. When he was fourteen years old he cut up Chet Baker to pieces.'[44] Also Fred Miles shares vivid memories of the Philadelphia jazz scene: 'In the '50s Philadelphia still had many jazz rooms, but the accent was on out of town "name artists" often with set groups of their own. Much of our local talent concentrated their efforts on the swinging Tuesday night sessions at "Music City", a musical instrument store run by drummers Ellis Tollin and Bill Welch. These sessions did much to start young artists such as Sam Dockery, Billy Root, Lee Morgan, Ted Curson, Jimmy Garrison, Tuttie [sic] Heath, Henry Grimes, Bobby Timmons, Ruth Price, Curtis Porter and many others.'[45] People in the Philly scene also met privately to hear live music. One such place was bassist Steve Davis' house, where sessions regularly took place. Among the guests were Dizzy Gillespie, sometimes Charlie Parker, and the young Sonny Rollins. Davis' wife Khadija was herself a vocalist with many women friends who showed up at the sessions – John Coltrane met his first wife, Naima, at one of them.[46]

Thanks to his school education and his contacts with active musicians among his fellow students, Grimes became closely involved in Philadelphia's music life. 'Ted Curson, Bobby Timmons and other guys are just about my same age,' he recalled in a 2004 interview. 'We went to the same school, I mean to the same two schools. As I got older, I met guys like Lee Morgan, McCoy Tyner: we used to play around together, we would jam and experiment. Some guys were younger, some guys older but there was a strong relationship between the different generations. It was a very experimental thing, it's just the way it goes in the avant-garde.'[47] In a 2003 interview he stated that he and his brother had good contacts with Jimmy Garrison and Lee Morgan. The latter sometimes dropped by, and 'he and my brother would trade musical ideas and understandings.'[48]

Grimes' early jazz band activities in Philadelphia were also witnessed by people who played with him at the time, or heard him playing. One example is Lee Morgan, who at the age of fifteen (around 1953) formed a band with other teenagers to play in dance clubs. The changing membership included pianist Bobby Timmons, bassists Henry Grimes and Spanky DeBrest, and drummers Lex Humphries and Albert 'Tootie' Heath.[49] Archie Shepp remembers often being at a place called the Jazz Workshop around 1954, which belonged to a disc jockey. 'I used to go to after school [...] Lee [Morgan] frequented the place all the time. He and Kenny [alto player Kenny Rogers] were like local heroes, and this was about the time Lee was 14. He was a very young cat, but he was playing. Henry Grimes, Ted Curson and Bobby Timmons used to come in too. There was something like a rivalry between the north Philly and the south Philly musicians. Spanky DeBrest was from north Philly. It seemed like some very good bass players came out of south Philly, like Jimmy Garrison and Grimes.'[50]

The bassist's own memories, not only from this period, mainly involve the musical side of the jam sessions, concerts, and recording dates he took part in. Even some of the pieces he played stand out in his memory. The practical goings-on at these events are mostly forgotten; he was completely absorbed in the music. Asked in 2006 about playing with Sonny Rollins, he replied, 'There's a lot of things going back and forth there that I can't remember at all. But I know that, if I listen to something, it comes back, if I listen to a CD or something like that. I recognize the music. [...] I notice by the way you mention the music that it's all sort of together in an archived way. So that means, you know, the music is still alive and still accessible. That's the important thing.'[51] In a 2003 interview he said much the same about his solid musical memory: 'When they played my records back to me, I couldn't remember a single session, but I could remember the music note for note.'[52]

Compared to the surviving music, the events around the music are not so important to him. Henry Grimes is a musician who lives and breathes music. Except in the music he plays, this is nowhere more apparent than in his memories.

Commuter between Two Worlds – Studies at Juilliard (1952–54)

When Grimes was about seventeen he left Mastbaum Tech and enrolled at the Juilliard School in New York City. By that time he was exclusively a bass player and appeared in many rhythm and blues bands in and around Philadelphia. He also played in Boston, Cleveland, Rochester NY, and frequently at colleges and universities, including Pennsylvania State.[53] He toured with Willis 'Gator Tail' Jackson, 'Bull Moose' Jackson, 'Little' Willie John, and several other leading rhythm and blues and soul musicians of the era,[54] as well as with the Texas tenorman Arnett Cobb, who 'had a lot to do with not just playing rhythm and blues, but also teaching.'[55] Henry 'used to go on the road with all these bands. Playing Rock and Roll, you know, you have to play heavy. So they would always encourage me to have a heavy sound. I always did go for that tradition. That heavy bass sound.'[56] He compared the emergence of his characteristic sound at the time with trying to survive in the jungle. 'Guys like that, they show you something. These guys would complain, "I can't hear you! Play harder!" So, you're pulling the strings harder. [...] Then, I used to play with Buddy Rich. He played so loud and hard ... four beats on the bass drum ... it was like trying to survive in the jungle.'[57]

Alongside rhythm and blues, Grimes also moved in a wholly different parallel cosmos: European music of the classical-romantic period, or even earlier. His years of study at Juilliard remain firmly engraved in his memory. He auditioned and was accepted. 'They liked the way I played. A lot of young guys never had the kind of thing I had.'[58] To achieve this, 'one sort of started studying early at school. Well, some people didn't start studying early at school systems, you know; they started by knowing people like Percy Heath and others.'[59] But 'at that time there wasn't any jazz curriculum at Juilliard School, only classical music.'[60]

There were few African-American students at Juilliard.[61] For three years Grimes studied intensively at the renowned conservatory, then located in Manhattan's Morningside Heights, and thus bordering directly on Harlem. His studies included the basics of harmony and music theory, but also many hours in the orchestra.

He played for opera singers,[62] and for Fred Zimmermann, the principal double bass player in the New York Philharmonic.[63] 'At Juilliard I learned the necessary things that the artist must be. Juilliard deals with that kind of a way of life with music, art, dance, culture. I had a great teacher at Juilliard, Fred Zimmermann [...], and he took a special interest in me. He gave me private double bass lessons at his home that went beyond my training at the school.'[64] Grimes used to play with the opera orchestra, where he was the only bass player, and learned a lot about harmony and theory.[65] 'I played all types of music while I was there, even worked with students doing Gregorian chants and other types of religious music.'[66] It was also at Juilliard that Grimes developed his arco technique, which benefited his playing outside the conservatory. 'I usually played in piano-less combos with no chords in the background. That was a standard technique there.'[67] Shortly after his return to the music world in 2003, the *New York Times* wrote of him: 'He was known for his ability to alternate from long Eastern-sounding bowing to hard pizzicato plucking, all of which generated tremendous calluses on his hands.'[68]

While Grimes was at Juilliard, it was also possible to study English. 'That was great, but I used to dodge that kind of a thing. Now I sort of wish I haven't dodged it.'[69] The Juilliard years 'directed me towards the music that I wanted to play. I was able to incorporate a lot of things into my jazz playing because of that training.'[70]

Grimes left Juilliard without a degree. This resulted from both practical and musical issues: to attend the conservatory he had to commute daily between New York and Philadelphia, which brought him into financial and transportation difficulties: 'I was commuting between New York and Philadelphia every day. I just had to give that up.'[71] He also turned increasingly toward jazz music: 'I began to listen to a lot of players around New York and became more involved in that scene.'[72] He remembers an evening on which, still underage, he heard the Modern Jazz Quartet from the hallway of New York's Birdland. The music overwhelmed him.

While still commuting daily between Philadelphia and New York, he had already begun trying to play in clubs. Fluctuating between the academic music of the conservatory and jazz music, he must often have felt pulled to and fro as an artist. 'Actually I wanted that – to become a classical player. Then I became a jazz musician. When I started working with musicians like Anita O'Day or Gerry Mulligan – at that time I started working my way out of one era in music into another, and that was jazz, rhythm and blues before that. In the classical thing, music is more academic than anything else. I played it, but not on a professional level. It was interesting, but so was jazz.'[73]

Finally the desire and perhaps the financial need to play music won out, and Grimes dropped his studies at Juilliard: 'Henry attended Juilliard wholeheartedly from 1952 to 1954, but one night, too young for admission, he was standing in the hallway at Birdland in New York City listening to the Modern Jazz Quartet, and that music swept over him, and he knew he had to devote himself just to playing jazz music. He was still commuting from Philadelphia to New York each day to attend Juilliard, while also trying to play in clubs at night, and the urgency to play took precedence.'[74] During his conservatory years he had acquired comprehensive musical skills probably attained by few other Juilliard graduates, even those with degrees. To sum it up in the words of Andrew Cyrille: 'The academy is not the goal of a great performer. But it's good that we have them – Bach and Beethoven and these people. We get some information and learn from them.'[75]

3

First Big Successes – The Years from 1956 to 1959

First Meeting with Sonny Rollins (1955–56)

After leaving Juilliard in 1954, Grimes continued to work and tour with various rhythm and blues bands. He also visited New York's jazz clubs whenever possible, scouting for gigs and absorbing the music, especially from his idols Oscar Pettiford, Percy Heath, Ray Brown, Charles Mingus, and Richard Davis.[1] At some point in 1955–56, in Philadelphia, Grimes met Sonny Rollins, who in those years was often on tour with the Clifford Brown and Max Roach Quintet, perhaps the most renowned avant-garde group of its day.[2] 'I met Henry Grimes in Philadelphia. I was playing with Max Roach and Clifford Brown. And then I met him – he was in the audience. I found out that he was a bass player. When we came from the bandstand I was talking to him and to some other people. Somebody introduced me to him. I think he was well known with the people in Philadelphia.'[3]

Grimes clearly recalled the meeting in an interview from 2003: 'I remember playing with Max Roach, Clifford Brown, and Sonny Rollins at a matinee at the Showboat Lounge. I don't think they put me on their short list. They were testing me; I was very young, and then they showered me with compliments.'[4] Asked in 2006 about this first meeting, his memory of the jam session was more muted: 'I wasn't playing with him at that time. I talked to him in some way. He was interested in me as a musician. I played with Sonny in Max Roach's band – Max Roach and Clifford Brown. We jammed – at that time in Philadelphia.'[5] This meeting must have taken place before June 26, 1956, the day when trumpeter Clifford Brown, pianist Richie Powell, and Powell's wife Nancy died in a fatal car accident on their way to the Brown–Roach Quintet's next gig.[6]

More than two years would pass after that first meeting before the already famous Sonny Rollins hired Henry Grimes, now much sought-after in musical circles, to play bass in his trio at the Newport Jazz Festival in July 1958, with Roy Haynes on drums.[7]

Besides the outstanding Sonny Rollins, Grimes met another musician in the mid-1950s with whom he would later work closely: the clarinetist Perry Robinson.[8] He even shared an apartment with him for a while. In his biography, which appeared before Henry's re-emergence, Robinson acknowledges that 'Henry Grimes was a major influence and one of the most important people in my life. I met him in the mid-1950s right after high school; I used to go to jam sessions at lofts like Dave Amram's, then one night I went to a jam and there was Henry playing bass. [. . .] I started going over to his house every week; the two of us would play together [. . .].'[9]

First Jazz Concerts with Anita O'Day and Gerry Mulligan – Marriage – Relocating to New York (1956–57)

When he first came to New York, he immediately went right to the top and there was no gap.

Andrew Cyrille, 2008.[10]

Grimes' first booking in a jazz music context came in 1956–57 from the swing vocalist Anita O'Day. It was limited to tours with her band; there are no phonograph or broadcast recordings.[11] At one of her concerts, at the Red Hill Inn in Pennsauken, New Jersey, Gerry Mulligan was in the audience.[12] He was so impressed with the bassist's playing that he regularly hired him for his group: 'We worked all around New York.'[13] Grimes calls Mulligan his first truly important experience in jazz music: 'That was about the first jazz gig I had; before that I used to have rhythm 'n' blues gigs.'[14] Anita O'Day was important to him mainly 'because on that occasion I met Gerry Mulligan.'[15] 'Playing with him was very good, as with all or a lot of the musicians at that time. Very good player, but not too good for other reasons.' Still, because of Mulligan's constant problems with addiction, Henry 'might have to get away from him, because first thing he'd wanna do is come up and ask me to borrow some money. He's the leader, you know, and he's supposed to have it [Laughs]. I'm not supposed to give him money. And you know, that's the thing: A lot of the musicians are musically really tops.[16]

At some point, the logical consequence of Grimes' regular work with Mulligan around 1956–57 was to move to New York. At the age of twenty-one he married his first wife, Sarah, whom he had known from Philadelphia,[17] and moved to the musically promising city with her.[18] They rented an apartment at 62 West 91st Street. Finding the apartment was, Grimes says, 'a matter of money'; there were no other obstacles. Experiences on this point could obviously vary widely. Sonny Rollins composed his *Freedom Suite* in 1958 precisely because of the racism he experienced when searching for an apartment in Manhattan.[19] Grimes, however, had felt the racist 'ambiguity', the 'social *a priori*', more acutely in Philadelphia. It was also partly because of his exposure to prejudice that he left for New York, saying that he finds it 'more tolerant here'.[20] No less important was the fact that, as an aspiring jazz bassist, he had far more job opportunities there than in Philadelphia.

Grimes' wife Sarah took a training course in administration in New York and very quickly had problems with her husband's life-style. As a professional musician, he was very often out and about. Each time she had 'problems with being alone'.[21] Apparently music was not her world.[22] The couple separated in the early 1960s.[23]

Even if it meant the end of his first marriage, the master bassist's musical career catapulted upward beginning in 1957. He was regularly hired for top-flight bands, whether live or for recording sessions.[24] In early 1959, having just turned twenty-three, Henry Grimes went on his first European tour with Sonny Rollins. All in all, the extraordinary versatility and comprehensive skills that Grimes had acquired from 1947, first on the violin and then especially on the bass, now began to pay off. He himself attributes his meteoric career mainly to luck. In a 2003 interview with Marshall Marrotte, he argued that 'most of the work I got was due to luck, being in the right place at the right time.'[25] In a 2004 interview he claimed that '[a]t that time it wasn't hard [to find work] but I call it luck the way it went.'[26] These self-pronouncements pay no heed to his remarkable musicality, creativity, and energy on the bass.

However, his early successes derive from precisely these factors; luck was simply a catalyst. In this connection, he said that he let things happen as they would and always focused on the thing at hand rather than worrying about the next one.[27] This basic attitude goes some way to explain why, rather than firmly planning his musical activities, he tended to wait for others to hire him.

'Cool' Studio Debut – First Recordings as a Sideman (1957)

It's a strange thing. Like an effect of battle. Listening to these records I made with all these guys, I couldn't remember the place or how I got there playing. But I remember every note of the music. I mean every note.

Henry Grimes, 2003[28]

The first phonograph recording with Henry Grimes on bass dates from September 1957. It was headed by the saxophonist and painter Shafi Hadi,[29] who was then a permanent member of Charles Mingus' band.[30] Over the next three months Grimes played bass in five recordings for three other leading musicians: Lee Konitz, Tony Scott, and Gerry Mulligan. With Mulligan he recorded no fewer than three albums in December 1957, including *The Gerry Mulligan Songbook Vol. 1* and *Reunion*, which marked Mulligan's

musical reunion with Chet Baker after a five-year hiatus.[31] John A. Tynan, who reviewed *Songbook* for *DownBeat Magazine* in September 1958, gave it four out of five stars, the maximum awarded by the magazine, praising its 'perfect time' and 'consistently cooking' rhythm group as well as the 'powerful rhythm trio' pushing the saxo-

Reunion: Gerry Mulligan, with Chet Baker, Henry Grimes, and Dave Bailey, recorded December 3, 11 and 17, 1957 (insert of CD released 1988).

phone.[32] The critic also reviewed *Reunion* for the same issue of *DownBeat*, conceding only three stars and calling it a relatively unspectacular meeting of two stars. The rhythm section, especially Henry, came off more lightly: 'Bassist Grimes, also, gets off his most spirited solo, but it's Gerry's track.' Tynan praises 'the fine Grimes–Bailey rhythm team' while lamenting the absence of 'swinging cohesion' that he recalled from Mulligan's and Baker's 1952 recordings.[33] On 30 April 1958 the Gerry Mulligan Quartet, with Art Farmer (trumpet), Henry Grimes (bass), and Dave Bailey (drums), made a TV recording,[34] and three months later they appeared again at the Newport Jazz Festival.[35] There were no further recordings with Mulligan and his young bassist.

Grimes' intensive work with this highly regarded baritone saxophone player formed an important springboard for gigs with other leading figures of jazz music. This is especially and impressively evident in his many appearances at the 1958 Newport Jazz Festival. As will be shown later, the twenty-two-year-old Henry Grimes was perhaps the most sought-after bass player at this multi-day summer festival, where he was booked for six fundamentally different ensembles.

Henry's next important musical encounter after Mulligan was with a musician likewise assigned to the 'cool' style. Indeed, he was one of its founders: the renowned teacher, composer and pianist Lennie Tristano.[36] 'Right after Mulligan came Lennie Tristano's band, where I stayed for six months. Warne Marsh and Lee Konitz were often there.'[37] They were working at the Half Note and Grimes just got in there.[38] 'I learned a lot about harmony from Lennie. Several bass players worked with him, and it was my luck to be one of them. [...] I loved his way of stretching harmonies, beginning with very low notes and letting them end way up in the melodic form ... Very interesting.'[39] Grimes emphasizes Tristano's 'musical character': 'The stories about him are interesting up to a certain point but when you start playing with him like I did you'd understand that those stories are [...] second rate. What it really is all about is playing the music.'[40] The Half Note was also the scene of a recording (unfortunately with substandard equipment) that Grimes made as a member of the Lennie Tristano Quartet on August 9, 1958, with Warne Marsh on tenor and Paul Motian on drums, called *Continuity*.[41]

Toward the end of the 1950s Henry also played in the trio headed by the pianist and music professor Billy Taylor, who still had a lively recollection of his bassist's skills in 2005: 'Here's a guy who whenever he had an opportunity to really express something in the context of the trio… he did it. No trio that I had, before or after that, sounded like that.'[42] When Grimes learned about this high appreciation, he simply stated, 'I didn't think I was liked that much.'[43]

In April 1958 Grimes had also worked for a while in the Miles Davis Quintet. At that time it frequently played in Cleveland, with almost the same members who made the famous album *Kind of Blue* in 1959. Henry replaced Paul Chambers, whose arrival in Cleveland had been delayed: 'And then I played […] for four days with Miles […] together with Cannonball, Coltrane, Bill Evans, and Philly Joe.'[44] Asked about the occasion in 2006 for the eightieth birthday of the great trumpeter, Grimes reported: 'It was an inspiring and edifying feeling to play with Miles. […] He's one of the greatest musicians from the Charlie Parker connection, and the myth started even back then.'[45] Grimes remembers learning from Davis and from Coltrane: 'Miles was very able and really on top of you, but, I mean, it's a good thing. […] What you don't know about music at that age is a lot. You need to learn. A lot of times a musician like Miles Davis or Coltrane are taskmasters in the sense that the younger musicians might be doing wrong so they have to put them down firmly at times.'[46] Especially important for Grimes' development as a professional jazz bassist, besides the bookings with such leading figures as these, was the Newport Jazz Festival of 1958.

'that's what stands out in my mind' – Six Gigs at the Newport Jazz Festival (1958)

Before Grimes' reappearance, Ron Carter and John Goldsby had this to say of him in their *Jazz Bass Book*: 'Henry Grimes was one of the most brilliant young jazz players of the 60s – until he dropped out of the music scene in 1967 at age 31. […] A brilliant versatile player, Grimes could and would play with anyone, anytime. A measure of his versatility is the 1958 Newport Jazz Festival: Grimes

Henry Grimes with the Sonny Rollins Trio, Roy Haynes (drums), Newport Jazz Festival July 6, 1958 (© Burt Goldblatt Estate Archives/CTSIMAGES).

played with Benny Goodman's Orchestra, Lee Konitz, Sonny Rollins, and Thelonious Monk, all in the same week!'[47]

Scott Yanow was equally amazed that Grimes could play so outstandingly with such wide-ranging musicians at a single event.[48] Yet these laudatory writers present an incomplete list of the bassist's appearances at the festival: he also features on the bass in the bands of Gerry Mulligan[49] and Tony Scott.[50] Four of these six formations were either trios (Konitz, Monk, Rollins) or a piano-less quartet (Mulligan) that called for especially strong and inventive bass playing. Awareness of Grimes' skills in this respect must have spread through Newport like wildfire; his bass playing probably convinced bandleaders on the spot. The name of Henry Grimes does not, however, appear in the printed program of the 1958 Newport Festival,[51] suggesting that almost all his appearances were spur-of-the-moment decisions. Nor did he have a reputation in commercial musical circles, and he received less attention *per se* as a 'sideman'.

Grimes himself has vivid memories of his many Newport appearances in 1958: 'I was playing at the Newport Jazz Festival, that's what stands out in my mind. It was just like a job ... I preferred the small bands.'[52] All in all, he views his many Newport appearances – with his usual modesty – merely as a lucky coincidence. Asked about them by *DownBeat* journalist Michael Jackson in 2005, he replied that 'They didn't have enough bass players. I was there and they told me to stand by. [...] One thing led to another.'[53]

His first gig took place on Friday evening, 4th July, in Benny Goodman's big band, where, let it be noted, he was the only bassist.[54] It was Goodman's first time in Newport and he was the main feature of the evening, and consequently the band played at length: six pieces including a medley.[55] Grimes recalls: 'Well, that was one of those lucky things at Newport Jazz Festival. I did a lot of rehearsing for that and was with the band for quite a few months. Sometimes we'd play at his house, I think it was in New Haven, Connecticut. [...] He was sort of a sergeant. You know that's the way a lot of bandleaders become when they are working with a lot of different personalities. Especially when it is an older musician like Benny Goodman working with younger musicians like me.'[56]

The reviews of Goodman's Newport concert tended on the whole to be negative. Denise Jokinen, in her discussion of the Festival for the French magazine *Jazz Hot* (September 1958), even emphasized that most critics considered Goodman's offerings shoddy, though she felt that this opinion was overstated in view of musicians of the stature of Kenny Burrell.[57] Eric T. Vogel, for the German magazine *Jazz Podium*, called Goodman an out-and-out 'disappointment'. Many of the band's musicians had been hired at the last moment, he claimed, and consequently the ensemble playing was ragged. Only the 'undemanding part of the festival' had brought him ovations, and Goodman himself seemed not very pleased with his appearance.[58] In another passage Vogel speaks plainly of the 'inadequacy of the Goodman orchestra'.[59] *DownBeat* was a bit more differentiated in its opinion: 'Goodman, despite the ragged, often distorted, sound of his band, appeared in excellent spirits. [...] But the inability of Butterfield to make it with the rest of the trumpets made the band a painful experience to undergo.'[60] None of these reviews mention the 'sideman' Henry Grimes. But even if Goodman and parts of his band did not exactly excel in the luxurious harbor town's Freebody Park, the booking gave a healthy boost to Grimes' career. He also played in Goodman's band later, and following the appearance he was virtually handed from one major bandleader to another at the festival.

On the evening of the next day, Saturday 5 July, Grimes played in Gerry Mulligan's Quartet, with whom he had already worked intensely in previous months. The evening bore the motto 'Blues in the Night', and the other quartet members were Art Farmer on trumpet and Dave Bailey on drums. The critics were very positive. 'They should have stayed on stage, for what followed was dreadful,' wrote Denise Jokinen, who quite obviously disliked the next act: Chuck Berry.[61] Eric T. Vogel thought much the same: 'This appearance [by Chuck Berry] was even less intelligible in that it took place before [*recte*: after] the supreme musical level of the Gerry Mulligan Quartet. Gerry's interplay with Art Farmer [trumpet], Henry Grimes [bass], and Dave Bailey [drums] had a rare homogeneity. Mulligan himself, equally outstanding as player and arranger, seems always to be in top form, no matter what style he plays.'[62] The band, including Henry Grimes, must have meshed perfectly.

The afternoon of the final festival day, Sunday the 6th, bore the motto 'An Afternoon Of Modern Jazz' and found Henry Grimes in no fewer than four appearances with four different bands.[63] The first was with the clarinetist Tony Scott, with Jimmy Knepper on trombone, Kenny Burrell on guitar, and Ed Levinson on drums. Grimes had already worked on a recording with Tony Scott in 1957. In Newport they played Scott's 'Blues For An African Friend', the standard 'Moonlight In Vermont', and another Scott composition, 'Blues For Charlie Parker'.[64] The critics do not single out the individual musicians, but stress a violent argument with the

Tranquility: Lee Konitz with Billy Bauer, Henry Grimes, and Dave Bailey, recorded October 22, 1957 (insert of CD released 2011).

projectionist that must have had a lasting adverse effect on the performance.[65] Denise Jokinen, while reporting much the same thing, found the music 'very moving'.[66]

The next three appearances placed special demands on the bassist, for all three were trios. The first was headed by the alto saxophone player Lee Konitz, then already renowned worldwide. Grimes had first played a recording date with him in 1957. In Newport they were joined by Ed Levinson on drums.[67] 'One wants to hear more,' Jokinen curtly noted.[68] The *DownBeat* critic was also positive: '[...] Lee Konitz, with Henry Grimes and Ed Levinson backing, played three tunes very well: "Some of These Days", "Lover Man", and "Will You Still Be Mine". He maintained a high standard of creativity throughout his performance.'[69]

Next came the Sonny Rollins Trio, Henry Grimes' first concert appearance with the famous tenor saxophonist. Roy Haynes sat at the drums.[70] The contemporary reviews did not single out the bass and drums and ranged from positive to subdued. 'Sonny played two pieces: the theme from the *Threepenny Opera*, then "I Want To Be Happy",' Jokinen reported. 'His simple playing and beautiful tone are much appreciated.'[71] *DownBeat* informs the reader that 'Sonny Rollins, with Roy Haynes and Henry Grimes, played a two tune set. On both "Moritat" and "I Want To Be Happy" Sonny played well, but without the usual continuity and occasional ferocity of which he is capable.'[72] The tenor saxophonist's biographer Peter Niklas Wilson views the Newport recording 'hardly an indispensable addition to Rollins' already well-documented trio work' and laments the 'technically uneven tape'. But he finds that the music 'on the other hand, is first-rate: the 1924 Vincent Youmans hit ["I Want To Be Happy"], performed at a frantic clip, once again inspires Rollins to intricate explorations of interval and rhythm.'[73]

Henry Grimes' final appearance at the 1958 Newport Festival was perhaps his most famous: with the Thelonious Monk Trio. Once again the much sought-after Roy Haynes sat at the drums. There exists a three-and-a-half minute recording of the piece 'Blue Monk' on *Jazz On A Summer's Day*, a live documentary of the festival by Bert Stern.[74] Henry has seen the film and remembers the gig well, though not every detail.[75] Besides his own piece 'Blue Monk', the pianist played three further titles: 'Just You, Just Me' and his compositions 'Round Midnight' and 'Well, You Needn't'.[76] The critics refer only to Monk, and sing his praises. Things about Monk's music that used to be called 'ultramodern were no longer so far out,' Jokinen notes in her review, ending with the statement 'his success was well-deserved.'[77] Eric T. Vogel was surprised at Monk's 'amazingly simple and uncomplicated delivery'.[78] *DownBeat* found Monk's playing 'fine, provocative, and quite witty', mentioning that he left the stage with cries for more from the audience.[79] Compared to his Prestige recording of 1952,[80] Monk took 'Blue Monk' at a relatively slow tempo. The off-scene narrator of *Jazz On A Summer's Day*, Willis Conover, introduces the pianist at the beginning as a man dissatisfied with the half-step intervals on his instrument: 'Henry Grimes and Roy Haynes remain on stage [right after their appearance with Sonny Rollins] to accompany one of the complete originals of music, a man who lives his music, a man who thinks his music, and it is possible to say that he lives and thinks of little else. We can't describe him exactly as daring, because I think he is unconcerned with any opposition to his music. He concerns himself with such elements as the quarter tone, which he doesn't find in our western scale, so he will strike two adjoining notes on the piano, two adjoining keys to imply the missing notes in between.'[81] The camera zooms in twice for a few seconds on Henry Grimes. He lets himself be swept away by Monk's music – a style that band member Oscar Pettiford had found difficult[82] – and accompanies 'Blue Monk' with relaxed

Henry Grimes at the Auditorium Theatre in Rochester, NY, *ca.* 1959, probably performing with Sonny Rollins (© Paul Hoeffler/CTSIMAGES).

concentration. Unfortunately, Monk's improvisation is drowned out by Conover, who chats at the same time about the weather and the sailboats on the water next to the festival grounds. The audience applauds wildly after Monk rises from his chair.

Asked by Ken Weiss, in his 2003 *Cadence* interview,[83] whether Monk told him how to play, Grimes said 'No, he gave you direction from sort of an inward manner. He would look at you and just nod his head and you start playing when he starts playing.'[84] At the Blue Note in 2007, when again asked about his work with Monk, he replied, 'He was the kind of guy who would just turn around and point to the musicians and just let them know what he wanted them to do as a band. He was a technical master but was a very . . .

kind of low profile type of guy. But *Jazz On A Summer's Day* was a great thing. I did work with him one other time at some places that aren't around any more in New York City. It was with Billy Higgins and myself, and I wasn't even hired for the gig. I think the bass player was late or something like that, but I went up and played a short thing with Monk. I think during that song he was just dancing around and looking for the bass player anyway!'[85]

In 2004, when Grimes was asked about his strangest experience in the world of music, he named Monk, but qualified the widely held view of the pianist as a sort of 'kook': 'One day he showed up with a small truck. He was just getting out, and he wore a black cape. He ran up to the piano and didn't play. You couldn't let yourself get fazed by his theatrical antics. In his own way he was very level-headed.'[86]

Newport was a sort of jump start for Henry Grimes. It was immediately followed by three big band recordings in New York: one with the tradition-minded Benny Goodman on July 7 (one day after the festival), another with the modernist Sonny Rollins for *Sonny Rollins And The Big Brass* on July 10 and 11 (revealingly, the album also has three pieces for trio),[87] and again with Goodman on July 14.[88] Demètre Joakimidis, in his review of *Sonny Rollins And The Big Brass* for *Jazz Hot*, called Henry Grimes on double bass 'an excellent accompanist who gives the orchestra solid support. [...] The musicality of Henry Grimes and 'Specs' Wright [on the three trio pieces] is so strong that we do not regret the absence of the piano for a single moment. [...] The recording is excellent, clear, and perfectly balanced. This is not only a good disc with tenor saxophone, but one of the best recordings by a leading figure in today's jazz.'[89] Joakimidis gives the record four out of five stars.[90] Peter Niklas Wilson, proceeding exclusively from Sonny Rollins' innovative trio classics, came to a quite different opinion of the album's trio pieces in 1991: 'The B side shows a newly staffed Rollins trio that has a hard time living up to the standards established in *Way Out West* and *Freedom Suite*.'[91] Remarkably, Grimes stands out even in the full-voice big band pieces, where he is the only bassist. Power and energy had already become typical of his playing, qualities he claimed resulted mainly from his period of rhythm and blues.[92] Discussing this point in an interview from 2007, Sonny Rollins vociferously agreed – 'that's true' – and added: 'He was a person who seemed to live for one thing: for music. He is a person I was very happy to be able to work with.'[93]

A good month after his Newport gigs, Grimes, as mentioned above, played bass with the Lennie Tristano Quartet for a live recording in the Half Note.[94] Then, toward the end of the year he joined Miles Davis' group for a couple of days.[95] And he appeared often with Sonny Rollins in concerts in and around New York.[96]

Pianist Larry Vuckovich remembers having 'heard Henry in San Francisco, circa '58/'59 at the Jazz Workshop in a piano-less quartet setting which, I believe, also included the young Freddie Hubbard.' There exists a photo from around that time of Sonny Rollins and Henry Grimes playing at this Club.[97] The tenor player Don Menza also has lively memories of a Sonny Rollins gig from this period: 'It was New Year's Eve 1959. Sonny Rollins was playing at the Red Rooster in Rochester. Five of us got in a car and drove through a snow storm to go hear Sonny Rollins. Sonny was supposed to quit at 1:30 or 2:00 am. He played until almost 3:00 am. It was Sonny with Frankie Dunlop on drums and Henry Grimes on bass, playing "Be It Ever So Humble, There's No Place Like Home", at a break-neck tempo [...].'[98]

At some point between 1958 and the early 1960s Henry Grimes played regularly with Sonny Rollins in a New York loft, as described by Mose Allison biographer Patti Jones: 'One session spot which had a notable impact on the New York jazz scene was held in a loft downtown at 335 East 34th Street. Clyde Cox, a trombonist from Mississippi, founded and organized the sessions in his loft apartment, beginning in 1956. They continued into the early 1960s, when the building was demolished [...]. The location at 335 East 34th Street was not typical of most lofts. Sandwiched between two woodworking shops on the middle floor of a three-story building, the physical accommodations on 34th Street were smallish, resembling more an apartment than the cavernous shape of a traditional Manhattan loft. [...] The steady stream of musicians patronizing the loft on 34th Street included many New York jazz players whose careers were on the rise. [...] Among other regular participants at the loft were pianist Don Friedman and popular bass player Henry Grimes. [...] Among the more celebrated musicians who played the sessions regularly on 34th Street were [...] renowned tenor saxophonist Sonny Rollins, often with bassist Henry Grimes.' Jones also records Clyde Cox's memory that 'The loft was not a competitive place at all. We had what I really guess you could call a "cutting session" one time but it was wonderfully friendly. [...] The whole idea of the loft was not to exclude.'[99]

The collaboration with Sonny Rollins was an especially important and intensive experience in Grimes' early career. Luckily, the quite varied music they made together in 1959 is well documented on live radio and private recordings and taped TV broadcasts.[100]

'You play things with him you play the rest of your life'[101] – First European Tour with Sonny Rollins (1959)

Sonny Rollins, an innovative trio leader and rhythm-driven tenor saxophonist, helped to liberate the bass and drums both musically and beyond. He gave gifted musicians like Henry Grimes a chance to express themselves and to evolve artistically. His special appreciation of the rhythm section *per se* comes to the fore in a statement he gave to *DownBeat* on the topic of trios in 1958: 'I think this trio can work. It's very good practice for musicians. Makes them listen to each other. It's very demanding, but it's also a very good thing. Of course, if one guy is off, the group is off. And that way, the group never is as good as I play, but rather as all three play. ... When I look for a drummer or a bass, they have to be very positive. It's very difficult for them to play without a piano player. With a piano, it's easy to relax and maybe shirk what they should do. They lean on the piano player. That's why I have to have a strong bass player, and a very strong drummer. That's not the easiest thing to find, either. I look for guys who can stand on their own two feet, who can solo, and who can accompany. They have to be good musicians. The caliber of the men has to be high.... I know what I want, and I don't think it's hard. I've heard that I'm hard to work with. But I think what I do is clear.'[102]

Henry Grimes himself, in a 2005 *DownBeat* interview, describes the beginning of his close collaboration with Sonny Rollins as a more or less lucky break that he seized at the time: 'I just wanted to play music, whether free or loud or whatever.... I got the call and went to Europe with Sonny.'[103] When Bret Primack, also in 2005, asked him about his work with Rollins, he recalled: 'It was 1958. I know, I used to jam with him a little before that – when he was with Max Roach and Clifford Brown in the Band, in Philadelphia. Sometimes, a couple of times I did go and jam, play with them [...]. But after I got to New York I met Sonny around 1958 [...]. That was the first time he called me for Europe [...]. It started out with Pete LaRoca, Kenny Clarke. Kenny Clarke was at the beginning when they couldn't find Pete LaRoca and then there was [...] a drummer from Philadelphia. And these drummers were playing with Sonny [...] and there was something going back and forward about who did the gig and finally there was Pete LaRoca.'[104] Peter Niklas Wilson's discographical details and various other sources show that initially Pete LaRoca sat at the drums (also Joe Harris in Stockholm) and Kenny Clarke only toward the end of the tour.[105] But it is also possible that Clarke, who lived in France from 1956,[106] played drums in several of the Paris concerts of February 23 to 28 at the beginning of the tour, and again at the end on March 11.

Grimes himself repeatedly emphasizes the music he played with Sonny Rollins at that time.[107] As a participant on many legendary recordings of innovative jazz music in the 1950s and 1960s, he attaches hardly any importance to the quotidian events surrounding the music. He generally does not recount his memories in linear, predictable anecdotes, still less in gossip.[108] In a 2003 interview, he recalled Sonny Rollins as 'very tactful, a natural. You play things with him that you play the rest of your life.'[109] In another interview from the same year, he was asked how his collaboration with the tenor saxophonist came about. Once again he stressed the musical things he learned from Rollins: 'About my second or third time in New York, I worked with Anita O'Day and Gerry Mulligan's groups. I met Sonny Rollins and he enlisted me for his group. The music was great. Sonny is a great teacher without realizing it. The reception for the music in Europe was tremendous and also here too. I know that when I first met Sonny, he was working with Clifford Brown and Max Roach, their group. I sat in

Henry Grimes and Sonny Rollins at the San Remo Jazz Festival, February 21, 1959. Europe tour of the Sonny Rollins Trio, Pete LaRoca (drums) – Grimes' first tour outside the United States (© Sergio Pedroli / Riccardo Schwamenthal Archives/CTSIMAGES).

with them in Philadelphia and that is how I knew him in New York after that. The reception for his music was very great.'[110]

It need hardly be said that the learning process was not always easy. Bill Crow, who succeeded Henry at the bass in Gerry Mulligan's band, recalls that Henry Grimes worked hard at the bass to keep up in Sonny Rollins' trio: 'Sonny had cut the group down. But I thought Henry was doing yeoman work, hanging in there with Sonny. That was a hard combination. It looked like he would have liked to have a piano player [laughs].'[111] When asked in 2007 about Grimes' qualities as a trio player, Sonny Rollins singled out the intensity, earnestness, and lack of fear: 'One thing about Henry: He was always a very intense musician – and he was a very serious musician – and he was fearless – whatever I attempted to play, he would never flinch – he was ready to play anything. [...] He is serious about his music – this is the type of person I wanted.'[112]

At that time Sonny Rollins' importance extended far beyond

the borders of the United States. This is nowhere more apparent than in a concert announcement published in the German magazine *Jazz Podium* in February 1959 under the heading 'Silver-Rollins Package'. The editors admitted that they knew nothing precise about Rollins' band members: 'Soon the Sonny Rollins Trio and the Horace Silver Quintet are expected to appear in Germany. [...] Nothing definitive is known about Rollins' accompanists. Both groups will play in the Stuttgart Liederhalle on March 6 in South German Radio's "Treffpunkt Jazz" series.'[113]

Sonny Rollins' European tour started with a concert at the San Remo Festival on February 21.[114] The London jazz bassist Coleridge Goode (born in Jamaica in 1914), who was touring with the innovative alto saxophone player Joe Harriott at the time, has lively memories of this booking in his autobiography:[115] 'I drove to San Remo. Our spot was on the first day of the festival, Saturday February 21st, and it went well. [...] A couple of American stars were on the bill, too. Sonny Rollins appeared with his trio of Henry Grimes on bass and drummer Peter Sims (later known as Pete LaRoca).' Coleridge Goode mentions an on-stage argument between Rollins and Grimes during the concert,[116] whereas Grimes denies that he ever argued with Rollins. Asked about it in December 2006, he said that '[t]he only problems I did have were musical problems – not personality things.'[117]

The next stop on the tour was Club Saint-Germain in Paris, where they played for almost a week from February 23 to 28.[118] Goode attended these Paris concerts on his return trip to London and reports that disagreements – he may have misinterpreted the situation — were still going on.[119] Surviving sound recordings of some of the subsequent concerts reveal that at least there was no harmful effect on the music – on the contrary.

The tour continued to Stockholm, where the Rollins–Grimes–LaRoca Trio played in Club Nalen (March 2), Swedish Radio, and the Södra Theater (March 4). At the latter they were joined by gig drummer Joe Harris who lived in Sweden at the time and was making studio recordings with his band in Stockholm. A live film of the Södra gig is available on the internet and shows the trio masterfully performing 'It Don't Mean a Thing', the Rollins original 'Paul's Pal', and the standard 'Love Letters'. The urgent reading of the last one is virtually a solo performance by Sonny Rollins, discreetly accompanied by a highly focused and attentive Henry Grimes, with Joe Harris listening enraptured to the tenor saxophone and the bass.[120]

All the live Stockholm cuts available on CD contain superb music in every combination of musicians.[121] At the end of the Ellington piece 'It Don't Mean A Thing If It Ain't Got That Swing', Sonny introduces 'one of the outstanding young bassists in the world – Henry Grimes – who is my bassist,' thereby expressing his high opinion of the young musician to the audience.[122] A Swedish Rollins fan made a private recording of the Nalen gig and circulated it in a tiny run of ten 45-rpm records – 'a discographical treasure that was made available to a wider listening audience only in 1984 with the Dragon release.'[123] Peter Niklas Wilson specially emphasizes Sonny Rollins' 'technique of tension-filled displacement to the note lengths' on 'There Will Never Be Another You' and 'How High The Moon', finding that Pete LaRoca and Henry Grimes 'prove themselves [...] a well integrated, impressive rhythm section.'[124] On 'How High The Moon', a rehearsal recording made before the broadcast, Grimes and LaRoca play an elaborate exchange of 'bass-drum fours that show off their solo abilities.'[125]

On March 5, one day after the final Swedish gig, the trio moved on to Switzerland for a Zurich concert, recently released on CD.[126] By now they had blended into a telepathic unity. A fiery and propulsive Grimes is given ample solo space, which he fills with melodic finesse at sometimes acrobatic tempos. He and Rollins develop a sensitive melodic interplay on the standard 'It Could Happen To You'.

On March 6, one day after the Zurich concert, the tour continued to Germany, where the Rollins–Grimes–LaRoca Trio appeared in the Stuttgart Liederhalle. Dieter Zimmerle recorded his impressions in a rather skeptical review for *Jazz Podium* that seems out of tune with what the trio had presented in Zurich. Unfortunately, in the absence of recordings, his observations cannot be corroborated: 'Rollins stands like a rock, a musical mid-point, brilliantly combining progressive melody lines and a harmonic framework in his playing – all by himself on the horn! – and proves to be an individualist who has trouble fitting into an ensemble. So he leaves it that way with the accompaniment from bass (Henry Grimes) and drums (Pete LaRoca). [...] What his fellow [...] colleagues offer is usually neither a response nor a true addition. It was this experience that caused him to form a trio, in which he alone is responsible for both melody and harmony (!). But whether this is the right path for his undoubtedly great talent seems very questionable. Here and there we already sense stagnation, and his dialogues with bassist Henry Grimes and his somewhat unconvincing drummer LaRoca prove how much he wants to grow from the friction.'[127]

On March 7 the tour moved on to Paris, where the trio performed two more concerts at the Olympia. In this case there are two contemporary accounts from *Jazz Hot* critics Gérard Brémond and Aris Destombes. Brémond's observations are especially germane, for he took an interest not only in the tenor soloist but particularly in the bassist's playing techniques. Perhaps no critical statement on Henry Grimes from this period is more detailed. The magazine also ran a photo of Grimes smoking a cigarette – something that otherwise he never did.

Brémond describes the two concerts of the Sonny Rollins Trio at the Olympia as 'an event for all lovers of modern jazz'. It is the piano-less line-up that makes the Trio distinctive and original for him; he emphasizes the suppleness and delicacy that it gains through this. Especially interesting for him is to watch the three musicians search and discover new musical ideas – without any distraction from a chordal instrument – and to experience the original character of the tenor saxophone in this setting. Brémond also is struck by the distinctive personality of the bassist and his playing technique: '[H]e strikes the strings casually [*slappe*], magnifying the volume of sound. I found an interesting approach in his solos: he sometimes plays the melody line with two or three fingers and the low notes with the thumb, which considerably enriches his playing. Perhaps his technique is not yet secure, but Henry Grimes is young, and we can only rejoice when he opens up new possibilities for the bass in jazz.'[128]

The 'counterpart' of the review, entitled '*Pro ou Contre*', was given to the critic Aris Destombes, who wrote mockingly of the rhythm group: '[...] Sonny Rollins' two accompanists – were they there for any reason? I guess so, for the bassist was very restrained and the drummer terribly busy. I was told a particular Rollins quote – one among many ('Lark, I'm gonna pluck you'), which aptly renders the heated discussion that took place behind the scenes after the concert – between the leader and his drummer.'[129] Grimes, too, remembers that Rollins had problems with LaRoca's playing style, which led to arguments.[130] But however painful the effects of the leader's high expectations at the time – not least on himself – they did the trio no musical damage, and probably even released new forces.

Following a Brussels appearance on March 8,[131] the trio returned to Germany the next day and held a concert in Frankfurt am Main. The four pieces they played there have only recently been released, not least because of the mediocre recording quality:[132] 'It Don't Mean a Thing' at breakneck speed (with a short but fiery solo from Henry Grimes), a solemn 'Cocktails For Two', a swinging 'I've Told Every Little Star', and an almost aggressive 'I Want To Be Happy' – with a cheeky solo from Grimes and a forceful one from LaRoca. All four pieces are noteworthy for their inventive dialogues between tenor and bass.

On March 10, the trio presumably continued to Holland, where they played in the Singer Theater in Laren.[133] The live film recording of 'Weaver of Dreams', available on the internet today, offers an improvised interpretation of this standard that is masterly from beginning to end. True, the bass and drums play with restraint, but the trio forms a convincing and creative whole.[134] The camera swings to Grimes several times, with his eyes and ears following the tenor saxophone.[135]

In the last two appearances on the tour, on March 11, Pete LaRoca was replaced by Kenny Clarke[136] – 'he is one of Sonny's favorites – and one of mine,' as Grimes puts it.[137] Sonny Rollins' relaxed announcements of each piece are not the only thing that shows this was the right decision. First they played in Marseille in a school theater, then later that same evening in a club in Aix-en-Provence.[138] The second concert survives in a live private recording that can be called, to quote Peter Niklas Wilson, a 'real sensation'.[139] The electrically charged music, often with only scraps of melody lines, differs markedly from the comparatively introverted, melodious playing of the Rollins–Grimes–LaRoca Trio in, say, Stockholm or Laren. Here we can see – hear – that each member of the trio essentially defines the music. With Kenny Clarke on drums, Sonny Rollins' improvisations are more daring and adventurous, which in turn grants Henry Grimes more leeway on the bass. 'The widely held opinion,' Peter Niklas Wilson writes of the Aix-en-Provence concert, 'that the "conservative" Rollins only attained to a modern style in 1962, under the influence of Coleman sidemen Don Cherry and Billy Higgins, is belied by these three tracks. Rollins preserves the form of the compositions (unlike the 1962 recordings), but within this framework radically deconstructs the motivic, harmonic and rhythmic structures from the ground up.'[140] Owing to the poor recording equipment, Grimes' bass is unfortunately difficult to hear. This is especially regrettable in the passage where Sonny Rollins, with the words 'Stretch out!' expressly invites him to take a solo, which he does, humming along in full concentration. When Jacob Larsen wrote his liner notes, he could not have guessed that for thirty years after this remarkable concert the bassist would be living in Los Angeles isolated from the world of music. 'During the tour he [Sonny Rollins] introduced himself along with bass player Henry Grimes (1935–1984) [sic], who was to become the avant-garde companion in the 60s – and Kenny Clarke (1914–1985) replacing Pete LaRocca [sic] after [the] Parisian concerts.'[141] And we can only second Larsen when he adds: 'Life wouldn't be the same without these few moments of joy! ... as on the night of March 11th 1959 in Aix-en-Provence, France.'[142] At the end Sonny Rollins cries out 'Henry Grimes! Henry Grimes' and, 'Thank you very much, thank you! That was a ball!'[143]

In the course of the tour, Grimes not only met the challenge of Rollins' extremely high artistic demands, but grew along with them. Asked in 2004 what he learned from Sonny Rollins, he replied 'more powerful harmonies' and continued: 'With him, you had to stand up to the pressure, to follow him, then he could break out unchecked on his high-altitude flights.'[144] Two years later he emphasized: 'The thing is with Sonny with his striving for perfection, a lot of musicians with him are under a lot of pressure, they really have to be playing; they can't be doing any halfway thing and not doing it, you know. That's what I know myself: If you play with him, you come under a lot of pressure about playing, not about any drug thing or anything like that, but about playing, playing the music, the music, and knowing what it's about, pragmatically what it's about – music, and that is the point I'd like to emphasize. [...] It's just that when you played with him, he played so well that [...] you're under pressure. I mean, if you've ever heard of bein' under pressure, that is really the epitome of being under pressure. [...] I was workin' hard. I didn't pay too much attention to how it came out. That's really hard work, but that's what I want, you know. It's really very enjoyable, Sonny, you know, really just swinging.'[145] He went on to sum up the learning effect he gained, expressly referring to all the innovative musicians he played with at the time: one man might influence another playing dynamic speeds up at a certain level, 'and it doesn't go lower than that; it either goes higher than that or gets above the level. That's what goes above playing. And it's right up at that level, no lower.' [146]

Henry Grimes' first European tour with Sonny Rollins had given him invaluable experience in the collective exploration of free musical expression – a development that already pointed to a new musical era.

4

'there are always transitions behind the names of the music' – The New York Years (1960–66)

Freedom Now! – Political and Musical Changes from the Late Fifties

A revolution is unfurling – America's unfinished revolution. It is unfurling in lunch counters, buses, libraries and schools – wherever the dignity and potential of men are denied. Youth and idealism are unfurling. Masses of Negroes are marching onto the stage of history and demanding their freedom now![1]

A. Philip Randolph, *ca.* 1960

1960 was the year of the first sit-ins, when black students sat at lunch counters previously declared off-limits to them in the cities of the American South. A pictorial document of these acts of protest appears on the cover of the album *We Insist! Freedom Now Suite*, recorded on August 31 and September 6, 1960, by Max Roach together with Abbey Lincoln (vocal), Booker Little (trumpet), Julian Priester (trombone), Walter Benton and Coleman Hawkins (tenor saxophones), James Schenck (bass), Michael Olatunji (congas), and Ray Mantilla and Tomas DuVall (percussion). A few weeks earlier, in July, the leader of the Black Muslims, Elijah Muhammad, had demanded an independent black state.[2]

In these years of social and political turmoil, jazz music underwent a process of rapid change, driven by an increasingly openly expressed need for liberation and independence among various social groups. First and foremost among these groups in the United States were the country's African-American citizens.[3] Amiri Baraka summed up this development as follows: 'Just as the civil rights movement was transformed (and we can identify Malcolm X as its catalyst) into the Black Liberation Movement, so the music went from hard bop to the avant-garde. And along with Ornette, Sun Ra, Eric Dolphy, Pharoah Sanders, Oliver Nelson, Ted Curson, Freddie Hubbard, Bill Dixon, Henry Grimes, Wayne Shorter, Bernard McKinney, Jimmy Lyons, Scott La Faro, and many others moved onto the scene.' The new music wanted to get back to its basic 'African rhythms, blues orientation, the primacy of improvisation'. It introduced 'the extended form of Ellington and Mingus and Rollins', and opened itself up to the 'search for the new expression of Coltrane'.[4]

The new improvisational and compositional approaches of Sonny Rollins, Charles Mingus, Ornette Coleman, and Cecil Taylor are inseparable from the burgeoning civil rights movement, driving and inspiring it. But they cannot be boiled down to this movement: they equally involved a genuine musical renewal. Jazz music *per se* is well known to be an art in a constant state of flux. Henry Grimes in particular is a musician who puts great stock in music's spiritual autonomy and independence, who distrusts conceptual definitions and interpretations or a philosophical superstructure for music, and who considers it impossible to explain the one (music) by means of the other (logical concepts).[5]

Pianist Paul Bley, who lived in New York during the early 1960s, summarizes the highly charged musical atmosphere of these years: 'As a musician there are some decades in which you can't help but become really good at what you do, and there are some decades that are a waste of your time. And it's not based on your talent; it's based on the calendar. And 1959 and this period, everything was so alive that just to be in New York City, it would be impossible not to absorb what was important in music.'[6]

'I woke up and found myself in the place I was thinking about' – Early Contacts with Free Music (*ca.* 1960)

Henry Grimes played on many albums now considered milestones of free jazz: Albert Ayler's *Witches And Devils* and *Spirits Rejoice!*; Don Cherry's *Complete Communion*, *Symphony for Improvisers*, and *Where is Brooklyn?*; Cecil Taylor's *Unit Structures* and *Conquistador!*; and Pharoah Sanders' *Tauhid*. It is these albums that mainly underlie his present-day image as a 'free jazz legend'. He also played in many other innovative ensembles not associated with free jazz, including those of Gerry Mulligan, Sonny Rollins, Charles Mingus, Lennie Tristano, briefly with Miles Davis (in the Sextet with John Coltrane, Julian 'Cannonball' Adderley, Bill Evans, and Philly Joe Jones),[7] Roy Haynes, and McCoy Tyner. His playing with all these major groups demonstrates musical abilities capable of being applied independently in any style. He clearly remembers this busy phase in his early musical career: 'Yeah! At one time I couldn't raise my elbow and not bump into someone who wanted me to play with them. It was coming from all sides! It really felt great to be playing so much.'[8] In 2004 he let his interviewer know: 'I like to switch from avant-garde, to modern, and cool, be-bop, I'm doing everything. [...] That's what motivates me as a player, trying to convey emotions to the listeners while interacting with other musicians.'[9]

Musicologist Marc Medwin, who heard Grimes in 2010 at a trio concert with Marc Ribot and Chad Taylor, summed up his universal musical skills: 'As the band jumps abruptly into one final assault, it occurs to me that Grimes, like his younger bandmates, is a natural postmodernist. Rock, swing, modern classical composition – this trio does it all, with style and passion. I'm reminded of what Grimes said the day before, as we sat in his studio: "It's all music."'[10]

His special affinity for free music was connected with the fact that it gave him personally the greatest potential for emotional expression and interplay – and it still does. From roughly 1959 Henry Grimes was, in musical terms, no longer a sideman or accompanist. Time and again it has been shown, since then, that trios and free music ensembles offer him the greatest scope to develop his powerful orchestral sound, his ideas, and his group charisma. Mike Hobart sees Henry Grimes' pioneering role as a free music bassist in the following terms: 'At the time, there was no template for advanced jazz double bass. There had been Scott LaFaro's light-toned fluency and Charles Mingus' use of complex chords and scales and modern classical music, but nobody had put this together into a role-defining style. Grimes is the one who at the turn of the 1960s anchored the bottom end of the free-jazz ensemble while joining in the free flow of ideas.'[11]

Journalists often ask Grimes how he experienced the change from so-called swing and hard bop to so-called free or avant-garde jazz, and why he made this 'big step'. His replies are sometimes monosyllabic and noncommittal, but some of them give deep insight into his musical creativity and the associated mental processes from which he drew musical knowledge. Labels such as hard bop or avant-garde jazz play a subordinate role; instead, it becomes clear that Henry Grimes, as a musician and as a living part of New York's music scene, evolved in the direct enactment of the music itself. He thereby both brought about and reflected this development. Like other musicians of the period, he personified free music and its evolution. Rather than coming to this music, Grimes came to himself as an historical agent with an individual way of perceiving his art. He enacted an artistic evolution within the currents of the day rather than consciously deciding in favor of 'avant-garde jazz', 'free jazz', or any other musical concept. Grimes views the freedom of the avant-garde expressly as a consistent evolutionary step within freely improvised music, i.e., within jazz music *per se*.

Amiri Baraka put it this way:

> The new music is always rooted in historical certainty, no matter how disconnected from history it might sound to the casual or neophyte listener. But it *uses* history, it is not paralyzed by it!
>
> So that the truly new expresses where we are or will be. It also lets us know that what we feel or think *will be*, often *already* is! The new music, as any new expression, tries to impress us with motion, its constant; and with change, its persistence![12]

Deciding in favor of a concept is an idea propagated by onlookers (critics, journalists, enthusiasts), who understandably seek historical handholds in the maelstrom of musical creativity. Henry Grimes, in contrast, describes himself as a musician who always joined other musicians when they approached him. It was in these ensembles that he helped to develop the music that came to be labeled, among other things, 'free jazz'. David Keenan is right when he characerizes Grimes as 'a key architect of the free jazz revolution in the '60s'.[13]

In 2003 the social worker and music enthusiast Marshall Marrotte, who tracked down Henry Grimes in Los Angeles in late 2002, and without whose commitment and initiative Henry would most likely never have returned to music,[14] received an unpretentious answer when he asked Grimes what had motivated his switch from hard bop to avant-garde jazz: 'Well, those musicians became interested in me and I played with whoever I could, and was lucky enough to get work with Benny Goodman, Sonny Rollins, Gil Evans, Tony Scott, and Gerry Mulligan. [...] Later on I played with Cecil Taylor, Albert Ayler, and other avant-garde musicians, and I just stayed with them to see what they were about.'[15] When Lynell George of the *Los Angeles Times* asked him what prompted his transition 'from straight-ahead gigs to more abstract ensembles', Henry answered: 'The music was a feeling. And if you understand that feeling, [...] it goes right through you.'[16] Similarly, when Fred Jung asked him in 2004, 'what attracted you to free jazz?', Henry emphasized that he had always had a notion of what free music was and the challenges it poses to freedom of the will:

> I had an idea about what free music was and so I guess having an idea, it automatically enlists you into what a lot of free playing musicians are. That is what happened to me. Before I could realize anything, they were all kind of interested in what I was doing. Before I could even recover from my own surprise, I was in with Albert Ayler, Denis Charles, Mingus, Cecil Taylor, and on and on and on. I really enjoyed playing free music. The freedom of expression, that was the main point with me. The expression, you just have free will to play just what you feel. Your own free will dictates to you to play. There were no other influences that could override your own influences to play free music. I encourage a lot of classical musicians to get with some jazz musicians and see what it is to develop free music. The free music of jazz outweighs a lot of expressions in other music because it is moving forward and ahead and it has very much to do with free sounds and things that have never been heard before, being done.[17]

Again in 2004, Ken Weiss wanted Henry to explain what led him to embrace the financially unrewarding 'avant-garde jazz' movement. Grimes pointed out that he had already worked in Cecil Taylor's group before he realized how this music was affecting him.[18] Weiss continued by asking whether he could express himself better in 'avant-garde jazz'.

The answer:

> Yes, it was more challenging. The thing is that it is the desire to play something new, something different, and when the challenge

of it comes along it's double. You not only want to play something new; you want to play something you never heard played before. You say you want to do a certain thing and it comes that you get to do that certain thing over abundantly. [...] Yeah, I saw myself there. I was following my own thoughts. When I turned around I saw that I had done that before. I was in the same place so I sorta transported myself from where I was to the new groups. I woke up and found myself in the place I was thinking about. That's the only way I can describe it, I woke up to find myself in these groups and that's just because I was thinking about it, it seems to me. But it was a very enjoyable thing working with Pharoah Sanders and all of them. I worked with all of them. [...] when I started that type of playing I didn't realize exactly how it was going to stand up. It just became that music was part of my thoughts and before I knew it I was just following my own thoughts. That's what happened.[19]

When Hans-Jürgen von Osterhausen asked Grimes how he came to 'free jazz', the answer was utterly noncommittal: 'It always turned out that the musicians hired me. It might sound surprising, but I never chose what to play.'[20]

In 2007 Grimes gave a particularly revealing interview in New York's Blue Note jazz club. Again he was asked, 'How did you get from playing swing and bop music to avant-garde? Was it a natural transition?' He answered by pointing to another aspect of jazz practice. The music, he said, no matter what it was called at the time, evolved in the hands of committed people who not only played rhythm and blues, but who showed young musicians what music is about. It was in this connection that he mentioned Arnett Cobb as his personal mentor: 'Yeah, well first of all, we called that music from back then cool jazz. It came from be-bop, re-bop, hard-bop, and all those other names that were popular at the time. I used to play with Arnett Cobb, who as I understand, caused a lot of musicians to steer in that direction of educating others and seeing the music for what it is. He had a lot to do with not just playing rhythm and blues, but also teaching.'[21] In the same interview he was asked what he would call his own music. His answer avoided any and all definitions: 'I call it avant-garde jazz. Or free jazz. I just see it for what it is, and that has a lot to do with people's opinions regarding what's different, whether it's avant-garde or fusion, whatever it be. There are many titles that everyone uses, and jazz is just one of them. I heard Duke Ellington once say that he didn't like the name jazz, so that should really tell you a lot. That was back in the '50s. Jazz, the name itself, was something that he didn't appreciate at that moment in time.'[22]

In the course of the Blue Note interview, the question also arose as to what Grimes felt about the classification of musical styles altogether, and whether he was surprised, when he returned to music in 2003, to find that avant-garde jazz still existed. His answer shows once again that he did not find historical tags for musical styles particularly relevant. Instead, what he found important was the essential core of jazz music that all 'styles' have in common – improvisation: 'No, because there are always transitions behind the names of the music. People pay attention to how it's described, the names – like the name "jazz" for example. What I'm trying to say is that the problem has always been labeling the music. Charlie Parker did it, Monk did it, Cecil Taylor. For some reason the style of playing is created by improvising. That's the common theme that holds it together. When you think about the application to music and what it means to play it, improvisation is the common thing. Monk did the same thing as Parker – not the same thing, like copied it, or technique-wise – but held the same concept.'[23]

Interviewed in 2006–07, Grimes again stressed that the musical discourse in the jazz world changed during the 1950s and 1960s, but that something remained constant for the performance of the music, despite all the differences in the result. The main focus in the 1950s, he explained, was on such figures as Charlie Parker and Miles Davis and the respect they commanded, and the idea of spirituality did not become widespread until the 1960s: 'Whatever goes on to create that situation in music, the bottom line is the same thing as before that and after that. The musicians that really influenced other musicians always were known and followed.'[24] When asked whether this constant factor was more important than the musical discourses (like the idea of spirituality), which change from time to time, Grimes did not give a clear answer. He merely added, with respect to the 1960s, that the spiritual idea emerged from the loft scene, where it was formulated altogether. As he describes it, the idea arose from a mixture of social and musical events and only coalesced much later into a primarily musical matter: 'It happened in lofts. The musicians just played in these lofts. Pretty soon that was the really spiritual thing. Later on that spiritual unity kind of a thing and the spirit in music came together. That was thirty or forty years after these musicians were playing in these lofts. That's the kind of music that developed. That's what they were playing. So it wasn't a spiritual matter, but it had something to do with being in those lofts instead of this spiritual matter, the place of these lofts. Now they don't play there, but it's still there, the same music, still circulating tunes, still developing.'[25]

Amiri Baraka sees the new lofts of the 1960s as resulting from a lack of musical open-mindedness among established club owners: '[T]he lofts and coffee shops came into prominence as places where the music could be heard simply because there were not enough club owners open to the new music.'[26]

Recordings in the New York Loft at 821 Sixth Avenue (1960)

Grimes' playing in lofts was frequent and at least partially documented, beginning in January 1960, when four tape recordings with Henry Grimes on bass were made in the legendary New York loft at 821 Sixth Avenue. Eugene Smith, a photographer from *Life* magazine, moved into the building's fourth floor in 1957 to write a photo-essay on Pittsburgh. The Pittsburgh project soon came to a standstill, and instead he made thousands of photos of the musicians who had long been gathering in the building for jams and recording sessions. The five-storey building was a nocturnal meeting place for such musicians as Charles Mingus, Zoot Sims, Thelonious Monk, Roy Haynes, Sonny Rollins, Bill Evans, Roland Kirk, Alice Coltrane, Don Cherry, Paul Bley, and, of course, Henry Grimes. It was also visited by underground figures. Smith shot 1,447 rolls of film with roughly 40,000 pictures.[27] 'He wired the building like a surreptitious recording studio and made 1,740 reels (4,000 hours) of [...] audiotapes, capturing more than 300 musicians, among them Roy Haynes, Sonny Rollins, Bill Evans, Roland Kirk, Alice Coltrane, Don Cherry and Paul Bley.' The musicians included 'pianists like Eddie Costa, Sonny Clark, drummers Ronnie Free and Edgar Bateman, saxophonist Lin Halliday, bassist Henry

Grimes and multi-instrumentalist Eddie Listengart. Also dropping in on the night-time scene were the likes of Doris Duke, Norman Mailer, Diane Arbus, Robert Frank, Henri-Cartier Bresson, and Salvador Dali, as well as pimps, prostitutes, drug addicts, thieves, photography students, local cops, building inspectors, marijuana dealers, and others.'[28]

The drummer Frank Amoss remembers the loft in 1961, when he lived there: 'In those days you had to go down to the corner of Sixth Avenue and Twenty-Eighth Street, where there was a phone booth, and call to the loft, and someone would open the window and throw a key out down to the sidewalk, and that was the way to get in and go upstairs and play.'[29]

On January 29, 1960, Grimes played there with Fred Greenwell and Zoot Sims (tenor saxophones), Dave McKenna (piano), and Eddie De Haas, Ronnie Free, and Roy Haynes (drums). Smith's recording of the session offers '120 minutes of music in excellent sound', though no details are available.[30] Grimes was included in another 110-minute loft recording made on May 25, this time with Manny Duran and Alan Neese (trumpets), Jean Cunningham (piano), and Ed Livingston (drums).[31] A 112-minute tape recording, probably likewise from 1960, features Zoot Sims (tenor saxophone), Jimmy Raney (guitar), Eddie Costa and Hall Overton. And Grimes. Sam Stephenson's *Jazz Loft* picture book reproduces the original label on the cassette of this recording: '*Ca*. 1960. Hall O. Apt session. Strong piano (2 players). The two piano players on this recording are Overton and Eddie Costa, sometimes playing at once on Overton's side-by-side upright pianos.'[32] Also from around 1960 is a 110-minute recording with Fred Greenwell (tenor saxophone), Manny Duran and Warren Fitzgerald (trumpets), Gary Hawkins (drums), and Henry Grimes.[33]

Partly because of these many loft contacts, Henry's professional career accelerated. Top-quality musicians brought him into the studio for radio and phonograph recordings. On February 4 and March 26, 1960, he played with pianist Billy Taylor, on both occasions with Ray Mosca on drums, and on June 30 he backed up the piano and vocals of Mose Allison along with drummer Paul Motian. On July 6 he stood at the bass for a recording by vibraphonist Ollie Shearer; the other band members on this New York studio date were Bill Barron on tenor, Pepper Adams (bass), Freddie Hubbard (trumpet), Urbie Green (trombone), pianist Bobby Timmons, and drummer Lex Humphries.[34] In a 2004 radio interview, Billy Taylor, still remembering his work with Henry in the late 1950s, expressed his high esteem for the bassist's musicality and his strengths as a trio player.[35] Though there is no recorded evidence, a WKCR interview on September 25, 1997, at least implies that he also worked with Sam Rivers in the early 1960s. Here Rivers talked about a recording he never released: '*Fuchsia Swing Song* music I had done four or five years earlier. I thought it was much too old to record.' The interviewer, Ted Panken, then asked him, 'That was the music you had recorded in that quartet with Hal Galper, Henry Grimes, and Tony Williams?' Rivers confirmed this as well as Panken's next conjecture: 'So the music performed on *Fuchsia Swing Song* was all music from 1959 and 1960.'[36] In September 1965 Grimes played with Sam Rivers once again, this time live at the Village Vanguard in a trio led by drummer Tony Williams.[37]

There were other outstanding figures of the new music in the early 1960s who wanted Henry Grimes to play bass in their projects.

First Collaboration with Cecil Taylor and Others (1961)

Bob Rusch, in a *Cadence* interview of 1986, said to Buell Neidlinger in his Los Angeles home (not far from Grimes at the time): 'I thought Henry Grimes replaced you.'[38] Neidlinger denied this on every level: 'Henry Grimes is a much greater bassist than I would ever hope to be, so I would never say he "replaced" me. I believe that Alan Silva was selected to be the bassist after me, if I'm not mistaken. Henry also worked with Cecil. But he came to Cecil via another group. I think that Alan Silva was the first one.'[39]

However it happened, Grimes' major musical encounter in 1961 was with Cecil Taylor, whose group he soon joined. The contact with the pianist arose as follows: 'When I was playing in Birdland one night [he came] to listen to me play and we became friends and pretty soon I went downtown to work with him.' Henry played with Cecil Taylor's group, and their first three joint recordings were made in the Van Gelder Studio in Englewood Cliffs, NJ, on

October 10, 23, and 25, 1961. Besides Taylor and Grimes, the musicians were alto saxophonist Jimmy Lyons, tenor saxophonist Archie
Shepp, trumpeter Ted Curson, trombonist Roswell Rudd and
Sunny Murray on drums. The studio date on the 10th was sponsored by Gil Evans, who wanted to make Taylor's music known to
a broader public.[40] Over the next five years Grimes and Taylor continued their musical collaboration, resulting in Taylor's famous
recordings *Unit Structures* and *Conquistador!* of 1966 with Grimes on
bass.[41]

Cecil Taylor was, of course, not the only musician Grimes
played with in 1961. It is known that he gave a concert with the
pianist John Bunch in New York's Hickory House at the beginning
of the year. Whether the group was conceived as drumless from the
outset can no longer be determined. Whatever the case, Grimes
absorbed the role of the drummer, as is known from a laudatory
DownBeat review of January 5, 1961, that praised his percussive
skills. It was written by the then already renowned pianist Marian
McPartland: 'Bunch and Grimes make a good team. Grimes is a
resonant, percussive player, and his forceful attack and hard-
driving beat amply compensate for the lack of drums. The duo
plays well on a diversity of tunes ranging from Harold Arlen's "Ill
Wind" and Cole Porter's "Every Time We Say Goodbye" to John
Coltrane's "Giant Steps". Some of their best numbers are tunes by
Thelonious Monk, such as "Crepuscule for Nellie"; "Well, You
Needn't"; "Straight, No Chaser", and "Rhythm-a-ning". Their
version of Charlie Parker's "Au Privave" and, at a slower tempo,
Duke Ellington's seldom-heard "What Am I Here For?" are relaxed
[...].'[42] *The New Yorker* calls them 'a consummation that has long
been devoutly wished'.[43] Grimes may have met Bunch during a 1960
recording date led by clarinetist Rolf Kühn on which Jack Sheldon
(trumpet), Chuck Wayne (guitar), and drummer Ray Mosca also
took part. The two men met again in 1961 at another recording
date, this time headed by tenorist Carmen Leggio.[44] With Leggio's
quartet, Grimes also appeared on Sept 16, 1961, together with
pianist Dave Frishberg and tenor saxophonist Booker Ervin, at a
free event at Hubbard Park in Meriden, Connecticut, which was
broadcast by many different radio stations.[45]

In the summer of 1961 Grimes contributed his 'services at a

concert organized by Metronome for the benefit of the Harlem Community Council on Drug Addiction, founded by Assemblyman Mark Lane and the Rev. Eugene Callender'. Max Roach, Ted Curson, Booker Little, Eric Dolphy, Walter Perkins, Bill Barron, Eddie Kahn, and Eddie Thompson also appeared.[46]

Two further well-known yet highly contrasting musicians brought the much sought-after bassist into the studio in 1961. First on November 17 with Shirley Scott on piano and Otis 'Candy' Finch on drums for a trio album entitled *Shirley Scott Plays Horace Silver*,[47] and again on November 29 with Don Cherry on cornet and Ed Blackwell on drums for Grimes' first working date with Cherry. The live recording of the Cherry-Grimes-Blackwell trio playing compositions by Ornette Coleman ('The Idiot') and Cherry himself ('Harlemite' and 'Black Elk Speaks') apparently still exists,[48] but is currently unavailable on sound media.

'at twenty-six already a veteran in terms of experience'[49] – Playing Bass with Mingus, Haynes, and Tyner (1962)

By 1962 Henry Grimes had definitely arrived on the New York jazz scene. In this year he was contacted by Charles Mingus, who not only played bass, but also was a fine piano player and arranged his own compositions. He thus urgently needed a bassist equal to his own stature. '[W]e played gigs in Baltimore and some around here. Most of them were in Baltimore and he played piano and I took over the bass chair so he could get the arrangements going. He directed me in terms of what he wanted me to do, and that's how I got to know all of the guys in Mingus' band. [...] He was encouraging just by calling me up. Mingus was also a decent piano player. He didn't play that much but he had ability.'[50] Their collaboration apparently came off well, for on May 5 and 12 Mingus fetched Grimes (and Herman Wright) for two concerts in Birdland that were taped from radio.[51] The other band members were Charles McPherson (alto saxophone) and Booker Ervin (tenor saxophone), trumpeter Richard Williams, pianist Toshiko Akiyoshi, and drummer Dannie Richmond. At the first session, on May 5, Mingus enlarged his band to include two bass players (Grimes and Wright) so that he himself could play piano.[52] A week later, on May 12,

Wright was dropped from the roster, and Mingus along with Grimes took the bass parts.[53] As Henry remembers it, they usually alternated on bass in concerts rather than playing duet.[54]

Asked whether Mingus cracked down on him during concerts, as he did with many other musicians, Grimes replied with fairness and magnanimity: 'I know what the stories say. He did have temper tantrums at times but really light temper tantrums. You know, if a guy like that hits you he's liable to get decked. You're liable to come back and hit him. Now, if it's a bass player like Charlie Mingus and he is threatening you have to settle that because you don't want to get into hitting any musician while you're playing. [...] No, I never had any problem with Mingus or any other musicians like that.'[55]

In these years Grimes' collaborations with leading musicians continued without a gap. In May 1962, Roy Haynes went into the studio with his then quartet, consisting of Grimes along with multi-instrumentalist Roland Kirk (tenor saxophone, manzello, strich and flute) and pianist Tommy Flanagan to record his album *Out Of The Afternoon*.[56] Michael Cuscuna, in his 1995 liner notes, remarks that Henry Grimes was a veteran at the age of twenty-six, having already gained experience with Sonny Rollins, Thelonious Monk, and Charles Mingus.[57] Especially worthy of mention on this album is Henry's distinctive arco playing on 'Long Wharf'.

Henry Grimes has vivid memories of his work with Roy Haynes: 'Roy (giant drum roll) HAYNES!! Master of percussion, most musical of drummers. Working with Roy Haynes meant every musician had to shape right up under his understanding of music. His attitude is a kind of demanding equanimity, expecting and knowing that you will give him what he wants in the music. We worked together in the early '60s someplace on Long Island two or three times with Jaki Byard and Rahsaan Roland Kirk, and as I remember, another time the pianist was Harold Mabern, and then Roy called me to record *Out Of The Afternoon* with Rahsaan and Tommy Flanagan in 1962 for Impulse!. People still come up to me and say that's their favorite album of all time, especially young musicians.'[58]

Three further Grimes appearances from 1962 have to be mentioned here: In spring the bassist appeared at the Village Vanguard with pianist and singer Blossom Dearie, 'whose Mona Lisa face,

The cover (*above*) shows the four musicians standing relaxed in a springtime woodland scene together with their instruments, or parts of them (only Flanagan stood empty-handed, the piano being too cumbersome). The photograph was taken in the woods behind Rudy Van Gelder's studio in Englewood Cliffs, NJ, where the album was recorded on May 16 and 23, 1962.

baby voice, and precise piano are supported by such good men as Henry Grimes and [drummer] Al Harewood'.[59] Somewhere in that same summer Grimes performed with trumpeter Johnny Coles' quintet along with alto saxophonist Sonny Red and pianist Duke Pearson, and on July 5 in the Museum of Modern Art with Blossom Dearie's already mentioned trio.[60]

Grimes' intensive work in the Roy Haynes Quartet led to another remarkable studio date whose results, likewise, have lost nothing of their freshness today: on November 14, 1962, McCoy Tyner, then a permanent member of the John Coltrane Quartet, recorded the album *Reaching Fourth* with Grimes and Haynes.[61] Their tight blend on this session belies the fact that they had never played together before as a trio. 'These three musicians really were together,' Dan Morgenstern enthused, 'they sound like a love match.'[62] Especially noteworthy is Grimes' melodious pizzicato solo on the Tyner piece 'Blues Back': 'Besides Tyner's solo, there's a strong solo from Henry Grimes, but that's no surprise. [...] "Blues Back" starts out a slowdrag, picks up for a few bars, accelerates to hard swing and, after Grimes' fine solo, retards into a slowdrag,' reads a 1962 record review published in *Kulchur* magazine, whose editor at that time was the poet and activist LeRoi Jones (Amiri Baraka).[63] Almost four years later, in summer of 1966, Grimes again played with McCoy Tyner – at Slugs' Saloon in the pianist's quartet with Joe Henderson and Jack DeJohnette.[64]

At the end of 1962, Grimes once again appeared with Roy Haynes at the Gaslight Inn in Philadelphia along with Frank Strozier on alto saxophone and flute and Kenny Barron on piano. Fred Norsworthy has this to say about the bassist here: '[...] Grimes is developing into a logical soloist without faltering. He managed to keep good time with Haynes on all the up tempos. His bow work was inspired by [Paul] Chambers' past efforts, achieving a tight rhythm with Roy to give the front line a backing.'[65] In the beginning of 1963 Grimes performed with Roy Haynes at The Tenament in New York City, again with Frank Strozier on alto saxophone, and this time Harold Mabern on piano.[66]

Funk Dumpling (1962)

Another remarkable musical event took place in 1962 (possibly February), though its exact date can no longer be determined. Clarinetist Perry Robinson, pianist Kenny Barron, Henry Grimes, and drummer Paul Motian met in the Medallion Studio in Newark, NJ, to record the album *Funk Dumpling*, named after a Henry Grimes composition that appears as the sixth of the album's seven pieces. Grimes had already met the leader of the session, Perry Robinson, in New York in the mid-1950s and had since played many concerts and jam sessions with him.[67] Robinson especially remembers Grimes in his 1987 liner notes: 'Henry Grimes, the bassist, [...] got the guys together. [...] We did a minimum of takes. [...] I've been very happy with the album through the years.

[...] A very quiet guy, who didn't like the show biz stuff but had a great reputation among musicians.'[68] As was to be expected in the 1980s, Howard Mandel's liner notes end with the words, 'Henry Grimes has dropped from sight, and is suspected to have died in California, though details are unknown.'[69]

In his autobiography *The Traveler*, written with Florence Wetzel and published shortly before Henry's reappearance in 2002, Robinson recalls many details surrounding the recording. The subsequent owner of Savoy, Herman Lubinsky, and music producer Tom Wilson had decided to rebuild the legendary Savoy label. One day, Robinson recalled, Wilson came to him and offered him a recording date. Robinson immediately thought of Henry Grimes. The drummer he chose, Paul Motian, was familiar to him from Minton's, where he was playing at the time with Tony Scott and Bill Evans.

Henry, Robinson remembers, liked Paul a lot and was happy to play with him. 'So I had a bass player and a drummer, but what piano player? Henry suggested Kenny Barron, who was 19 at the time. I didn't know Kenny, but I trusted Henry. The recording session itself was so nice. It was in a beautiful studio in Newark, New Jersey [...] Henry and I collaborated on the album, and we used my compositions and his. We did Henry's songs "Sprites Delight", "Farmer Alfalfa", and "Funk Dumpling". [...] The whole session was magic; it went very smoothly and wonderfully [...] And to this day whenever I see Kenny Barron he always says *Funk Dumpling* is one of his favorite albums ever. [...] *Funk Dumpling* was just effortless to make; something wonderful definitely happened.'[70]

Grimes' abilities as a melodically sensitive, inventive, and swinging bassist are on display in every piece on the album. His own three compositions are noteworthy for their rhythmic energy, forming early examples of funk music. He also accompanies Robinson's more balladesque pieces with great originality and empathy. Scott Yanow finds the music 'warm, lyrical, and thoughtful'.[71]

Shortly after recording *Funk Dumpling* the two men worked in Birdland with pianist Richard Wyands.[72] 'Grimes and Robinson played numerous gigs in many different settings, including a psychiatrists' convention in Atlantic City, NJ. 'We had a big lobster

dinner and played a little jazz,' says the clarinetist. Robinson has a
great fondness for the bassist and over the decades has continued
to perform and record pieces by Grimes and also dedicated a composition, 'Henry's Dance', to him on his 1977 Chiaroscuro album
The Traveler.[73] Three years after recording *Funk Dumpling*, Henry
Grimes and Perry Robinson met for another studio date, this time
for Henry's album *The Call*, recorded during the period when they
shared an apartment on the Lower East Side.[74]

Paths to Free Form (1963–66)

> *But it's not the note being played that's important. What's important is
> the note that follows. That's the note I'll play.*
>
> Henry Grimes, 2003.[75]

Judging from the surviving sound recordings, the year 1963 marked
the moment when Henry Grimes turned noticeably toward free
jazz. Especially important was his work with Sonny Rollins, who in
turn was striving more intently toward free forms. It was here that
Grimes also met Don Cherry and Billy Higgins. Two other form-
ative companions on this evolutionary path were Steve Lacy and,
above all, Cecil Taylor.

On Uncharted Trails with Sonny Rollins (1963)

> *Henry has always been a serious, intense and fearless musician whose
> personal life reflected those exceptional qualities. I admire him greatly.*
>
> Sonny Rollins[76]

Sonny Rollins has vivid memories of Grimes' skill at fearless, powerful, and inventive improvisation in the early 1960s. Four years
after their long European tour of 1959, he again hired the bassist
for his latest musical explorations and several big concert tours.
One of them led to Europe at the very beginning of the year;
another took them to Japan in September – a first for both of them.
Luckily, many of these concerts were recorded live, though sometimes only by tape pirates, and can be re-experienced today on
technically remastered CDs. In contrast, there are no sound
recordings of the American concerts Henry gave with Sonny

outside the jazz music metropolis of New York City.[77] However, Lee Konitz was an eye- and ear-witness to an especially inspired concert that Rollins gave on one of his US tours, with Henry playing bass: 'And one time in the early sixties, in San Francisco, Sonny was late for an afternoon set, and Paul Bley asked me to sit in. [...] Henry Grimes was the bass player and Roy McCurdy was the drummer. I was just in the audience, and I don't know how come I had my horn with me. So I played a set, and then Sonny came in, and played the most fantastic set you could imagine – non-stop outness! He just played stunningly creatively. It was very free, though with a groove.'[78]

In 1963 Sonny Rollins formed a quartet, rather than a trio as he had done in 1959. Besides himself and Henry Grimes (and sometimes the bassist Bob Cranshaw as well), the new group featured two musicians who had previously played with Ornette Coleman: the trumpeter and cornetist Don Cherry, and the drummer Billy Higgins. The quartet ventured into uncharted musical territory. In the course of roughly eight months of collaboration, they developed a highly distinctive music and inspired the leader to extended free forms of improvisation. Henry Grimes' bass playing likewise underwent a fundamental change. In 1959 he gave Sonny Rollins' musical explorations a tight, inventive, and sensitive accompaniment. By 1963, however, he was presenting long solo excursions, plucked and often bowed, that made listeners sit up and take notice. Particularly remarkable was the quartet's increasing tendency to create musical dialogues.

In 2007 Sonny Rollins was asked to explain his reasons for working so intensively with Henry Grimes again, whether his decision was related to the musical transformation he had undergone after his sabbatical of 1959–61. He didn't confirm this transformation, explaining that he never listens to his own music. Though he didn't say anything about the music of his 1963 quartet, he excitedly talked about the day-to-day life on the tour: 'In Düsseldorf, I remember, I had one of my best concerts. Henry, Don Cherry, and Billy Higgins. I remember very well, we were traveling in those days with our instruments and our luggage, we were carrying all our own bags, and we were trying to get the right train. So we were going to the station and finally we got the train to

Düsseldorf, ran in at the last minute, the doors closed, and we had all our luggage and everything. And we were tired, we were traveling all the day. We got to Düsseldorf and we had one of our best concerts of the whole tour.'[79]

Grimes himself, in a 2005 interview with the music and video journalist Bret Primack, delved for the first time more deeply into his collaboration with the tenor saxophonist, especially emphasizing Sonny Rollins' outstanding technique: 'He plays well straight-ahead into everything with technique and you have to come around with him, which is good. We always worked out that kind of form. It was beautiful to know. [. . .] Very fantastic technique, his technique is amazing, you know.'[80] The same interview reveals that their joint tours often came off with few words spoken: 'He didn't talk to any of us much. That was not because he wasn't talking to us but . . . I don't know he had something on his mind, maybe he was working on arrangements, something like that, you know, but as I said, he is a quiet man.'[81] Evidently the concerts were not always preceded by rehearsals; sometimes they walked directly onto the stage: 'We went on the bandstand and sometimes we worked out what we were going to do that night. Other times we were working on some arrangements that he did before we started the gig going to Europe. Sometimes we worked both ways.'[82] It was Grimes' impression that, at their reunion in 2004, they picked up exactly where they had left off in the early 1960s: 'I spoke with him a short while back in Lincoln Center in New York, where he was playing with his group. We talked exactly the same way as we did years before. There was no difference. [. . .] when we spoke together he was the same as always. Our conversation turned on the same subjects; he was completely natural.'[83]

Rollins' music of the early 1960s is freer than in the 1950s. Yet free form is always present in his playing, even before the 1960s. Like Ornette Coleman at the beginning of the 1960s, the Sonny Rollins Quartet of 1963 played music that abandoned the traditional jazz music framework. However, this freedom is reached on different levels in each case.[84] Though half of the Sonny Rollins Quartet was made up of Ornette Coleman veterans, on closer listening the mark they left on the music as a whole is not as deep as it is sometimes made out to be.[85]

In this respect, Ekkehard Jost, in *Free Jazz*, comes closer to the truth: 'Coleman is consistent in eliminating the bonds of functional harmony and divisions into bar-patterns. But he holds fast to what could be called the traditional superstructure. The schematic order of the theme, solo improvisation and theme, with the tempo remaining constant. Rollins takes the opposite path. While the inner structures of his music, their melodic and harmonic content, are largely in line with the laws of Fifties' jazz, the overall form of his pieces is permanently open to spontaneous alteration. [...] Following Rollins' lead in a process of continuous interaction, the group attains a variety of structure only rarely encountered in the free jazz of the early Sixties. In this respect, the music of the Rollins Quartet is closer to that of Charles Mingus than to Ornette Coleman. Like Mingus, Rollins does not eliminate traditional models in general, but calls them into question by playing with them, thus stripping them of their normative value. [...] Sonny Rollins usually takes the lead in initiating structural alterations, he proves as well to be perceptive to every musical idea his colleagues suggest while the piece is in progress.'[86]

Rollins likewise relates his musical ideas of 1963 closely to the musical figures he worked with at the time.[87] In short, if there was an influence at all, it came not primarily from Ornette Coleman, but directly from Don Cherry, Henry Grimes, and Billy Higgins, though Cherry and Higgins naturally made use of Coleman's innovative musical approach (later named as 'harmolodic') in their playing, among other things. Conversely, what Ekkehard Jost wrote of Don Cherry in 1970 applies equally to Henry Grimes: 'Working with Rollins laid the foundation for many things that continue to distinguish Don Cherry's music today. It is likely that one of the most important lessons he learned was that traditional models and improvisational freedom are by no means incompatible.'[88]

The European tour of January 1963 took the Sonny Rollins Quartet to Copenhagen's 'Folkonercentret' on January 15,[89] and to Stockholm on January 17 (both concerts are noteworthy for their high degree of free form).[90] On January 19 they held two concerts in the Paris Olympia,[91] and on the next day they traveled to Rome.[92] On January 29 they gave a concert in the Stuttgart Liederhalle,[93] having probably appeared previously in Milan and Düsseldorf.

There are several black-and-white photographs from Milan showing the quartet in elegant suits, including a photo taken by Riccardo Schwamenthal during a concert at Teatro Dell'Arte, Milan, Italy.[94] Apparently neither the Milan nor the Düsseldorf concert was recorded, for there is no known discographical information on them.

During the Paris concert, Rollins personally introduced his ensemble with special words of praise for his bassist, as in 1959: 'Our bassist, a guy that was here with me a few years ago right on this stage and he is proved to be a favorite of yours and he is of mine: Henry Grimes!! Contrabasso.'[95] Two reviews of 1963 show

Henry Grimes, Don Cherry, Billy Higgins, Sonny Rollins, Milan, January 1963: the Sonny Rollins Quartet on tour in Europe (© Riccardo Schwamenthal/CTSIMAGES).

how the quartet, always rubbing against the grain of old listening habits, was received in Paris and Stuttgart. Jef Gilson and Claude Lénissois of the French magazine *Jazz Hot* detected the alleged influence of Ornette Coleman, not only in Rollins but even in John Coltrane. They also complained about the poor acoustics of the Olympia and praised Grimes' propulsive drive and wealth of ideas while lamenting his 'approximate' and 'arid' playing style and the fact that he often made use of the bow.

Lénissois wrote that: 'On January 19 we again found bassist Henry Grimes at his side, this time with Billy Higgins (drums) and Don Cherry (cornet). [...] The influence of Ornette Coleman is decisive in both great tenormen, Coltrane and Rollins, and this in the same sense – a sort of pure madness. [...] As for the acoustics, the Olympia still has much room for improvement: Henry Grimes in particular could be heard only in the second part of the concert at 6 pm. [...] Grimes has wonderful drive, but his sometimes approximate intonation and arid sound, especially with the bow, hinder the clear expression of his many good ideas. [...] The team of Grimes and Higgins is surely one of the best rhythm sections today. [...] The order of the choruses was conspicuously the same in every piece (of the first concert): a series of choruses from the two horns, a chorus for bass (too often with the bow), and a drum chorus, after which Sonny took up the chorus [...].'[96]

Dieter Zimmerle, founder and chief editor of the German magazine *Jazz Podium*, reviewing the Stuttgart concert, had this to say about Grimes' playing: 'In Henry Grimes, who already accompanied him on his last trip to Europe, he has ideal rhythmic support. This magnificent bassist unflinchingly strikes his swing beat with voluminous sound and enters the musical events wherever needed as a soloist, often using the bow. He is equalled in this respect by drummer Billy Higgins, like Don Cherry a former member of the Ornette Coleman Quartet, so that we always have the impression of a homogeneous group in which each player is intently following what his colleagues are doing at any given moment.'[97]

When Peter Niklas Wilson wrote about the quartet in the original German version of his Sonny Rollins biography (1993), the new technically remastered CD releases of these European concerts were not yet available, and he criticized the substandard recording technique of the pirated editions at his disposal: 'Unfortunately the Rollins Quartet's European tour of January 1963 is documented only on bootleg editions. This is especially regrettable since this formation, as we can tell even from the technically deficient recordings, reached a level of ensemble playing that few other Rollins groups were able to attain.'[98]

One can only agree with this high 'level of ensemble playing'. As regards Wilson's description of the live recordings from

Copenhagen, particularly 'Oleo' and 'You Don't Know What Love Is': 'In "Oleo" Henry Grimes breaks the shackles of thirty-two-bar form with an unusual arco solo. And in the fourth piece, Rollins proves that he no longer needs to be anchored in a well-known theme in his interplay with Cherry, Grimes, and Higgins in order to break out and depart from it into free structures: a curt saxophone introduction develops into a completely open and thematically unfettered musical process that touches on a wealth of instrumental combinations and sound textures, from solo cadenza to collective improvisation, from rubato soundscapes to passages of metronomic regularity. Here Rollins, probably owing to the experience he has gained from working continuously with this group, sounds much more self-assured and focused – and more relaxed – than on the free "Oleo" version of July last year[99] (almost paradoxically, it is the avant-gardist Cherry who introduces the most traditional element with a quote from 'You Don't Know What Love Is'). The last item on the CD, also freely improvised, sounds at once more unified and conventional, as it is oriented almost entirely on a two-bar riff stated by Rollins at the beginning.'[100]

Here Wilson is presumably writing about the 'Improvised Medley' that also appears on the new CD release of the Copenhagen concert.[101] No less remarkable about the 'Oleo' version from this concert is the cello-like tone of the saxophone immediately after Henry's bowed solo. The Paris concert left Wilson less excited than the Copenhagen date: 'The only outstanding thing here is the wide-open version of "Solitude" – a fantasy from the two horns on motifs from Ellington's melody, with only occasional shading from the bass and drums.'[102] However, to evaluate the quality of this music primarily on the degree of free form it achieves is to overlook the high level and remarkable density of the quartet's ensemble playing even in more 'conventional' passages based more closely on the underlying theme.

A television appearance taped in Rome on January 28, 1963 and available on the internet since 2007 (and as a bonus track on the CD *Sonny Rollins and Don Cherry*: New York 1962/Stockholm 1963, released in 2009), conveys a vibrant impression of the elegantly dressed group playing '52nd Street Theme'. It also gives the listener an opportunity to experience Grimes' high-spirited arco technique in a lengthy solo.[103] For the Stuttgart concert, which follows the Rome date in Grimes' discography, the same thing applies as for the evening at the Paris Olympia: a blanket verdict of 'conventional' hovers over many inspired moments and distinctive aspects that the quartet produced at its Liederhalle concert.

Peter Niklas Wilson, again with a technically inferior bootleg edition at his disposal, writes of the concert: 'The live recording from Stuttgart shows the group's conventional side. The two titles (the "52nd Street Theme" is only a short fragment) suggest nothing of the openness that had impressed listeners at the Village Gate six months earlier (*Our Man In Jazz*). The design of the numbers and the sequence of solos follow traditional norms; the only thing that is free (and virtuosic) is the way the soloist handles the unbroken formal and harmonic patterns. Among the technical peculiarities of this production are not only the thin, distorted, unsteady sound, but the fact that all the pieces sound a half-tone too low: evidently the bootlegger's equipment wasn't running at normal speed.'[104]

These technical shortcomings have been expunged as far as possible on the new release of 2009. In 'On Green Dolphin Street' Grimes has a convincing extended solo excursion with hints of Sonny Rollins' technique of thematic improvisation. Now and then, as on several other live recordings from this period, one can hear him humming along to his own bass line in rapt concentration. Also impressive is the way Sonny Rollins intersperses the theme from 'On Green Dolphin Street' in the next piece, 'Sonnymoon For Two', which is indeed propelled by Henry Grimes' 'voluminous sound' and 'imperturbable swing beat' for long stretches at a time. Just how varied the quartet could sound from one venue to the next is demonstrated by the great receptivity of its music to external influences, whether from the audience or from the concert hall and its acoustics. The varying amount of free form does not, therefore, automatically indicate a difference in quality. All these surviving concerts merit close listening, particularly because of the differences between them.

Immediately after their return from Europe, the quartet entered the recording studio. On February 20 they recorded three pieces – 'You Are My Lucky Star', 'I Could Write A Book', and

'There Will Never Be Another You' – for the RCA sampler *Three in Jazz* (1964), which combined music from Gary Burton, Sonny Rollins, and Clark Terry on a single disc. Seven days later came another studio date whose music, however, was not released.[105]

In 2005, the *DownBeat* writer Michael Jackson asked Henry Grimes about the February 20 studio date. Grimes remembered initial difficulties for Don Cherry and Billy Higgins, adding that they gradually lessened. He also emphasized the lasting influence of Sonny Rollins' ideas on his own music to the present day: 'Don felt a little negative about his playing, and it was initially difficult for him and Billy Higgins. We all have some uneasiness about our playing, but it came together. Playing with Sonny, even if you leave that band, you don't leave that music. I'm still trying to figure out certain things he does. His knowledge is fantastic.'[106]

A *DownBeat* review of *Three in Jazz* singled out Henry's prowess as a soloist: 'Grimes solos with imagination and triphammer strength.'[107] In contrast, Miles Davis, in a *DownBeat* blindfold test with Leonard Feather that same year, gave a muted response to the bass playing in 'You Are My Lucky Star': 'Now, why did they have to end it like that? Don Cherry I like, and Sonny I like, and the tune idea is nice. The rhythm is nice. I didn't care too much for the bass player's solo. Five stars is real good? It's just good, no more. Give it three.'[108]

Henry Grimes seldom displays his mastery of the bass in melody lines suitable for daydreaming. His playing tends toward the abrasive; it is marked at once by an oddly rich-hued abstract quality and by a swinging, primeval force that can give rise to familiar melody lines but recedes the moment they threaten to become superficially 'pretty'. Nor can one agree with Peter Niklas Wilson when, in the *Three in Jazz* titles, he misses the free interplay that had so often distinguished this quartet in the preceding months: 'The finale of this innovative collaboration is surprisingly conservative.' Wilson describes the three tracks, each with thirty-two beats in the familiar pattern, as being 'played at medium tempo' and 'with the usual sequence of (brief) solos'. His critical view is that: 'The strength of this outfit – the interaction, the spontaneous breaking down of traditional contexts – is really only heard on the coda to "There Will Never Be Another You".'[109] Those who listen closely to the three standards will also discover free form. But here the musical freedom was squeezed into the conditions of a studio production. Probably decisive for the allegedly 'conservative bent' is the fact that Sonny Rollins, a man acutely sensitive to social surroundings, rarely plays as freely in the studio as he does in concert – with consequences for the entire group. Another probable factor was that the record producer, owing to the limited length of the pieces and the taste of the prospective buyers, did not grant him the freedom he needed. Viewed in this light, the Sonny Rollins Quartet still manages to play amazingly freely on *Three in Jazz*. Whatever the case, after the RCA date, the members of this extraordinarily productive ensemble went their separate ways.

Henry Grimes, Newport Jazz Festival, July 6, 1963. Appearance with the Sonny Rollins Group (SR, Paul Bley, HG, Roy McCurdy) and special guest Coleman Hawkins (© Joe Alper, courtesy the Joe Alper Photo Collection IIC).

Sonny Rollins as he appeared with HG at the Newport Jazz
Festival, 6 July, 1963 (© Joe Alper, courtesy the Joe Alper
Photo Collection LLC).

Sonny Rollins nevertheless continued to work with Henry
Grimes.[110] Here the bassist had a musical experience which, as
Grimes recently put it, 'knocked him out!' Immediately after his
rediscovery in late 2002, Marshall Marrotte asked him in an
interview which recording date was most strongly emblazoned in
his memory, and received the following answer: 'My favorite would
have to be with Coleman Hawkins and Sonny Rollins (the LP *Sonny
Meets Hawk*); that really knocked me out! I remember those tunes,
the way we were playing them, very bluesy.'[111] Before Grimes

entered the studio with Sonny Rollins, Coleman Hawkins, Paul Bley, and Roy McCurdy on July 18, they had appeared at the Newport Festival on the 6th of that same month.[112] Apart from a *DownBeat* review by Ira Gitler, the concert was completely undocumented – until recently. Since 2012 a live radio recording lasting about ten minutes has been available on the internet.[113] In a blanket review of the 1963 Newport Festival, the prominent jazz journalist limits his discussion almost entirely to the musical anomalies he claims to have heard in this unusual booking while faulting the sound equipment:

'When the other saxophone Sonny Rollins, and one of his original models, Coleman Hawkins, locked horns on Saturday night, the results were not so happy,' Gitler opined. 'Rollins, with pianist Paul Bley, bassist Henry Grimes, and drummer Roy McCurdy, began the set with a blistering 'Remember?' in which Rollins inserted a particularly inventive unaccompanied section. Then Hawkins came on stage for 'All The Things You Are' and 'The Way You Look Tonight'. The sound system, generally excellent throughout the four days, was in imbalance here, leading to distortion of Rollins' already very powerful sound. Meanwhile, Hawkins' mike seemed to be failing, and it was hard to hear him. In 'Things' Hawkins played well, but the 'Tonight' tempo proved too much for him, and Rollins' staccato style [...] overpowered him. The most consistent musician of the set was Bley, who swung hard and probed ideas deeply.'[114]

The taped radio broadcast of 'All The Things You Are', available on YouTube, conveys a quite different impression. Perhaps the sound was improved on this recording but, quite apart from the technical side, what we hear is a charismatic modern reading of this standard. Hawkins is the first to improvise, with elegant, energetic melody lines, followed successively by Paul Bley and Sonny Rollins with inspired hard-swinging solos verging on atonality. Henry Grimes plays forceful non-stop pizzicato, sustaining the entire architecture of the piece and constantly propelling the ideas of every participant.

Twelve days later, at the studio date for *Sonny Meets Hawk*, Henry Grimes again stood at the bass to play 'Summertime', 'Just Friends', and 'At McKies' with Bob Cranshaw playing the other three pieces.[115] In a *Jazz Hot* interview of 2004, Henry singled out this LP as the favorite of all the recordings he made with Sonny Rollins.[116] John Goldsby and Ron Carter, in their *Jazz Bass Book* (published before Grimes' re-emergence), have special praise for the bassist's independent counterpoint in 'Summertime': 'Check out his work on "Summertime" from *Sonny Meets Hawk* (RCA, 1963). Grimes plays the bass function, and then he jumps into thumb position to add his own contrapuntal comments. He had a Mingus-like tone and a LaFaro-like delivery.'[117]

Peter Niklas Wilson considers 'At McKies', with Grimes on bass, the most striking piece on the album: 'The most unusual product of the two studio dates is perhaps Rollins' piece "At McKies". It is less a "theme" in the traditional sense than a four-bar phrase, used as the starting point for a free improvisation around the key of B flat. Hawkins demonstrates that he can make something of this exotic material even without the harmonic support of the piano, which sits out for long stretches.'[118]

The musicologist and journalist Marc Medwin was similarly enthusiastic in 2010: 'A moment symbolizing Grimes' transition from post-bop to free jazz can be heard on the July 1963 encounter of tenor giants Sonny Rollins and Coleman Hawkins, released on RCA as *Sonny Meets Hawk*. The band laid down a version of Gershwin's "Summertime" on which Grimes adopts the dual role of melodist and percussionist, adding layers of intrigue to Paul Bley and Roy's swung rhythms as Sonny and Hawk create intricate webs of polyphony. Later in the track, Grimes' solo finds him taking the bass out of its assumed role, his pizzicato full and punchy, his accents bold and decisive.'[119]

In August 1963 Grimes was scheduled for a one-week appearance with the Sonny Rollins Quartet at The Village Vanguard. He became ill and Bob Cranshaw subbed for him.[120] A little later the same Sonny Rollins quartet – but now with Grimes on bass again and joined by the illustrious Clark Terry, Coleman Hawkins, and Ben Webster – entered the RCA Victor studio, for a recording that regretfully never has been released.[121] Around that time the much sought after Henry Grimes also appeared for one week with Al Cohn and Zoot Sims at the Half Note[122]

The final milestone in the musical collaboration between

Coleman Hawkins, Newport Jazz Festival, 6 July, 1963. Appearance as special guest with the Sonny Rollins Group: SR, Paul Bley, HG, Roy McCurdy (© Joe Alper, courtesy of the Joe Alper Photo Collection, LLC).

Rollins and Grimes was a three-week tour of Japan in September 1963, sponsored by the Art Friends Association, which marked the first time either of the two men had visited the country. Joining them was vocalist Betty Carter as guest star on the entire tour, Grimes recalls, as well as trumpeter Reshid Kamal Ali, Paul Bley, and Roy McCurdy.[123] Several pieces from this highly successful tour are captured on a live private recording made from the Hotel Marunouchi in Tokyo on September 19.[124] Among the other stops on the tour was Osaka.[125] Even as they arrived at Tokyo International Airport, the Sonny Rollins Quintet was greeted enthusiastically by a crowd of some three hundred people consisting of fans, critics, reporters, and a television team from Nippon Broadcasting Co. Each member was given a bouquet of flowers, and Roy McCurdy is said to have quipped, 'I feel like an ambassador.'[126]

The band was driven to its hotel, the Tokyo Ginza, where the next day a press conference was held in the ceremonial hall before four hundred and fifty assembled reporters and critics. Sonny Rollins explained that the band he was taking on tour differed from his standard formation, and he introduced each band member as they sat at a table. 'We taped a TV show today,' he explained, 'and the main question that came up was the racial problem in the United States. My answer was this – I, as a musician, have my job to do. My place is to bring happiness and joy to the public with the music that I – we – play. This is what we hope to accomplish. It's obvious how I feel about the racial problem. I'll do my job – on the stand, with my instrument.'[127] Nine months later, in July 1964, Fred Miles and Jean French interviewed Sonny Rollins for the now defunct periodical *Abundant Sounds* and asked him, among other things, about his initial experience of Japan. He spoke of the many presents the band had received from its enthusiastic audience: 'It's a wonderful place. The people are very nice. We had to buy a trunk to bring back all the gifts we had and they liked the music.'[128] Henry Grimes describes the Japanese as being especially 'knowledgeable' listeners.[129] Paul Bley remembers the tour of Japan as '[o]ne of the highlights of my year with Sonny' and emphasizes that '[w]e were all good friends with Henry [...] he and Sonny were particularly close.'[130]

The qualities that prompted Rollins to resume his close collaboration with Grimes in 1963 were the same as in 1958–59: his intensity and earnestness as a musician. 'I can't differentiate the styles – but it was always those qualities of his musicianship and as a person. He was always very intense and very serious about his music. I liked that very much; I related to that very much.'[131] With wonted discretion, he also recalled Grimes' personality: 'Henry was a very private person. I respected Henry very much. You know, if I have respect with someone, I don't like to gossip. I respected Henry and his personality, his serious nature. That's what I remember about Henry. We had a good working relationship together and we had some good musical evenings playing together. There is nothing more that I remember about anything, except his dedication to what he was doing, his conscientiousness about his music, and that's the highest praise I can give him, and he deserves it.'[132]

Henry Grimes relates similar things about Sonny Rollins, emphasizing the high level of their playing and the benefits that accrued to his own music.[133] Rollins was pleasantly surprised: 'He said that? I'm honored, because Henry is playing with a lot of different people. That's wonderful, I'm very glad to hear him say that. I am very pleased.'[134] It was here that Sonny's great appreciation for Henry Grimes became truly manifest. When asked in conclusion why his work with Henry ended so abruptly after the Japan tour, he returned the question in amazement: 'Are you sure?' He was uncertain whether they might have continued working together after all.[135] However, there is no evidence that they did.[136] 'I think it was the last time I worked with Sonny.'[137] Grimes remembers that he needed a rest and a break after he came back from Japan, and then he began working with Albert Ayler and Cecil Taylor. However, he feels that the music he played together with Sonny Rollins continues to influence him until today.[138]

Probing Freedom with Steve Lacy and Others (1963)

Beginning in 1961, Henry Grimes played intermittently with the soprano saxophonist Steve Lacy, whose quartet then included trombonist Roswell Rudd and drummer Denis Charles. Lacy recalled the group in a 1993 interview: 'The band lasted from 1961–1964, hustling gigs everywhere including [...] an Armenian restaurant.'[139] Denis Charles remembers: 'We played Monk compositions ... We didn't make much money. I never felt comfortable.'[140] None of this discomfort is evident in his playing. In March 1963 the venturesome group played in New York's Phase Two Coffee House. A live recording of their performance was later released under the title *School Days*. Steve Lacy on Henry Grimes: 'As for the bassist, about thirty bass players have passed through this quartet. Twenty-seven, exactly. John Ore, Steve Swallow, Henry Grimes, Wilbur Ware were among the best.'[141] All the pieces on the album are by Thelonious Monk,[142] who served as a demanding mentor with his jagged compositions. To quote Steve Lacy – as per Peter Kostakis' CD liner notes – once again: '[T]he liberty was what interested us – a liberty through this discipline. And sure enough it worked – it was something on the other side, and we began to get through to a kind of freedom, a kind of looseness. It got looser and looser until it sounded like some New Orleans stuff after a while.'[143]

The process of liberation and the collective advance into surprising new musical territory is viscerally audible on this CD. Henry Grimes (on tracks 2 to 6) and Denis Charles go far beyond the conventional roles of bass and drums as timekeepers. Bursting with ideas, they contribute to the odd swing of the music. Peter Kostakis: 'Grimes adds imagination to technical command of the instrument on statements such as his Brilliant Corners solo, where a growling squally voice mock-"harmonizes" with pizzicato bass. This composition doubles the tempo every second chorus, and Grimes embraces the bewildering maze as if warding off a case of the scares. His moans in flat goofy accompaniment to the bass' dark intonation sound like Slam Stewart discovering existentialism. Elsewhere in the same performance, Grimes shows strength as a supporting player, setting off the humour of the theme's ominous angles and stopped-short cul-de-sacs with Inspector Cl[o]useau-like stalking/walking and ironic embellishments.'[144]

The liner notes for the 1993 CD release are silent on Henry's subsequent history: 'Grimes' present whereabouts since his move to the West Coast are, sadly, unknown; but *The Call*, his recording as a leader, is back in print along with a host of other ESP titles featuring him as sideman.'[145] When the jazz historian Steve L. Isoardi played Grimes this album on CD in February 2003, shortly after his return to music, he claimed that though he could remember nothing about the recording session, the band members, or the studio location, he remembered every single note.[146] Once again one can see how intently Grimes enters into the processes of the music; in such moments he apparently leaves everything else behind – the people, the place, the time.

In March 1963 Grimes also played on three recordings headed by musicians of the 'moderate' avant-garde: two studio dates with the tenor saxophonist Bill Barron, and another with vibraphone player Walt Dickerson.[147] The drummer on the latter recording was Andrew Cyrille, whom Henry would frequently meet over the next few years in his work with Cecil Taylor.[148] The musically complex yet swinging pieces on the album *Jazz Impressions of Lawrence of Arabia* draw directly on Maurice Jarre's original film score.[149]

Some months earlier, in fall 1962, Grimes was scl
European tour with Cecil Taylor – the pianist's very
Europe. It was to last six months, and it granted Taylor
umphs beyond his wildest dreams in his native country　　──ɔ ɑɪɪ.s
his cooperation with Henry Grimes at that time: 'Then I went out
to a place called the Take 3, and I got the job performing. And it's
been going and stopping like that ever since for me. We – me,
Jimmy Lyons, Sunny Murray – worked there for thirteen weeks; it
was the longest gig I ever had in America. Sometimes the magnificent Henry Grimes would come in: I remember one night he did,
and we played for three hours but I thought we'd played for about
ten minutes. Coltrane heard us there, and arranged for us to make
our first Scandinavian tour.'[150]

The drummer in Taylor's outfit, Sunny Murray, precisely recalls
the 1962 tour. When Dan Warburton asked him in 2000 whether
Taylor's saxophone-piano-drums formation was originally meant to
include a bassist (the saxophonist on the tour was Jimmy Lyons),[151]
he replied: 'There was supposed to be Henry Grimes, but he got
sick just before we left, so when we arrived in Europe we were just
a trio. I remember Nils Henning Ørsted went over to Cecil's table
once – he was sixteen.'[152] Grimes too remembers having health
problems that first cropped up around this time and constantly
recurred, but were finally overcome toward the end of the 1970s: 'I
did have some problems then. It had been going on for some time.
I had to take medication, Thorazine, to help with it. I had to go
into the hospital for a while. They diagnosed me with [...]
depression, and it was really hard on me. The medication helped
me out though, for a while. [...] The [...] depression bothered me
for a long time, but about 1978 I just started feeling better. I haven't
had much of a problem since then. [...] No medications.'[153]

On New Year's Eve, 1963, the collaboration with Cecil Taylor
finally came about. The quintet, now including Jimmy Lyons on
alto saxophone, Albert Ayler on tenor, and Sunny Murray, held a
concert in New York's Philharmonic Hall that was recorded privately but is still unavailable.[154] Yet Henry Grimes' true period in
Cecil Taylor's band only began three years later.[155]

Henry's discography for the next year, 1964, lists two recordings
with Albert Ayler, indicating that he consistently pursued his free

music activities. His awareness of civil rights also came to the fore in this period.

Henry Grimes and the Civil Rights Movement (1963–64)

When life itself offers no order and meaning, the musician creates an order and meaning from the sounds of the earth which flow through his instrument. It is no wonder that so much of the search for identity among American Negroes was championed by Jazz musicians. [...] Much of the power of our Freedom Movement in the United States has come from this music. [...] And now, Jazz is exported to the world. For in the particular struggle of the Negro in America there is something akin to the universal struggle of modern man. [...] In music, especially this broad category called Jazz, there is a stepping stone towards all of these.

Dr. Martin Luther King, Jr.,
opening address to the Berlin Jazz Festival, 1964[156]

Jazz is the transforming aesthetic of an oppressed people becoming free.
Henry Grimes, 2012[157]

In 1963–64, the politicization of thought and life brought about by the civil rights movement reached the predominantly white world of the music industry. Thus the program director and organizer of the 1964 Berlin Jazz Festival, Joachim Ernst Berendt, invited Dr. Martin Luther King Jr. to write a preface to the event's program and the prominent civil rights activist delivered the words quoted above. American music critics began to address the social contradictions and tensions between black and white, as is evident in a two-part article published in *DownBeat* in 1963. Here Leonard Feather, Red Mitchell, George Shearing, James L. Tolbert, John Tynan, and Gerald Wilson issued public statements beneath the headings 'Racial Prejudice in Jazz' and 'The Need for Racial Unity in Jazz: a Panel Discussion'.[158]

The renowned New York jazz club, the Five Spot, openly sided with the demands of the civil rights movement and organized two benefit concerts for the Congress of Racial Equality (CORE) on October 20 and 27, 1963. James Farmer, the organization's then national director,[159] sent written words of gratitude to each musician who participated actively in the concerts – including Henry Grimes, who had played at the Five Spot on October 27:[160]

November 5, 1963

Mr. Henry Grimes,
c/o Five Spot Café
2 St. Marks Place,
New York, New York

Dear Mr. Grimes:

All of us at CORE are deeply grateful for your help in making the benefit performance at the Five Spot Cafe a resounding success.

In the extremity of the Civil Rights battle that now confronts us, this kind of tangible and practical support is essential.

Thanking you again, I remain

Yours in freedom,

James Farmer,
National director, CORE.

Although not detailed, Henry Grimes remembers his performances and political participation with Amiri Baraka, and his participation with the poet and activist in civil rights movement strategy meetings that took place in Harlem at Babatunde Olatunji's loft and probably other fairly secret locations.

In a statement about his history with Amiri Baraka from January 14, 2014 (five days after Amiri Baraka's decease), Grimes explains: 'I cannot begin to describe the power of Amiri Baraka's influence on my life or the many ways he enlightened me and uplifted my spirit, making it possible for me (and millions of others) to be proud of who we are and the people we came from and to live courageously, as he did. I remember first meeting Amiri in the '60s at Babatunde Olatunji's loft. Cecil Taylor first took me up there. Amiri started a movement right there of bringing in people with various literary talents and a lot of musicians and a lot of speakers. He organized this himself. Musicians were joining up and going up

```
CORE BENEFIT - FIVE SPOT CAFE - 2 ST. MARKS PLACE

Oct. 20, 1963

M.C.'s - Billy Taylor and Don Heckman

Ted Curson - trumpet                    Edgar Bateman - drums
Bill Baron - alto                       Dick Kniss - bass
Dick Berk - drums                       Don Friedman - piano
Ronnie Boykins - bass                   Helen Merrill - vocal
Kenny Burrell - guitar                  Ben Reilly - drums
Ray Draper - tuba                       Dick Katz - piano
Ben Webster - tuba                      Thad Jones - trumpet & flugel
Billy Taylor - piano                    Tommy Williams - bass
Joe Newman - trumpet                    Roy Haynes - drums
Horace Parlan - piano                   & Frank Strozier - alto
Frankie Dunlop - comedy mimic


Oct. 27, 1963

MC's - Ira Gitler & Alan Grant

Bill Evans - piano                      Bobby Hutchinson - vibes
Gary Peacock - bass                     Joe Chambers - drums
Paul Motian - drums                     Ron Carter - bass
Al Cohn - tenor                         Freddie Redd - piano
Zoot Sims - tenor
Sal Mosca - piano
Dick Scott - drums
Hal Dodson - bass
Sheila Jordan - vocal                   Booker Ervin - tenor
Jack Reilly - piano                     Henry Grimes - bass
Dave Sibley - bass
Prince Lasha - alto
Paul Bley - piano
J. R. Monterose - alto
Eric Dolphy - bass clarinet, alto & flute
```

List of musicians who played at the Five Spot, NY, on October 20 and 27, 1963, two benefit concerts for the Congress of Racial Equality (CORE), (reproduction courtesy Margaret and Henry Grimes).

there. It was kind of an artistic and political and intellectual gathering under the banner of Amiri Baraka's poetry. I played up there a few times with Cecil and various others. Amiri and I also played benefit concerts for the civil-rights and black-power movements in downtown Manhattan and the Village of Harlem and Brooklyn, and participated in strategy meetings at Babatunde Olatunji's loft and other secret locations in Harlem, coordinated and run by a number of organizations of that time – SNCC, CORE, the NAACP, a few of the Panthers, Malcolm X and his people, members of the Organization of African Unity, etc. I seem to remember Ralph Abernathy, Harry Belafonte, John Coltrane, James Farmer, Clifford Jarvis, Yusef Lateef coming through these meetings.'[161]

Further evidence bearing witness to Henry Grimes' awareness of civil rights and dedication to justice dates from 1964. This time

Grimes openly expressed his claim to equal rights, not only in his music, but in his everyday behavior on tour. On July 2, 1964, the famous Civil Rights Act was passed, abolishing segregation in all establishments open to the public, including schools, restaurants, and hotels, and thereby granting equal rights of admission to everyone irrespective of race, color, or creed.[162] In the same week that the legislation was passed, Henry Grimes, then on the Music for Moderns tour, showed beyond the shadow of a doubt that he intended to live on the basis of the new law. The singer Helen Merrill, who took part in the same tour, remembers the occasion. Asked by Wayne Enstice, for his book *Jazzwomen*, 'When did you first notice a big change in racial attitudes?' she replied: 'You know, Henry Grimes was on the Music for Moderns tour, too. The law changed the week that we were booked into a very fancy hotel in Memphis. According to the new law, the hotel had to accept black and white. Most of the black musicians chose not to tackle the new law and stayed at a friendly motel that they were accustomed to. But Henry, being aware of the law change, and knowing that we had reservations at this famous hotel, walked up to the desk and checked in. He had a suitcase with a rope on it. The receptionist looked shocked. But we were booked as a group, and Henry was clearly on the list. He was a very, very courageous man. It touches my heart every time I think about that picture. It still goes on as we all know, but there's quite a difference today.'[163]

The fearlessness that Grimes displayed in this everyday matter – evidently all by himself – is also present in his music, as noted by Sonny Rollins, who came to value this artistic stance in his former bassist and still mentions it today.[164] This quality was equally important for the ensembles of the innovator Albert Ayler, with whom Grimes worked closely on many occasions between 1964 and 1966.

'Spirits Rejoice' – Collective Improvisation with Albert Ayler (1964-66)

When Marshall Marrotte tracked down Henry Grimes in downtown Los Angeles in the fall of 2002 and visited him in his hotel room, one of his first questions was, 'What caused you to leave music, and your recollections of friends and musicians like Sonny Rollins, Don Cherry, Albert Ayler …?'[165] Grimes immediately wanted to know, 'How is Albert doing?'[166] He was unaware that his former musical companion had drowned in the East River in November 1970, under circumstances that have never been entirely explained. In 2002 he envisioned Albert Ayler as a living person and felt just as closely attached to him as in the 1960s.[167] He spoke of his special rapport with Ayler in an interview with Ben Young for the *Ayler Anniversary* CD Box in 2003: 'I feel that Albert understood me in certain ways. I don't remember when we talked about the kind of union we had, but we had it. I just couldn't know exactly why I had this feeling. We were on a very friendly basis; there was never any other way. On the one hand he didn't talk to me too much about it and I didn't talk to him too much about it. But still on the other hand, it seemed like we had talked about this somewhere, you know — that kind of feeling of extrasensory perception. Kind of a strangely beautiful thing. It's like he knew every word I was thinking, and I knew every word he was thinking, some way. But with no connection I could make about 'When did that happen?' – I never had that experience with anybody but Albert Ayler. He's a beautiful musician.'[168] Note the use of the present tense.

Intuitive rapport was a basic condition for Ayler's free, spiritual music, and his powerful sound transferred it to those who took part in his performances. Guitarist Marc Ribot, who worked with Grimes in his Spiritual Unity project and still works with Henry in his Marc Ribot Trio: 'What you get from an Albert Ayler record isn't a polished aesthetic gem where everything is perfect. It's more like an artifact of a ritual experience, as if you were standing in the back of a room while a ritual ceremony or sacrifice was being performed and you can't quite see what's going on but you know something is going on.'[169]

In 1966 the musical press began to take notice of Ayler's message on a more lasting basis. From then on he was discussed in many leading jazz music magazines and sometimes allowed to speak for himself. Nat Hentoff, for example, asked the brothers Albert and Don Ayler how they would recommend listening to their music: 'You have to relate sound to sound inside the music,' Ayler explained. 'I mean you have to try to listen to everything together.' Later in the same interview he added, 'It's really free, spiritual music, not just free music.'[170] In a *Jazz Podium* interview conducted by journalist (and since 1989 chief editor) Gudrun Endress in New York, he found especially probing words for his spiritual approach: 'Why do I have to live? Why do I have to die? Just to be reborn where the Spiritual dominates even more fully.'[171] *DownBeat* writer Henry Woodfin aptly noted of Ayler at the time: 'The direction that seems more promising for him – and it demands talent and control – is to work further with the technique of 'free' improvisation. Such a procedure requires that both Ayler and his fellow performers achieve the highest sensitivity to each other and their respective styles.'[172] Grimes' sharp intuition, sensitive ear, and powerful delivery were tailor-made for this approach.

In the years between 1964 and 1966 Henry Grimes and Albert Ayler jammed and toured extensively with each other, and Grimes felt ties of friendship with the saxophonist without actually spending much 'free time' with him. They were musically attached by the fact that both had started their careers in rhythm and blues bands.[173] At the same time, Henry maintained his own artistic standpoint in their collective improvisations: 'A fantastic improviser, amazing musician. He would come up with things completely out of nowhere, and from everywhere. We played together a lot, just jamming, and Albert had all these sounds going on [...]. The music had a spiritual element, but I didn't want to get too caught up in it and overplay, do too much, you know? Didn't want to overcontribute. Albert and I didn't hang out too much unless we were touring or in a studio or something, but I considered him a friend, a buddy.'[174]

In 1964 Ayler returned to America after a fairly long stay in Scandinavia: 'I decided to go back to America, so that's when I started playing with Cecil Taylor at the Take Three.'[175] Take Three was a Greenwich Village coffee house in Bleecker Street.[176] 'Eric Dolphy and John Coltrane used to come and listen to Sunny Murray, Jimmy Lyons, Henry Grimes, and myself and Cecil [...] and Eric would come in to listen with Coltrane after they had finished at the Village Gate. Because they knew it was some new music that was happening. That was very strange. They couldn't understand it, but they could feel it. We would play with Cecil and we would make five dollars. He would give it all to us for food and take nothing, so we would come back the next day and play with him again. [...] This was in 1964.'[177]

Originally Ayler and Murray also considered taking Grimes along as the Scandinavia tour's bassist, but Henry, as Murray recalls, was confined to hospital at the time, and the tour was ultimately joined by Gary Peacock, who was also unwell – suffering from a stomach ulcer.[178] In Europe, too, audiences had just begun to warm to Ayler's improvisations in 1964: 'I remember one night in Stockholm [...]. I started to play what was in my soul. The promoter pulled me off the stage. So I went to play for little Swedish kids in the subway. They heard my cry. That was in 1962. Two years later I was back with my own group – Don Cherry, Sunny Murray, Gary Peacock. The promoter woke up. He didn't pull me off the stage that time.'[179] Some listeners dismissed his polarizing music as "Salvation Band on LSD",[180] others immediately recognized 'many elements of previous jazz styles [...]: the free shaping of a composition based on underlying melodic ideas, an emphasis on improvisation, an ensemble spirit in collective performance, polyphony à la New Orleans jazz music, and distinctive and easily identifiable personal styles.'[181]

Peacock, writing in 1966, described how Ayler's novel performance style exploded the classical concept of 'note': 'In the improvisation, the melody line is replaced by structures created on the instrument by means of intervallic leaps from note to note, with each note ceasing to exist as an integrative factor. Ayler is interested in all possibilities inherent in a single note. In his playing, he can make the note completely unrecognizable – multiplying it, transforming it, and thus departing from the actual concept of 'note' in the conventional sense.'[182]

When Henry Grimes speaks of Albert Ayler's music, he emphasizes: 'It seems to me that he had a religious approach in his music, as far as I can tell. I can say that he moved in this direction, even if I don't know the inner motivation.'[183] Though Ayler himself rarely talked about his spiritual context to his fellow musicians, he did so in public. In 1969, for example, he published an apocalyptic, sermon-like text in the underground magazine *The Cricket*.[184] He also spoke to journalists who asked him about it: 'For me, the only way I can thank God for his ever-present creation is to offer to him a new music impressed of a beauty which nobody had previously understood [...]. The music we play is one long prayer, a message coming from God. [...] Like Coltrane, I'm playing about the beauty that is to come after all the tensions and anxieties. This is about post-war cries; I mean the cries of love that are already in the young and that will emerge as people seeking freedom come to spiritual freedom.'[185]

Ayler already found apocalyptic words in a *DownBeat* interview of 1966: 'I'm trying to communicate to as many people as I can. It's late now for the world. And if I can help raise people to new plateaus of peace and understanding, I'll feel my life has been worth living as a spiritual.'[186] Like his mentor John Coltrane, Albert Ayler was convinced that music can free people from inner constraints: 'Our music should be able to remove frustration, to enable people to act more freely, to think more freely.'[187]

What Grimes especially values in Ayler's music and performance style is its energy, which for him possesses an inexhaustible presence and vitality: 'Most of his recordings were made around 1965, but even today you can hear his energy. He and his brother played with lots and lots of power.'[188] He describes Albert Ayler, the man, as 'very avant-garde, if you can imagine such a thing as an avant-garde person.'[189] '[...] his personality and the way he would pick up his horn and play. He would just pick it up and play and the sounds would just go all over everywhere, indoors and outdoors and everywhere else. That's just what you would have to deal with. Him and his brother, they really wrote these things out together and made it work out. It was beautiful. I would like to know more. I didn't know as much as I wanted to. I realize now that I wanted to know much more. [...] It really inspires me now that the old music from that age is still the new music that it is. The way it sounds now [...] we must have exploded.'[190]

Henry Grimes still remembers the challenges that Albert Ayler posed on improvisation: 'You had to pay attention. It was very demanding.'[191] He stresses its 'abstract design'[192] along with its 'unique take on gospel' that 'never lost its "roots in the church".'[193] Altogether Henry Grimes played on four Albert Ayler albums, sometimes alternating or playing synchronously with another bassist.[194] The period during which he played in Albert Ayler's groups is often called the zenith of this innovative saxophonist's roughly ten-year artistic career.[195]

The first two albums, *Witches And Devils*[196] and *Goin' Home*,[197] differ fundamentally in conception. Both were recorded in Atlantic Recording Studios, New York, on February 24, 1964, by practically the same musicians. For Sunny Murray, *Witches And Devils* (originally entitled *Spirits*) was 'the most spiritual session I had with Albert. In this session we felt like we were on LSD, but we had spiritual hallucinations.'[198] *Goin' Home* is a 'long unpublished spirituals session by Ayler that had to wait until 1982 before George Coppens released it on his Osmosis label.'[199] Sunny Murray excitedly recalls Albert Ayler's idea of recording traditional spirituals, i.e., pieces in which the 'religious rhythm and blues groove' – that was at the core of the saxophonist's true originality – could come into play.[200]

Witches And Devils is 'entirely the work of Albert Ayler. He chose the themes and also the musicians: one of his friends from Cleveland, the very young trumpeter Norman Howard, and two of his friends from Cecil Taylor's ensemble – Henry Grimes and Sunny Murray. And in the end a second bassist, Earle Henderson. [...] As for Henry Grimes, he contributes to the piece's complexity wherever necessary by introducing small, accurate attacks, a sort of playful sizzle, and quick-witted accents.'[201] 'The album', Peter Niklas Wilson sums up, 'contains thirty-six minutes of liberated music. Yet the prevailing impression is not one of unfettered energy, but of relaxation. This lies partly in the fact that two of the four pieces – the title theme and 'Saints' – are *rubato* ballads, and partly on the fact that Sunny Murray and the two bassists are usually spare and dynamically restrained, always intent on keeping the music transparent and giving lots of space to the lines of the horns.'[202]

LeRoi Jones (Amiri Baraka) noted about Grimes in this context that he 'can sound like a string quartet, but the complexity and subtlety of his playing never obscures the hot rhythmic core of his driving "accompaniments". One of the tunes, "Witches and Devils", should frighten anyone given to mystical involvement or even simple impressionistic reaction. It is a scary tune, going deep beneath what we say is real to that other portion of our selves that is, finally, realer, and much less familiar.'[203]

On *Going' Home*, on the other hand, Albert Ayler offers 'an almost literal reading of the traditional melodies, albeit with powerful vibrato and much fervor, yet with no improvisatory license at all.'[204] The traditional material on *Goin' Home* allowed Ayler to reveal the basic lineaments of his style,[205] with Call Cobbs 'festooning Ayler's *rubato* delivery with *ex tempore* arabesques and conventional solos.'[206] In contrast, Henry Grimes on this album reveals himself as the strong rhythmic bass player he is: 'at home in the metronomical freedom that is available, and an outstanding contrapuntal voice. "Ol' Man River – Take 2" is an object lesson in how he uses his leader's comparatively basic line as a sounding board for his own inventive process. The nature of the material demands that he observes certain thematic disciplines but, at every turn, he is seeking to extend the listener's perception of them. This makes him naturally compatible with Murray, a drummer who is a master of rhythmic displacement.'[207]

Marc Ribot emphasizes the wholly innovative type of ensemble on this Albert Ayler recording – his favorite album altogether – and especially singles out Henry Grimes' contribution: 'Listen to what Henry Grimes is doing on *Goin' Home* – a different role for the bassist. So the changing of the traditional roles of instrument, different forms of counterpoint, different kinds of collective improvising. [...] There are all the different combinations of collective improvising, which you could call an innovation. [...] It's a treat for me to work with the musician who played bass on my favorite recording of all time.'[208]

Six years later the guitarist again mentioned Henry Grimes' extraordinary contribution to *Goin' Home*, noting his unique blend as a soloist and a member of the rhythm section: 'Especially on that album, Henry established a role that is somewhere between a soloist and a rhythm section player. He's soloing but he's not soloing. He's supporting but he's not supporting. He didn't invent this out of thin air. He's not the only one, but he did it and still does it in a very particular way. And aside from that there's a certain gravitas to everything he plays. That's what I value most in the musicians I work with – that's what I seek out.'[209] The tapes for

Goin' Home were left unreleased for decades. In 1964 Albert Ayler
played them to ESP's director Bernard Stollman, who, lacking a
deep training in and sensitivity for music, took a dislike to them
and was 'upset to hear spirituals played in that way'.[210]

The next Albert Ayler album that Henry Grimes worked on was
Spirits Rejoice, 'one of Ayler's most energetic sessions',[211] recorded
on September 23, 1965, 'at New York's Judson Hall, selected by
engineer David Hancock for its acoustical individuality'.[212] Ayler,
wanting two bassists for this recording, hired Henry Grimes and
Gary Peacock. This was the last time Peacock would meet the saxophonist.[213]

The French music journalist Guy Kopelowicz, then visiting
New York, was accidentally given an opportunity to take part in the
recording: 'A few hours after my arrival, I ran into Sunny Murray
who was standing outside Slugs' on the Lower East Side. Murray
was helping there in the capacity of a club bouncer. He had been

Albert Ayler, Donald Ayler, Sunny Murray, Charles Tyler, Henry Grimes, Gary
Peacock, recording session of Albert Ayler's *Spirits Rejoice*, Judson Hall, NYC, September 23, 1965 (© Guy Kopelowicz).

offered the part-time job through Henry Grimes, with whom he was sharing an apartment. Grimes was playing at the club that night as part of the Charles Lloyd quartet. [...] The full band assembled for a quick sound check, and at 4:30 pm the recording proceeding started. Two hours later, all the music for the album had been recorded. [...] There were no second takes. "It's always like that with Albert," Murray told me. When the tunes were done, the musicians went to the control booth to listen to the tapes. They seemed happy with the music.'[214] Afterwards the musicians were in such high spirits that they all went to dine at an Indian restaurant.[215]

Besides Albert Ayler, Henry Grimes, Call Cobbs, Gary Peacock and Sunny Murray, this recording included Charles Tyler on alto saxophone and Donald Ayler on trumpet. Originally Ayler wanted Cobbs to play vibraphone, 'but eventually settled for a harpsichord, the instrument that provides the luxuriant waves of tinkling sound on "Angels", and the later Impulse recording, *Love Cry*.'[216] The upshot is that the session, *Spirits Rejoice*, 'is mainly a collective improvisation [...] in which the seemingly caricatured "military" phrases return periodically. Each horn has a period out front, but even then basses and percussion are busy with their disjunct yet complementary patterns. [...] There are other advances, for instance on Coltrane's use of two basses. With Coltrane they still marked time, in however complicated a fashion, didn't alter speed and didn't play lines really independent of the horn(s). Here they do. There is greater – and significant – freedom between basses and percussion, both among themselves and in relation to the horns. And hear the bass duet on "Prophet".'[217] Grimes plays in a two-bass configuration with Peacock on every title. 'Such a setup became more frequent during this time and Grimes also performed in this tandem configuration with Bill Folwell, Alan Silva, J.-F. Jenny-Clark, and Charlie Haden. He was flexible in playing pizzicato or arco and worked well no matter which was his partner's strength.'[218] Especially worthy of mention is Henry Grimes' solo part in 'Spirits Rejoice', where he delicately explores Ayler's propulsive improvisation.

The fourth and last Ayler recording in which Grimes took part was a taped concert held at New York's Village Vanguard on December 18, 1966. Indeed, it is his last recording from the 1960s;

the next live recording on which Grimes can be heard dates from 2003.[219] Besides Albert Ayler himself (tenor saxophone), the Vanguard concert featured his brother Donald (trumpet), Call Cobbs (piano), Michael Samson (violin), Bill Folwell and Henry Grimes (basses), and Beaver Harris (drums).[220] John Coltrane, who was in the audience, arranged the concert for Albert Ayler and ensured that it was recorded: 'Shortly after returning from Europe, the quintet, augmented by Call Cobbs, piano, and Henry Grimes, bass, played at the Village Vanguard, where they were recorded by Impulse. [...] John Coltrane was present at this show, observing the progress of the recording he had arranged. His compositional and instrumental style had progressively become more and more influenced by Ayler.'[221]

Ayler's biographer, Peter Niklas Wilson, sees this concert as the most mature and opulent of the surviving versions of Ayler's approach at that time: 'Taken together, the Village recordings are a final document of Ayler's conception of Universal Music in full flower, with titles such as "Spirits Rejoice", "Our Prayer", "Truth Is Marching In", "Omega", or "Infinite Spirit". Though the titles can already be heard on other recordings of 1965 and 1966, the versions are rarely as mature and timbrally opulent. Ayler's gift for inventing and spontaneously varying melodically expressive and harmonically cohesive obligato parts was seldom as manifest as here in the versions of "Truth Is Marching In" and "Our Prayer".'[222]

A few months before the concert, in a *Jazz Podium* interview, Ayler himself discussed the process of collective improvisation: 'It starts with a feeling that then gets taken up by an instrument and adopted by the other musicians. We toss it back and forth, and the feeling grows with the music.'[223] In another interview, in 1966, he expressed ideas readily audible on the Vanguard recording: 'I'm trying to get more form in the free form. Furthermore, I'd like to play something – like the beginning of *Ghosts* – that people can hum. And I want to play songs like I used to sing when I was real small. Folk melodies that all the people would understand. I'd use those melodies as a start and have different simple melodies going in and out of a piece. From simple melody to complicated textures to simplicity again and then to the more dense, the more complex sounds.'[224] Still, it is regrettable in the Vanguard concert that Don

Ayler, with his domineering, relatively one-dimensional trumpet, constantly drowns out the multi-layered refinement of Albert Ayler's playing and that of the other musicians. When Don Ayler falls silent, the collective musical flow is more vibrant, lively, and complex for long stretches, and the subtlety, idiosyncratic soft sound, and charisma of Albert Ayler's tenor saxophone become audible after all. Moreover, Sunny Murray, with his pulsating drive, would surely have been superior to Beaver Harris, who sometimes thumped conventionally in time. Peter Niklas Wilson points especially to Henry Grimes' contribution to the collective sound developed in the Vanguard concert: 'Not a small part of this opulence is contributed by the extended formation: for his guest performance at the Vanguard, Ayler had augmented the quintet of his European tour with the seasoned bassist Henry Grimes.'[225]

Grimes' orchestral playing style today, whether on bass or on violin, still reflects Albert Ayler's approach to improvisation, where he frequently added his part to the collective. Today he is more aware of Ayler's musical force than ever before. But in retrospect Henry recalls that in those days there was only a small, select audience for this music, and thus practically no payment: 'There was no money for recordings; those were the conditions avant-garde musicians had to face.'[226] ESP director Bernard Stollman, who issued both Henry Grimes' and Albert Ayler's music, remembers clearly that his label did worse and worse after 1967, and that he finally had to refer Ayler to a different record company which, unlike ESP, could afford to pay him and take charge of marketing his records: 'By 1967, '68 my company was on the way down. [...] I said, "Albert they can give you the money and the distribution that I can't give you."'[227]

Ayler was deeply depressed that he could hardly gain a foothold in the United States with his music. 'He needed engagements, concerts, promotion and he wasn't getting any help from anyone.'[228] That said, ESP was 'not a purely philanthropic operation' and was tardy in paying royalties, if paying at all.[229] Ayler spoke about these debilitating material problems with Nat Hentoff in his 1966 interview for *DownBeat*: 'I'm a new star, according to a magazine in England [...] and I don't even have fare to England. Record royalties? I never see any. Oh, maybe I'll get $50 this year. One of my albums, *Ghosts*, won an award in Europe. And the company even didn't tell me about that. I had to find out another way. [...] I went for a long time without work. [...] Then George Wein asked me to come to Europe with a group of other people for 11 days starting Nov. 3. I hope to be able to add five or six days on my own after I'm there. Henry Grimes and Sonny Murray will be with Don and me.'[230]

This European tour actually came to pass from November 3 to 15, 1966, but with an entirely different lineup: the new rhythm unit consisted of Beaver Harris and Bill Folwell, 'who scarcely seems an adequate substitute for a Gary Peacock or Henry Grimes. [...] Ayler, with his few concert opportunities, did not always have a leading bassist like Henry Grimes at his disposal.'[231]

Like Albert Ayler, Grimes, who now played almost entirely in a free music context and usually worked with top-caliber ensembles, also had to struggle financially.[232] Until late 1966, however, he managed to earn a living in New York City with his music.

'A new alertness'[233] – Free Music and Precarious Living in the Lower East Side

When the Baroness Pannonica de Koenigswarter, working on her *Three Wishes* project, asked Henry Grimes what three things he would wish for his life, he answered – or is said to have answered:

1. Health. If I had the health, I could do anything else.
2. The second would be money. Not a large sum of money, but just a constant flow of money to keep me in comfort the rest of my life.
3. Everlasting peace and everlasting goodwill amongst everyone. So there'll be no wars, and no excuse to drop that H-bomb, and all that shit. So I'll live in peace, and spend all that money in peace![234]

The exact day when she asked him is uncertain, but it must have been somewhere in the 1960s – a time when Henry Grimes had long since made a name for himself in New York's music world. Although there is no evidence that Henry Grimes really said these words, Henry's 'three wishes' – like many other musicians' wishes presented in the book – name the three pillars essential to everybody's life: health, money to make a living, and peace, all three of which he evidently lacked in some way. Yet Henry possessed the ability and inner strength to lead a constructive life as far as possible while accepting severe material and, increasingly, artistic deprivation. His material circumstances did not, as with some of his fellow musicians, drive him to ruin.

Around 1963, the precarious living conditions for professional free musicians took a noticeable turn for the worse. It was extremely difficult to obtain a gig in a regular jazz club with this style of music. Usually the new music was played in lofts and coffee houses where the sponsors could hardly pay their performers. In 1963 LeRoi Jones addressed this dilemma in *DownBeat* and complained that, under these conditions, highly talented people would atrophy artistically and, worse still, go hungry:

'There seems, frankly, no way to get the owners of these various clubs interested in hiring men like Coleman, Taylor, or any of the younger musicians associated with what's been called the "New Thing". Most of these musicians get no work at all, except now and then a party or session in somebody's loft. [...] Almost concomitantly with the development of jazz in coffee houses (an idea still not completely off the ground by any means) is another manifestation of New York's messed-up jazz scene – the beginning of loft jazz, i.e., not just sessions but formally arranged concerts in lofts featuring some of the best young New York-based musicians. For the concerts, little advertising is used because of the extremely limited finances at the sponsors' disposal (the sponsors are in a great many instances the musicians themselves).'[235]

Jones' critique, aimed at the established jazz clubs, also mentions Henry Grimes, who frequently stood in for the already legendary bassist Wilbur Ware in the loft concerts of the Cherry-Ware-Higgins Trio – in Jones' opinion 'more than adequate[ly]'. He uses Grimes as an example of the upcoming generation of highly talented musicians who could not evolve artistically, much less make a living, under the prevailing conditions: 'The other loft concert listed the Cherry-Ware-Higgins trio on the placards, but most times Henry Grimes played bass in place of Ware. [...] There are a lot of the younger jazzmen around the city now. They could be used, say, as the second group opposite some name. It's bad enough to let so much talent go to waste, but it's worse to let it starve. Meanwhile, the coffee houses and lofts are beginning to take up some of the slack.'[236]

Drummer Sunny Murray, in a *Paris Transatlantic* interview by Dan Warburton of 2000, tells of still more virulent problems that even free music giants such as Ornette Coleman had with club owners in 1963–64. He too mentions Henry Grimes as one of the central figures of the new music: 'At that period they paid Ornette not to play for two years. The Mafia, or whoever it was, said "Keep these cats *quiet*" [...] Steve Lacy was OK, he was playing Monk. George Russell was playing sort of neo-bop, so he was OK. No, it was to stop *us* [...] When we opened up at the Five Spot, the old Five Spot, we opened with a whole band: Cecil, Archie, Jimmy and Henry Grimes. The place was packed – Eric [Dolphy], Monk, John [...] that's where I met all those guys. They came over to the drums, took me up to the bar, bought me drinks, told me they didn't know what the hell I was doing but "keep it up, sounds great...". I remember that very well, and right after that a period went down when we didn't work *at all*.'[237]

Cecil Taylor was fired several times by club owners, e.g. from the Coronet in Brooklyn, although the audience valued his music; as Murray recalls: 'Cecil was very hurt, very dragged. The people were digging it, they dug Henry, they dug me. They dug Cecil. It was the power in the music that they really dug.'[238] One club manager, Murray said, pulled a switchblade on him when he refused to stop playing, and Jackie McLean was beaten up for playing experimentally with Tony Williams.[239]

Some three years later, in April 1966, *DownBeat* writer Gus Matzorkis debated the musicians' economic problems from the standpoint of racism: 'To say that Negro avant-garde jazzmen are scuffling for work and a bare minimum financial support *because they are Negroes*, which is exactly what many of their followers do say, is illogical. They simply ignore the fact that white avant-garde jazzmen are having similar frustrations and that many Negro musicians playing a more immediately accessible kind of music are achieving varying degrees of commercial success. The argument also is dangerous, for it can tend to breed a group feeling of self-righteousness and self-satisfaction about the music that it may not merit.'[240] The above statement from Sunny Murray suggests that he would have put this quite differently.[241]

Eighteen years later, the German bassist Peter Kowald, during a month-long stay in New York (1984), was struck by the unequal professional opportunities for black and white musicians in the New York scene:

The legal progress achieved by the civil-rights movement was massive, but in actual practice most of the system was still working very much as before throughout the '60s, and it took time for civil rights for African-Americans to take hold and become general practice. To some extent that is certainly still to be achieved. [...] I was amazed to see that whites often play more interesting stuff.' (In German Kowald says *die interessanteren Dinge*, which can be translated as 'more interesting jobs'). 'But this starts to get a bit boring [...] because so little of it comes from inside [...] because it's often so conceptual. And it can lose its value quite quickly. I've also seen how much easier it is here for whites. The promoters, club owners [...] people who run the places [...] where you can play they're mostly white. And I'm amazed how much I myself could do here [...] when blacks surely wouldn't have gotten the gigs. [...] All the music for TV or films [...] white rock music, of course [...] so much here is influenced by jazz. Jazz is behind everything. Yet the people who seriously practice it [...] have very slight cultural importance here [...] in contrast to Europe. So they're paid much worse here [...] the people play for very little [...] and that, of course, means – since rent [...] and many other costs are so high – that a lot of people are barely existing [...] even famous people [...] you see at European festivals.'[242]

This was no different – indeed, worse – in the mid-1960s.[243] Roughly a month after the publication of Gus Matzorkis' article, the avant-garde pianist Andrew Hill, when Don Heckman interviewed him for the *DownBeat* issue of May 5, 1966, expressed his thoughts on the matter from the viewpoint of public subsidization and record producers. As an experienced musician with a deep knowledge of the predicament, he sharply criticized the musicians' working conditions and the lack of musical education among many music managers:

It comes as a shock to many jazz fans to discover that their favorite players often are subject to fearsome economic difficulties. [...] The important fact [...] is that there are two often-contradictory pressures that dominate the life and work of the jazz player –

commercial interests and an artistic esthetic. [...] In classical music [...] the artists are subsidized by different foundations and grants; so why aren't the artists in jazz subsidized the same way? Often they make money off one music, and they give it back to another music.[244]

Hill, like his colleague Cecil Taylor,[245] thus adopts a fiercely negative attitude toward such 'New Thing' producers as the ESP label, criticizing their lack of musical knowledge and blatantly calling them exploiters:

'I just call them white liberals because they act like they're going on a peace march somewhere [...]. Before they step into the music, they should go to different libraries and read things. They're neo-phytes, know nothing about the music, and about what has transpired before. [...] What their artistic views are like, which aren't like the views of the subculture they're exploiting, is really a great contradiction. Even though we're not interested in money, we have to live. But they say, "Well, screw it, your music's out there, it's being heard, and it's beautiful."'[246]

Don Heckman sums up in the same article: 'If the music has changed, Hill is convinced it is because of a changing social environment and a new alertness.'[247]

Roughly a year later, in April 1967, lawyer and ESP label owner Bernard Stollman gave an interview with the French magazine *Jazz Hot* that probably no musician of the 'New Thing' ever read. Given Andrew Hill's statement, Stollman virtually personifies the lack of credibility among white producers. 'Do you think in commercial terms?' asked the *Jazz Hot* journalist, to which Stollman responded: 'No, commercial success is not my aim; it's the path of least resistance. I will never take that path. The public has stopped acknowledging the music of ESP. I knew all the obstacles before I began. I hope to see more clearly in this respect before the end of the year. Seven new albums are about to be released (including Henry Grimes Trio, ESP 1026).'[248] Asked what his greatest failure was, he replied: 'The impossibility of bringing about an immediate change in the musicians' lives, despite my good will. Some of them still have to struggle as before.'[249]

In sum, the problem of making ends meet with the new music was known to all.[250] It was even discussed in the mainstream media from about 1963 on. But the record companies and clubs did not really seek a solution to the problem. The result was a tragic material predicament for many outstanding musicians, including Henry Grimes. LeRoi Jones' prognosis of atrophy and starvation, the widespread professional decline of the new music scene reported by Sunny Murray, hit Henry Grimes with full force beginning in 1967. Until then, however, he was given regular opportunities to play music at the highest level and to take part in legendary recordings. During this artistically productive period his living conditions were anything but comfortable, but he experienced a sense of family cohesion among his fellow musicians – for the time being.

After separating from his wife Sarah, Grimes lived alone in various New York apartments, first in Little Italy, then on 7th Street and Second Avenue.[251] One of them was near the apartment of Ed Blackwell, whom he frequently met for jam sessions: 'Yeah, Blackwell lived near me and we used to play together all the time. We did a lot of experimenting with musical forms, times and things. We did stuff that no one had been doing before, we did things just for the heck of it, I mean music we didn't even know we could do! (laughter).'[252]

In 1965 he shared an apartment at 272 East 3rd Street with the drummer Tom Price and the clarinetist Perry Robinson.[253] It was a block away from Slugs' Saloon, at that time a favorite but now nonexistent jazz club where he often played. LeRoi Jones, in his *DownBeat* interview with Archie Shepp, referred to the Lower East Side as 'a place where many poets, painters, and others of artistic bent hole up because of cheaper rents and the presence of empathetic types.'[254] The same applied to Henry Grimes' apartment: it allowed the three and sometimes more musicians to save living costs and to exchange musical ideas directly whenever they felt like it.

In late December 2006 I drove with Grimes to the building at 272 East 3rd Street (between Avenues C and D) where their apartment was located. We had an opportunity to reach the stairwell, but could not enter the apartment itself, which is occupied today. Henry told me that it is difficult for him to remember details, but he misses the trees that used to stand in front of the building. He

The apartment, 272 Third Street, NYC, where Henry Grimes used to live on the first floor (on the right half of the building) together with clarinetist Perry Robinson and drummer Tom Price in 1965 (© Thomas Rösch, 2009).

also vaguely remembers that Perry Robinson arranged for the apartment, that each man had his own bed, if not his own room, and that the apartment had a piano.

Tom Price, in a 2003 interview with Michael Fitzgerald, remembers musical discussions and jam sessions that took place in the apartment: 'It was there that they developed their musical concepts, jamming together almost every day. Price says, "So much so that people began to complain after a while [laughs]." They were joined by neighbourhood friends such as trumpeter Marc Levin and saxophonists Archie Shepp and Frank Wright. They also met the drummer Frank Clayton and his wife, vocalist Jay Clayton. Grimes was working steadily with clarinetist Tony Scott at The Dom, a nearby club, and the environment was fertile for creative expression.'[255]

Grimes also played with Scott elsewhere: in 1966 (probably February 23rd) he played with the clarinetist's quartet, which also included pianist Horace Parlan and drummer Eddie Marshall, at a barely documented happening of Salvador Dali which took place at New York City's Philharmonic Hall. Grimes remembers this event as grand, splendid and elegant, with many famous people in attendance, but he can't remember anything more specific.[256]

Perry Robinson has vivid memories of his time with Henry Grimes in their East Village apartment: 'The East Village was full of jazz musicians at that time, it was very high energy. [...] That first apartment with Henry and Tom was on Third Street between C and D close to Slugs' [...]. We were living on army unemployment, and we lived very cheaply. We used to buy twenty bottles of baby food for three dollars, custards and creams that we'd mix with liver, it was delicious and nutritious. We also cooked a lot of Rice-a-Roni, which was my specialty. We also had a cat; it was a wonderful scene, a real home. That's when we recorded Henry's 1965 album *The Call*. It was a terrific thing because we were all living together and were very close.'[257]

The journalist Guy Kopelowicz, who arrived from France in summer 1965, conveyed his sharply observed impressions of the Lower East Side to the French magazine *Jazz Hot*.[258] The area was then already undergoing a period of economic and social decline. On his tours of the clubs he met Henry Grimes several times: 'My next visit was to Slugs' Saloon, one of the rare new places where jazz can be heard. The saxophonist Charles Lloyd, who will leave the Cannonball Adderley Sextet, heads his own group there. Slugs' is located in a district where one shouldn't necessarily be out and about by foot at night. Along the poorly lit streets, one sees buildings only in silhouette and dubious figures emerging from the darkness. Young people in search of the next bad escapade? Policemen in search of some bad young people? Paper and trash lie strewn on the street. But the atmosphere is more relaxed in front of Slugs'. As I arrived, some ten people were standing in front of it, trying to get in. [...] Slightly confused, I asked Sunny Murray whether he was Albert Ayler's drummer. "Sure am," he answered, "but this evening I'm here just as a spectator. The situation's not so great at the moment, and you can only earn money every now and then. Henry Grimes, who's playing here with Lloyd, told me he'd drop by this evening. That'll earn me a couple more dollars. For we share the same apartment, which lets us pool our resources." [...]

Charles Lloyd has freed his music from the influence of John Coltrane, but he's not one of the young tenor players who excites me most. On that evening he had remarkable sidemen: Herbie Hancock, Henry Grimes, and Pete LaRoca, whose dry and accurate playing fits in perfectly.'[259]

Kopelowicz's report, and Sunny Murray's 2000 interview with Dan Warburton,[260] reveal that the drummer lived at least intermittently in Henry Grimes' apartment and that the roommates shared their earnings. Grimes himself cannot remember this, though he considers it plausible, as he told me in December 2009. At least one thing is clear: it was this exciting atmosphere of communal living and musical interchange in the Lower East Side that gave rise to Henry Grimes' first and, until 2003, his only album issued under his own direction: *The Call*.

Cover photo of Henry Grimes' album *The Call*, 1965, (© Ray Gibson, courtesy ESP-Disk).

The Call (1965)

Henry Grimes made his album together with Perry Robinson and Tom Price in New York on December 28, 1965.[261] The black-and-white cover photo, taken by Ray Gibson, shows a portrait of Grimes with a symbolism whose meaning is left to the interpretation of the beholder. Only the right half of his face is illuminated; down his cheek runs a bead of perspiration which, given its location, might also be a tear. The left half of his face is shrouded in darkness; the bridge of his bass is visible – at least the outline of it. In 1966 and again in 1968, this riveting photograph would be reproduced in an issue of the African-American cultural magazine *Liberator*.[262]

Hans Schreiber and Tom 'Tornado' Klatt, in their liner notes for the CD reissue of *The Call* (*ca.* 1990), could only pose this question about Henry Grimes at the end: 'After all his activities and his excellent bass playing, he got lost in jazz history after 1966. Does anybody know what happened to him?'[263]

Grimes has clear recollections of the recording: 'We recorded in a low-priced studio.'[264] ESP-owner Bernard Stollman was not present at the session, Henry said, for at the time he was in the office of his record company, which was located in a loft. Many musicians wandered in and out. His own compositions on the album – 'Fish Story', 'For Django', 'Saturday Night What Th'', and 'Song Of Alfalfa' – were composed directly in the studio, and the titles were added spontaneously afterward. 'The people in the studio didn't come up and say do this and do that about which composition that should be. I didn't have any compositions when I went into the studio. [...] I had some tunes in my mind, but on that album they came out for the first time. [...] When I feel that way it's very intense, spontaneous and alive, you know.'[265] '"Fish Story",' Grimes says, 'could be talking about a woman.' Particularly striking are its changes of tempo; it opens at breakneck speed with a dramatic bowed bass, then suddenly becomes slower and more melancholic. 'For Django' is dedicated to Django Reinhardt: 'It goes back to the time when I was at high school. I went to a record store thinking of finding Miles Davis and then discovered Django.'[266] The piece features Grimes with an emotionally powerful arco solo. 'Saturday Night What Th'' deals with a feeling he often had on Saturday night: 'I just made a remark that people mess around, and there were bunches of hippies who mess around on Saturday night.'[267] There is anger in the title, he says, but not in the music. 'Son of Alfalfa' relates to his composition 'Farmer Alfalfa', released on *Funk Dumpling*,[268] and to the cartoons he had drawn in high school, which in turn relate to 'Farmer Alfalfa' from the animated cartoon 'Betty Boop'.[269]

In his book *The Traveler*, Perry Robinson remembers his composition 'Walk On': 'I Think "Walk On" came out of conversations I had with Henry about swing. Henry said that when he played he used to imagine himself walking on an endless conveyor belt, just constantly moving forward at a regular pace. Because what is it to swing? It's a magic momentum that's always moving; you're walking, but at the same time you're being conveyed because the rhythm is carrying you.'[270] 'The Call' is a composition by Perry Robinson, but the title came from Henry: 'You come up to this title because you try to get the most from it, you know, to get all that you can get from it, and also I can find that new image of my own work, [...] force it out into the open, [...] from where it was, always hidden, a hidden art form.'[271]

When Grimes was asked if anything is revealed in it, he replied: 'Yeah, it has to be revealed, but actually it doesn't tend to being able to come out of it that way. – You know, sometimes it's not a real philosophy to say someone has a philosophy, has a call. Sometimes it's not a real philosophy to say you are philosophical, and someone will reckon that, or they may reckon something else altogether, you know. You might have two people come up with ideas so, by the time it's over, it's four people, four or five people comin' up with ideas. It makes you study things more deeply of find the way they operate best. [...] It's a very interesting theory, type of theory.' A method? 'Well, I don't know. I guess that there is a method if I would study. – But there was no method to this at that time, I say, but I might be wrong on my own stuff there.'

Then asked whether 'The Call' might refer to a calling, maybe that of a preacher, Henry adamantly denied it. 'No. It's getting away from that kind of a thing. With music, there is no standard or philosophical group of words you can give to different persons [...] It's spontaneous, free improvising. Actually, you can't call music philosophy. Music is music. It might be like in philosophy that it comes out, but it's not in the same philosophical place as a philosophy, you know, argumentation, ideology. All those are not musical terms. You have to have musical terms for it to be music. [...] That has nothing to do with having titles. I mean, you have titles within that music, but it's only found within that scope of music, not outside of it in philosophy or what that thing is called –

emotion. I mean, all those things are true, but they're not music.'
Asked what he meant by these musical terms, he replied: 'You have
to operate that within yourself.'²⁷²

A day before we talked about 'The Call', Grimes wrote down his
thoughts on 'music and innovative strength.' Right at the beginning
of his memorandum he wrote that the terms he used are philosophical and expressionistic at once:

> Here is an idealistic, avant-garde, or expressionistic answer to your
> question. We're all (or – must be) under the auspices of one form
> of ordering or another that is responsible for our own personal
> audition into exposure by or of another form that is created by
> pressure, or by ideation into the free forms which have ordering by
> the power of freedom (or freedoms) that 'come' to the places of our
> knowledges, understood while perhaps being not understood at all;
> by the social norms around us. That is because expressions that
> arrive via the conveyances of freedom are in every sense 'power' or
> powerful. (think of anyone – from here or now, from Albert Ayler,
> all the way back to great music created by Charlie Parker.)
>   Its existing or (existentiality) is infinite or profound living in the
> 'forces profundities' of music or art that has lived for the length-
> wise perception in many persons' art that is a large position for
> anything to be in, by, or of.
>   One condition of music it has is fed to another.
>   That condition of music 'in place' is very often the feeding and
> place of other musicians. The magic of it all, the innovator is often
> taught to us simply by the way you're conditioned to respond.
>   By aesthetic
> art forms which take place 'in the head' when time becomes the
> rendition of assuming the form of art you will understand.
>   That form of art is alive. It will live with you in time, in the
> past, in the present (as Charlie Parker wrote), in the future (as by
> Sun Ra).
>
> Henry Grimes²⁷³

When Grimes reflects on music, he develops his concepts directly
from musical practice. I mentioned this point to him in connection
with his album *The Call*, and with his reflections on the musical
innovator in his notes. He then reworded the entire thing as a
joyous process of knowledge acquisition that takes place during
collective improvisation: 'An innovator goes inside of a thing and
comes out on the other side in another person – it's the same

Henry Grimes, Perry Robinson, Tom Price, ESP-recording session of Henry
Grimes' album *The Call*, NYC, December 28, 1965 (© Raymond Ross Archives/
CTSIMAGES).

process, making a man improve, understanding something that you
didn't understand before, and then he understands it by going
inwards of that person he's playing with or who presented this
music [...] It's hard to explain, you know – but it's something that
is very joyful.'[274]

Grimes' thoughts resemble the visionary approach recognizable
in other pioneers of the New Music – Ingrid Monson has charac-
terized them in her study *Freedom Sounds*: 'The cultivation of
utopian visions in music has been particularly associated with musicians of the avant-garde, whose sonic explorations longed to give
musical expression to these ideals. Every musical parameter –
melody, rhythm, timbre, instrumentation, harmony, counterpoint
– was opened to exploration. [...] In the context of the civil rights
movement and black nationalism, the abstract cries and shrieks of
the 'New Thing' were often taken as anger rather than as the spiritual exploration they were to many of its practitioners, such as
John Coltrane, Sun Ra, and Albert Ayler. [...], [AACM founding
member Richard] Abrams and Roscoe Mitchell viewed melody,

rhythm, and timbral exploration as the primary musical means of achieving spiritual transcendence, which they defined as a place where intuition and intellect meet through collaborative action.'[275]

Apparently *The Call* was not truly noticed and accepted until long after its release. Gerard Rouy, writing for *Jazz Magazine* in 2004, claimed that it manifested 'a will to freedom in its every nuance, and does so almost bucolically.'[276] In 2008 a writer by the code name of Medjuk excitedly recommended *The Call* on an internet music page: 'Listen to it and you want more, especially if your tastes run toward Albert Ayler or Don Cherry.'[277] Max Harrison, writing in 1976, was reminded of Ornette Coleman's violin playing: 'Something close to Coleman's actual violin tone is found in Grimes' playing on his own disc, *The Call*.'[278] In contrast, American jazz music magazines of the 1960s did not review the album at all, and two reviews in the French magazine *Jazz Hot*, published a good year after *The Call* was released, were decidedly skeptical: Philippe Nahman found its music 'extremely tense [...] often repellent' and was reminded, owing to its combination of instruments, of *The Jimmy Giuffre 3*. 'Most of the themes are extremely severe: a single motif repeated two or three times in unison and in free improvisation by Perry Robinson (a clarinetist whose sound recalls Steve Lacy's), Grimes, and Tom Price.'[279] Nahman found that the trio 'completely lacked unity. The impression prevails that the group is still searching for its actual unity. This aspect is grievous owing to the inaccuracy of the playing of Tom Price (in his defense, the poor recording quality should be mentioned here). This arid disk is one of those that don't need to be heard often to recognize their actual value.'[280] In conclusion, Nahman recommended the album to 'lovers of extra-sensory perception',[281] and gave it no star at all.

Daniel Berger compared Henry Grimes, owing to the demand for him in New York's jazz circles, to Richard Davis, who was especially valued by the 'new-ists': 'We see him not only at Basie's in Harlem (e.g. with [not clear whether Stanley or Tommy] Turrentine), but also at Slugs'-in-The-Far-East, playing both mainstream and staunchly 'in': we can hear him a bit with Cecil Taylor or Don Cherry at the Blue Note. He's always there when needed. [...] This is a small trio which, incidentally, had also convened with another highly interesting bassist, Bill Folwell, whom we heard a bit in Paris with Albert Ayler. It is Robinson's clarinet that sets the mood of the album – very tormented, unbearably nervous, striking to the marrow. To name a few points of reference: less cool than Giuffre, but less *foufou* than [Tony] Scott. The most interesting thing about this album comes from the pieces, which are all well composed and usually attractive. Those by Grimes bear a strong similarity to Robinson's ('Walk On', 'The Call'). Very fine photograph by Ray Gibson on the cover.'[282] Berger, too, did not give the album a single star.

What *The Call* triggered in Marshall Marrotte in the mid-1980s speaks a wholly different language from the two negative reviews of 1967. His reaction shows that it was not only the album's compositions that were 'attractive', but also the bass playing of its leader, which holds the listener truly spellbound. Marrotte was so struck at first hearing by Grimes' improvisations on *The Call* that he set out in search of him sixteen years later, and ultimately found him.[283] With *The Call* Grimes had, indirectly, rescued himself, even if the rescue had to wait for Marrotte's research thirty-seven years after the album was recorded.

A short while after Grimes' re-emergence and resurrection (made possible by Marrotte), he was asked by Fred Jung why he did not make any more albums as leader in the 1960s after *The Call*. His reply makes it clear that, as an artist, his only concern was art, and that he was uninterested, to his regret, in career-advancing strategies, although he well knows how important such strategies are and where he stands musically: 'I wasn't offered too many. It is my own doing because I didn't drag my way into a lot of musicians and writers and try to get them to recognize me. That is the kind of feeling I had. I didn't want to be over-ego about it. That is something that I am still struggling with and I have to get over it. That is all there is to it. I don't seriously think that I am not able to play. I just love playing. That is my main impulse. I love it and when I get a chance to do it, that is the only thing that I want to do.'[284]

This strong devotion to music made Cecil Taylor (whose music 'didn't make a lot of money'[285] at the time) work more closely than ever with Henry Grimes, beginning in the summer of 1965.

CHAPTER FOUR 101

'collective compositions' – Working with Cecil Taylor (1965–66)

Henry Grimes' early collaboration with Cecil Taylor is spread over the years 1961, 1963,[286] 1965, and 1966. The most important musical documents of their collaboration date from the most recent year. That Cecil Taylor's music throws listening habits out of kilter is well known. At times it reached a point where he was physically attacked for his music.[287] Yet 'at every stage of his development, Taylor has played with total sureness and the tremendous drive that is his hallmark. Sometimes he will have several melodies going on at once, all of them in different keys.'[288] In the 1950s he had trouble finding musicians who could follow him at all when he tried to combine particular ideas of musical order with creative improvisation: 'Most of his sidemen admit that it takes a minimum of three years of steady rehearsal to fully assimilate his music. Cecil's approach to group improvisation is so demanding that it usually requires a thorough re-evaluation for the musician.'[289] This changed in the 1960s as a number of top-flight free jazz musicians reached maturity. Suddenly there were musicians such as Sunny Murray, who 'considers the musicians cowards for refusing to play with Taylor: "... They didn't have enough faith in themselves to believe they could handle as much music as Cecil plays, which some of them can. Cats like [tenor saxophonist] Archie Shepp, [bassist] Henry Grimes, and Jimmy Lyons have proved that."'[290] Cecil Taylor's music even began to have a considerable impact on musical evolution: 'With some of the best players of the day, Taylor was successful in evolving a form of ensemble playing that came to have an enormous influence on many free-jazz groups.'[291] The influence even extended to improvisation ensembles outside the realm of jazz music.[292] In Cecil Taylor's musical approach, spontaneity and order form an organic whole. Its freedom resides in the possibility of making a deliberate selection from a limitless body of material. He and his ensemble shape this material in a way that does more than map the psyches of the players: it creates a musical structure representing emotion and intellect, energy and form in equal measure.[293]

In 1966 Cecil Taylor, in a *Jazz Podium* interview with Gudrun

Endress, explained that a concert hall is more suitable for his music than a club. What constitutes music, he said, is the musician's concern to transform the ugliness of everyday life into beauty, the symbol of music. 'Not that we can escape ugliness: we just move it into the transcendental.'²⁹⁴ In relation to this, Endress asked him whether he had found his ideal ensemble, which at that time featured above all Jimmy Lyons, Henry Grimes, and Andrew Cyrille. 'Sure thing,' was his reply; 'we've been working together for three years, and I'm convinced that we're capable of mastering what we've set out to do. The music is very different from what it was when we started.'²⁹⁵ At present, he continued, 'the emphasis is not so much on chords and keys. It's focused on tonal centers, and the standard thirty-two bar song form is completely negated. The interest lies increasingly on ideas of sound, on pure sound.'²⁹⁶ 'It's not so important that listeners are informed about the music's structure. The main thing, it seems to me, is that they are moved by the music. I want them to have an experience of a kind and intensity they've never known before.'²⁹⁷ In another interview from the same period, he describes the process of existential transformation initiated when performing collectively before an audience: 'When you work, what happens to your psyche – the metamorphosis of you as a human being – is so complete that you live on a different plane. All your energies and capabilities are realized or in the process of being realized.'²⁹⁸

Henry Grimes and Cecil Taylor valued each other from the outset.²⁹⁹ Taylor sums up his opinion in a simple phrase: 'Henry is a giant.'³⁰⁰ Grimes in turn calls Taylor one of his favorite musicians: 'Cecil has always been very impressive to me. He is sort of this wild pioneer that would sort of come up to the piano and play more notes than there are on the piano. Musicians like that: You don't just stand up there; you study. That is what happens when you are standing up there playing with them. You don't just stand on the bandstand and play music and forget about it. You have to study certain things that you learned then and there. That is really beautiful about Cecil [...]. Cecil is definitely one of my favorites.'³⁰¹ 'It's whirling pools of ... I guess the word is "happening". That's the only way I can describe it.'³⁰² 'He played very much like a classical musician: He would get all over the piano, you know?'³⁰³

Cecil Taylor Quintet, Newport Jazz Festival July 2, 1965, Cecil Taylor, Henry Grimes, Andrew Cyrille, Jimmy Lyons, Bill Barron (© Joe Alper, courtesy of the Joe Alper Photo Collection LLC).

Cecil Taylor and his group, which in 1965–66 consisted of Jimmy Lyons, Henry Grimes, Andrew Cyrille, and sometimes Bill Barron, Ken McIntyre, Alan Silva, and Eddie Gale, had few opportunities to appear in clubs. Appearing at a renowned jazz festival seems to have worked better: on July 2, 1965 the Cecil Taylor Quintet with Lyons, Grimes, Cyrille plus Barron played the Newport Jazz Festival.[304] But the club owners were intent on receiving easily digestible 'fare', and most regarded Cecil Taylor's music with suspicion. When he gave his *Jazz Podium* interview in 1966, his previous club appearance – at the Village Vanguard in July 1965 – already lay months in the past.[305]

Buell Neidlinger, Taylor's bassist until the early 1960s, summed up the situation: 'Trying to make a living playing with Cecil is absolutely unbelievable, because there is no economic advantage to playing music like that. It's completely unsalable in the nightclubs because of the fact that each composition lasts, or could last, an hour and a half. Bar owners aren't interested in this, because if there's one thing they hate to see it's a bunch of people sitting around openmouthed with their brains absolutely paralyzed by the music, unable to call for the waiter. They want to sell drinks. But when Cecil's playing, people are likely to tell the waiter shut up and be still.'[306]

Only a few television programmers and concert halls appreciated Cecil Taylor's art. Thus on September 19, 1965, his quartet, with Jimmy Lyons, Henry Grimes, and Andrew Cyrille, played two short pieces ('Number One' and 'Octagonal Skirt And Fancy Pants') at New York's Village Gate for the WNET TV broadcast *The Arts In America*.[307] It was a praiseworthy effort – indeed, sensational by US standards – to give the avant-garde ensemble a television forum. Listening to these pieces, or perhaps they should be called morsels, on their 2009 CD release[308] makes it clear, however, that Taylor's collective improvisations cannot be squeezed into three-minute tracks. Their refined complexity, orchestral power, and tendency to expand in time are obliterated in 2'33 and 2'44 snippets.

In June 1966, the Cecil Taylor Quartet (Taylor, Lyons, Grimes, and Cyrille), augmented by Makanda Ken McIntyre (alto saxophone, bass clarinet, oboe), Alan Silva (bass), and Eddie Gale (trumpet), held a concert in New York's Town Hall.[309] Critic Dan Morgenstern was especially impressed by the bass playing in Taylor's composition 'Steps', which 'also contained [...] a vigorous bass duet (throughout, Silva played arco, while Grimes plucked and strummed; both bassists performed with impressive dexterity)'.[310] 'Steps' also appears on the album *Unit Structures*, recorded by the same group a few weeks before the Town Hall concert, one of the two Cecil Taylor albums considered milestones of jazz music today.[311] It was recorded in Rudy Van Gelder's studio in Englewood Cliffs, New Jersey, on May 19, 1966,[312] Grimes is especially impressive on the second piece, 'Enter, Evening (Soft Line Structures)', with brilliant arco lines in the low register. Cecil Taylor, in his idiosyncratic liner notes, says of *Unit Structures* that he was concerned with an equal interplay of personal modes of perception, with the goal of achieving a new sonic synthesis and collective musical knowledge: 'The player advances to the area, an unknown totality, made whole thru self-analysis (improvisation), the conscious manipulation of known material; [...] Each instrument has strata: timber, temperament; internal dialogue mirror turns: player to nerve ends, motivation "how to" resultant Unit flow. The piano as catalyst feeding material to soloists in all registers, character actor "assoluta".'[313]

Grimes sums up his recollections as follows: 'You really have to be careful [...] There's a lot of ground to cover.'[314] Andrew Cyrille remembers this collective musical process while calling it one of the foundations of jazz music:

'If I write a composition and I give the notes to certain musicians or to the members of the band and I have certain rhythms, I also want them to play the music with their own signature, which very often is one of the foundations of jazz. You want to play with a person – a particular person – because of his or her way of self-expression within a composition. When you have a composition and five or six bands playing that composition, you might like one better than another. That was more or less what was going on with the music that we played with Cecil. And he would tell us, he would say, "This is our music, not just my music – our music." He was making the notes. It was interesting too, because sometimes he would say: "Everybody is soloing." It's almost like an oxymoron, but that was more or less how he put it and it kind of was that way. [...] Jazz is not through-composed music.'[315] Accordingly, Ekkehard Jost refers to Cecil Taylor's compositional practice as 'collective compositions'.[316]

'We belong to those who place *Unit Structures* among the three greatest recordings of jazz history.'[317] Thus the critic's assessment for the French magazine *Jazz Hot* (1967). In the same year, the *DownBeat* critic gave the album five stars, its highest evaluation: 'This music breathes, more like human breathing, more like music, from phrase to phrase. [...] The bass duo (Henry Grimes, Alan Silva) is so well entwined that I couldn't tell the players apart (which is intended, I believe).'[318] The final remark suggests that the critic, Bill Matthieu, could have listened more closely. Henry Grimes and Alan Silva can be clearly distinguished by the registers and techniques they employ: Grimes plays low-register pizzicato, Silva high-register arco.[319]

On October 6, 1966, Cecil Taylor again entered Rudy Van Gelder's studio to record the album *Conquistador!*.[320] Once again, the lineup included Jimmy Lyons (alto saxophone), Henry Grimes[321] and Alan Silva (basses), and Andrew Cyrille (drums), this time joined by Bill Dixon (trumpet). Cecil Taylor, in Nat Hentoff's original liner notes, explained that he viewed his life as a musical process, and that every music has its order, provided that it comes from the inside, from the musician's gut. This order does not necessarily relate to external ordering criteria: 'If you take the creation of a music and the creation of your own life values as your overall goal, then living becomes a musical process. It becomes a search to absorb everything that happens to you and to incorporate it into music. [...] There is no music without order – if that music comes from a man's innards. But that order is not necessarily related to any single criterion of what order should be as imposed from the outside.'[322] Hentoff recommends listening specifically to the album's bass part: 'I would [...] counsel separate listenings to both sides just for the evocative and provocative bass interplay between Alan Silva and Henry Grimes and between them and the rest of the ensemble.'[323] It is unclear why he (like Bob Blumenthal in his *Conquistador!* liner notes of 2003) categorically names Alan Silva before Henry Grimes. A choice of alphabetical order would have done greater justice to the two bassists' equivalent contribution to the collective improvisation. Both Grimes and Silva 'establish distinct and sympathetic angles on the music.'[324]

A close hearing of *Conquistador!* shows how often the pianist is spontaneously channeled in a new direction by Grimes' pizzicato. In a collective *DownBeat* review of several outstanding jazz music recordings beneath the title 'Four Modernists', the author Bill Quinn gave Cecil Taylor's *Conquistador!* five stars and singled out the bass playing of Henry Grimes and Alan Silva: 'The tandem bass work is a dichotomy in arco and pizzicato [...] and expanding digits of Grimes and Silva.'[325]

When Val Wilmer interviewed Andrew Cyrille and Alan Silva about working with Cecil Taylor, she learned that 'Silva found working with Taylor too demanding at first, but when he decided to concentrate on the bow, he was able to develop certain *arco* techniques that fitted perfectly with Henry Grimes' intricate *pizzicato*. On "Unit Structures" [...] and "Conquistador" [...] the two bassists interact almost demonically at times, a relationship they were to continue to expand with Albert Ayler. As far as the prodigious Grimes was concerned, he and the pianist shared an empathy that was, according to Andrew Cyrille, "like radar".'[326] John Litweiler said much the same of Grimes' contribution to Cecil Taylor's ensemble: 'Henry Grimes, with his big tone and drive, was one of the most powerful and forceful jazzmen of the sixties, with deep instincts for enforcing ensemble motions, as various Sonny Rollins and Albert Ayler groups, as well as Taylor's Unit, discovered.'[327]

Andrew Cyrille has vivid memories of the time he spent with Henry Grimes in Cecil Taylor's group.[328] The drummer first played with Taylor in 1958 and worked continuously in his ensemble from 1964 to 1975.[329] He and Henry both remember meeting for the first time in the early 1960s, when they gave a concert in Brooklyn's Sonia Ballroom with Grachan Moncur III, Harry Carney (only Grimes remembers him), Bobby Hutcherson, and Beaver Harris.[330] What set Henry Grimes apart, says Cyrille, were 'his sound, musical intelligence, creativity, and talent.'[331] 'It's the notes that he chooses, the rhythms that he plays, it's how he assigns the rhythms to his accompanying and to his solos [...] When I play with Henry, I hear him challenging me, I hear him supporting me, I hear him playing things with me in unison, I hear him playing things with me contrapuntally, also a certain kind of emotional give and take that we have.'[332] Usually, Cyrille adds, Taylor wrote the music and gave it to Lyons, Grimes, Silva, and himself. 'Of course the different musicians played the notes in a way that they felt that a note should be played. Sometimes there would be a comment by Cecil or a comment by the musicians that they felt that they should go with that. Or Cecil would say "No I'd like fourths to go with this." The only person that he ever asked not to do a particular thing, maybe two or three times at the most, was me, the drummer, you know. I had a free palette, colors, the rhythms. All I had to do was to construct the rhythm that would go with the rest of the music; that was left up to me. It was like an absolute freedom. [...] There would be certain notes that he would give to Henry, certain notes he would give to Alan Silva. Sometimes Alan would be assigned to play pizzicato [...] and then Henry would consider playing arco [...]. And sometimes both of them would play pizzicato or both of them would play arco. Very much of that was left to the musicians after the notes were given out.'[333]

After recording *Conquistador!* in October 1966, Henry Grimes and the Cecil Taylor ensemble went their separate ways. Andrew Cyrille remembers this in great detail: 'In 1966 – it was after a rehearsal I had with Cecil Taylor, Alan Silva, Jimmy Lyons – and Henry was part of the group that was supposed to go to Europe to play together. And at the end of the rehearsal, on a Saturday night, everybody said that we would meet at the airport on Tuesday. And Henry was one of the people who said "Yeah, we will see you at the airport," and I remember him saying he has some problems with his passport, but it shouldn't be a problem. We all came to the airport and then said "Where is Henry?" We waited and he never showed up. That was the last time any of us had heard of Henry. So the only thing I can say is at that time it was totally mysterious to all of us. We were looking at each other – we were friends, sometimes relatives – saying Henry was like a cat who just goes away. This was what happened, and it was a mystery. Now, why that was with Henry, I can't tell you. After I met him, years after, we talked about certain situations that had happened with him around that time and probably had to do with economics, etcetera [...]. As far as Henry was concerned, again, we thought about him collectively, we thought about him individually, and until a few years ago nobody knew where he was, until I saw him at the Jazz Bakery in Culver City, California in 2003. And I asked him "Henry, whatever happened to you after the rehearsal when you said you gonna come to the airport?" And he said he didn't remember.'[334]

In a 2003 interview, Grimes explained that he was already struggling with depression, 'and that was the end of my work with Cecil Taylor. His music was really *out* [i.e. very free], and I had no mental problems playing it.'[335] It was thus Grimes' health that brought about the end of their collaboration. Andrew Cyrille remembers that Henry was normally reliable in coming to prearranged meetings: 'I would have to say he would be there when he was supposed to be.'[336] So something extraordinary must have happened to prevent him from coming to the airport and joining Cecil Taylor's European tour. The exact reasons can no longer be determined.

Even then, as Andrew Cyrille later explained, Henry Grimes

had difficulties earning a living as a musician. The fact that he consistently worked with outstanding colleagues from New York's free music scene did nothing to alter this fact.

'somnambulistic empathy' – Working with Don Cherry (1965–66)

Henry Grimes and Don Cherry first met in 1961 'when I was hanging around the Lower East Side. We did a lot of jam sessions and he asked me to work on a few things with him.'[337] In the same way, Grimes met Ornette Coleman, in whose ensemble he played for several weeks, substituting for Charlie Haden.[338] In November, 1961, Grimes took part in Don Cherry's first studio recording together with Ed Blackwell, who was then working frequently with Coleman. They recorded three pieces.[339] In 1962–63, Grimes and Cherry played lots of gigs in the Sonny Rollins Quartet (with Billy Higgins on drums) that survive in sensational live concert recordings.[340] The third and final phase of their musical collaboration took place between late 1965 and late 1966, when Don Cherry and his groups made three recordings that are milestones in the history of jazz music: *Complete Communion* (1965), *Symphony For Improvisers*, and *Where Is Brooklyn?* (both 1966).[341] Here Grimes proved once again that he had developed into an outstanding improviser and leader as a bassist.

For *Complete Communion*, cornetist Don Cherry entered the Van Gelder studio on December 24, 1965, along with tenor saxophonist Leandro 'Gato' Barbieri, Henry Grimes, and drummer and percussionist Ed Blackwell.[342] Both pieces on the album, 'Complete Communion' and 'Elephantasy', are suites in four sections with poetic titles: a) 'Complete Communion', b) 'And Now', c) 'Golden Heart', and d) 'Remembrance'; and a) 'Elephantasy', b) 'Our Feelings', c) 'Bishmallah', and d) 'Wind, Sand And Stars.'[343] Ekkehard Jost remarks of Grimes: 'For the rhythm section, Cherry called in [...] bassist Henry Grimes, with whom he played in the Rollins Quartet, and who had become one of the ablest bassists in free jazz during his work with Cecil Taylor (1961), Albert Ayler (1963) and Archie Shepp (1965).'[344]

In the liner notes for *Complete Communion*, Nat Hentoff refers to Henry Grimes and Edward Blackwell as being 'among the most resourceful and flexible musicians involved in the new jazz' and emphasizes their ability to enter into dialogue[345] – probably the result of their many jam sessions together:[346] '[A]ll previous jazz has been dialogue in whole or in part. But in the new jazz, as here, the conditions for conversation have been greatly extended. [...] Blackwell and Grimes [...] are full-scale contributors to the dialogue inside the steadily evolving, undulating time of this particular collective musical experience.'[347] Those who need convincing about Grimes' contribution to the *Complete Communion* suite should listen to his melodic part at 5'00, his solo at 12'00, his pizzicato at 15'00, or his solo at 16'57.

As so often with free jazz albums at the time, the reviews were mixed. The *DownBeat* critic, arranger, and instrumentalist William Russo gave the album three stars on July 28, 1966, justifying his evaluation with high-brow verbiage that is both academically stilted and coarse, particularly as regards the bass.[348] Daniel Berger practically took the opposite view in his review for the French magazine *Jazz Hot* and gave the album 4.5 stars.[349]

On September 19, 1966, barely nine months after *Complete Communion*, Cherry returned to the Van Gelder studio with the same ensemble plus Pharoah Sanders (piccolo, tenor saxophone), Karl Berger (vibraphone, piano), and, as second bassist, Jean-François Jenny-Clark, to record *Symphony For Improvisers*. Once again the album is made up of two four-part suites: 'Symphony For Improvisers' and 'Manhattan Cry'.[350] Compared to *Complete Communion*, *Symphony For Improvisers* is, as its title suggests, more open in its form, despite its almost identical design as suites with interlocking thematic complexes. In the latter, the two bassists (like the two tenor saxophones) always play consecutively, with fluid transitions from one to the other.[351] Equally fluid, in most cases, are the transitions between the thematic sections and the boundaries between composed material and improvisation. 'A great deal more time is spent on the improvisations, as opposed to the themes, which become more and more fragmentary.'[352]

The poet and publicist A. B. Spellman refers to four of the album's musicians as leaders, owing to their instrumental contributions to the new music: 'A clue of the strength, depth and breath of the New Music is the number of musicians who have grown to maturity in it. Four such musicians are represented here: Don Cherry, Henry Grimes, Pharoah Sanders, and Ed Blackwell all have handled several jazz disciplines at various points in their careers but have spent most of their still young lives working in the milieu of the New. Each has that big, mature ear that makes for virtuosity in a jazz man; each is a leader on his instrument, influencing in technique and styles not only the younger musicians, but also their contemporaries and those of the antecedent generation who want to keep their tradition alive in these times.'[353] Henry Grimes, Spellman continues, 'is thought by his contemporaries to be the premier bassist of the day. [...] Grimes [...] has been in the vanguard of jazz bassists for ten years now, and every day has been a day of growth. His intelligence, strength, and virtuosity sustain, from the first chord to the last, the impeccable vitality of this record.'[354]

Reviews of this album, too, appeared in *DownBeat* and *Jazz Hot*. The latter review barely mentions the musicians singly and gives the album three stars.[355] Ira Gitler, writing for *DownBeat*, was definitely favorable: 'The musicians are really improvising, collectively and individually, and do not get hung up in blind alleys. [...] He [Blackwell] is most musical, and together with the bassist, sets up rhythms that surge with the elastic joy that has been the jazz pulse through all eras of the music.'[356]

Complete Communion and *Symphony For Improvisers* are considered among the most significant free jazz albums of the 1960s.[357] Both are sustained by a common idea of several thematic complexes integrated into a suite. Owing to their contradictory thematic material, their movements are clearly identifiable yet interrelated.[358] 'We improvised from the flavor of the tunes,'[359] Don Cherry said of *Symphony For Improvisers*, and the same can be heard in *Complete Communion*. In both albums the musicians improvised on the themes.[360] Especially for *Complete Communion*, Ekkehard Jost aptly spoke of 'ensemble precision achieved in an utterly unpedantic way'.[361] The complicated transitions among the musical figures are accomplished with amazing facility, 'as though they were the most natural thing in the world'.[362] The reason for this facility is, above all, the interconnectivity that had emerged among the musicians during their intensive collaboration before the album was recorded. Jost speaks of a 'veritably somnambulistic empathy between Henry Grimes and Ed Blackwell, who not only produce a stable rhythmic foundation, but – more important – react quickly and accurately to changes in direction taken by the horns.'[363]

In the same year, 1966, three further recording sessions followed in quick succession. A concert again featuring Cherry, Barbieri, Grimes and Blackwell, along with vibraphonist Karl Berger and bassist Charlie Haden, took place at New York's Five Spot on October 25 and was recorded live, though the tapes have never been released. Besides a few unknown titles, they included Charlie Parker's 'Ah-Leu-Cha'.[364] Barely two weeks later, on November 11, Don Cherry (cornet) was joined by Pharoah Sanders (piccolo flute, tenor saxophone), Henry Grimes (bass), and Ed Blackwell (drums) in Van Gelder's studio to record the album *Where Is Brooklyn?*[365]

Ornette Coleman wrote the original liner notes; like A. B. Spellman, he singles out Don Cherry, Pharoah Sanders, Henry

Pharoah Sanders, Henry Grimes, Ed Blackwell, Don Cherry, at The Five Spot, NYC, 1966 (© Raymond Ross Archives/CTSIMAGES).

Grimes, and Ed Blackwell as torchbearers for the new music, with a potential everyone (and every musician) could learn from: 'Blessed are the musicians of tomorrow because today's musicians are building the eternal houses of being and Don Cherry, Edward Blackwell, Pharoah Sanders, and Henry Grimes do exist as their existence is in the form of music, if you question the meaning and placement of this music in your life living, then you have been baptized, if the music doesn't cause you to question its meaning and placement in your life don't blame Cherry, Blackwell, Pharoah, and Henry.'[366]

Thanks to his marked ability to evolve individually and to contribute a propulsive and even commanding bass to a very wide range of ensembles, Henry Grimes was given further opportunities to record seminal free music albums in 1965 and 1966.

'remarkably attuned to the questing spirit' – Recordings with Archie Shepp, Sunny Murray, Burton Greene, Pharoah Sanders, and Others (1965–66)

In August 1965, Archie Shepp fetched Grimes, Bobby Hutcherson (vibraphone), Rashied Ali (drums tracks 1-3), J. C. Moses (drums track 4), Joe Chambers (drums track 5, tympani track 1), Ed Blackwell (rhythm logs tracks 2-4), and Christine Spencer (soprano voice track 1) into the studio to record *On This Night*.[367] The material on the album is deliberately heterogeneous; Shepp's concern was to achieve, with maximum range and variety, a proclamation of faith in the heritage of African-American culture.[368] The original LP version has four pieces, including a rendition of the Duke Ellington classic 'In A Sentimental Mood' and three compositions by Archie Shepp himself.[369] The 'centerpiece' of the album is the title song, 'On This Night (If That Great Day Would Come)', which Shepp views both as 'a synthesis of how I sum up contemporary America as a man of color' and a tribute to the civil rights activist, sociologist, and journalist W. E. B. DuBois.

In the first half of the piece, Shepp plays piano to accompany the obviously classically trained vocalist Christine Spencer, who delivers his political poem of the same title.[370] This emotionally accessible song is heavily influenced by contemporary European and American art music, which, together with the politicized words, creates a certain disconcerting effect. Roughly midway through the piece, it transmutes into a section of purely instrumental free improvisation ending in a slow, traditional twelve-bar blues. The song returns at the end, with Spencer's voice now highlighted by flowing harmonies from Shepp's tenor saxophone.[371] In the first half of the song, Grimes applies his deep knowledge and experience in European classical music, accompanying Spencer's voice with a dark-hued orchestral bowed bass in flowing lines and suspended meter, as if he wanted to help channel the words of the poem to the listener. Particularly impressive is his effortless switch to pizzicato, and thus to the sharply rhythmic second half of the song, ebbing away in a traditional blues. Here he brings things into play that he had already employed during his studies at Juilliard, flipping the inner musical 'toggle switch' back and forth between European and African-American music. In those years he had studied European music by day and played in rhythm and blues bands or visited jazz clubs by night. These two worlds are still alive in him today; he can effortlessly summon them at any time and thereby, more importantly, create new things. 'The two, with Henry Grimes and the rest of the rhythm section, evoke a tidal wave of determination, a rise of consciousness of a need for power, that cannot end until the American fabric is fundamentally changed,' wrote Nat Hentoff about 'On This Night'.[372]

The title of the next piece, 'The Mac Man', alludes to a black slang expression of the 1950s for what would be, in today's jargon, a 'womanizer'.[373] Here Grimes proves to be a solid and inventive accompanist who brilliantly adopts the vacillating moods of the 'mac man', now gentle and balladesque, now tentative and driven, now furiously irate. Again and again he departs from the melody lines of the tenor saxophone to pursue his own ideas, which blend naturally with those from Shepp, Hutcherson, and Ali. These four musicians in particular generate an astonishing sense of unity and facility on this recording (pieces 1 to 3). Another Shepp composition on the album is 'The Original Mr. Sonny Boy Williamson'. He wrote it in Copenhagen in 1963 after meeting an African-American blues singer and instrumentalist who had adopted the name of the legendary Chicago blues singer, and who left a lasting impression on Archie Shepp as an artistic personality.[374] Once again Henry Grimes can be heard as a more than solid accompanist who, however, recedes further into the background, as on 'In A Sentimental Mood' and the second version of 'The Mac Man.' In any case, there are no extended solos from individual musicians on the original album. Instead, the point was mainly to generate a dense interplay among all the participants, whether on the written or the improvisatory level. It thus comes as no surprise that Harvey Pekar, in his *DownBeat* review of 1966, gives a favorable lump assessment: 'All of the bass playing is fine.'[375]

Like Archie Shepp's *On This Night*, the next recording on which Henry Grimes worked, Sunny Murray's *Sonny's Time Now*,[376] has a political message conveyed not only in its music, but also in the form of a poem. Perhaps it was artistic experiences such as these that prompted Grimes himself to begin writing poems a short while later, albeit far less overtly and aggressively political than those of Archie Shepp or LeRoi Jones, who declaims a radical poem on *Sonny's Time Now*. Murray recorded his album for LeRoi Jones' Jihad label in the Crown Heights area of Brooklyn in November 1965.[377] Besides Henry Grimes (bass) and Sunny Murray himself (drums), the participants were Albert Ayler (tenor saxophone), Don Cherry (trumpet), Lewis Worrell (bass) – all musicians who had played in Albert Ayler's ensembles – and LeRoi Jones (spoken word).[378] Probably proceeding from this fact, Peter Niklas Wilson misses the 'subtle balance' and 'floating lightness of Ayler's 1964 groups' on this album. He also finds that 'Murray's vestigial compositional specifications (in "Virtue" hardly more than a descending fifth from D-flat to G-flat) were obviously not [...] very inspiring,' adding that his 'growing predilection for insistent strings of pulses on snare and cymbals tend more to retard than to propel' the music, and that 'the combination of two basses reinforces this ponderousness.'[379]

Though Sunny Murray was deeply inspired by Albert Ayler, the very title of the album, *Sonny's Time Now*, clearly announces that he was concerned with making his own statement, and especially with demonstrating his fundamentally new understanding of jazz percussion. For Murray, sound for its own sake is a key feature of the new music. Traditional drum sets had, he felt, become obsolete:

'They only have a certain pitch, and that's all that can be played. They can't sustain, and with this music more of a sustaining, ringing kind of thing, it's even getting beyond rhythms.'[380] Murray developed a new kind of percussion which, with the aid of electronics, is capable of sustaining, thereby becoming 'more in touch with the human voice in terms of humming and screaming and laughing and crying'.[381] His innovative playing allowed him, as Val Wilmer so aptly put it, 'to lay down a shimmering tapestry behind the soloist, enabling him to move wherever he wanted.'[382] Unfortunately the recording technique, 'with its clogged sound and sometimes violent distortions',[383] did not exactly make the subtleties of this sort of interplay easy to hear. In any event, the point of the album was not only to project subtleties, but also, as in 'Black Art', to excoriate the reality of white racism in America. In the piece in question, LeRoi Jones recites a 'gross poem' (*krasses Poem*)[384] from which the piece 'Black Art' takes its name.[385] The poem can indeed rightly be called 'a manifesto of Black nationalism'.[386]

For long stretches on *Sonny's Time Now*, Henry Grimes and Lewis Worrell play in duet, generating a constantly humming sound that, like Sunny Murray's drumming, conjures up the collective improvisation, both holding the music together and driving it forward.[387]

Briefly interviewed in Dudelange (Luxembourg) in 2007, Sunny Murray was asked what he particularly valued in Henry Grimes as a musician. His answer could hardly have been more concise: 'Gettin' together into the right trance – that's what it's about.'[388] Henry's ability to enter completely and utterly into Murray's music, and to move freely and intuitively within it, is palpably evident on *Sonny's Time Now*. The two basses are the sustaining element of the ecstatically unfolding sound on 'Virtue', 'Justice', and especially orchestrally in 'The Lie.' Bill Quinn, in his *DownBeat* review of March 23, 1967, gave the album four stars with the words, 'This LP [...] is an allstar effort by the new musicians and should contribute something to the kinesis. Murray has gathered some formidable exponents of the genre. [...] Cherry vaults over the chugging and throbbing Grimes and Worrell. [...].'[389]

Roughly a month after the recording date with Sunny Murray, Henry Grimes worked with another leading figure of New York's free music scene: Burton Greene. If Grimes hadn't vanished from New York hardly a year later there would presumably exist even more recordings with him and Greene from the latter half of the 1960s. Even today Greene highly praises Grimes' musicianship, especially his powerful pizzicato: 'Henry Grimes, a great pizzicato player [...] played more pizzicato without an amplifier than most cats with, you know, he could be heard over that free scream, and I don't know how he did it, you know, he must have had 8 inch calluses, I don't know, this cat could play some pizzicato.'[390] The sound matches the personality: 'He had the biggest sound in the business. [...] And he had the heart and the personality, too.'[391] Greene precisely remembers Henry Grimes playing a legendary gig with Albert Ayler, Rashied Ali, Marion Brown, and Frank Smith in Slugs' Saloon in 1965 or 1966.[392] He considers Henry Grimes one of those who embody the philosophy of free music: 'All of us that had the chance to play with Henry remember how he could help kick a band out to the outer stratosphere and back, which of course was just what the explosive sixties were about.'[393]

Greene recorded his debut album for ESP, *Burton Greene Quartet*, on December 18, 1965. Actually it was scheduled with a different set of musicians: 'Originally I proposed a quartet with Marion Brown and Henry Grimes and Rashied Ali, but Rashied couldn't commit himself to the recording because he was going with Trane, so Dave Grant and Tom Price did two tracks each on the album.'[394] Burton Greene himself can be heard not only at the piano, but also on piano harp and percussion, with Marion Brown on alto saxophone. The guest performer on 'Taking It Out Of The Ground', tenorist Frank Smith, stands out from the otherwise tight and sensitive quartet with his self-absorbed, uninspired, slapdash playing.[395] Like every other member of the quartet, Henry Grimes received ample opportunities for solo improvisation. What distinguishes his playing, again and again, is a dry, wooden, abrasive pizzicato with which he creates a sound that blends with the sounds of Greene's piano harp. These inventive bass sounds generate an energetically propulsive force, heard to particular advantage in his roughly two-minute solo on 'Cluster Quartet' (from *ca.* 6'56). In 'Ballade II', a piece reminiscent of Arnold Schoenberg, Henry delivers an orchestral arco solo more than two-and-a-half minutes long (from *ca.* 6'12), revealing both great emotional urgency and a grasp of classical music. It is too varied and complex to be called simply 'sorrowful' or 'melancholy' – two moods that it nevertheless manages to strike. On 'Taking It Out Of The Ground', Henry, in a roughly one-minute arco solo (from *ca.* 9'30), again reveals his ability to shape and propel the collective improvisation with highly inventive melody lines and sudden changes of tempo.[396]

Three further albums on which Henry Grimes took part in 1965 cannot entirely be assigned to the new music: *Cullen Knight Music*, recorded live at Philadelphia's Starlight Lounge on June 26;[397] a lost album recorded for Atlantic by Mose Allison on October 7 (the tapes were presumably destroyed in the Atlantic warehouse fire);[398] and a trio album recorded by tenor saxophonist Frank Wright for ESP on November 11 with Tom Price on drums.[399] On the last of these, Henry Grimes' playing can barely be made out, a result not only of the poor recording equipment but also of Wright's ponderously dominant style, which at least here is incapable of forming a dialogue. Roughly six weeks later, on December 28, Grimes recorded *The Call* with his own trio, consisting of Perry Robinson (clarinet) and Tom Price (drums). Unlike Frank Wright's trio album, it demonstrates inspired and intensive interplay among everyone involved.[400]

Grimes was also hidden far in the background on his first studio date of 1966 – the ESP album *Ensemble* by alto saxophonist Charles Tyler, a close companion of Albert Ayler. Tyler recorded it in New York on February 4 with Charles Moffett (orchestra vibes), Joel Freedman (cello), Henry Grimes (bass), and Ronald Shannon Jackson (drums).[401] The music, though heavily beholden to Ayler's ideas, did not seem to inspire Grimes' gifts for improvisation, as did his studio dates with Cecil Taylor,[402] Don Cherry,[403] and Albert Ayler himself[404] a few weeks later.

In contrast, an outstanding album from 1966 which Henry took part in is *Tauhid* by Pharoah Sanders (tenor saxophone, alto saxophone, piccolo, voice), recorded in Rudy Van Gelder's studio on November 15 with Sonny Sharrock (guitar), Dave Burrell (piano), Henry Grimes (bass), Roger Blank (drums), and Nat Bettis (percussion).[405] Here we can witness a truly 'imperial' Henry Grimes.[406] On the first piece, 'Upper Egypt & Lower Egypt', he plays a heavy, dark arco solo (*ca.* 4'50). A short while later Pharoah Sanders (who said in an interview at this time, 'I feel closest to Hell when I'm thinking about money') enters with the piccolo, giving rise to subtle, variegated interplay lasting a good three minutes. Then Henry launches into a vigorously swinging pizzicato solo (*ca.* 8'50) that introduces the theme with rhythmic elegance, gradually and movingly ushering all the musicians into the piece (*ca.* 9'20). On 'Japan', Grimes again proves to be a more than powerful and inventive pizzicato accompanist. And on the final piece of the album, a sequence consisting of 'a. Aum, b. Venus, c. Capricorn Rising', Grimes can be heard right at the beginning with a breakneck pulsating arco foray that demonstrates his rich experience and proficiency in free music. A busy interplay between Grimes' pizzicato and Sanders' free, expressive tenor saxophone (*ca.* 9'00) follows and leads ultimately to a haunting, roughly two-minute pizzicato solo from Grimes (*ca.* 11'00). Here he generates a state of deep languor to introduce the concluding sequence, moving the piece, to quote the reviewer Bill Quinn, 'from pain to peace'.[407] 'Throughout this work, and the album, Henry Grimes' playing on bass is remarkably attuned to the questing spirit of Sanders' music,'[408] reads Nat Hentoff's summary of Grimes' contribution to this album.

Some three weeks after the studio date with Pharoah Sanders, two more followed on a single day, December 8. Both took place in New York for ESP and partly used the same personnel: Karl Berger's album *From Now On* included, apart from Berger, Carlos Ward (alto saxophone), Grimes, and Ed Blackwell (drums);[409] and Marzette Watts' album *Marzette Watts And Company* with Watts (bass clarinet, soprano saxophone, tenor saxophone), Grimes and Berger, Byard Lancaster (flute, bass clarinet, alto saxophone), Clifford Thornton (trumpet, cornet), Sonny Sharrock (guitar), Art 'Juni' Booth (bass) and J. C. Moses (drums).[410]

From Now On is made up of two suites: 'Scales / Turn Around / Steps', and 'Blue Early Bird / Like That / Greenbird / From Now On'. Both are clearly inspired by Ornette Coleman yet dominated by Berger's cheerfully swinging vibes. Once again, Grimes proves to be a musician who not only has a distinct command of contrasting styles, but also invariably finds room for personal artistic expression. He switches spontaneously from largely non-metrical free playing to something akin to traditional swinging bass lines, coaxing fresh ideas from Berger and brilliantly providing a low-register counterpoint to Berger's bright vibraphone sounds.

Marzette Watts And Company is a dense ensemble performance dominated by horns and guitar, with especially impressive and inventive wild free playing from guitarist Sonny Sharrock. The two basses and drums tend to work in the background, and Grimes, despite his powerful and unique pizzicato playing, is usually difficult to hear. For large stretches other musicians drown the two basses out – a quality for which the poorly balanced recording is to blame.

Henry Grimes' last recording, before the year 2003,[411] was the live concert with Albert Ayler at the Village Vanguard on December 18, 1966.[412]

The impending radical break in Grimes' life around 1966/67 does nothing to change the fact that he had long been numbered among the major figures in African-American free music: a 1966 issue of the now defunct magazine *Liberator*, published by the African-American Research Institute in New York, contains an article with photographs by Ray Gibson under the title 'Spiritual Voices of Black America'. The photographs are searing portraits of Marion Brown, Henry Grimes (the cover photo of *The Call*), Grachan Moncur III, Sunny Murray, and Sun Ra. The text reads, beginning in large capitals:

THESE MUSICIANS ARE AMONG THE STRONGEST FORCES IN EMERGING BLACK AMERICA. THEY ARE THE REPOSITORIES OF THE SPIRIT OF FREEDOM AND EXPRESSION IMBEDDED IN THE SOCIAL HISTORY OF BLACK PEOPLE.

Sun Ra, the spiritual prophet, understands the cosmic forces in music. He is constantly moving his music to new planes of wonder and fulfillment. Sonny Murray believes that it is movement – spirit. Marion Brown's playing probes deep into unexplored regions of the General Black Psyche. Grachan Moncur is one of the most proficient trombonist[s] on the music scene. Henry Grimes' playing exhibits a great range of mood and feeling. Take a good look at them; they assume great importance as we come to understand our spiritual selves and the world around us.[413]

Almost two years later, the *Liberator* issue of April 1968 (vol. 8, no. 4) placed the same portrait photograph of Henry Grimes directly on the cover. The editorial, dedicated to Byard Lancaster and bearing the title 'Black Music', was written by Errol Green, who worded his thoughts as follows: 'It is generally true that the ethnic group that is most continuously caused to suffer within a society will have a more urgent need to give existence some meaningful purpose. Therefore, this same ethnic group is most likely to make the most universal and truly meaningful artistic contributions.'

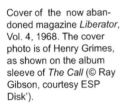

Cover of the now abandoned magazine *Liberator*, Vol. 4, 1968. The cover photo is of Henry Grimes, as shown on the album sleeve of *The Call* (© Ray Gibson, courtesy ESP Disk').

By this time Henry Grimes, listed here as one of the leading figures among these artists, had probably already moved to Los Angeles. In the minds of New York's avant-garde musicians he was as present as ever before, but this was of no further use to him.

Many outstanding 'New Thing' musicians of the late 1960s found themselves in the paradoxical situation that they produced artistic achievements recognized as being of the highest caliber, but received practically no financial recompense.[414] Between 1968 and 1970, Henry Grimes, still in his early thirties, drew the most radical consequence from this state of affairs and abandoned the musical profession altogether. The effect that this materially imposed silence caused within him will be described later. But for the moment, in 1967, he experienced a perilous transitional phase into a life without a bass.

5

In Transition – 1967–68

> [T]his is a materialistic society and no one ever asked you to be involved
> in spiritual values. If you are, you have to accept the responsibility of
> that, and if you're a Black man, this is complicated in many, many
> different ways.
>
> Cecil Taylor[1]

Henry Grimes and Paul Chambers, both born in 1935 and both outstanding bass players, traveled quite different paths in music and in
their lives. But toward the end of the 1960s they both faced the
same problem: they couldn't earn a living with their tremendous
talents and had been unable to create a social network to protect
and nurture that talent. The reasons for the absence of a social
network are many and varied, and they do not lie entirely in their
personalities: they also lie in the social conditions under which the
two men grew up and lived. In the end, both developed a skeptical
detachment to the society around them and a sort of resignation
toward their minimal chances of influencing that society as artists.
Chambers died in New York on January 4, 1969 of tuberculosis, a
consequence of heroin addiction.[2] In the same year Grimes bid
farewell to the world of music for more than three decades – a
world for which jazz music had in any case become increasingly
irrelevant. As Sonny Rollins puts it, 'This is what happens in life
when musicians, artists have to live in this commercial world. It's
really unfortunate.'[3]

Viewed as ideal types, Paul Chambers and Henry Grimes are
separated by a historical watershed in their mentality. Paul
Chambers embodied the fast life-style of the bebop era, which
was often associated with heroin addiction and drove many

musicians to an early death. In his own way, Henry Grimes adopted the health-oriented, vital, meditative life-style of the free music pioneers. Burton Greene summed up his observations of this latter group of musicians, to which he himself belonged: 'Thus we find that the apt practitioners of the new music are essentially positivists, great practitioners of life itself. [...] Several of the new breed that I know are health addicts as well as competent writers, painters, actors, teachers, social commentators.'[4] It was this spiritual attitude toward life that helped the new music pioneer Henry Grimes to survive his decades of artistic silence.

Musical Changes from the Mid-Sixties

For many jazz musicians, not only in the new music, the latter half of the 1960s was a period of turmoil and imperiled livelihoods. Rock and Motown became increasingly popular, changing the nature of the record market. Producers who previously gave jazz a prominent place in their catalogues now preferred the new styles, or expected jazz musicians to incorporate the new commercial elements into their music in order to make it more marketable. In purely musical terms this was certainly not a problem: jazz music is, after all, 'the umbrella under which all other musics exist'.[5] But not every jazz musician was willing or able, like Miles Davis or Weather Report, to swim with this new current. Moreover, many jazz clubs had to shut down for lack of an audience.[6]

'When you are someone like Henry – and Henry is not gonna change, he is still a serious person – you end up just disappearing and leaving the world scene. You are alone someplace; this can happen, I can understand that very well. [...] It's very difficult for an artist and it's very difficult for a Black artist in the United States. So you always have that problem plaguing you. [...] Well, Henry could do all of this stuff, but when the electric bass came in, the trend was changing. I can see why Henry might have been beginning to have some difficulties surviving.'

Thus Sonny Rollins, speaking of the period and of Henry Grimes, his musical confrère in the years 1958–59 and 1962–63.[7] Rollins, too, entered a period of reorientation in 1968. His spiritual quest took him to India, 'where for five months he studied meditation and Vedic philosophy with Swami Chinmayananda in the Ashram Sandeepany Sadhanalaya at Powai near Bombay.'[8] In 1969, disgusted with the music business and with American society as a whole, he withdrew completely into private life for roughly two years and even considered abandoning music altogether.[9] What Sonny Rollins had seriously considered doing was, at roughly the same time, translated into action by Grimes, not of his free will, but in response to material pressure. Rollins later analyzed the situation: 'Henry was in a very unfortunate position which a lot of musicians were in. Because during the seventies and these years there were a lot of stylistic changes going on in the music world. So it's very possible that Henry might have found himself less able to find work.'[10]

'I didn't want to be subject to the cold' – Grimes Decides to Leave New York (February 1967)

We may never know what befell Grimes out west. Whatever it involved would have broken a weaker heart.

Marc Medwin[11]

By the 1960s Henry Grimes was already aware that the music he played and the musicians he worked with were outstanding. From this standpoint there was no reason for him to give up playing. The only musical aspect that drove him into 'isolation' was the fact that his 'perceptions' – his awareness of and receptivity for collective improvisation – regularly were being drowned out by disruptive emotions: 'Emotions can get you in a lot of trouble or hassle [...]. And you can either let them bother you or you can find a way to get something out of them.'[12] At this time, as he recounted in a 2003 interview, he was 'overwhelmed by emotions'.[13] In the same year he told Los Angeles reporter Lynell George, 'it just kind of hit me. I don't know where it came from. It was a strange thing. I remember it all accumulating. I started a scuffle with one of the musicians. Wasn't like me at all. And after that I was kind of embarrassed. I had to get out of there.'[14]

Other external factors came into play, ultimately causing him to turn his back on New York. Perhaps all these factors mutually reinforced each other. For example, Grimes mentions 'the violence that affected Manhattan's loft community in the 1960s, which influenced his decision to leave New York.'[15] He recalls 'people ripping other people off in violent ways,' and those 'who would want to hurt you because of the kind of music you played.'[16] However, he does not single out any particular incident that motivated his decision.

Another reason – indeed the principal factor in his decision to leave – was his financial straits. Again and again he emphasizes that young musicians such as Albert Ayler, who often hired him at the time, earned so little money with their music that they could hardly pay him: 'I was often booked in New York, but I couldn't manage to make money. When musicians like Albert Ayler came up in the Sixties, the financial situation was very bad. They were all younger than me. Age may not have anything to do with it, but professional experience does. They were all happy for every gig they got, but they never had any money. The economic situation was a real disaster.'[17]

In 2003 he told Marshall Marrotte that he made his decision to leave New York '[...] more for economic reasons [...] than anything else. I was involved in a lot of jam sessions, you know, but there was very little money. [...] I was getting paid, [but] it just wasn't enough money. I didn't want to say "Oh, I want some more money" you know, because these guys were great players and I was enjoying playing.'[18]

Being an artist, Henry Grimes' primary concern was (and is) music. When he felt good about it, money was secondary, provided things somehow worked out. But at some point they stopped working out. He watched the New York music scene gradually disintegrate before his eyes: 'I had to get a few things going, and discovered that when I did, the things around me started to fall apart.'[19] As he explained to Ken Weiss: 'I got out of New York before I totally broke down. [...] I didn't feel secure so that's why I left. I just didn't want to be in any way out on the street. [...] Depending on that [performing and recording] for income was not a steady business at that time at all. A lot of recordings were made, but no financial benefit.'[20]

When *DownBeat* writer Michael Jackson asked him, 'Did you and Sonny Rollins share a pact to go on sabbaticals, then you forgot to come back?' Henry ignored the insensitive irony in Jackson's remark: 'No [...] I just had to get out of New York City. There just wasn't enough money, and it forced me to consider something else. I tried San Francisco and then L.A. I wanted to get work in Hollywood but could never do it.'[21]

Because of his dire financial straits in New York, Grimes was afraid he might succumb to the cold. By the time he left the East Village, 'Economically I was in no shape at all [...]. My money was down to nothing. So I came to California, where the sun shines. Mostly that was the idea. I didn't want to be subject to the cold.'[22]

In 2005 Ssirus W. Pakzad wanted to know, why he 'didn't ask his New York friends for help or support.' Henry Grimes just shook his head: 'No, I never would have done that. First, I don't like to ask people for favors, and I didn't want to borrow from anyone, because the moment I have money, it's gone.'[23] But he does not only brood on his 'weaknesses': he keeps his skills and his good times in mind as well. This source of inner strength has kept him walking tall: 'I knew that one day my time would come again. Through all the years I always did special exercises to strengthen my hands. I wanted to be prepared to start playing again.'[24] As he put it in 2009, he never lost hope in himself.[25]

Henry Grimes was, he admits, not the only one to vanish from New York or drop out of music: '[A] lot of musicians in the past have gone missing. I don't know what the analogy is or anything, but a lot of musicians have played, and disappeared, just like I did.'[26] As for his own decision, '[i]t wasn't a conscious choice to stop playing music, but it was a conscious choice, [...] to get out of the way of the New York scene, so I went to San Francisco.'[27] Andrew Cyrille wondered whether Henry might have stayed in New York if he hadn't been living alone at the time: 'If he had Margaret [Henry's partner since 2003 and wife since 2007] back then maybe he wouldn't have disappeared. You have to have somebody who understands and wants to be with you, wants to give you that love and attention, to nurture whatever art that you have.'[28]

In all his years of isolation, Henry Grimes remained inwardly in touch with music. His disappearance from the world of music loses its aura of mystery the moment one speaks with him about it. He had solid, intelligible reasons for disappearing – and many other leading avant-garde musicians were in the same predicament: 'The history of jazz is made up of (many) disappearances, (unusual) reappearances, and stories taking place underground. Sonny Simmons and Henry Grimes reappeared after twenty or thirty years and asked: "Where did we leave off?" Sunny Murray plods along in Paris, loaded with cymbals and drums, playing gigs in front of twenty persons at best. Milford Graves, the explorer of percussion, teaches music therapy a long way from the limelight. The case of Giuseppi Logan is notorious [...] And what about Marzette Watts? Whatever happened to him? In the Seventies he had made a space to play out of the former ESP office in Cooper Square. It's all darkness after that.'[29]

There are also some solid arguments why Grimes did not tell his closest family members, such as his sister or his musical companions, that he was leaving New York. As his wife Margaret analyses it: 'He was not close to or even in contact with his family members. He had had a falling-out with his parents when he was in his late teens or early 20s and never spoke with them again, and in fact he was having horrible financial problems then too and struggled back to Philadelphia in a huge storm to ask them for help, and they turned him away and told him never to come back. And Henry was also estranged from his twin brother and his sister, though he's never really explained why. Also, Henry may have thought going out to the West Coast was just another tour at first. Also, he did not contact his fellow musicians because he didn't see any examples of music community happening where musicians gave money or other forms of support to the ones in trouble. In fact, such forms of caregiving did take place in those days, but Henry just didn't know about them. And Henry would have been mortified at the very thought of asking and still to this day has a horrible time asking anyone for anything. He really just can't do it. And finally, another reason Henry didn't ask for help is most mundane, but real: On his way from San Francisco to L.A., he lost some of his few possessions, including his address book with all his contacts in it.'[30]

Relocating to the West Coast (February 1967)

. Whether it was during his stint in Jon Hendricks' band that Grimes
resolved to move to the West Coast, and thus to a region known
for its mild winters, or whether he made the decision beforehand,
can no longer be determined. The idea of leaving New York must
have been in his mind for a long time. He had just come through a
long New York winter, and with his lack of money he would not
always have stayed warm. Perhaps his engagement in Hendricks'
band, which took him on tour via Chicago and Vancouver to San
Francisco in early 1967, gave him the final incentive to put his plan
into action. At that time the band was looking for a new bass player,
and eventually found one in Henry Grimes.[31] 'So I went to San
Francisco to see what I could do there. The avant-garde thing had
not made any full circle to come to San Francisco. San Francisco
musicians at that time weren't like New York musicians, but they
were good players. Playing mostly standards. Technically, it was
alright.'[32]

The Jon Hendricks band traveled from Boston to New
York, where they picked Grimes up. Clarence Becton, Hendricks'
drummer at the time, has clear recollections of the tour.[33]

Riding in Jon Hendricks' Car from New York via Chicago and Vancouver to San Francisco – Henry Grimes and Clarence Becton Remember[34]

*Born in Mississippi in 1933, Clarence Becton moved to Buffalo, NY, at
the age of twelve. He grew up with church music, began playing music
himself at nineteen, and learned to play drums, tenor saxophone, and
piano. He worked locally as a drummer with Pete Johnson, Don Menza,
Don Ellis, and Wade Legge, playing at the Royal Arms Club in Buffalo
and working with soloists such as Coleman Hawkins, Clark Terry, and
Jon Hendricks. He left Buffalo with Hendricks, with whom he toured
the USA and Canada until 1968. In 1967 he met Henry Grimes, who
briefly played bass in Hendricks' band, but there are no known
recordings of the two men playing together. Then, in 1969, Becton moved
to Munich, where he worked at the Domicile Jazz Club and other locations with Pony Poindexter, Benny Bailey, Slide Hampton, Lucky*

Clarence Becton, Amsterdam October 14, 2007 (© Thomas Rösch).

Thompson, Mal Waldron (including the ECM album Free At Last),
Dusko Goykovich, and many other artists. Upon returning to the US in
1970, he worked with Thelonious Monk, Bobby Hutcherson, Ernestine
Anderson, Woody Shaw, Mark Levine, Michael White, Joe Henderson,
Milt Jackson, Pepper Adams, Eddie Henderson, 'Captain' John Handy,
Julian Priester, and others. In early 1979 he went on the road for nine
months, touring the US, Canada, and parts of Europe with Earl 'Fatha'
Hines. At the end of the tour he moved to New York and began per-
forming with artists such as Joe Albany, Jon Hendricks and Family,
Pepper Adams, and Slide Hampton. He also worked with such avant-
garde musicians as Marilyn Crispell, Julius Hemphill, Oliver Lake,
Hamiet Bluiett, and James Blood Ulmer. Moving back to Europe in
March 1981 and establishing a home base in Amsterdam, where he
taught at the conservatory, he has performed and recorded over the years
with many fine local and international musicians, and appeared with
his own group, The Clarence Becton Society.[35]

By the time Clarence Becton and Henry Grimes met each
other, Becton had already been working with Hendricks for twelve
years. In February 1967 the band needed a new bass player, for their
previous bassist had family obligations that forced him to return to

his home near San Francisco. 'We played in Boston and we came to New York in between gigs to get a bass player, and we got Henry, picked up Henry.'[36]

Pianist Larry Vuckovich, who then belonged to Jon Hendricks' band, remembers quite the same: 'In 1967, while I was working with Jon Hendricks heading the trio that included Clarence Becton on drums and Bob Maize on bass, Jon had a tour set up that took us to the East Coast. The cities and the clubs included Buffalo (Royal Arms), Toronto (The Town Tavern), and Boston (Lennies on the Turnpike). The regular bassist, Bob, was unable to make the tour, and for our first performance in Buffalo at the Royal Arms, Jon called New York and was able to get Henry Grimes to come up and work with us. When I heard that Henry was going to join the trio, I was very excited. I already was aware of Henry's strong reputation in jazz, having heard him on recordings with McCoy Tyner and Sonny Rollins.'[37] Becton remembers that they had a vehicle with a trailer for the instruments – he vaguely recalls a Dodge station wagon while Grimes remembers a 1965 Studebaker Cruiser or something around that size and style. Clarence Becton: 'In some interviews with Henry, one can read that we traveled with Henry's bass on top of the car. To my memory, we had the bass and the drums and the luggage in the trailer and we drove in the station wagon.'[38] Becton and Vuckovich both remember that this tour took place in February 1967, but a few press articles place the entire tour in 1968.[39] Some evidence points to February 1967, and there is not any hint of Grimes' staying in New York City after February 1967. Hendricks moved to London in 1968 and toured Europe and Africa while based there.[40]

Becton recalls that, first 'we picked up Henry in New York and we drove to Chicago. With Jon and, I guess, somebody of his family and myself and Henry. In Chicago Jon decided that he wanted to fly to Vancouver. We had a job in Vancouver at a place called The Shanghai Junk.'[41] Hendricks wanted to stay there to give a couple of interviews and generate publicity for the gig. He put Becton and Grimes in charge of the car for the roughly two-thousand-mile drive to Vancouver, a trip lasting about two days, if each man drove half the trip.

'He told me, "Okay, you and Henry can share the driving." So we got on the way, and I drove the whole day or something. So I got tired and said to Henry, "Maybe you can drive some," and he said, "Oh, yeah, I can drive, " and I said, "Is your license up to date, your driver's license?" And Henry said, "What license?" And so I had my doubts, so I said, "Well, I can drive a bit longer." So I drove, I think, 24 hours, and I got so tired that in the evening I hallucinated, I saw trees hanging upside down [laughs], and I said, "Henry, could you drive?"

'And he was ready, he got behind the wheel, and he started doing this [swerving with his hands]. It was about eight o'clock in the evening. We were somewhere between Chicago and Vancouver, fortunate for us that there was not much traffic on the road. People were in having their dinner. We were all on the wrong side of the road, almost going off the road.

'I said, "Henry, Henry, what are you doing?"

'He said, "Give me a chance!"

'I said, "Henry, stop!" I couldn't take it any more.

'I said, "Henry, pull over and stop!"

'He said, "Why? Why? Give me a chance!" I said, "Man, a chance to kill us?" He was resistant to pulling over and stopping.

'He said, "We're gonna be late for the gig if we stop in a motel overnight. We might be late for the gig."

'I said, "It's better to be late for the gig than to be late – the late Henry Grimes and the late Clarence Becton." He wasn't happy about it, but we slept and then we continued on.

'And we would have made it in time for the gig, except that then we had mechanical problems with the car. We had to stop, and we spent some money. We also had a problem because Jon had left the car documents at home, and the police stopped us and checked, and they wanted to take us to jail, but we could be allowed to continue on if we paid a fine, so they took some money from us. When we got to the Canadian border, we were down to our last few cents, we had spent money to repair the car and to give to the police, and when we got there, Jon had neglected to leave the contract for the gig at the border. If you come with the instruments and all that stuff, they don't let you come into Canada unless you have a contract, or otherwise you have to pay about a $500 bond to bring the instruments in. We didn't have the money. We were in trouble. I had just enough change to make a telephone call to the club and explain the situation. And the club owner drove to the border and brought the contract. So we finally got to the gig.'[42]

In spite of this account, Becton recalls Grimes as a man who never gave him any trouble — apart from the trip to Vancouver: 'I always found Henry a beautiful person. I didn't find Henry to be obnoxious or anything. When we were together on the trip in the car it was quiet, but not in an unfriendly way; it was a comfortable quiet, you know. Henry just scared me to death with his drive and we had a conflict of ways to do things at that moment. He wanted to continue on by him driving and I decided definitely against that. So I had to exercise my authority, because Jon put me in charge with the car, and to get the car and myself and Henry to Vancouver. So I had to do that the best way, and I did not see it the best way to have Henry driving. So I had to insist Henry get out from behind the wheel. And he wasn't happy about that, about missing the first gig. And we missed the first night, but we were alive.'[43]

The Jon Hendricks Quartet, with Grimes, Becton and the Philippine pianist Joseph 'Flip' Nuñez, played for a week in Vancouver's Shanghai Junk before traveling on to San Francisco. Becton vaguely remembers that they drove in tandem, with Nuñez driving his own car (together with Hendricks) and Becton and Grimes in Hendricks' car.

Becton recalls that 'Henry always had his dog with him.'[44] Grimes remembers the dog as well — a female named Chica that lived with him for one or two months at the end of his New York period and again in San Francisco, where she suddenly disappeared.[45] In New York he also had a Siamese cat named Jasper that he gave away to a female employee of Blue Note Records when he left. Grimes' eyes still glow today when he thinks of Chica and Jasper, with whom he shared his long-ago New York apartment.[46]

The trip to San Francisco took them through the deserts of Utah and Nevada. During the trip Henry Grimes' bass was seriously damaged, whether on the roof of the car or in a trailer is anyone's guess. The instrument lacked a travel case.[47] 'It was hot and dry, and the drive was pretty shaky. You know, when you are in the desert, it's hot and dry, and that's not good for a bass. It can make the bass crack.'[48]

More than four decades later, when Grimes spoke with his wife Margaret about his bad time starting in the late 1960s, he said that he went through the desert and put it inside him and kept on going.[49]

Stopover in San Francisco – Working with Jon Hendricks, Al Jarreau, and Sunny Murray (1967)

After spending a couple of free days in San Francisco, Henry Grimes and Clarence Becton played a four-week booking at the Trident, a club in the San Francisco suburb of Sausalito.[50] Becton recounts: 'After that we were on our own. Jon didn't have more work. [...] There was not much going on, so it was a struggle.'[51] Jon Hendricks, Grimes recalls, returned East after this gig, 'but I did not want to go so I stayed there.'[52] Grimes also remembers that he 'was actually leaving with Jon Hendricks, was in the car, and Hendricks made some nasty remark about Cecil Taylor and his avant-garde playing, and Henry was insulted on his friend's behalf and got out of the car, and Hendricks drove away without him.'[53] Grimes had to pay a horrendous price for his powerful qualities of loyalty and dedication.

At the time Clarence Becton 'didn't see in Henry any expectations; I just saw that he is there and just can see what he can do there, survive there, do what he can do.'[54] Henry Grimes' San Francisco period was to last only a couple of months. Becton knew a few people in the area and lived there for a couple of years.[55] He had a small one-room apartment in San Francisco at the time, but he does not know exactly where Grimes lived – nor does Grimes himself. 'We met up sometimes and played. I think we played a couple of local gigs together – with some people that I knew – and they knew who Henry was. But it wasn't that much going on.'[56] Occasionally, 'somebody called me, they needed a drummer and a bass player, and then we got in touch with Henry. We had each other's telephone numbers.'[57]

During his months in San Francisco, Grimes also worked with other musicians, including a singer who would become internationally famous in 1975: Al Jarreau.[58] Grimes is also known to have played a multi-day gig in Sunny Murray's Band at the Both/And club. The drummer remembered it quite well in an interview with Dan Warburton for *Paris Transatlantic* in 2000: 'I was invited to play at the Jazz Both/And in San Francisco in 1967. Beaver Harris had told me a guy called Delano or something had been asking for me down at Slugs' Saloon, and that he wanted me to be a house drummer for the Both/And. I met the guy and told him being a house drummer was a little far-fetched, considering the way I played, so he offered me an engagement of four days or something like that instead. He got Ralph Gleason to write a whole thing in the [San Francisco] *Chronicle*, 'Welcome Sunny to California.' I'd never had that before. Amiri Baraka was trying to produce a lecture tour of Californian universities at the same time, so we rented a big van together, a tour bus like the rhythm'n'blues bands used to have. I took Al Shorter, Pharoah [Sanders], Henry Grimes.'[59]

The Both/And concert is the last gig of the 1960s corroborated by Henry Grimes' fellow musicians.[60] Marshall Marrotte asked him in 2003 when he last played the bass, and he replied, 'It must have been in 1970, in a church with some younger guys, I forget their names, but it was a trio thing. This was in San Francisco, not long before I sold it.'[61] Clarence Becton dates Henry's departure from San Francisco to the end of 1967 or early 1968 at the latest.[62] Whenever it exactly was – Henry Grimes took his bass, now riddled with cracks, and moved on to Los Angeles to seek his fortune.

'Follow the Yellow Brick Road' – The Move to Los Angeles (1967–68)

Unlike his move to San Francisco, when Grimes arrived in Los Angeles he 'didn't have any standards to follow [...] I just did it.'[63] Nor did he have any friends there. 'I just followed a notion. I followed a feeling in my heart, like they say, follow the yellow brick road.'[64] But before long he felt 'lost because I didn't know any musicians there and the club scene was pretty lame.'[65] He remembers that the last person he played with there was the pianist LaMont Johnson:[66] 'LaMont Johnson had a band that I played in for a while. I lived in the house they occupied. Then they all became Scientologists, and I left them because I didn't want to have anything to do with it. So I found myself out on the street. My bass was in bad condition. [...] I thought someone would call me sooner or later and I'd find work. So I waited.'[67]

The bassist Roberto Miranda, speaking to the journalist Lynell George in 2003, remembers an event that probably relates to this period: 'Miranda caught a glimpse of Grimes at a jam session near Loyola Marymount University. "It was about thirty years ago at someone's house: seven bass players, four or five drummers and thousands of horn players. I ended up standing right next to Henry.... In the middle of all this, Henry stops playing, sets his bass down, walks to the couch [and] immediately falls asleep."'[68] Grimes may not have had any other place to sleep at that time, was exhausted, and fell asleep in the middle of the jam session.

At some point Henry Grimes' bass became unusable. He took it to a violin maker who quoted a high price for the repair work:[69] 'For one thing, it needed repairs and the repairs were expensive. I just sold it to this violin maker and that was that. [...] It was about five hundred dollars, I think. That was in 1968, when I came down here from San Francisco to L.A. That is when I sold it.'[70] The price he received for the bass was far too low: 'I didn't make enough money from the sale.[71] But I still sold it anyway. I was feeling that was what I had to do, so I just did it.'[72] Assuming that Grimes, as he confirms himself, stopped playing music altogether after selling his instrument, not even on someone else's bass, the sale probably took place later than 1968: Clarence Becton met Henry Grimes again by accident in Los Angeles in 1969 and jammed with him several times.[73]

At first Grimes thought he would be able to buy back 'Brunhilda', as he called his German bass, but it never happened.[74] Without a bass, he had to take on jobs of any and every kind: 'I was in good physical condition and could earn money as, say, a construction worker.'[75] Yet he did not abandon music inwardly and maintained a waiting posture, as he puts it, for more than thirty years: 'After that, I just waited in Los Angeles, and I was just waiting for something to happen. And it lasted thirty some years out there in Los Angeles, waiting for something to happen.'[76]

Early in 1969 Clarence Becton, who was living briefly in L.A., ran into Henry Grimes: 'In February 1969 I moved to Los Angeles. I met a girl, I fell in love, and I moved down to Los Angeles with her. After a few months I ran into Henry – in Los Angeles.'[77] He could not discover how Grimes had fared in the interim or how he was doing at the time of their accidental meeting. To Becton, Grimes always 'was kind of inscrutable. It is hard to read in his expression what is going on inside him. He didn't talk about it. When we met up in Los Angeles, he came to a session to play or something like that and we played and that was the communication. I didn't get much of an insight into his state of mind or what had happened in the period in between. Usually, in a gig or in a playing situation [you are] kind of focused on the music anyway. [...] He played well. It felt good playing together. If there was any change in his attitude, musicality, I didn't receive it. [...] Music can bring you up, and other people around you don't realize that you're down in a hole. So, it could have been that with Henry.'[78] They played together a few more times, meeting, he recalls, at someone's house and jamming. 'And then he disappeared again.'[79] Or rather, Becton lost sight of him once again.

Clarence Becton, too, had trouble finding music work in L.A. and moved away the same year that he received an offer from Munich: 'I didn't have a lot of work myself when I lived in Los Angeles, because I just moved down there. I didn't stay there very long. Los Angeles turned out to be kind of a commercial scene. I didn't feel right. My relationship broke up and I had an offer to go to Munich and playing in a club called The Domicile [...] and being in the house band there. So I went and lived in Schwabing [a district of Munich] about nine months.'[80] Nine months later he returned to San Francisco to study music. 'From time to time I asked people if they heard anything from Henry Grimes. And I heard some different stories. Somebody has told me that Henry was hired on a ranch and riding horses. And then I heard another story that he was selling insurance, and somebody said, "I think he died" – different stories.'[81]

6

'Waiting for something to happen' – Thirty-four Years in Los Angeles (1969–2003)

> *In L.A. it's possible to work, but not as an artist.*
> Henry Grimes, 2007[1]

Grimes had chosen to live in a place not exactly known for its appreciation of jazz music. Sonny Rollins, too, had experienced this side of the city: 'I don't want to generalize. But Los Angeles, as compared to New York or Chicago or other cities, is very much of a commercial place, and they are very much interested in shows, big cars, big clothes, things of this sort – entertainment values. [...] They had jazz all over, of course [...] there were jazz clubs in Hollywood [...] Charlie Parker played out there in the forties, I played out there in the fifties [...] But basically Los Angeles was more of a place of entertainment value than musical value. [...] I think if Henry had been in New York, he would have had more friends.'[2] The tenorman Don Menza, in a 2006 interview, likewise expressed a disheartening view of Los Angeles' music scene in the late 1960s: 'When I got to Los Angeles in 1968, I was really disappointed. Everybody was scuffling. In Europe I had a steady gig. Here, I was just a tenor player. Nobody knew who I was.'[3] Grimes' situation was much the same: even those who knew him in Los Angeles could not, in the long run, arrange any gigs for him.

The saxophonist and flutist Sam Rivers, in a 1999 interview, called Hollywood a money trap that robbed musicians of their freedom: 'There's a lot of talented Hollywood musicians. But in Hollywood, when you're working in the studios, you get all this money and you sort of get trapped. I know a lot of guys like that. They say, "I hate it, but I can't leave it!" So for me, that's a lesson not to get trapped by a financial situation where you can't leave – it takes away your freedom.'[4] Bassist Buell Neidlinger, a great admirer of his colleague Henry Grimes[5] and a member of Cecil Taylor's band in the 1950s, held a different view of L.A. He moved there from New York in 1971 and availed himself of the Hollywood 'money trap'. In a 1986 interview for *Cadence*, he felt perfectly satisfied with the decision: 'A musician of reputable quality can work and create a pension he can retire on through the movie business. That's impossible to do anywhere else. That's why I moved here.'[6]

Neidlinger, however, is not Henry Grimes. Interviewed in 2007, Clarence Becton stressed that Los Angeles was not a city for Henry, and it would have been better if he had immediately returned to New York: 'Henry? Not in L.A.! Henry is not a hustler, to get out and relate and talk and sell himself. [...] Also, he was in a place where there was not much to be found. He was well known among musicians – people had heard about Henry Grimes and his work, people in a hip circle. But there wasn't that much going on. There were two clubs, the Lighthouse and Shelly's Manne Hole. Those were about the only two big clubs. There were a few small clubs and there was another club up in Hollywood – I forget the name of it. I never went there and I wasn't in the studio thing. A lot of it is just bullshit, if you don't mind the expression. For the rest, there was not that much going on. I did a few local gigs here and there. When my relationship broke up, I didn't see any reason to stay in L.A. So I can see why Henry had a hard time in L.A.: it was the wrong place. He would have been better off to stay in New York.'[7]

Grimes' reasons for moving to the West Coast are thus not intelligible on the surface. In 2004 he explained in a *Cadence* interview, with admirable self-awareness, 'I just didn't feel like trying to make deals for myself. That can be difficult.'[8] Proceeding from this self-analysis, his decision to settle in Los Angeles in the late-1960s seems almost daredevil. At the age of thirty-three, he probably had the subliminal notion that, having long been a musician of high repute, he too could gain a foothold in Los Angeles. He presumably relied on the many positive experiences he had gathered in New York between 1956 and 1966 as a much sought-after bassist. However, his decades of isolation after 1969 show that this intellectually demanding yet diffident musician did not stand a chance in L.A.'s anonymous, commercially oriented music scene. 'There also is some kind of a psychological situation that exists there,' said Andrew Cyrille in this connection. 'All of us for the most part are social beings, and Henry too. That is obvious. But there was something that was not connected.'[9]

This is not the place to probe the psychology of Grimes' journey through life. In any case, judging from his own statements, he seems to have deliberately sought seclusion, which allowed him to reach a deeper understanding of himself. '[H]e did survive – because he walked away,' is Lynell George's apt summary in her 2003 article for the *Los Angeles Times*.[10] 'Grimes doesn't refer to being lost in Los Angeles,'[11] reads another article. He himself once called his time in California, during which he was separated from music, 'the time I was getting to know myself'.[12] He also explained to Fred Jung in a 2003 interview: 'I stopped playing in order to eyeball my own perspective better. That had nothing to do with music. As I was waiting, it is a matter of waiting to see if I would run into some way of musical expression like I wanted to. It didn't happen until about thirty years or so after that. I wasn't thinking of how long it was taking. I was just trying to gain perspectives. It was a way of imposing self-isolation. That is the only thing I can think of [...]. Only publicly, I stopped playing. I wrote a lot of poetry to make up for it, so I could express myself with words instead of with music. [...] I was able to do it in my private environment, no audience. I was going through experiments like that. I don't think I am really an introvert, but I think what I really like is to try to have more things to say and more interesting points to make.'[13]

In this statement, Grimes works his way toward a truth about himself: his strong will toward expression. 'Introvert' is a label pinned to him by onlookers who see only that he does not speak much, and when he does it is never small talk. Grimes displays a high degree of artistic expression. Outside an artistic context, he maintains a fundamental detachment from almost everyone and everything. In this light, by moving to anonymous Los Angeles, he maneuvered himself into solitude. Perhaps only gradually did he realize that he had to wind up being the person he is.

Grimes never abandoned his hope that at some point, as before, a musician would show up and invite him to play music: 'Yeah, I was waiting for that to happen and it did happen when Marshall

Marrotte found me. [...] I was very surprised, but that's what I was waiting for.'[14] This hope was both a source of strength in his everyday life and an expression of his unsought predicament, which made him feel as if he were dead: 'In the end, I waited thirty years to return to life. In some mysterious way, I no longer existed.'[15] In the fall of 2005, after his appearance at the Frankfurt Jazz Festival, he told me much the same thing: 'I was like a dead man.'

Between the late 1960s and the late 1970s, Grimes went through a period of massive health problems and bitter poverty. He learned what it meant to go hungry. The final lines of his poem 'Peace', written some time around 1984, speak of wishing for a full bowl. Here hunger is 'more than just a metaphor'.[16]

Peace[17]

Face was made a form.
  The instincts
  that are bade must telegraph
  the distincts found,
  the woe of breath,
  the numberless,
  the less

  that fate: a cockatrice
  shall not alight a poisonous bite,
  atop the den of the adder
  where a little child shall play
  and where, in all delay,
  a little child shall lead them.

  Feet found the calm
  that long before it started to be the priority
  of this occasion, yet, as all must delve,
  distinction of amorphus state, the only place
  the cow and bear shall feed.

  The seeds remain, all cause,
  as adventure, stay in metaphor, domain.

  Heart, sought for the bearing that
  represents to it
  the whole rime of old beginning
  and acceptance, and the universal mind of God,
  the peace of the mind
  contained the law.

Each seed: domain.

Hands gave the only right of way,
not diligent as pro or con,
not feeling
avant, over-drawn,
nor cursed especially,

but the forceps of a dawning year,
to draw the time
with measures oblique of filling,
to the satisfying of the soul:

So, to God – that we may all fill – our bowls,

until we are delivered.

In Los Angeles, in spite of the hunger, Henry Grimes could at least rest assured that he would not die of cold.[18] He took his chances with that area's unfamiliar music scene – and suffered the inevitable consequences. In L.A. he soon had to become used to the fact that there was no longer an instrument in his life, and thus no opportunity to express himself professionally and earn a living in music. No one in his new surroundings knew him or took an interest in him, simply because he was unknown and made no attempt to approach other musicians.

Compared to his highly active New York years from 1956 to 1966, which took him as far afield as Japan, Grimes' new life in Los Angeles must have seemed like a shock with every new day. Since he had had a falling-out with his parents when he was about twenty, he didn't contact his family either.[19] When interviewed by Thierry Pérémarti for the French magazine *Jazzman*, he put it this way: 'After 1968 I never tried even once to renew contacts with my family. And then it became impossible for me to stay in contact with my fellow musicians. It's easy to say that you can always get in contact with people again.'[20] But living in downtown L.A. without a car, without a telephone, and having lost his address book made this almost impossible for Grimes, and going to clubs, looking for musicians he knew, would have been too painful.

Henry Grimes settled down to his life of seclusion with remarkable inner strength. At some point, probably in the late 1970s, he again became artistically active, though for a long time without audience or instrument. In retrospect, it seems clear that the conventional time frame that guides people in industrial society did not exist for him. In the final analysis, thirty-five years were for him what thirty-five weeks might have been for someone else: normally few professional artists will wait longer than that for new opportunities to arise. This personal sense of time may also be related to his dispassionate attitude toward money, which he always considered secondary in importance to art. When Marshall Marrotte asked him in 2003 whether he played his gigs and recording dates for free, he replied, 'No, I was getting paid; it just wasn't enough money. I didn't want to say "Oh, I want some more money," you know, because these guys were great players and I was enjoying playing.'[21] In 2004 he was asked whether he ever considered returning to the world of jazz music during his Los Angeles years: ''Esthetically, which is to say the only thing I thought about was playing and not making money. I would have played if the conditions were viable, but they weren't.'[22]

Gerard Rouy, in his 2004 interview with Grimes, noted: 'it seems incredible that someone could simply disappear like that and no one cared.' Grimes' reply was typically detached: 'Nobody knew where I was, and I didn't have a phone.'[23] Thus, over the years, he grew increasingly remote from his early life in jazz music, which had sustained him almost by itself: 'I wasn't thinking about music at all. I was thinking about it, but not in a sense of creating some new music. So I'd say about thirty years I've been under that kind of a cloud.'[24] Beneath that cloud, he regained his composure and channeled his activities toward other things, with all the energy and independence of the musician he always remained.

'measures oblique of filling'[25] – Struggling to Survive (1969–2003)

After leaving San Francisco, Grimes moved to the downtown district of Los Angeles, where he lived until 2003, and 'where there were a lot of missions; I used to work in a mission out there. I did guard work; I was working behind the reception area. I was able to eat and sleep there. I got five or ten dollars a week.'[26] Thus, at first he was homeless himself,[27] '[…] but I managed to get by. I worked a lot and tried to keep my hands in OK shape, you know, because if I messed them up, then I couldn't work.'[28] Grimes, it is plain to see, never gave up the hope that sooner or later he would again play bass on a professional basis.[29]

In his early days in L.A., Henry Grimes' professional aspirations still focused on art. He toyed with the thought of becoming an actor and took a course in a theater workshop. But his acting career came to naught: 'I wasn't really involved. I wanted to know how it goes. I did it from pressure to be myself. But nothing came from the movies. Nobody called.'[30] Nevertheless, rumors arose that Grimes performed street theater, dyed his hair green, and many other things. In reality, from 1971 to 1987 he earned his money as a porter, a security man, and handing out food in a refuge for homeless people where he himself lived in the 1970s. In 1987 he spent several months working as janitor and cleaner at a bowling alley in Long Beach, only to give it up when the operation moved elsewhere. He then spent two months doing telephone marketing for a home renovation outfit. He soon left this job, for which he had no aptitude. His explanation is found on a form he filled out for his job placement agency (he still owns a copy today): 'I tried it for a while but decided I was not naturally a salesperson.'[31] In 2007 he elaborated his standpoint: 'You have to be a beast – calling somebody to sell him something.'[32] Finally, from 1987 to 1998 he worked as a janitor and guard at a large Jewish educational and community center in Los Angeles. He held this secure job for eleven years, only to be dropped when the center hired a facility management company. Again and again, even after 1998, he did odd jobs on construction sites.[33] 'I worked in construction, demolition. I carried away rubble and things like that, hard work. But I always looked out for my hands.'[34]

With inexhaustible inner strength, Grimes performed and endured all these jobs for some thirty years, working by day and by night.[35] There exists an official certificate from his job placement agency attesting to his personal competence and reliability in all of them. The impression arises that, no matter how poorly paid, over the years they gave him stability and financial security. 'Physical work […] releases some of the tensions,' he explained to the journalist Lynell George in 2003.[36]

Still, Grimes' life in his early L.A. years seems to have been unstable and beset by crises. The drummer Donald Dean recalls a visit from Henry Grimes in Los Angeles around 1970, when Dean lived near the beach.

The meeting is recounted in a report by Steven L. Isoardi on Grimes' return to the music world, beginning with gigs in various L.A. venues in 2003: 'After the gig, I chatted with drummer Donald Dean, veteran of the Pan Afrikan Peoples Arkestra and bandmate of Eddie Harris, Jimmy Smith, and Horace Tapscott, among others. Shaking his head in amazement at the story of Henry's last thirty years, he told me that he had last seen Henry in L.A. around 1970, at his home near the beach. Henry was visiting and at one point took off his shoes. He said he was going for a walk along the beach and headed out the door. Donald said that he never came back, leaving behind his shoes and other items. That was the last time Donald had seen him ... until this Saturday night.'[37]

There is no way of knowing today whether this story is true, but at the least it demonstrates that Grimes had a need to wander away from social environments.

From the late 1970s, Grimes' life took a new turn. His situation, though still difficult enough, began to improve; his health stabilized.[38] He began to devote himself to writing, and in the early 1980s he moved into an SRO (single room occupancy) hotel in the downtown district. Shortly thereafter, in its March 1986 issue, *Cadence Magazine* noted in its obituaries column that 'Henry Grimes (bassist) is reported to have died in late 1984.'[39] This death notice demonstrates the slovenliness of journalists who don't do their fact-checking before publishing; on the other hand, it was hardly an inappropriate pronouncement, given Grimes' subliminal frame of mind during his entire Los Angeles period ('I was like a dead man.')

In the hotel – the Huntington, 752 Main Street – Grimes had a tiny room (No. 335) where he lived until he left Los Angeles in July 2003.[40] The hotel stood at the edge of 'LA's homeless city-within-the-city.'[41] Here, too, 'were a lot of homeless people' declared Grimes. 'They had certain stipulations to work, maybe for two weeks for one time, and then another time. At some point they had to pay for getting a new place. You know, very complicated. [...] That is very depressing there.'[42]

The hotel was set up by the welfare service, which then left it to its own devices. In other words, every resident had to pay rent to a shady rent collector who usually charged more than the legal price. Practically everything Grimes earned and received in welfare benefits from 2000 was spent on rent for this hotel room. Margaret Davis Grimes, who visited Grimes there in 2003, describes it as a prison with bars, locks, and screams – 'a hell hole'.[43] The residents lived only for themselves. 'It was a house full of troubled people,' as Margaret Davis Grimes puts it.[44] Henry recalls 'very bad conditions, low finances, you know. These people were really poor.'[45] Thierry Pérémarti, who visited and interviewed Grimes in L.A. in 2003, describes the SRO hotel as something 'between Skid Row and South Park. A Blade Runner atmosphere from the moment you opened the door. Bewildering noise. Disturbing. Bellowing drunks [...].'[46]

Both Henry Grimes and his wife Margaret, in different ways, see parallels between the life Henry led for some two decades in the SRO hotel in Los Angeles and the story of the title hero in the film *The Soloist* – 'a movie about another musician, a black guy who went to Juilliard,' Margaret explains. 'He is classical. He plays cello, and he's played by Jamie Foxx. It is really weird. But he also ended up in LA. He had a violin with two strings on it. His cello he didn't have [...] We went to see the movie and Henry recognized the whole area.'[47]

Grimes left his hotel room as often as possible. After work he regularly went into nearby MacArthur Park 'to rest and think and to catch some fresh air'.[48]

Over the years the construction work kept Grimes in good physical shape.[49] But in the end he regarded all his jobs as burdensome: 'They were all pretty bad. I worked truly hard [laughs].'[50] Moreover, his financial situation deteriorated as he grew older.[51] In 1998, when he lost his job at the Jewish community center, he urgently sought new work. A form that he filled out at his placement agency for this purpose lists the following potential areas of employment: 'Immediate work as a janitor to gain a sufficient income (now) so as to be available for other positions' possibilities' – such as work in the music field.' This shows that after some thirty years, despite all the hardships, Grimes never

Lost In Park, drawing by Henry Grimes (2012). The drawing shows the MacArthur Park in L.A. where Henry used to relax after work (courtesy Margaret Davis Grimes and Henry Grimes).

abandoned the prospect of returning to music. He was proved right, but it was only at retirement age that he was able to return to the bass. When he reached retirement he was entitled to Social Security only on the basis of his bread-and-butter jobs in L.A., not for his extensive early work as a professional musician.[52] The Social Security benefits amounted to $500 per month. Someone helped him to receive this money, to which every sixty-five-year-old who has paid into the state retirement program is entitled.[53] Of this, he had to spend $400 for his hotel room alone, leaving him $100 to cover all other expenses. He did not have a telephone. Often he had to go hungry.[54]

There is a photo from the year 2000 that shows him standing next to a parking meter, stoic and emaciated. An employee from the reception desk took the shot from the hotel door: 'I don't know. I worked before that. I stood there and he caught up to me and made this shot [laughs nervously].'[55] Later the employee gave the photo to Grimes.[56] Asked whether they were friends, Grimes replied, 'No. I knew him pretty well for a few years [...], but we didn't help each other.'[57]

In 2009 Grimes said of the photo: 'During that time my income ran out. [...] I hate to see that picture: it looks terrible. [...] I wasn't still working. But that particular time I just couldn't make the ends meet.'[58] As already mentioned, even after retirement, Grimes tried to find work in order to get by on a day-to-day basis – with intermittent success.[59]

Henry Grimes in front of the S.R.O. Huntington Hotel, Los Angeles, 2000 (name of photographer unknown; courtesy Margaret Davis Grimes and Henry Grimes).

'Who is this person? You will gain wisdom if you can understand who he is and get a feeling of what he has gone through. He has been parked there at the parking meter for a long time. The man in the picture is a known person, but unknown even to himself. He is Henry Grimes in the year 2000, before rescue came. Who could another one be on your street in such a situation? If you knew he was an artist in trouble, would you help him? If you didn't know whether he is an artist or not, would you help him? If he is not an artist, would you help him? If you are the one in the photo, will we help you?'

Henry Grimes (2013)

Grimes' social contacts during his Los Angeles years were meager: 'The people that I was around were not exactly up to par on musical or literary things.' It was only after the call from Marshall Marrotte that Henry Grimes again found friends, as he explained in an interview in 2007.[60] For a while he had a girlfriend in Los Angeles, the singer Heather Evans.[61] The undated poem, 'signs along the road being put there',[62] mentions a 'she', though, of course, without naming a real person (and also another 'she' – his bass Brunhilda – comes to mind):

signs along the road being put there

Signs read all along – as roadside signs are –
claim to absolute newness and mastery of all mystery
as signs are, the ones that you see go down the road –
with you, as are trumped all universal sorts of energy
that emerges from them – are mystery
(I said, as I thought if I would ever see her again)
and the condition of them being put there
seen all along the highway.

Signs are called then, these original works of art
designed to snare and hold the human heart – before,
like on a prior occasion when you have seen them
in the city's heart, you know –
out there they are the same as
seen all along the highway.

'You are so naïve' (we who are the country-born),
clumping even all the fallen leaves coming along the
roadside-way.

And lo, the bend is steep.

And, all along the silent time the earth had grown terrifically.
battered in green, the life we lead
as seen all along the highway.
and 'When can it be that I will see her again' – thinking only to myself,
trying to remember all the shades of scenes put there
to filter in through the warm sunlight in her apartment –
by trying a – desire to clamp them into time – all together –
all the heart things, all the soul –
as seen all along the highway

Henry Grimes' life in Los Angeles seems to have passed without incident – or at least none that he could report. That Percy Heath met him there was told not by Grimes, but by Margaret Davis Grimes, who learned of it from Heath himself. Similarly, Bennie Maupin saw Henry in Los Angeles, but was unable to speak to him, as Margaret later recounted:

'Bennie [Maupin] saw Henry somewhere probably in the nineties. He was driving in downtown L.A. and he looked out the window and he said, "That's Henry Grimes. I just saw Henry Grimes." He told me that. He turned, he tried to go back and get him, but he never found him again. And Percy Heath saw Henry in L.A. and he asked Henry if he would play a gig that Percy couldn't play because Percy was leaving town, and Henry said "Yes, please, I really wanna do the gig. You just have to bring me a bass and you have to bring it back after work because I don't have a car and I don't have a bass." And Percy said "Sorry man, I can't do all of that. I have to go back to New York." This was right before Percy died, when Percy told me about it.'[63] Grimes himself does not recall the meeting.

Grimes' connection to the outside world came mainly from the television set he owned. He remembers precisely the death of Princess Diana and the attack on the Twin Towers. Asked what it felt like to confront New York again, he said, 'Very strange.' He then spoke of his complete consternation at watching the planes fly into the Towers: 'You don't believe it. You are looking at it, but it doesn't make any sense. [...] I got up in the morning and I saw the crash, and then there was another, there were two of them. [...] I found no logic, you know.'[64] Grimes never saw the World Trade Center with his own eyes. By the time it was inaugurated, he had already been living in Los Angeles for four years, and it was destroyed one-and-a-half years before he returned to New York.

Toward the end of his time in manual labor, Grimes 'was writing some poems, and other things I was leaving unfinished.'[65] He had already begun doing so years earlier. Many things were left unfinished for lack of time, but fortunately he was able to work on them with greater concentration when he began to receive Social Security.[66]

'I conquered it by poetry'[67] – Literature, Writing, Yoga

No other group of people in the Western world has so completely utilized the medium of music to define, make tolerable, and give meaning to their lives.

Errol Green, 'Black Music', *Liberator* 8, no. 4 (1968)

After the 1960s, music was merely incidental to Grimes' life. When he heard music somewhere in his surroundings, he was interested in people's reaction to it and observed them.[68] But he had neither a radio nor a record player in his room, only a television set. 'I used to listen to fusions of all kind: church, rock 'n' roll, rhythm and blues, a lot of different kinds of music, Mexican, all kinds of music. I listened to it on television programs. That was interesting. But it wasn't jazz.'[69]

He frequently ate dinner in a Mexican restaurant where he heard 'a lot of mariachi music' from the jukebox.[70] In a 2004 interview he recalled hearing some jazz music in these years, broadcast in Ken Burns' TV series,[71] and in a 2007 interview he again emphasized not only Mexican but also Chinese music, which he listened to regularly at the time.[72] Grimes lived sealed off from the outside world and settled down in his own mental universe. Being a serious artist, he discovered a new language: 'I conquered it by poetry, you know.'[73] That is what he now concentrated on, what kept him – the musician he has always been – inwardly alive.

As early as 1970, Grimes had already begun to visit the downtown Los Angeles Library (a magnificent building, outside and inside) to acquire a knowledge of literature. He read works of literary theory, poetry anthologies, and writers' guides. 'I read Yeats, Auden, Williams – I had a library close to where I lived, and I was there almost every day.'[74] Sometime after 1993 he also bought Nancy Sullivan's *Treasury Of American Poetry* (1978, 1993). In late 2006, it had a bookmark on which he had jotted down names of writers and technical terms: 'Walt Whitman [the bookmark was at his poem 'O Captain! My Captain!'], Teleology, Jean Garrigue, Emily Dickinson, Free Verse, Mark Strand, Ezra Pound.'

He himself wanted to write, and his path to this goal was self-instruction: 'I walked around and ended up in the library and started writing. First I wrote in the library; then I wrote at home when I was in the hotel. I wanted to write, you know, started studying that, how to write. I did prose analyses; I just kept things going that way – the thought of being creative.'[75] – and to remain mentally alert.'[76] 'Every night when I came over from work, I gave myself something to do, work out, you know, problems, literally, and that worked very well. [...] I read to just try to map out the inspiration, and maybe the problem with artistic concerns. So I did that in a sense of life, pulling myself to work, put myself to some work, you know, in association to working.'[77] As he further explained to Lynell George, 'I've been writing some poetry too. It's the same place of expression. It's the way I like to do it. Everything coming through me.'[78]

Alongside his literary studies and writing activities, he also began in the 1970s to learn yoga in the tradition of Paramahansa Yogananda ('The Self Realization Fellowship') and regularly visited a chapel in L.A. where a large portrait of the master hung in a recess. He explained that he 'wanted to be able to be spiritually in control of things,' and that he aimed not to be a victim of circumstances.[79] Grimes still owns a picture of Paramahansa Yogananda that hung in his room during the whole of his Los Angeles period.

Asked in 2005 about the most important influence on him during his time in L.A., he replied, 'A major influence to me during those thirty years was the writing of poetry and prose; it occupied a place within me that you can say is somewhat the same place I felt and experienced as a musician.'[80]

'the time is full of times'[81] – Henry Grimes, Poet

Grimes has some ninety handwritten notebooks dating from his years in Los Angeles.[82] They bear no resemblance to diary entries, which invariably contain trivial matters, such as a current frame of mind, the weather, or a news event. Rather, they are his mostly undated notes for a collection on philosophy of life, excerpts from textbooks, writing exercises (including a sort of horror story), poetic sketches, and poetry. He used these notebooks alternately for his own writing and for learning purposes, waywardly reworking passages from textbooks to obtain mental guideposts and stimuli for his own texts. An initial broad picture of his poetry can be found in the volume *Signs Along The Road*, published in Germany in 2007.[83] It is a gathering of his texts from the years between 1978 and 2005, most of them dating from the early 1980s.

In an interview in 2009, he explained that he began to write in 1970, at first only a few lines at odd intervals, then with increasing regularity beginning around 1980.[84] Asked to say something about *Signs Along The Road* in 2007, he outlined a real-life, poetical, and musical level from which he writes his poetry: 'The contents of the book is poetry, and what is reflected in people's minds. [...] A lot of people don't have an understanding – they think they're into it, but they're not into it – and that can be anyone. The whole question – "What is poetry?" – is what the book is all about. The poems are sketches. They are different but they have that sameness about them, the subject that ties them together. Poetry allows you to really view a subject in different lights. I love poetry. I used to go to the library and get all my information there, and I really enjoyed it. At that time I was alone, and this is what I did at the time. It was my way of expressing myself without the bass in hand.[85]

In 2009 Eli Dvorkin, now co-director of the Silent Barn arts collective, asked the 'relentless innovator' about the connection between the world of music and that of the written word. Grimes replied that writing allowed him to express something he had wanted to say his whole life long, something closely akin to his work as a musician.[86] In this sense, he comes close to the poetic art described by Amiri Baraka: 'Black poetry, in the main, from its premise (unless the maker be considerably "bourgeoisified") means to show its musical origins and resolve as a given. Just as Blues is, on one level, a verse form, so Black poetry begins as music running into words.'[87]

It need hardly be stressed that a musician who writes will produce a language brimming with musicality. Yet even if one knew nothing about Grimes' background, his writings, whether lyric poems or prose, are strikingly oriented in sound and rhythm. The close and multi-faceted parallels with the music he played in the 1960s are far more likely to strike professional musicians than non-musicians. The New York guitarist and composer Marc Ribot, who has worked with Grimes on a regular basis since 2004, describes the artistic procedures of 'free jazz' as, basically, a willingness to respond to spontaneous improvisation and to break with the tradition of opening title themes and the conventional expectations of bebop soloists. The result, he explains, is the creation of new forms in the relation between composition and improvisation, adding that the ties have gained in depth through the power of unconscious association: 'The techniques and experience of this musical process were what Henry took with him into the L.A. wilderness, and I read Henry's poems exactly as a continuation of this work: as consciously choosing to establish a different relation between conscious/unconscious, between signal/noise, between composed "head"/improvised body, as consciously choosing to display − or more accurately, to represent − to the reader (or listener) elements of unconscious process.'[88]

'The poems "Water Wax" and "Signs Along The Road Being Put There", both from *Signs Along The Road*, convey a vivid impression of Henry Grimes' diction − rich in imagery and splashes of color, always guided by music. Like Surrealist art, it draws its strength from the wellsprings of the unconscious.

'The poem "Water Wax" was written sometime between 1984 and 1999. It is a poetically analytical flow of ideas, ranging across a number of pages along which one can feel the rhythm, the poignant sense for colors, the toying with rhyming expressions ("heaven's skies"/"heaven's guise") and alliterating chains of words ("Water Wax"; "worlded and worded world"), seemingly without specific significance at first, but as a whole evoking a startling harmony of content. The poem neither requires nor indicates an exact dating, since it ignores all current affairs, but instead rather timelessly flows past particular events or obvious incidents. The focus is on fundamental issues. What evolved in time is subjected to an anthropological, sociological, and philosophical analysis in "Water Wax": it is a trigonometric influence dividing up the human landscape and the poet's society into court, city, and country. What authority separates matters into three remains a mystery.

'Henry Grimes is interested in the mysterious and searches for those signs that go beyond the simple straightforwardness of road signs, searching for the origins, including those of language and the spoken word. Grimes poses questions that lie buried under the present-day mindset, dominated as it is by technical, scientific, and other pragmatic considerations. Of course, Grimes lives in this demystified world too but has not assimilated himself to it. The title "Water Wax" addresses this to a certain degree, consisting of two words that sit side by side and yet maintain a fine distance from one another: water is repelled by wax, as is the poem from the surface of public life that it really is part of. But this title contains far more: Henry Grimes elects to converse with the cosmic powers as a poet, and even if their signs and the contradictions they produce remain inscrutable for him, he does not react to them with incomprehension, but rather by producing a free flow of words that seem to be tracing these mysteries. Reading "Water Wax" out loud leads one to hear this impenetrable depth and yet obtain new insights – but only if one is able to free oneself from the desire to rationalize any alleged meaningful relationships, and instead is prepared to get into the images that Grimes draws with words. It may well be that, amongst other things, his reflections and visionary thoughts were spurred by the spirit of his generation, which was critical of the status of civilization. However, primarily there is someone busy here with talking and writing who has remained remarkably independent in the ways he thinks, feels and creates.

'The origins of poetry can be traced back to rhythm and music, and "Water Wax" and "Signs Along The Road Being Put There" also specifically suggest that Henry Grimes' wordplay is just as much part of the African-American musical tradition, and specifically about raising awareness for the less obvious and unpredictable. Examples are his abstract, rhythmically colorful flows of thought that are pierced by familiar statements such as "When can it be that I will see her again" or "You are so naïve."[89]

Another example is the poem 'The Chime Around Above Time', dating from the early 1980s, with the interruptive lines: The birch trees would follow / Hitler or Mussolini / down into the root – /where 'ere they went.[90]

Marc Ribot observes of these formal shock effects: 'Henry's poetic, in both words and music, is one in which unexpected structures of great beauty arise like a phoenix from a sharp bed of broken syntax, in which meter may at any moment shift or undergo a metric conversion, sudden as a rip tide.'[91]

Thoughts flash forth that Grimes may once have read in a

textbook and that cropped up in his mind while writing: 'Henry's familiar statements include historical, analytical thoughts such as the one that human laws are a further development of archaic customs and conventions. Grimes views the linguistic standardizations, e.g. of human law, as a poem that has already made it to heaven, and he points out that poets escape from subjects that require sophisticated language in order to be conveyed. Here, too, poetry and the cited musical tradition of jazz music touch upon one another somewhat, since they both avoid virtuosity as an end in itself and draw their persuasive power from deeper and hotter spiritual sources of energy. Prose, the ubiquitous more or less meticulously carved-out form of narration, is the pyre of consciousness, the artificial, the civilized, the surface that barely covers the simmering poetry (and music) about to fuse as a white, blue, amber-green water flame. This is what results at the end of 'Water Wax' and is to a large extent all that is left over at the end. It is not the well-established heaven that virtuosic legal rhetoric aspires to, but the hell of consciousness, which embraces the truth.'[92]

Several poems from *Signs Along The Road* contain names or statements directly related to the world of music, which Grimes left behind in 1969, but from whose tradition he constantly drew sustenance: 'Cecil Taylor was still at large, waiting for a piano – high above the ground' reads the final line of an untitled poem from the early 1980s, and 'The Infant of Attention', likewise from the early 1980s,[93] explicitly mentions the blues and its leading exponents. At the end it reads:

[. . .]

Bessie Smith, that's who.

Who – set the black blues down
on paper,
and informed, in one, a nation of its existence?

W. C. Handy: conforming forms

the blues have taken many forms

throughout the years.

Another poem, 'A Pre-Revolutionary Cabin',[94] speaks of the woods in Fairmount Park (Philadelphia) and of the bass made from that wood, while the word 'garrison' recalls the legendary bassist of the John Coltrane Quartet. The poem leads back to Henry's existential origins:

> [...]
> No woods there now, yet still it must be cludded with the still-ringing sounds of musket-balls
> Instead of the modern bullet, clinging as though –
> it was still lust,
> clipping the green eucalyptus branches
> in their sway and tell.
> But no! This by far was not a garrison,
> it could have been – a home.
> it must – have been!
> string, stringly straightness wood and splintery, which in its horizontal bar(n')ss'
> its wood would pass the test of time – all by its dampness and willingness to absorb.
> [...]

In an interview in 2009, Grimes said that the wood of the violin and the bass contains emotions: 'Especially the violin or the double bass – with that wooden scheme – that wood holds emotions itself [...].'[95]

The first stanza of 'To Adopt A Child',[96] written around 1983, speaks of the rhythm of life, of love, of a sense of belonging. The jazz music tradition and Henry's (absent) bass immediately spring to mind:

> Godly care
>   is started where
>   the pulse is found
>   that makes the heart beat fonder.
>   Coming where adjoined
>   the sweetness of the breath is shared
>   by that one impulse that gives fond charity
>   as extension of the self
>   is found
>   to be the only way to help another.
>   [...]

The next four stanzas describe loss: pain, hunger, struggle, tears, helplessness, solitude. The poem ends with the words:

[...]
So let your love drive the clouds away,
from the life and tears
of every helpless
lonely
    child.

The poem 'Back To Down Along Spring Street'[97] (*ca.* 1985) reads like a search for traces of New York's 'free music' scene of the 1960s ('the many cultures by activities / will never cease / their leading to the cacaphone / leading feet.'), which Grimes had done much to create but had involuntarily left behind long ago: 'Where all things, lending – / dead upon the past – or / smashed by pressures as / they hold / barometers and / swelling.'[98]

Like the poems in *Signs Along The Road*, Grimes' unpublished texts are pervaded by a freely associative interplay of ideas, as is apparent in several prose notes, poems, and a story inspired by Gothic Romanticism from his early period. All the texts are taken from a notebook dating roughly from 1979 to 1981 that Grimes specifically chose for my research. The notes bear witness to a deep study of Western literary history, from Greek Antiquity to the 1960s, of the sort conveyed by the standard academic textbooks of the day.[99] At the same time they document a specific form of assimilation of this theoretical material, which Grimes primarily sought to use for his own writing. They shed light on writing experiments, hand down remarkable poems, and demonstrate over and over again that their author moved aesthetically in the world of music.

Marc Ribot sees a peculiar analogy between Grimes' poetic techniques and the musical devices of 1960s 'free jazz' as well as the 'free improv' movement from the 1970s to 1990s: 'It's true, there are moments of broken syntax, mis- and disarticulation, yet a type of sharp meaning arises out of and because of them, in exactly the way it did in the music of Albert Ayler and other musicians of the "free-jazz" movement of the sixties, or of Derek Bailey and the "free-improv" movement of the seventies through the nineties. That Henry managed to create this textual analogue for musical processes is, to me, amazing; that he's managed to do it without even a hint of the clichés of "jazz poetry" is astounding.'[100]

Grimes' texts from this notebook, including his reflections and original summaries of academic works, usually maintain this 'free jazz' syntax, and are thus initially puzzling to onlookers. They are sprinkled with neologisms and unusual spellings. His textbook excerpts, rather than being dry abstracts, assimilate the material in a creative fashion that might be termed verbal improvisation. A similar syntactical liberation from common sense can be found in the written commentaries that Cecil Taylor published as liner notes to his album *Unit Structures* (1966). They, too, read like a linguistic analogy to the music, leaving their intelligibility to the inspiration of the reader.

Those expecting standard jazz-music liner notes, which invariably seem to smooth out the turmoil of the music, will be disappointed: 'Hearing is sight face away academy's superfluity. There are not separate parts: one body and the mind enclosed. We procede inventing. The interpretation has occurred. Emotion being aggressive participation defines the 'acts' particularity the root of rhythm is its central unit of change eye acting upon motor responses directing motions internal movement (wave).'[101] The musical message of things new, unusual, and alien to the recipient, flows smoothly into the writing. The theoretical level itself is presented as art and embodied in art. Grimes' notes also reveal this impetus in surprising neologisms and idiosyncratic spelling of common words, which, in their 'correct' form, would otherwise be blandly conventional. Here are some examples of his neologisms, which lay bare the thought and perception of their creator:[102]

'chantroeme' – alluding to the close relation between music ('chant') and poetry ('poem') and suggesting Grimes' path from music to writing;

'artitude' – replacing the customary attitude with the artistic stance;

'pragmagic' – imparting an inexplicable aura to things otherwise pragmatic and quotidian;

'misogymystical' – combining the adjectives 'misogynist' and 'mystical', perhaps pointing to deep-seated reasons for misogyny, which in turn ties in with Euro-American racism;

'ratiocinature' – restoring a natural, Dionysian dimension to conventional rationality (Latin: ratiocinor), again alluding to Grimes' mode of thought;

'symbolicaholic' – describing the perception of symbolic connections as an addictive process;

'proantagonist' – referring to the protagonist as an antagonist – a remarkable neologism from an experienced bass sideman;

'con/tra-gedy' – this word is preceded by 'con/tra/diction', from which it probably emerged. Perhaps Grimes' absent double bass (contrabass) reverberates here, too.[103]

Grimes' prose writings are often arranged spatially on the page like poetry. They also manipulate textbook material that he found important. As mentioned above, his language already aspires to poetic form in its reception of writings from other sources. Perhaps this reflects his learning method, in which the visual rhythm of a text is intended to make its meaning readily comprehensible. Viewed in this light, Grimes is thus buoyed by the visual rhythm of written information, which he reads in the same way as musical notation:

> The world (and – its existentialism) is – word. – that is, it is summed-up to mean that it is the emblematicism of which the things of the senses are secretly – sewed up – to those whose lives evolve by the charms of eso-teric sound, revealed as emblematic of motives in the social order, so that all visible entities – discerned – become tangible energies: and – tangible enough, so as to release one from the entities of materialism and the produce-magic of equity and the giant part in all of the things,
>
>   from which the senses are secretly revealed as emblematic of the motives in the order of society, so that, all
>   visible entities that are discerned become tangible energies, and entities become a materialization, a metamorphosis, and a part of all pageantry:
>   and poets-prose ritual
> and symbol become – one, of all the phenomena of aesthetic enigma.[104]

The above note is devoted to the all-embracing mystery of nature, to things lost and buried for millennia beneath the civilized, material, tangible surface – things that the poet has divined, sought, and found lacking. This motif, perhaps inspired by the yoga tradition, is found regularly in Grimes' poetry.[105] As Marc Medwin aptly concluded in 2010, 'indeed it's the mystical – that which is beyond words – that is the central focus of his art.'[106]

Asked in an interview of 2010 whether there is any aspect of art he has not yet explored, Grimes pointed to the connections between mythology and creativity: 'Well, I don't know. To answer that, you end up considering, you know, the literary fountain; the fountain of knowledge. The links between mythology and creativity. It's hard to even approach a definition. And sometimes those moments come easier than at others – sometimes it's the recognition of something you find true, and sometimes it's a reaction to something you find false.'[107]

This same sequence is equally apparent in his visual rhythmic presentation of texts presumably freely reworked from textbooks:

> [...] the duophony of time and destiny.
> There is a spatial development:
>   and, that is – in
> between, that it takes the
>   minds of characters which animate a form,
> within the drama and story of the last spark – or of fire within the drama
> that is this enacting of man – enacting his most feeble drama – in the
> aura of the presence of the GODS. [...]'[108]

Many of Grimes' textbook excerpts serialize words in a distinctive manner by repeating them with altered spellings. When read aloud, the written sentence then develops a sound that forces the meaning into the background, if not drowning it out altogether. Such passages, reminiscent of the musical devices of Thelonious Monk or the sound-based diction of James Joyce, directly mirror the improvisation of music.[109] One example of this procedure is an excerpt presumably drawn from a stylistic guide for beginning writers. Its furious verbal transformations are variations on the word 'misogynic'. This note also contains willful misspellings of common words ('intensifie' instead of 'intensify', 'modifie' instead of 'modify') that seem to underscore the written 'Don't', as well as the neologism 'duodifie', which sets another sonic accent:

> Don't – over-intensifie! you need only to intensify – to – modifie – (what actually is there) finish at the end of it. the rest! just – duodifie to bite! don't try - to be The all-out misologist woman hating misogynist misogy-nistical – misogymous misogynist of a misogamy that is everything of a misnomer or – misoclere – except – 'a misocapnic', blowing your smoke all in somebodys face oblivious of intent's real meaning.[110]

Marc Ribot's comments on the poems Grimes published in 2007 also apply to the note quoted above: 'Henry's leaps of association occur within a framework or formal and conceptual cohesion and deep familiarity with the history of the form [...] playing with repetition in exactly the same way Monk did in his compositions and solos [...].'[111]

The poems in the notebook examined here confirm the observation that Grimes also realized his musical ideas in his poetry. The notebook includes twenty poems signed by Grimes with titles in slightly larger script compared to the rest of the text.[112]

Two of the poems bear specific dates,[113] but none of the other texts in the notebook is signed or dated. Like the poems in *Signs Along The Road*, a sound often leads to a surprising revelation of meaning, rather than vice versa. Meaning, far from being presupposed, must first be created.[114] The point is the infinite plenitude of the unseen, the unheard, the unread – the unrealized. Clichéd turns of phrase such as 'dream factory' stand out in Grimes' texts as in a wasteland. In some poems (e.g. 'Heteronym') the reader cannot but think of the personal situation of their author, an African-American confronted with a fundamental ambivalence and a degrading racist animus. Grimes' poems cannot, of course, be reduced to this basic social predicament, but neither can they be viewed entirely apart from it.

Faro – Faro![115]
Meanings drawn then withdrawn, regain again in
certain polyseminous term, the meanings
               that are gained – by number:
adultero – faro: faro – faro!

Pina Colada[116]
        There am I!
playing – full around with my girl
while I am. Locked out. In the rain.
When she will – return. Yet – not the same. While there – and
               not wistfully at all, there she is.
Locked-in, safe and tight and warm. What a bane! Some game!

The OCEAN from – above – beyond:[117]

(The tragic hero feeds catharsis action:)
    The heart –
aware – in glory, of only its own synthesis and purity,
        sleeps in this action
            through all eternity, an art
                that retreats its path – from the pathway of solipsism.

A failure would be commingling and tragic,
            whereas – it is a failuring of insight providing
                the crab of tragic drama,

in maintenance of the
            tension,

The sight of the mind,
            roceeds forth –

of a thing of failure:
and – a thinness lucidity occurs – to rime the synthesis of all dramatic
writing, to that which
        does – appear. The potency
of all – becomes as the
single – voice expressing, of the hubris and expression of a lyric
pathos, or of a stoic despair;
that all is upon the ocean floor, and is above – beyond.

O – moonlit cove[118]

O moonlit cove
what avails a storm cloud
accurate in form and color –

spontaneity?

one level
thrilling pictures hide
full of mysterious likelihood
of smuggling exploits
and deep schemes
of dark melodrama.

You must hide:

Odd – In living monochrome foreground of stars

the boom and wailing land mass –
full of vapor which
the universe must hide
odd formations
mental formulations
boom in blend of indistinguishability
of inky darknesss plightgating light
and making it all – but invisible
to mind to – mare to see

bold silhouettes
through which that grade-pervading moonlight
and brightness breaks!

The pallid and intense quality
of all but colorless light – makes.
The paint is as thick as

the feeling is itself
intense and reckoning with
the breaks of resounding waves
asunder
breaking through of that which is
as undefinable as all detail – is
swallowed up on the aura
made of unrecognizeable forms:

The pallid and intense quality
of light blue all but colorless
and naked skin
and light.
The impressionists – were not moon painters

notably accurate in his evocation of the moonlight:

O moonlit cove
all but perfectly well-suited to become
the slave of detail
once painted
as to so become
the expression in a thought
and not the surface of it:

When the moon was full
and walked all nite
returning in her words
soaked up in moonlight

(Epi)[119]

Gentle spirits, do preside, with heart, so to do marvel
                    At these subtle truths that – do hide,
The fountains of youth – so do abide.
                    and therefore, on – and into forever:

Heteronym[120]

I could shun the very meaning of a hope!
          Engraved in mundane empathy and braced in the amphibioticae
of old meanings.

Then-turning empathic soundings to pay and epiglottis rumourings,
stay –
          hailed onto the clock of bind and seep dispersion mystery.

My clock, – then on, and bound to rime – too tight,
          the conspire rithims intramural.

Then [...] turned against me,
wheel and circle, bind and fortune,
played the wrong cards, the fates assail me.

The spirits hate me! for, as I
duell, how deep the well – for twilight,
pericardium – do keep me.

For, lo! I knew, and now the time,
the thing that always knew, I knew, I knew, has
ascended,
then descended on me.

Pericardium round and round, wind
and cycle, wheel and fire one
plane, the same as game and
fortune,
          when polygon, and all is lost
and gone.

The following note, entitled *Points*, likewise bears a signature.
It falls into sections in the manner of a suite (I, II, III). Unlike the
other poetic texts, it extends over six pages.[121] *Points* contains vivid
images reminiscent of short film sequences while moving on a
scholarly meta-level with terms such as 'onomatopoeticism'.
Grimes' poetic stream-of-(sub)consciousness often interweaves a

rational urge to knowledge and discovery with an intensive verbal expressivity guided by music. The chosen material – street scenes, technical terms, conceptual clichés, and much else – assumes aesthetic form in a process of verbal improvisation.

Points[122]

I

Images – gist,
the powers of native Americans,
powers gist,
the images as they are, and point all actions toward
                the forces that [...] come alive – on top',
                        in inner speech, and point all speech towards the
forces which – are,
inherentingly are. and – watching it, that we are they who come to know, watching action!
and listening thru the mind. and – drawing the bind to
                        inner mind, those of speech which come to mind,
individuals, watching and waiting, that we come to know,
individuals – at large, both externally and internally:
personalities both overt as they are or other quiet,
        the wish of onomatopoeticism, those who, indicative of all the
        external signs,
who probability hides, the worshipped ancestor of Weltanschauung and hope unborn,
unrelative, unused, and [...] – undone, the spoils of the dramaturgicality, who age thru all the agency of the external

signs: the images of the archimagis;

II

[...]

(dream)

We are – suddenly here, in the dream factory,
when, with rings of steel and iron, the things of dreams – come – off,
then and up into cans. And the realm of secret [...] – fact, facts of the nature of event,
        events about to come, to meet and rise and fall, turn swirls of fancy into realms of metaphore (and – of mystic bore,) only to cumiliate solidity informs and cattificate, only to culminate by their actual resistances to the forces and their existances and then become

    the show – of forms they
are.

Cats in cars: feline drivers, and girls in leotards. More to lore,
   the things they are – in base rugs made of leopards skin and bear,
   and shadowing, the wars made out of inducement, in causing mystic
   twins – [. . .] to the mystic twins of the minds of man, who tenure, in
   philosophisements [. . .]

   the ocean of all plans,
with swift – philosophising, as a gallant suck upon a straw.
This is sewn
     these implications which, in the dramatising quality of the whole
elemental
guise the spirit
    of this – earth has,
includes in the spirit of poemic gravitations the power of the fact – and
fee
that –, as
that oblivionite feature – in the grass', old – prose dealings – dramatise
the
elements in the diapogrom of through course and implications,
by implications viewing in conviewing empathy
towards one and another – one,
[. . .]

III

It is – this the U.S.A. a dream anatomy, the prototype of an archetype
the anatomy of
a figure; the pure essence
of a dream anatomy of a theatre anatomy the fires
have vxx

visualised the points – indubitability of the implications
    of an action' – might be the fires of exposition. The sight alighted on
a thing
of disposition –
    or condisposition of an old precise eternal theme, the anatomic –
disposing:
    the
anatomy of motivation: the scene – produced an obligatory scene and
theme. and – the one
that has or had – its tie to nature in the beginning of the seaming of
psychic notions. The processes
despoiled [. . .], the mundane atomic particle whereby – by natural tenderness and the cosmic seat of mercy',
nature knew that she
    was indubitably outraged

natural tenderness – outraged and brutalized, mind raped and bruised
hard
    by sordid
conditions in which – a large part of the population lived. [...]. out
brutalized by its own conditions, that – the burlesqued implications of
an action – might be, the anatomy – of motivation:

Besides the poems, Grimes' notebook also contains a single
prose narrative.[123] It bears the title 'A Metaphor – of: How great the
distances' and resembles a horror story or nightmare. Whether it
is a fragment or a finished narrative is difficult to say. Its ten
chapters contain many neologisms and idiosyncratic spellings of
common words. Unlike the twenty poems, Grimes did not sign this
text and the material obviously derives from secondary sources,
both literary and cinematic (TV). Following the story, inserted
between pages 209 and 210 of the notebook, are ten loose leaves
with willfully formulated thoughts on literary theory (presumably
taken from a textbook) in which the story's title is adopted in
abbreviated form and 'hellish darkness' – a romantic motif that
plays an important role in the story – is translated into a state of
pure desire:

Phenomenologicality
The 'subject' of imaginative energy generates the exclusion of images
on world causes of mind – to – overextend – itself, until, that it finds
itself – empty – again (again – empty / faced with the void; (suddenly –
all it can imagine is a hellish darkness)
Mind, the conqueror of space, is – again, reconquered by space.
Thought, - left to itself traverses – 'everything' finally – done; it loses
itself in an 'imageless' night. The will – or desire – that shaped a world
– suddenly[124]

The eyes
and ears ... of spectators is the obvious reality the performer ... obviously possesses. Talking ... is the direct subject of imitation here. The
tragedies,
[leaf 6:] turns destructive and not only – annihilates the world but
threatens to dissolve the self. Even though – the characters in that
world may avoid = this self destruction, they sink into an apathy caused
by an awareness of – HOW GREAT THE DISTANCE is – that has
again separated – or does, separate them from the objects of their
desire. Feel – in – impotency, they will be left solely with their desire.
They seem caught-up – and in an inevitable temporal drift toward aging
and death. This is called – enervation[125]

Pages 247 and 248 of the notebook contain a section headed *Behind the Rococo* that seems taken almost verbatim from a textbook on literary theory. Here we find further thoughts on the literary motif of 'darkness':

> Think of the lone solitariness of the genius in the dark writing about
> the dark, as dark places secret the role of darkness on which the writer
> pits
> the total emphasis of the terror and misery in the human existence. The
> gothic,
> a basis of flex for the horror film and stage play basic of the
> melodrama, [page 248:]
> Is also a presence of the romantic notion of literature.

In his story, Grimes magnifies the darkness into a nightmarish atmosphere, leaving it unclear whether the character sees nothing because of the absence of an external light source or because he has suddenly become blind. In particular, the scenes with the figure called Jane Somers, set in a room in a hotel or hospital, display emotional states recalling Grimes' own predicament: intense yearning and oppressive isolation. The story takes place mainly in Los Angeles and involves a fairly large number of men whose names refer more or less clearly to real persons, literary figures, or stereotypes: Al Davis (perhaps the American football manager, 1929–2011), Al Dir (perhaps the mythical king of the Slavs from early medieval literature), Cauky Greene, Eddie J. (perhaps the TV actor Eddie J. Fernandez), Fats Dozier (perhaps the jazz drummer Carl 'Fats' Dozier), Franck Scott – the Scandinavian (perhaps the Canadian poet and lawyer Frank R. Scott, 1899–1985), Jim (Jim Crow?), Joe (Average Joe?), Manuel Jack – the D.J. (perhaps the Mexican boxer Manuel Jack Hernandez, who was active in the 1960s), Wil Simpson, 'the receptionist', 'the doctor', and 'those big-heavy guys, attendants in mental hospitals.' Among the female figures, one finds a Jane Somers mentioned by name (perhaps borrowed from Doris Lessing's novel *The Diary of a Good Neighbour*, published under the pseudonym Jane Somers)[126] as well as a 'nurse' and a 'female bank teller.'

The story takes place in various spots in the city, including a hospital (sometimes a psychiatric wing becomes detectable), a theater, an adjoining hotel room, an airport hangar, a bank, a place

Some of Henry Grimes' notebooks from his time in L.A. (© Alex Levine).

called 'at Francis", and the streets of Los Angeles. Of the latter,
'Beverly Blvd.' and 'Flower St.' are explicitly mentioned; they are
always crossed by car and lie approximately where Grimes himself
lived and worked at the time.[127] The story is dominated by constant
cacophony, loud din, and a 'hellish darkness' in which the figures
suddenly have to find their way. One regularly recurring term is
'circuit action', which opens up a new literary meta-level and reveals
the setting to be an illusion. Time and again the images recall
Grimes' personal situation in Los Angeles and seem, when taken as
a whole, to be a metaphor for the city. At the same time, the text
reads like a writing exercise with a strong affinity to Gothic
Romanticism.

Until his rediscovery, Grimes wrote continuously and studied
the works of English and American poets on a regular basis. On 15
December 2001, roughly a year before Marshall Marrotte located
him in Los Angeles, he wrote a long note on the blank final pages
of an anthology of American poetry he had bought some time after
1993.[128] This note, subdivided into ten sections, expresses his
assessment of various nineteenth- and twentieth-century poets

while capturing thoughts on philosophy of life. By now sixty-six years old, he had acquired a deep knowledge of Anglo-American poetry after about twenty years of self-instruction in literature and intensive writing activity. This body of writings had become his spiritual home. The note's main figures are John Berryman (1914–1972), Richard Howard (born 1923), Robinson Jeffers (1867–1962), Pauline Hanson (1917–1991), Jean Valentine (born 1934), Emily Dickinson (1830–1886), Hart Crane (1899–1932), Frederick Goddard Tuckerman (1821–1873), and Hilda Doolittle ('H. D.', 1886–1961), with special admiration voiced for Emily Dickinson and 'H. D.'. In this note poetry manifests itself as an indispensable interlocutor. Shown this list many years later, Grimes responded that he also admires and read deeply the works of Amiri Baraka, Countee Cullen, Paul Laurence Dunbar, and Langston Hughes, among other black poets. His list at the time he wrote it in the back of the poetry anthology may have been restricted to the writers included in the collection.

Poems form the points of reference for Grimes' own reflections. The following sequence is made up entirely of hints and allusions:

> [...] it is – all that we, as adults, are the rejoinder – to, and – so, our children know. 4. Jean Valentine ... wrote it in a line from her poem – anaesthesia – 'I knew them as my own, their cries took on the family whiskey voice, refusal, need, – their human need peeled down, tore, scratched for her life'[129] – (Thereby thrust'd upon the open shores of Gods' knowing – anthology – for this;) still, it seems strange to see and know, to experience and reexperience to vitalize and revitalize, all we feel, all we know. This bares lots of strange or 'unreasoning' purpose 'with' or Life-times or renditions. That – 'outhere' there exists reasons we have never known! Realities, that we cannot now call – our own. When time seems to grow still, or seems to stop in its way, it has become (to us) a stopcock. This is not speaking of a symptom – nor a rendition of relief. (I feel) turtles or the Gilamonster eat this way with their all-consuming traps of steel – as stomachs.

Grimes then goes on to express his great admiration for Emily Dickinson, only to write about the thoughts of sleepless nights that take shape as poems in the morning:

> One of America's all time – in any broad concept of greatness occurred with the blend of her life and poetic genius of [...] Emily Dickinson's subterfuge of writing and pure conceptuality thru – passage and pas-

sages of fire – pure art of poetry – who wrote – 'I reason, Earth is short' […] many, – who – are poets, get up from long and sleepless nights, to embrace thoughts that <u>still from</u> the night before have only – to – see (that is, to realize, an aspectrae of their own conundrum.)

In a later passage Grimes takes up a poem that praises the passive state of waiting as true to life (he was very familiar with waiting at the time):

The Poet Richard Howard composed 'Waiting is the poem of waiting' – I believe that we do some of our best quality – of living – while 'waiting' attentively, to do – it. It – lives in a mass sobriety. Submerged – in what – is called – Life (for that is all – it can be called) we're really – drunk!

In another sequence, 'meaning' and 'unrealization' are counterposed, with the latter remaining indomitable and superior to 'meaning'. Grimes states that: 'the Poet Hart Crane – put it with an excellent piece of poetry' and quotes:

Frosted eyes there were that lifted altars;
And silent answers crept across the stars.[130]

He continues:

Poets always knew – that by having the list – of – meanings subjected – to an unrealized – unrealization that is always apparent – and always a succinct element which is <u>drawn</u> upon by the best poets.

The ending is a ringing proclamation of hope in the future. Grimes quotes the last stanza from Hilda Doolittle's poem 'Garden' here – and then notes:

Let all lights be the dramaturgy of your communicates desires to be, to do, the things you want to be and do, and order (hearts) or – things that have no other desires – except those things which are your very own Life will go – on – in order to gauge[131] them. Henry A. Grimes 12-15-01

7

'I would be interested in playing again; I just need an instrument' – Rediscovery by Marshall Marrotte – Olive Oil – First Gigs (2002–03)

Henry Grimes had never been forgotten

When Grimes was asked if he ever thought of his former friends and fellow musicians while he was in Los Angeles and wondered whether they still thought of him, he replied, 'I envisioned them as all being busy workers, making their music, but I didn't give it a whole lot of thought.' Margaret Davis Grimes added, 'He really thought everyone had forgotten him six months after he was gone.'[1]

This notion was far from true, as is known from Bennie Maupin's and Percy Heath's accounts and the memoirs of Perry Robinson, published before Grimes' return.[2] Other renowned musicians remembered him as well. When Sonny Rollins was asked whether Henry Grimes occasionally crossed his mind, he said that he hoped Henry had only left music and was still alive: 'Being the optimistic person I am, I was hoping that it was true that he had just gotten disgusted with the music business. So I thought that maybe he just needed to get away from the music business.'[3]

Andrew Cyrille, who regularly thought of his former companion, also felt that Grimes had not died but had merely vanished: 'He was always in my mind, of course not all the time – things revolve like clips of a film. I thought about Henry often and spoke about him with different people to find out whether anyone had seen him or heard about Henry, especially with Perry Robinson. And Perry didn't know where he was. As far as my feelings, I was absolutely perplexed; it was a mystery. You know, it was one of those things, the police records are full of people who disappear, and it happens all over the world. So for thirty-some years Henry was in that category. No musician I know had seen him.'[4]

For many years after Grimes' disappearance, fellow musicians and fans would speculate about his whereabouts in conversation. Henry Grimes the bassist had always remained in the memory of the jazz world as an outstanding figure.[5] He was given a memorial day in *The Golden Age Jazz Calendar*, as is known from an article in the *New York Times* (February 9, 1997):

> Lawyers in the Fox News v. Time Warner antitrust case met recently in the Brooklyn courtroom of U.S. District Judge Jack B. Weinstein to schedule their jury trial. Yosef J. Riemer (representing Fox, the plaintiff) wanted an early date. He didn't quite get it, but he and his opponent, Robert D. Joffe, got a lesson in judicial cool. THE COURT: May I have a calendar? ... Wait, I have it. I have my Golden Age Jazz Calendar. ... Let's see. December is John Birks (Dizzy) Gillespie month. That seems like a good month. JOFFE: It sounds right for this case, Your Honor. THE COURT: October is Billie Holiday month. RIEMER: We are liking the music better every month you go backwards, Your Honor: Who is, say, May? JOFFE: The difference, Your Honor, between April and May is not substantial. Not meaningful. THE COURT: May is Lester (Prez) Young. RIEMER: We've always been a big fan of his. THE COURT: Charlie (Yardbird) Parker month seems to me the right month. That's November. RIEMER: Yes, Your Honor. THE COURT: Jury selection on Monday, the 3rd of November, which is Henry Grimes-bassist-day.[6]

Also, people outside the jazz music world regularly thought of Henry Grimes. Musicians and fans of punk and rock discovered his innovative playing style at a time when he was long considered dead and gone. Guitarist Robert Quine, as quoted in Marc Ribot's preface to *Signs Along The Road*, calls Grimes a major influence. It was also Quine who drew Ribot's attention to Henry: 'Although I'd been aware of Albert Ayler's music since the eighties, it was founding punk-rock guitarist Robert Quine who pointed out to me how important Henry Grimes' role was in it. Quine thought Henry's was the most beautiful, original bass playing he'd ever heard. To prove it, Robert played me Ayler's *Swing Low, Sweet Spiritual* record, later re-issued on CD as *Going Home*, and I still remember this first listening: It was one of a very few occasions when a piece of music made me weep. And I wonder how many of the thousands of guitarists and millions of listeners influenced directly or indirectly by Quine's punk style are aware of the influence of Albert Ayler and Henry Grimes in what they play and hear.'[7]

Marshall Marrotte, a social worker and music enthusiast from Athens, GA, who occasionally writes about improvised music, was so overwhelmed by Grimes' improvisations when he heard *The Call* in a New Orleans record store in 1986 that he ultimately decided in 2002 to search for him.

By the late 1990s rumors had spread that Henry Grimes was not dead at all but living in L.A. Nor did Marshall Marrotte ever seriously believe in Henry's death; there had never been a definitive answer as to his whereabouts.[8] Eventually his own research supplied the answer: Henry Alonzo Grimes was alive.

'from those first few notes I was destroyed'[9] – Marshall Marrotte discovers Henry Grimes (Fall 2002)

In 2002, sixteen years after he had first been deeply moved by Henry Grimes' art of improvisation, Marshall Marrotte set out to find him. Being a social worker, he had no trouble gaining access to official files and systematically examining them.[10] Marrotte 'sifted through all manner of legal records to solve the mystery of Henry Grimes,' the *Los Angeles Times* later wrote.[11] Finally, in the fall of 2002 he tracked down a Henry Grimes living at an SRO hotel address in L.A., and it turned out to be the legendary musician he had been searching for so intensively. A detailed account of his successful search appeared in the lead paragraphs to his *Signal To Noise* interview, published in early 2003:

> I have been an admirer of Henry Grimes since 1986, the year after I graduated from high school. I took a trip with some friends down to New Orleans and wandered into a record shop on Decatur Street. The guy working there had just put on *The Call* and from those first few notes I was destroyed. Clarinetist Perry Robinson and drummer Tom Price are amazing on that recording but it was the lower frequencies produced by Mr. Grimes which really messed me up. I bought the album (the first 'jazz' record I ever owned) and walked out onto the street with my head spinning. Over the years as I got more and more into creative music, I heard stories about

Grimes' mysterious disappearance: that he'd died in 1971, that he'd died in 1984, that he'd become a minister and turned away from music, that he was homeless [...], dyed his hair green and started to play electric bass with rock bands. [...] Last year [2002] I started doing some research into Grimes' whereabouts. Quite a bit of my spare time was spent examining the smallest of details concerning his 'vanishing': court records, death certificates, personal accounts of friends and musicians, family contacts etc. [...] yet I did not learn anything of substance from these efforts. All I really knew was that he was likely somewhere on the West Coast (whether he was alive or not was another matter).'[12] 'After a bit of detective work, I tracked down a Mr. Henry Alonzo Grimes, born in 1935 in Philadelphia, and apparently still very much alive in the greater Los Angeles area. I made contact and flew out to meet him at his room in an old Los Angeles S.R.O. hotel.'[13]

Grimes remembers the day exactly: 'I got a message up from the lobby. You have to get down there to answer it, hope you can get there before someone hangs up the phone.'[14] He walked down the five flights of stairs and took the call that would change his life.[15] Marshall Marrotte: 'After about 15 minutes on hold, I heard his voice.'[16] Henry Grimes: 'I felt elation at being called, and knowing that everything I wanted from it was coming true at once. I knew it was.'[17] On the other end of the line, Grimes recalls, Marrotte said that 'he was looking to find out who I was and he asked me if I play bass and if I am a jazz musician. I said yeah. We talked and then he came into the hotel and interviewed me, took a picture of me.'[18] Marrotte was impressed by Grimes' charisma: 'For someone who has endured rough times, Grimes has managed to remain a gentleman with a great sense of humour. He is quiet and reserved, but happy and excited about the prospect of getting involved in music again. He also writes a great deal of poetry and hopes to publish some in the future.'[19]

Two passages in the interview that Marrotte conducted with Grimes immediately after his rediscovery reveal how remote Grimes had become from the world of music. At that time he had no notion of critical changes that had occurred ages ago. When he sold his bass, he abandoned the world that had once been his life. In his mind, the world of music (but not music itself!) was frozen in the year 1968.

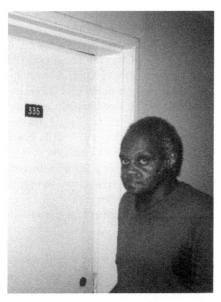

Henry Grimes in front of his SRO-room, LA, fall 2002 (© Marshall Marrotte, courtesy *Signal To Noise* archives).

Pete Gershon, chief editor of *Signal To Noise* (email from December 14, 2014, quoted with permission):

'I can vividly remember the day I received Marshall Marrotte's phone call. He asked if I'd be interested in publishing an interview he'd done with 'a legendary jazz musician.' Usually when people say that the musician is, in fact, not that legendary, so I was very skeptical. When he told me he'd located Henry Grimes, I nearly dropped the phone. I commissioned Michael Fitzgerald to write the supporting essay and tracked down the photos. (...) At any rate, being the first publication to break the news of Henry's survival was one of the highlights of my experience with *Signal to Noise*.'

'I wanted to ask you,' Marrotte began his interview, 'about what you have been up to all these years, what caused you to leave music, and your recollections of friends and musicians like Sonny Rollins, Don Cherry, Albert Ayler ...' Grimes answered with a question of his own: 'How is Albert doing?' Thirty-one years after Ayler's death he learned how things stood: 'Well, I hate to be the one to tell you, but Albert passed away in 1970 [...].'[20] Marrotte continued by asking about Grimes' 'unique, alien'[21] arco technique, and received a surprising reply: 'Oh, thank you. Yeah, I tried to come from everywhere, using everything, Indian music, all kinds of things, anything that inspired me. [...] especially Ali Ahkbar Khan and some Ravi Shankar. Mainly Northern Indian music. It had a lot of influence on my playing.'[22] The moment Grimes said this, he realized how remote he was from this era: 'I haven't thought about that in a long time. It's really amazing how much stuff I have forgotten about!'[23]

Another important topic in this exchange of thoughts was the outstanding recordings Grimes had made in the 1960s. The one that stood out most clearly in his memory, he said, was *Sonny Meets Hawk*. Marrotte explained that many of these legendary recordings were now available on CD: 'You know a lot of those records are being reissued on CD, the Impulse things: the Roy Haynes record, the Ayler records [I pull some of these CDs from my bag and show them to Henry].'[24] 'So this is a CD?!,' Grimes replied. 'Oh wow, you can see how out of touch I am. [*laughs*] You know, I'm not really one of those button-pusher kind of guys!'[25] In this way he alluded to the deeper reason for his information gap. 'I was amazed,' he later recalled at first hearing his music on CD, 'because I listened to some CDs of some of the Cecil Taylor and Albert Ayler things, and some of my music. At the time, I didn't pay that much attention to them. But when I listened to them again, it was amazing what I heard. There was more to it than I ever realized.'[26]

Marrotte gave him the CDs as a present, promising that 'I will [...] send you a portable CD player, you might get a kick out of listening to some of the records you played on.'[27] Grimes was enthusiastic: 'That would be really nice, thanks!'[28] He was then asked when he last played bass and whether he would like to play again. He wracked his memory: 'It must have been in 1970, in a church with some younger guys. I forget their names, but it was a trio thing. This was in San Francisco, not long before I sold it.'[29] Here he may be recalling a scene that occurred sometime between early 1967 and early 1968, for thereafter he lived in Los Angeles, where at first he still owned his bass.[30]

The second question brought forth a straightforward answer: 'Yeah, I still have a desire to play. I think once I got started, I could keep it going, as long as it was enjoyable, you know? [...] It would be difficult to have a bass here, too cumbersome, it might get broken in a place this small. But yeah, I would be interested in playing some gigs at some point, you know, if anyone is interested in playing with me.'[31] He precisely recalled this situation in an interview of November 13, 2003: 'The answer was that I wanted to play and that's really what I like to do. There I was, but Marshall, a man of understanding, helped me a lot with that. He still does.'[32] Indeed, Marshall Marrotte generously offered his assistance: 'Well, maybe me and some other folks can help you out with that.'[33] Grimes was excited: 'That would be really nice. I'm interested and

I think it would be enjoyable. I have thought about it at different times, but the economics have made it impossible. I would like to travel through, go to places I've never been.'[34]

Grimes maintains that he missed playing music all these years but always overcame the feeling with a sort of meditative exercise: 'I missed playing, [...] but I wasn't thinking about it. It wasn't that I didn't want to. It was like a concentration exercise. [...] Instead of worrying about "I don't have a bass," I just sort of got ahead of it.'[35] In an interview with Larry Blumenfeld in 2003, by which time he had already returned to New York, he nicely summed it up: 'I may have sold my bass a long time ago, but I've been thinking about music all the time.'[36] Speaking to Ssirus Pakzad in a *Jazzthing* interview of 2005, he said that his return to the world of music 'was as if I'd risen from the dead.'[37] These statements express a wide range of feelings from Grimes' years in L.A.. Again and again one finds that he struggled with his lack of an instrument, but it was never a lost battle. His enthusiasm for music was still unbroken in 2002, but for 'only' some thirty-five years he had never had a chance to act on it.

Immediately realizing this, Marshall Marrotte cautiously pointed out that the audience for creative experimental music was still tiny, relatively speaking. There were many small labels willing to cultivate it, but money remained a problem. It was still hard to earn a living from this music. 'Yeah, I guess some things never change,' was Grimes' reply. But there was no stopping his rekindled urge to play music: 'I feel like there is still more I can contribute,

Marshall Marrotte, 2013 (© Paula Marrotte, courtesy Marshall Marrotte).

though, you know? Things I could have developed if I had stuck with it.'[38] Marrotte assured him that he and many others were well aware of his outstanding contributions to free improvised music. Grimes, in his modest and undemonstrative way, thanked him for this recognition, all the more surprising for being so belated: 'Thank you. I think I would be interested in playing again, I just need an instrument.'[39]

Margaret Davis, William Parker, and Olive Oil (Late 2002)

When Margaret Davis,[40] a New York journalist and an activist for the free music cause, learned that Henry Grimes was still alive but did not own an instrument, she launched a nationwide campaign to obtain one for him. At that time she remembered him as a superb bassist of the 1950s and 1960s but did not know him personally. 'For me, a planet where the great Henry Grimes does not have a bass is not a place I want to be,' she exclaimed in her account of Grimes' return to the world of music.[41] Being unprepared to make long trips at the time, she decided in favor of a search operation, which went on for many weeks. She contacted roughly fifty musicians with whom Grimes had played and recorded before his disappearance, as well as a few bass players she assumed would acknowledge him as an influence. She focused her search primarily on the West Coast, it being very expensive to ship a bass. She also felt that West Coast musicians would gladly take the opportunity to contact Grimes directly, especially if they belonged to academic institutions and could place an instrument or practice room at his disposal. 'So with Marshall Marrotte's approval, I put the word out far and wide, and then we waited for a bass for Henry Grimes.'[42]

For a fairly long time nothing happened. Only gradually did a few people become active and promise to contribute something – a donation, a benefit concert, a bow – 'kind, good offers, but not a bass for Henry Grimes to play. A couple of afflicted souls responded negatively, cynically, or even with hostility. Most just didn't answer at all.'[43]

Margaret Davis' email correspondence throws interesting light on the situation at the time and her great commitment to artists like Henry Grimes. When she had almost lost her lifelong faith in the musical community 'as something more than a concept or an ideal, but as an actual living entity that embraces and sustains its own,'[44] she received a message from William Parker. Parker, himself an outstanding and much sought-after bassist, had just returned from a tour and was sifting through the many emails that had accumulated in his absence. He recalled the events in an interview of 2003: 'I received an email that Henry Grimes was not dead, that he was found, and he was living in L.A., and that he showed interest in getting back to playing. I didn't respond at first because I thought there was lots of bass players in LA and it would probably be easier for him to get a bass in L.A., which I think he would have eventually gotten if I wouldn't have sent that bass. Someone in L.A. would have eventually gotten him a bass somehow.'[45]

Finally he responded, initially by email:

The bass I have is a plywood bass that I refinished myself. It is both suitable to practice on or to do concerts with. The more you play it the better it sounds. I spoke to Ben Young the other week mentioning to him that there should be someone in the area where Henry Grimes lives that could get a bass to him. It would be easier to get a bass from the West coast than to ship from New York. Someone is always selling a bass at the same price it might cost to ship a bass. If a bass could not be found I have this bass called Olive Oil that I could give to Henry. Just have someone pick it up. This is not a problem. I was just hoping for convenience sake that a bass out there would show up. Have who ever is involved contact me to arrange pick up and shipping. If there is no money for shipping I will donate the funds myself or ship the bass myself. There must be someone on the other end to receive. I could even ask David Gage at the bass shop to ship the bass the way that he ships things. Please let me know. I leave town on December 3 until December 11.

William.[46]

Margaret Davis immediately relayed the message to Marshall Marrotte and discussed the details of shipping 'Olive Oil' to Los Angeles and setting up a donation account that would allow Grimes to buy bass accessories. Sonny Rollins had just told her that he would make a donation and she emailed Marrotte:

I just called David Gage's shop again to see how we're doing with the shipping of Olive Oil. [...] As to the bow, there's a chance that William sent one, so Henry Grimes may not need one, or at least not right now. My thought on this matter of bass accessories was to find out [the] best bass shop that's closest to where Henry Grimes lives and see if those who want to help can set up credit for him there so he can go 'round and get rosin and / or a bow and / or a gig bag and / or a wheel or whatever he might like to choose for himself. [...] Maybe Sonny Rollins will want to contribute to such a credit account too, since he'd said he'd contribute to 'a kitty'. [...] I talked to Henry Grimes for a few minutes on Saturday to let him know his bass should be coming this week.[47]

A short while later William Parker again called Margaret Davis personally to say that the bass and bow would be shipped: 'he [...] called me up to say he would send a bass and a bow to Henry Grimes. First he wanted New York's great bass specialist David Gage to make a small repair, and then David's shop would build a shipping crate for the bass and arrange and pay for the shipping. One of David Gage's employees, a bassist named James Royer, known as 'Sprocket', even put up $100 of his own money to help with shipping costs. Asked later on why he did this, Sprocket replied, 'When I was a kid, the first time I heard Henry Grimes play, I said, "I want to do THAT!"' Wendy Oxenhorn of New York's Jazz Foundation stood prepared to cover shipping if needed, & was happy to learn she could keep that money to help another musician in need.[48]

William Parker had given the bass a green finish – hence its distinctive name: 'When I got the bass, it was a regular colored bass. I stripped the bass and I refinished it in a green color, an olive green finish and I called it Olive Oil.'[49]

On December 9, Olive Oil was dispatched from Dave Gage's bass shop directly to Grimes' SRO hotel in Los Angeles. That same day Margaret Davis announced this to Marshall Marrotte, who replied, 'Margaret, thank you again so much for helping make this dream come true for him (and me). [...] it really would not have happened if you hadn't been involved.'[50]

A shipping company took the bass to Los Angeles,[51] where its delivery at the Huntington Hotel was scheduled for Friday the 13th. 'I wonder if Henry Grimes is as thrilled about the imminent arrival of Olive Oil as you & I are!,' Margaret Davis wrote to Marshall Marrotte on the scheduled day of arrival. 'I spoke with him on the phone earlier this week to let him know that today is arrival day & to give him contact information for the shipping people just in case of anything. [...] He said he would stick around at the hotel all day today.'[52] As it happened, however, Olive Oil did not arrive until three days later.[53]

Margaret Davis had a friend, Paulette Jones (now deceased), who lived near Los Angeles, had befriended Billy Higgins, and occasionally played bass herself. After some hesitation, Paulette agreed to contact Henry. As Margaret explained, Jones could do far more for Grimes on location than she could herself: 'She was the one who had a car and a cell phone. And I had met her in New York and I helped her find a concert [...]. She stayed here with me after I first met her. I helped her in New York, so I wanted her to help him. And I would call her on her cell phone. She was the first person I ever knew who had a cell phone. I would say, just go and see Henry, bring him to a concert, buy him a meal, and I'll pay you back or send you money as soon as I have some.'[54] At first Jones declined to visit Grimes in the SRO hotel, which was located in a dreadful area of the city: 'She didn't want to go there [...]. So we had this terrible argument. She hung up the phone. [...] I asked Paulette to go, so I was always bothering her about Henry, and she didn't want to go to that part of town.'[55] In the end she declared herself willing to do something for Grimes: 'And then she called back and said, okay, and she helped Henry. She did.'[56]

The three-day delay in the arrival of the bass must have been hell for Henry, who was struggling to believe that this great gift was actually a reality and that he would be able to play music again. Asked what the prospect of receiving a bass meant to him, Grimes spoke of cautiously awaiting the outcome: 'Before I got the bass, it just was an empty thought that I had. Carrying it, or playing it, or anything that I would do, you know.'[57]

Olive Oil was delivered on December 16, 2002 – a Monday.[58] Grimes remembers exactly how the bass arrived in the hotel lobby in a packing crate: 'They pried it open with crowbars, the bass was a big ray of hope. The best sounding bass I ever had.'[59] The instrument 'was in a casket-like box, like Dracula's coffin. I opened it up, took the bass, went upstairs to my room and started playing.'[60] In 2003 he was asked what it was like to play bass again after so many years: 'I guess I went over sketches of things in my own mind of things that I knew I had been familiar with in the past, a lot of free music, experimenting with my reaction. I enjoyed doing this in this kind of environment. I just gradually worked it out until it happened. I didn't forget. I couldn't forget. [...] I have been practicing a lot of Monk and stretching my fingers on *Brilliant Corners* and music like that. His harmonic experience is pure genius. You can sit there and seek out your own experience by his harmony and theory.'[61]

In another interview that same year, he added that he listened to old recordings on CD as he practiced (using the portable player Marshall Marrotte had given to him): 'Before my CD player blew a fuse, I listened to these records and I knew they were good but I didn't realize... I feel that the process is limitless, plenty of work to do, but it's all enjoyable.'[62] He elaborated his feelings to Lynell George: 'It's a strange thing. Like an effect of battle. [...] Listening to these records I made with all these guys, I couldn't remember the place or how I got there playing. But I remember every note of the music. I mean every note.'[63]

Grimes was enraptured by his new instrument: 'Olive Oil [...] was delivered to Henry Grimes earlier today,' Margaret Davis wrote to Wendy Oxenhorn, '& last I heard, he was ecstatically practising in his room.'[64] People told her that he practiced non-stop for two weeks, after which he was willing to appear in public again.[65] 'In fact, he recently was heard to wish for a pickup & an amp so he can go out to play, & the building manager reports that if someone knocks on Henry Grimes' door, he's been too engrossed in playing the bass to respond,'[66] she wrote on jazznewyork.org, adding: 'This leads me back to those offers of donations and benefit concerts & such. For all those who wish to help Henry Grimes on his road back into the music, here are some suggestions.'[67] The first suggestion was, 'If you were a close friend, band mate, or family member of Henry Grimes, please contact me or Marshall Marrotte and we will give you Henry's address (subject to prior agreement from Henry). Henry has neither phone nor email.'[68]

Before long the phone in the hotel lobby was flooded with calls from people all over the world who wanted to talk to him. Grimes' radical seclusion was about to end.

'I'm back for good' – First Gigs in Los Angeles and New York (January–June 2003)

From talking with Sonny on the phone, I can say that he is really deeply moved that Henry is alive & well.

Margaret Davis, 2003[69]

The news of Henry Grimes' return set the musical media abuzz. The first article, published in the winter issue of *Signal To Noise*, was written by the man who located him at his own initiative in the fall of 2002: Marshall Marrotte.[70] The good news he had to proclaim to the world quickly bore fruit: 'When Marshall found me and [...] let the world know I still exist, I immediately got calls and offers from everywhere.'[71] To the present day Grimes is deeply moved by his memories of this period: '[A]s soon as I started communicating to others that I was available and here, and not missing, I started to get jobs. [...] The hotel I was staying in didn't even have enough accommodations to handle it all. People were calling from Europe and everywhere else. I didn't even have a phone! But I've really enjoyed it so far, it's been wonderful. Thank you all for your support.'[72] Grimes told me in 2009 that the 'feeling was very exciting, you know: Lots of people were calling, but also people that I never knew before. It was really exciting. At that time I never had any intention to play and then I did certain things that would sort of suggest that I was wrong about that.'[73]

Val Wilmer, the author of the well-known free-music study *As Serious As Your Life*, was stunned to read the latest interview with Henry Grimes in *The Wire*. As she reported in a letter to the editor:

What a shock to open *The Wire* 227 and find a contemporary interview with Henry Grimes! ... [A]s someone responsible for perpetuating the belief that Grimes had died, both in the prefatory note to the new edition of *As Serious As Your Life* and elsewhere, I can only repeat that this was the belief of his community of peers.

I made many attempts to discover Grimes' fate, but felt that reports of his death had been finally confirmed by a conversation I had with bassist Reggie Johnson when he told me a story that he assured me was 'on good authority from someone in California'. A lifetime of research tells me that such claims need to be supported by official evidence, but at the time of my talk with Johnson, it was not possible to access the Social Security Deaths Index the way it is now.[74]

An exciting new era began for Grimes and has lasted to the present day. Marshall Marrotte and Margaret Davis, both living far from L.A., tirelessly helped him along his courageous path back to the music profession.

The first weekend of February, even before Grimes returned to the stage, a reunion took place with his longstanding musical companion Andrew Cyrille at the Jazz Bakery in Culver City near L.A.. At that time the legendary drummer was playing in the club with James Blood Ulmer and Reggie Workman. Margaret Davis reported the event to the Sun Ra Saturn group on the internet in an enthusiastic email of February 3, 2003. She also mentioned that in the meantime her friend from L.A., Paulette Jones, had visited Henry in his hotel:

The story of Henry Grimes gets more & more inspiring! At my request, a friend who lives in L.A. went to visit Henry Grimes about three weeks ago & came away very impressed by him & glad that she'd gone to see him. In fact, she invited him to be her guest at a concert at the Jazz Bakery in L.A. by James Blood Ulmer, Reggie Workman, & Andrew Cyrille the past weekend, & Henry said he'd love to go. He's been deeply engrossed with Olive Oil ever since the bass' arrival, the building manager having reported that nowadays when someone knocks on Henry's door, he's too busy practising the bass to respond! Last night my friend called to tell me about her evening with Henry at the Jazz Bakery. There was an emotional reunion with Reggie & Andrew (Blood didn't come to New York from the Midwest until Henry had already left for the Coast, so they wouldn't have known one another). Andrew dedicated a drum solo to Henry (on-mike), there was great applause at the mention of his name (Henry was amazed, because he'd always assumed everyone forgot about him after a few months!), the musicians spent the intermission backstage (my friend politely refrained from joining them, so she can't report on that part), &

Pharoah Sanders turned up on cue & went backstage too! ...
My friend said all the music in both sets was unmistakeably devo-
tional towards Henry, & Henry was thrilled & deeply moved.
Reggie had put Henry on the guest list, so she [Paulette] felt financially able to take him out afterwards for an enormous pastrami
sandwich at an all-night place ... Next weekend she's going to pick
up Henry & Olive Oil & take them to a practice space ... & if her
roommate is around, he may participate on drums, having actually
played with Henry in San Francisco in the short time they both
lived there .... [75]

The joy at Grimes' return to the world of music was enormous,
especially among those who contributed to it with such commitment. On February 5, 2003, Marshall Marrotte wrote an email
thanking everyone involved, especially Margaret Davis ('She has
been THE motivating force (and Henry!) behind the organization
of finding a bass for Henry [...] and helping to organize a fund for
his needs') and William Parker ('Thank you William Parker!! Your
donation of Olive Oil got Henry playing again'). Thanks were also
extended to David Gage's bass shop ('for their efforts and ongoing
support'), and to Pete Gershon of *Signal To Noise* as well as Michael
Fitzgerald and Rob Young of *The Wire* ('for running stories about
Henry').[76]

In the early days, support had also come from a young L.A.
musician, Nick Rosen, who was then just learning to play bass.
Shortly after they met, Grimes began to give him lessons in improvisation: 'After only a couple of months with Olive Oil, [Grimes]
began to emerge from his room, with sensitive, caring encour-
agement and assistance from a young music student named Nick
Rosen and classmates at the Oakwood School, where the youngsters persuaded the staff to pay Henry to give them improvisation
lessons.'[77] A rehearsal date was organized by the social scientist,
music historian and high school teacher Steven L. Isoardi, who had
established contact with the legendary bassist for some of his
students and who published a detailed account of it in 2010.[78]
Isoardi remembered that 'the first time Nick Rosen met with
Henry Grimes in January 2003, he was with Andrew Schneiderman.
Along with Nick Rosen and Joey Dosik, Andrew was the third
student who assisted in Henry's return.'

Rosen and his friend Dosik – two ambitious young men – wanted above all to learn about music from Henry Grimes. They also wanted to support him in his return to the world of music and to help him find an initial public appearance. When Rosen and Dosik visited him for the first time in the Huntington Hotel, he told them, 'I just want to play free.'[79] No sooner said than done: they arranged for a jam session on February 9, 2003, at the home of Rosen's mother in Van Nuys. 'Reed master and bandleader Vinny Golia played soprano saxophone. Alex Cline presided over trap drums. From the Pan Afrikan Peoples Arkestra came Joshua Spiegelman on tenor saxophone and alto clarinet, and bassists Roberto Miranda and Latif.'[80]

One day later, Grimes also appeared at the Oakwood School, where Rosen was still a student.[81] Lynell George wrote about it in her *L.A. Times* article of March 21, 2003, about which more will be said later:

> On a cloudy, late-winter morning, he stands before an eager group of about 50 high school students and their teachers at the Oakwood School in North Hollywood, his hands sunk deep in his pockets, his new bass leaning against him. It's an unlikely place for a comeback date, but this assembly will be Grimes' first semi-public performance since 1972. [...] He stands, stock-still, cradling the bass, plucking and bowing alternately – then simultaneously. His eyes seem focused on that middle space from which he emerged. In minutes, he is drenched in perspiration – his forehead glossy, his bow an unraveled mess. Rosen's eyes lock into his new mentor's gaze, picking up cues and clues.[82]

The journalist also took the opportunity to ask Grimes a few questions. The answers she received also brought out his soft-spoken humor: 'Grimes is alternately tentative and whimsical. To the question, "What does it feel like to have worked with all the greats?" he offers, "It kinda interferes with my sleep." He punctuates those one-liners with a teasing, slow-blooming grin.'[83]

After jamming with Henry Grimes, Alex Cline wrote to Isoardi: 'I was amazed at how fearless and game Henry was throughout the music making – plus he can still swing! He played most of the time and didn't appear to burn out, walk away with blisters, or just suffer massive overwhelm! What a guy!'[84] If Grimes had had his way, the jam session and his appearance at the Oakwood School might have gone on every week, and he was disappointed to learn that it would not be repeated.[85] But he received other offers, this time for professional gigs: 'After only a few short weeks with his new bass from William Parker,' Margaret Davis writes, 'Henry Grimes emerged from his tiny room to begin playing concerts with Nels and Alex Cline, Joseph Jarman, and others at Billy Higgins' World Stage, the Howling Monk, the Jazz Bakery, and Schindler House in the Los Angeles area in early '03.'[86]

On March 21 and 22, 2003, Grimes was given an opportunity, initiated by Paulette Jones in collaboration with Margaret Davis and arranged by Steven L. Isoardi, to play at the internationally acclaimed World Stage Performance Gallery in South Central Los Angeles – a tiny venue for literature and music that was founded in 1989 by the drummer Billy Higgins (1936–2001) and the poet Kamau Daáood, and was headed by the two men (and pianist Horace Tapscott) until Higgins' death.[87] There is a private recording of the concert,[88] and once again the gig was preceded by a rehearsal at the home of Nick Rosen's mother, this time on March 9. As recalled by Isoardi, 'Re-joining Henry were Alex Cline on drums, Nick on bass and Joey on alto saxophone. Fiery saxophonist/bass clarinetist Chris Heenan and Bobby Bradford-influenced trumpeter Dan Clucas joined the front line. Unable to make the rehearsal, but committed to joining the band for the gig, would be Alex's twin brother, prodigious guitarist Nels Cline, and multi-reed master Charles Owens.'[89]

Lynell George of the *Los Angeles Times*, along with a photographer, also attended the rehearsal. Her article, printed on the front page of the local events section of this great daily newspaper, bore the title 'A Jazz Mystery Unravels: Henry Grimes, the Juilliard-Trained Bassist Who Quietly Walked Away Decades Ago, Is Slowly Reemerging' and carried a photograph of Grimes. 'Once one of the most sought-after jazz bassists of the post-bop era, Grimes was as well known for his quiet demeanor as his big sound,' George accurately writes.[90] Her article opens with a few statements from Grimes about his return to the world of music: '"It's all a little overwhelming," Grimes will tell you in a mere rasp of a voice that only underscores the understatement. "Marshall told me that a lot of people thought I was dead. I thought, I could really use that plot for a horror film or something like that. [...] I've never had this kind of attention," says Grimes, 68, as bewildered by it as he is amused. "But I never stopped playing. Not in my mind.""[91]

Music historian Isoardi is also quoted with an assessment of Grimes' musical achievement, describing him as a musician who complements 'the new sounds that were coming from people like Ayler' and as 'the connection between the bass players of the last, say, twenty, thirty years and the ones in the '50s and '60s', an era in which 'he was one of the greatest artists.'[92]

Both concerts were hugely successful. After the first, Kamau Daáood turned to Grimes in the midst of the applause and said, audibly to everyone, 'Brother Henry, man, we missed you. Welcome back.'[93] Before the second concert on Saturday, Grimes, now dressed in suit and tie, made the acquaintance of the Nigerian poet and novelist Chris Abani, who had been incarcerated for a year as a political prisoner in his native country and was set free in 1991. Abani gave Grimes a copy of his poetry volume *Kalakuta Republic*, which deals with his harrowing experiences in prison, and an advance copy of his new volume, *Daphne's Lot.* Grimes immediately immersed himself in the poems and appeared alone on stage when the concert began. He announced that he would now play a piece inspired by a poem he had just read from Chris Abani's *Kalakuta Republic*.[94] 'Henry offered a haunting, meditative, five-minute performance. At the conclusion of the piece, and after a prolonged ovation, the band – minus George Harper, who had another commitment – joined Henry.'[95]

The Saturday concert attracted more listeners than the previous evening; the street outside the entrance to the World Stage was filled with people – Steven L. Isoardi: 'fans, old acquaintances, and the curious. Among the fans and artists, well-wishers and curiosity-seekers, were also people with offers, from gigs to documentary films.'[96]

Greg Burk reviewed Henry's World Stage performance for *LA Weekly*: 'Grimes, [...] cheek bent to bass neck, seemed to be in another world, but his fingers were right there, darting elegantly among the vines and thickets, or bowing deep, resiny foundations, just as they were with Ayler and Taylor and Rollins and Shepp. He must have been remembering why he once dedicated his life to this music, and also why he bowed out.'[97] In September 2003, Burk added a few more words about the concert in a *Jazz Weekly* article announcing Grimes' appearance at Eagle Rock Center: 'It was immediately clear that he had lost nothing, [...] perfectly balancing the passionate extremes of the seven other musicians who surrounded him.'[98]

Even today a concert report from an audience member named Adam can still be found in the *All About Jazz* internet forum, dated March 25, 2003: 'Grimes himself played without pause for the full 60 minutes, dripping sweat, sounding great, listening intensely, playing some walking lines. [...] everything he played sounded good to me. / The best moment for me from the two pieces was the end of the second piece, which was a lovely duet between Nels and Henry. I dreaded the possibility that everyone was going to come back in again, but they didn't.'[99]

Three further remarkable appearances followed in short order. On March 30, 2003, Grimes was a guest artist in the Pan Afrikan Peoples Arkestra and its chorus, The Great Voice of UGMAA, at the Jazz Bakery (Culver City), where the ensemble mounted its third memorial concert for its leader and founder Horace Tapscott, who had died in 1999.[100] On April 18 and 19, 2003, the Henry Grimes Ensemble (without Chris Heenan) appeared before a large audience at the Howling Monk, L.A., with a flyer bearing the title 'Henry Grimes Reappears'.[101] After the Howling Monk gigs, Alex Cline gave his impression of Grimes' musical development to Isoardi: 'The music grows more varied and focused, and Henry certainly seems to get stronger and more present and relaxed/confident in every way.'[102] His brother Nels Kline wrote ecstatically on his web site: 'I NEVER thought I'd play with Henry Grimes! He sounds better and better, and he seems to be doing quite well with it all. He says very little, and what he does say he says very softly. And when the bow is in his hand, it seems as though some things never go away. It's an extension of his hand, of his voice.'[103]

By late February a public appearance outside of L.A. was already being discussed,[104] namely at New York's six-day Vision Festival, founded in 1996 by bassist William Parker and his wife Patricia to promote freely improvised music, and held annually ever since. The festival was scheduled for the end of May, and Grimes was very interested in appearing there. An interview with William Parker conveys a lively impression from this period: 'Can I let the cat out of the bag and break that Grimes may be there this year?' Parker was asked, to which he replied, 'Yeah, we don't have a definite, definite on that, but we are working on that. That is all I can say about that just yet.'[105] Margaret Davis continued to maintain contact with Grimes via Paulette Jones: 'Henry's participation had been arranged among us in advance (Henry on Paulette's cell phone in L.A., Patricia Parker in New York, and I in New York).'[106] Together they arranged for his appearance at the Vision Festival on May 26.

But when the organizers tried to book his flight to New York, Grimes, for all his excitement at the impending gig, became mistrustful and agreed to fly there only on condition that they also pay for his return flight. His bad memories of New York in the late 1960s must still have been deep inside him, and at first he thought he wanted to continue living permanently in Los Angeles.[107] His request was granted, and as a result he could now appear on a New York stage for the first time in some thirty-five years. At this time, renowned fellow bassist Dave Holland, in an email to Margaret Davis, expressed his joy at Grimes' return: 'I am so happy to hear that Henry is playing again. He is one of the great individualists, and his absence left a space that nobody else could fill. I welcome his return to the music community and all that it will mean to us. I send love and respect to him.'[108]

A week before the event, Neil Strauss conducted a telephone interview with Henry Grimes and was told, from the lobby of his hotel, 'My calluses are in good shape, you know.'[109] Strauss wrote a *New York Times* article on Grimes that was published on May 26, 2003, the same day as Grimes' official appearance at the Vision Festival. The occasion was also announced in the event's flyer:

> Tonight, as part of the avant-garde jazz Vision Festival in New York, Mr. Grimes will perform with Mr. Parker and others as part of a memorial concert for the singer Jeanne Lee at Old St. Patrick's Youth Center (268 Mulberry Street, between Prince and Houston Streets). That performance will be his first in New York since he

left in 1968. [...] Despite his lost years, Mr. Grimes said he had no
regrets: 'I'm working on straightening things out now. But I'm back
for good.'[110]

Strauss' piece also features a statement from William Parker on
Grimes' forceful sound: 'On the records he was on, he stood out.
[...] He had a big sound, and it really punched out whatever
ensemble he was in.'[111]

Grimes arrived in New York on May 21.[112] Margaret Davis
Grimes remembers the day well: 'We met for the first time on May
21st of 2003 at La Guardia. At dawn [*laughter*]. We took one look at
each other — I could never have dreamed of this — and we've been
together ever since.'[113] His sensational stage comeback at the Vision
Festival just a few days later is noted on his website as follows:
'After having had his new bass for only five months, Henry
returned to New York to play as special guest in New York City's
great Vision Festival on Memorial Day, May 26, '03, in William
Parker's big band.'[114]

But the 26th was not the only day that Henry played at the festival. Margaret Davis Grimes describes what happened: '[T]here
was very much hubbub from the beginning of that year's festival on
Wednesday, May 21st because Henry was sitting in the front row
from the get-go, and everyone simply wanted to hear him!
Everyone knew he was scheduled for the 26th, but the excitement
grew and grew during the week, and finally on Saturday the 24th
Rob [Brown] and William [Parker] just decided to invite him up to
play with them. So the duo set became a trio set, and there was a
standing ovation for Henry, because everyone could hear that he
could still play!'[115]

The occurrence was also reported in *Jazziz*: 'Grimes [...] was
listed as one of the performers for the final night's memorial to
singer Jeanne Lee. But two nights before that, Grimes took the
stage unannounced along with bassist William Parker and saxophonist Rob Brown, who were scheduled to duet. Grimes played
without hesitation and with a full sound right from the start.'[116] A
live video recording available in the internet gives a vivid
impression of his playing.[117]

The final day of the six-day festival on May 26, dedicated to
Jeanne Lee, featured a thirteen-piece big band plus four vocalists;

the total personnel consisted of Thomas Buckner, Ellen Christi, Jay Clayton, and Lisa Sokolov (vocals), Rob Brown, Henry Warner (alto saxophones), Lewis Barnes (trumpet), Joe Daley (tuba), Cooper-Moore (ashimba, piano), Billy Bang (violin), Henry Grimes (special guest) and Nick Rosen (basses), William Parker (bass, balafon), Ngoni Omar Payano and Isaiah Parker (percussion), and Newman Taylor-Baker and Gerald Cleaver (drums).[118]

Grimes' stage comeback at the Vision Festival drew praise from Gary Giddins: 'Henry Grimes, who went from Sonny Rollins to Cecil Taylor to an absence of many decades, showed at the Vision Festival that he's lost none of the verve and technique that established him as one of the key bassists of the late '50s and '60s.'[119] No less enthusiastic was journalist Jim Eigo: 'You could hear a pin drop when Henry took his first extended solo during the Jeanne Lee Memorial Concert at the Vision Fest last June. Just amazing. The man still had it, like he never stopped playing. [...] Welcome back, Henry!'[120]

Grimes sensed this excitement and felt visibly at ease in New York. He remained there for a week after the festival to celebrate his comeback with more music. Margaret Davis Grimes wrote about it in the liner notes to his first CD released since his return: 'As if these events weren't dramatic enough, the young volunteers in the Jazz Department at Columbia University's famous radio station WKCR, headed by Ben Young, gathered to organize a five-day "round-the-clock" Henry Grimes Radio Festival that began two days after the Vision Festival ended [May 28 through June 1]. During the radio festival, Henry was on the air for some time each day listening to and responding to recordings he had made many years ago and had not heard since, recollecting fellow musicians long gone from his life, re-encountering some still with us, answering many questions about how the music was made, and opening up more and more to the huge significance of his musical past and to the tremendous possibilities of his musical future'[121]

The radio station WKCR had also made sure that Grimes' bass would be brought to New York.[122] Margaret Davis Grimes: 'This was a pivotal time in Henry's life, because when he finally decided that he did want Olive Oil brought back to New York, it meant that he'd cast his fate with New York City life and would give up his room at the Huntington and not move back to L.A.'

On May 31, Grimes played in the WKCR-FM studio with Perry Robinson (clarinet, oc) and Tom Price (drums), the original lineup for *The Call*. They played Grimes' 'For Django', Robinson's 'The Call' and 'Blasting Off', and a collective improvisation.[123]

On June 1st, the program included a collective duo improvisation with William Parker (bass, doussn'gouni [hunter's guitar]) and a forty-minute bass solo from Grimes, which was released on CD in 2004.[124] In her liner notes Margaret Davis Grimes goes into detail of the bass solo: 'On June 1st, the last day of the WKCR Henry Grimes Radio Festival, mention was made of the Philadelphia pianist known as the Legendary Hassan [*sic*], a great musician Henry had known and worked with when they were youngsters. The spirit of Hassan Ibn Ali entered and filled Henry's awareness that evening, and when Ben Young asked Henry how he would like to end the Henry Grimes Radio Festival, Henry decided to play a solo in gratitude to all, to express all his feelings at this momentous time, and to honor his long-ago young friend Hassan.'[125]

Grimes' elaborate musical tribute following a thirty-year recording hiatus is especially impressive for its orchestral arco improvisations on a basic theme, played pizzicato at the beginning and taken up again and again at varying tempos. The theme was a bass line Ibn Ali had taught Grimes for the pianist's composition 'Three-Four vs. Six-Eight Four-Four Ways.'[126] Once again Henry demonstrated that his decades-long absence from music in Los Angeles had done nothing to diminish his musical prowess.

Following his multi-day stint on WKCR Grimes 'offered a bass clinic at David Gage's shop on May 28th before nearly 50 New York-area bassists.'[127] Larry Blumenfeld, who called Henry Grimes the 'highlight of this year's Vision Festival', reported on the clinic for *Jazziz*: 'Not long after Grimes performed at the Vision Festival, he gave a bass clinic at David Gage's String Studio in Tribeca. [...] Grimes stood on the studio's small stage in front of a hundred or so musicians and fans. A dozen string basses against a wall – awaiting minor repairs – appeared at attention, as if to receive Grimes. Then [...] Roswell Rudd, unpacked his horn, and stepped up next to Grimes. [...] soon, the two began playing, and the sound recalled the music Grimes and Rudd made some 40 years ago in School Days, a band that also featured saxophonist Steve Lacy and the late drummer Denis Charles.'[128]

During this appearance in David Gage's String Instrument Shop, Grimes played a solo as well as a bass duo with Larry Ridley.[129] He also demonstrated the strength of his fingers to the onlookers: 'Many asked how he could play so powerfully. He did a few pushups on his fingertips and explained, that's where the strength in his fingers comes from.'[130]

Andrew Henkin likewise interviewed Grimes after his celebrated New York and Vision Festival comeback and summarized his musical impressions in a review. Here Grimes showed his delight at all the unexpected attention, adding that he had always known he would return and had drawn energy from this assurance: 'For a moment, the long layoff seemed immaterial. Grimes cannot help but be struck by the emotion. "It feels naturally good," Grimes says. "It's just a wonderful experience to have the attention. It's beautiful." [...] What may be surprising is that he always expected to be back here. "I have anticipated it," he says. "I have used that as the power to get here." [...] Though his recent performances show a certain rust, his approach is completely not tentative. There is no fear or restraint in his playing, be it with Parker or in duets with peer Larry Ridley at a benefit concert at David Gage's Instrument Shop downtown.'[131]

Further highlights of this initial New York tour were Grimes' receipt of a lifetime achievement award for jazz music from Long Island Public Radio (WLIU)[132] and a Meet the Composer grant for one of his concerts in California.[133]

After this moving and hugely successful New York visit, Grimes returned to L.A., where he was scheduled to appear on June 10 at the Jazz Bakery in Culver City, the site of his guest appearance the previous April. This time he played with three local musicians – Greg Dahl (bass clarinet), John Wood (piano), and Eric Steck (drums) – with whom he had rehearsed earlier in the year.[134] His second New York tour was already set for July.

In an interview given shortly before his departure, he registered his excitement at his Vision Festival appearance on May 26 and declared that from then on, he would play with greater introspection: 'It was fantastic. That is the only way I can explain it. It was fantastic. It was a very spiritual experience. I am going to New York tomorrow and I think I am going to be doing more of that playing. I get the same sense of enjoyment that I had except now, it is like, my study is more introspective. It is really enjoyable and a pleasure. It is actually fantastic.'[135]

Asked whether there had been any requests for studio recordings, he said, 'Yes, no definite ones yet, but the way they came forward, it is pretty definite. [...] I think I am going to be playing with William Parker and [... Roy] Campbell and musicians like that. A lot of musicians now play at top grade levels. There is more of them in New York, but there are some in Los Angeles like Alex Cline and Nels Cline, the Cline brothers, Roberto Miranda [...].'[136]

The interview ended on a high note: 'Your return is the best thing to happen to improvised music in this town in years.'[137]

8

'Everything that I've strived for came true' – Relocation to New York – Life as a Musician and Poet Today (2003–)

The Transitional Period to Mid-August 2003

The summer of 2003 is the third transitional period in Henry Grimes' adult life, and to date the shortest. The first lasted from 1954 to 1956, when he commuted between Philadelphia and New York, and hence between two musical worlds, before finally settling down for ten years in New York as a jazz musician. The second took place in 1967–68, when his life shifted from New York via San Francisco to Los Angeles for some thirty-five years. The third took him back to New York: he traveled back there a second time in early July 2003 and remained until the end of the month. His schedule included concert dates, radio appearances, and an awards ceremony. Though New York was still not his permanent abode, he had already decided during his first tour in May and June to leave Los Angeles for good.

On July 2, 2003, Margaret Davis sent an email to the publisher of *allaboutjazz.com* that said, among other things, 'Today Henry decided to have Ben Young & Brian Linde bring [Olive Oil] back here when they drive back from L.A. later this month by van. The arrangements are all made. So now we know this is a total commitment, & we are truly blessed.' And on July 6, she wrote an email to a Columbia student who was helping out with things in New York: '[W]e got a phone message today from Paulette in Long Beach, CA saying Ben Young & Brian Linde picked up Olive Oil tonight & she's on her way here!!'

Right at the beginning of the second tour, on July 5, Grimes received the Jazz Lifetime Achievement Award at the Wolffer Estate Vineyard in Sagaponack (Long Island), together with Gato

Barbieri, Bob Berg (posthumously), Teddy Charles, Carla Cook, and Anita O'Day. The next day he appeared at the Birdland Festival on Jane Bauermeister's property in North Madison, Connecticut, along with Sabir Mateen (reeds) and Warren Smith (percussion), under the direction of multi-instrumentalist Kali Z. Fasteau. A few days later, from July 8 to 10, he played at New York's Iridium Jazz Club with his own quintet, consisting of Roy Campbell, Jr. (trumpet), Rob Brown (alto saxophone), Andrew Bemkey (piano), and Michael Thompson (drums).

Shortly after this concert, Grimes expressed his excitement in an interview with Larry Blumenfeld: 'Something happened. It was like a thick air that came into the club and came right down on everybody in it. Everything that I've strived for came true, with bigger implications for the future.'[1] David Adler described his performance: 'Grimes was in excellent form on bass – rough around the edges, to be sure, but with a full, round tone and a very clear sense of musical direction. The music was free yet extraordinarily sensitive, with clearly delineated solo rotations and perfectly intuited peaks and valleys. This was a quintet without a weak link.'[2]

On July 20 and 21, as previously in May and June, Grimes was a studio guest at WKCR-FM. The program included an interview on his work with Albert Ayler, to whom the broadcast was dedicated (June 20), and the next day he gave a 'comprovised concert' with Roy Campbell, Jr. (trumpet), Perry Robinson (clarinet), Andrew Bemkey (piano), Chris Sullivan (bass), and Michael Thompson (drums). On the evening of the 21st, he played at the Lenox Lounge in Harlem in Roy Campbell's band TAZZ, featuring the same lineup of musicians apart from Perry Robinson. Finally, on the 31st, Grimes appeared at New York's Fez Under Time Café in the Charles Mingus Big Band, headed by Sue Mingus.[3]

During this four-week tour he lived with his new partner, Margaret Davis, listening to many of her CDs and discovering the German free jazz bassist Peter Kowald (1944–2002), whose name he had never heard before: 'When he first came back, he was living with me in an apartment where I had a small collection of music, maybe 100–150 CDs. And he went through them ravenously, over and over. I remember, he came running out one day, saying, "This bass player, this bass player!" I looked, and it was Peter Kowald

[...]. And he'd never known about him, because most of Peter Kowald's career took place inside those thirty-five years.'[4]

Another moving experience occurred during this period: on June 21, 2003, he received a letter from a nine-year-old boy in Sweden who already played several instruments (and still does) and who visited Grimes in New York in 2009. 'Hello Henry!,' the letter began. 'My name is Leo Lindberg and I am 9 years old. I listen to jazz music all the time [...] and play double bass, drums and trumpet.' Leo wrote that he had heard Henry on Don Cherry's album *Complete Communion*: 'I thought you were fantastic specially the bow solos and your sound.' He was also happy that Mr. Grimes was playing again, adding the words, 'You are my bass hero.' Enclosed in the letter was a photograph showing him holding the neck of his bass and wearing a T-shirt with a large photo of Henry on the front. Grimes wrote back, and their correspondence continued.[5]

In early August Grimes returned to Los Angeles to give two further concerts and to prepare for his final relocation to New York. On August 4 he played in Chris Heenan and Jeremy Drake's new music series *Line Space Line* in Los Angeles' Salvation Theatre. Joining him on the bandstand were Rob Brown (alto saxophone), Dan Clucas (trumpet), and Rich West (drums). A few days later, on August 8–9, he appeared at the Lillian Theatre, Hollywood, with his own group, consisting of Dan Clucas (trumpet), Joey Dosik (alto saxophone), Nels Cline (guitar), Alex Cline (percussion), Nick Rosen (bass), and, as guest performer, Vinnie Golia (soprano, tenor, and baritone saxophones).[6] It is noticeable that all of the musicians Grimes played with in L.A. were white.[7]

Definitive Return to New York (August 2003)

Grimes had never owned his own furniture in Los Angeles; everything in his room was the property of the Huntington Hotel. When he vacated the room in early August, after a good twenty years, he therefore took with him only his new bass, Olive Oil, which was shipped separately to New York, and roughly fifty notebooks, his books, and a few items of clothing.[8] His pupils Nick Rosen and Joey Dosik helped him move out: 'There were only two boxes of

Reunion after decades: Roy Haynes and Henry Grimes, after Haynes' concert in Marcus Garvey Park in Harlem, NY, August 2003 (© Ken Weiss).

belongings,' Steven L. Isoardi reported. 'The boys struggled with one large box down three flights of stairs, while Henry followed carrying the other.'[9] But before he definitively moved to New York, he spent a few more days in Los Angeles living with the parents of a Columbia graduate (the contact had been arranged by WKCR radio journalist Ben Young) and with the trumpeter Dan Clucas.[10]

Ben Young, who had driven the Columbia graduate back from New York to Los Angeles with his belongings, took Olive Oil along on the return journey. The bass had remained in Los Angeles the entire time since mid-December 2002, and had only been played there or in the near vicinity.

At some point in the first half of August, the same week that Olive Oil and two removal crates showed up in Margaret Davis' apartment, Grimes himself arrived in New York. Accompanying him on the flight was Margaret's Los Angeles friend Paulette Jones.[11] Around this time, shortly after his relocation to New York, Margaret Davis arranged for a joyous reunion with Roy Haynes, with whom Grimes had worked intensively in the early 1960s: 'I took Henry to hear Roy Haynes play in Marcus Garvey Park in

Harlem, and I wangled our way to the bandshell dressing room so Henry and Roy could meet up again. Roy took one look and howled 'HENRY!!!' and picked Henry up and threw him over his shoulder and ran all the way down the hall with him! And Henry is about twice Roy's size. I would say Roy was certainly glad to see him.'[12]

Grimes later summarized his feelings during this transitional period and final return to New York as 'a very big move': 'I got into motion. All the other time before was just like waiting.'[13] In L.A., the only things he kept in his hands at work were things he didn't want: brooms, telephone receivers, rags, bricks, rubble ... For a long time he had no other choice than to play an invisible bass. 'He dreamed the same thing over the years,' Margaret Davis Grimes recalls. 'When he first came to me he used to play the bass in his sleep. And this is what made me so sad, because he was playing an invisible bass.'[14] From December 2002 he again owned a bass, enjoyed many new encounters, mostly with young people who wanted to learn music from him or interview him, and again went on tours. All of this came unexpectedly, yet it was an experience that gave him courage.[15] The doubts and fears he had felt when looking into his new future were soon dispelled: 'It is hard work doing that, but [...] when you have to do something like that, I feel you better be doing that.'[16]

Grimes' life had now taken on a form he could only have dreamt of for over three decades. Once again he was completely immersed in the musical profession. The confidence with which he returned to New York also came from the fact that now someone was waiting for him there: Margaret Davis. He has been living with her ever since, and they married in 2007.

In the period that followed his move to New York, he plunged actively into the music world – an impressive achievement for a man his age. From May 2003 to the time of this writing (2012) Grimes has played more than five hundred concerts (including many festival dates) in twenty-nine countries and has toured the United States, Canada, Europe, and the Near and Far East.[17] In all these appearances he has been accompanied by Margaret Davis Grimes, who since 2003 has taken charge of the business side of his artistic work, including publicity.

'Moments are the echoes of a spectral explosion'[18] – Henry Grimes as Musician and Poet Today (Fall, 2003–)

In early September, 2003, Henry made his first tour as a newly reconstituted New Yorker to Los Angeles, where among other things he gave a concert with Joseph Jarman (reeds).[19] Back in New York, a number of major appearances were waiting for him: on October 30 the BBC interviewed him in the Village Vanguard, where he had appeared with Cecil Taylor and Albert Ayler in the 1960s; on November 9 he appeared in the WKCR studio with his *The Call* trio of 1965 – Perry Robinson (clarinet) and Tom Price (drums); and on November 13 and 20 he was a special guest in Marc Ribot's Django Reinhardt Project. This latter gig marked the beginning of a close musical collaboration with the guitarist that has continued to the present day. On November 23 he stood at the bass for a studio recording headed by Dennis Gonzalez (trumpet),[20] and on December 4 he played in the New York club called Tonic to mark the birthday of drummer Denis Charles (who had died in 1998), with whom he had played in the 1960s along with Cecil Taylor and Steve Lacy. Other notable guests on this memorial concert were Pheeroan akLaff (drums), Rashied Ali (drums), Ted Curson (trumpet), and William Parker (bass).

One highlight in the final months of this eventful year was Grimes' first European tour since the 1960s; playing with Perry Robinson (clarinet) and Andrew Cyrille (drums), he toured six cities in Italy from December 7 to 13, 2003, including Milan, Bologna, and Rome, and gave a concert in Ljubljana, Slovenia. Gianni Morelenbaum Gualberto, the artistic director of the Aperitivo In Concerto Festival (Teatro Manzoni, Milan), wrote of the trio: 'Henry Grimes' music is mysteriously profound, and we were astounded by the deep, dark expressive power that hit us from his bass. And we feel grateful also to the ever searching musicianship of Perry Robinson and the phenomenal skills of Andrew Cyrille. We were witnesses to a sound sculpture coming to birth.'[21]

Grimes' final concert in 2003 took place on December 18. It was also the first appearance of the free jazz ensemble Spiritual Unity, which had just been founded by Marc Ribot, and which also included Roy Campbell, Jr. (trumpet) and Chad Taylor (drums).

William Parker and Henry Grimes, Houston Hall, University of Pennsylvania, Philadelphia, February 16, 2004 (© Jaci Downs).

This project would probably never have materialized without Grimes' re-emergence. Margaret Davis Grimes precisely recalls how the contact between Henry and Marc Ribot came about in 2003: 'After Henry had been back in New York for couple of months, and feeling that the phone wasn't ringing as often as it should, I decided to send out an emailing to 150 of the New York musicians I thought worthy, in order to make sure they knew that Henry was back and available and how to contact him. The first person to call the very next morning was Marc Ribot, and he said, "If this is the same Henry Grimes who played bass with Albert

Ayler on my two favorite albums in the whole world, both recorded on the same day, I definitely want to work with him!'"[22]

As a crowning finish to Grimes' comeback year, he was named Musician Of The Year by the music magazine *All About Jazz, New York*.[23] A few months later, Ken Weiss for *Cadence* magazine asked him how it felt to be back in the music world as 'one of the hottest names in music'. Grimes returned the question with subtle irony ('Oh really, I'm the hottest?') and added that the completely unexpected attention he was now receiving came from the past: 'The way I look at it now is that I am experiencing attention that I never had before. I am getting attention from the past.'[24] He was right, but it soon transpired that the attention came at least as much from his current musical prowess.

In 2004 Grimes' activities redoubled compared to 2003. It was as if he wanted to make up for everything he had missed over the decades. He toured Europe no fewer than five times and Canada twice, concertized in various American cities (including, once again, Los Angeles), and made numerous appearances in his newly rediscovered home base of New York. He held bass workshops in California and New York City and carried out many concert projects of his own, including a quintet with Bennie Maupin, Dan Clucas, Jane Getz, and Alex Cline, with which he appeared in California in early 2004, and a quartet with Jemeel Moondoc (soprano saxophone, alto saxophone), Khan Jamal (vibraphone), and Hamid Drake (drums), with whom he toured Finland, Sweden, Italy, and Belgium in November.

Vibraphonist Khan Jamal, writing in 2009, waxed ecstatic about Grimes' musical skills on this tour: 'The tour I did with Henry Grimes was fantastic [...] We had packed houses every night. Henry is an exceptional musician. He can play anything. He's got a relaxed nature and he plays that way. He's got a fluid technique. He plays from his heart. He's among the long list of great Philadelphia bass players that we have.'[25]

But above all, Henry Grimes formed trios in 2004. He recorded the album *Sublime Communication* with Andrew Lamb (saxophones, flute) and Newman Taylor Baker (drums, percussion)[26] – an ensemble that *New York Press* voted Best Jazz Trio Of The Year in November 2004, prompting the editor Steven Psyllos to write,

'Henry Grimes plays the bass with absolute control, spinning tales without words, enriching the room with the depth of his bass.'[27] Grimes also played many gigs with David Murray (bass clarinet, tenor saxophone) and Hamid Drake, including one at the Kerava Jazz Festival in Finland on June 5. 'Henry Grimes' playing, technique, and sense of style are brilliant [...] supple and resolute,' wrote Jukka Haaru for Finland's great daily newspaper, *Helsingen Sanomat* (Helsinki News).[28] The concert was recorded and released on CD in 2005.[29]

Ben Young, writing in the liner notes for *Live At The Kerava Jazz Festival*, found that 'Henry's natural sense of collage brings him to use scraps of melody in an interpretive improvisation that [...] falls freely out of the cycle of the song as Grimes sees fit. He sits as happily in time as out, arco as pizzicato, and enjoys a contemporary freedom.' William Parker continued in the same liner notes: 'This music is truly a collective effort. In fact, in an improvising trio it has to be. Everyone is bringing something to the table that extends and expands the language of music while confirming all the elements that have lasted throughout the ages. The human heartbeat, the pulse of souls testifying.'[30] The critic Glenn Astarita, like so many others in these years,[31] praised Grimes' undiminished skills despite his long forced abstinence from the bass: 'Naturally, the first question that would come to mind is whether or not Grimes lost his stride or technique. Well, there's no hint of that here, as the bassist and Drake execute with the force of a revved-up locomotive. In addition, Grimes possesses a rather enviable tone, enamored with winding, arco passages, and a resonating single-note attack. In fact, he's in command, and his presence is an integral part of the trio's chemistry.'[32]

Marc Medwin's review is devoted particularly to Grimes' composition *Spin* and points out a difference in his sound as compared to the 1960s:

Despite fireworks of all colors and shapes from Drake and Murray, however, Grimes softly steals the show with his bass solo on 'Spin'. I hope it will eventually be the subject of a thorough analytical study; its conception and execution are so unified that it might have been a free-standing 'organic' composition. Its first half bowed and the remainder plucked, it begins nebulously enough, like Mahler's first symphony, with strong hints of the pitch A amidst clusters of rising harmonics. As melodic fragments gradually emerge, they still hover around B-Flat, G, sometimes intimating G-sharp, but often leaving A implicated if not achieved. The arco section exudes white heat, but key moments of silence, especially in the plucked passages, speak even further to Grimes' compositional leanings as a soloist and to his continued and re-invigorated power as a diversely gifted improviser. His sound is leaner but more direct than on much of his 1960's work, but his energy and evident enthusiasm remain undimmed.[33]

Marc Ribot Trio – Henry Grimes, Chad Taylor, MR at the Stadtgarten, Cologne, October 19, 2013 (© Jochen Fleeth).

From July 23 to 27 'Grimes, the returnee' toured France with his trio featuring 'the rare pianist Onaje Allan Gumbs and the decisive drummer Charli Persip'.[34] Another of Grimes' trios of 2004, with which he toured Europe in September, featured Perry Robinson (clarinet) and Andrew Cyrille or John Betsch (drums). Bill Shoemaker raved about the trio concert in his review: '[H]earing him at the helm of a trio with clarinetist Perry Robinson and drummer Andrew Cyrille at Wien Music Gallerie's annual cutting-edge festival confirmed that Grimes has reclaimed his world-class stature solely on the merits of his playing, which are considerable.'[35] Grimes also played in a trio with Charles Gayle (tenor saxophone) and Chad Taylor (drums), with whom he appeared, for example, at radio station WKCR-FM on December 16 and the next day in the

Vision series at the Church of St. Luke in the Fields, NYC.[36]

The fact that *Jazz Magazine* (France) could equate Grimes' ownership of a bass with the recovery of his voice says it all.[37]

No less numerous than his own projects of 2004 were his collaborations with other leading figures in free music, such as Marilyn Crispell, William Parker, and Marc Ribot, who invited him into their ensembles. In May he played in William Parker's *Requiem* for Peter Kowald and Wilber Morris, given at the Ninth Vision Festival on May 31, 2004. Besides Parker and Grimes, the bass quartet also included Alan Silva and Sirone, with Charles Gayle on alto saxophone.[38]

Equally worthy of mention is Grimes' involvement in Marc Ribot's quartet Spiritual Unity, which was devoted to the music of Albert Ayler and also included, up to December 2012, Roy Campbell, Jr. and Chad Taylor. In October, 2008, Marc Ribot formed a new trio, just with Henry Grimes and Chad Taylor, and a new kind of repertoire. This time, rather than focusing on Ayler's music, the group cultivated a wide range of musical connections, for example, John Coltrane, Jimi Hendrix, the American Songbook, country music, and rural blues. Daniel Graham fittingly describes this fusion as 'a pantheistic array of musical disciplines, from the 1960s love cry of Albert Ayler to the timeless, heartfelt patterns of country music and the untrammeled immediacy of its rather distant cousin, the blues.'[39]

Spiritual Unity played in Switzerland and Italy in August 2004 and entered the studio on October 27–28 to produce an album released under the title *Spiritual Unity* in 2005.[40] Ribot himself has spoken frequently about his project, explaining that it is related not just to Ayler's music,[41] but specifically to Grimes' contribution as well:

> Henry has unbelievable ears and what he plays will always relate to what's going on in some completely unpredictable and beautiful way. It's tempting to write off the density of his playing as just him going off the deep end, but when you listen to it, you hear the melody of the tune you're playing sped up, counter-pointed, harmonized, attacked, distorted, played backwards. He's really a Cecil Taylor of the bass. And he has his own version of playing grooves related to some strain of sixties funky jazz that we think we remember, but we don't. When I play with Henry, it's as if I'd only

seen synthetic fabrics my whole life, and I'm confronted with a hand-knitted wool sweater with all its oddities and imperfections – different, yet infinitely warmer. He's the living embodiment of the difference between groove and metronomic time, which we were all taught were the same thing, right? Wrong.[42]

Another important event happened in 2004: on November 3, Grimes' sixty-ninth birthday, the gift of a violin fulfilled a long-cherished wish of his. All his appearances since September 2005 have featured this instrument, which enthralled him even as a boy, and on which he soon developed 'his own language'.[43]

Grimes carried on his concert activities with the same intensity in 2005. In March he toured the United States together with Marshall Allen (reeds), a member of the Sun Ra Arkestra since 1958 and leader of the Arkestra from 1995. The tour, called Spaceship on the Highway, led on March 11 to 12 to a meeting with tenor saxophonist Fred Anderson, a founding member of the AACM (Association for the Advancement of Creative Musicians) who operated the Velvet Lounge Club in Chicago from the 1980s. Until his death on June 24, 2010, Fred Anderson worked with Henry Grimes on a regular basis. The Chicago journalist Michael Jackson, in his review of this 2005 concert, especially emphasizes Grimes' charisma: 'The free-form summit was dominated by stratospheric eruptions from Allen's unfettered alto, mellifluity from his antiquated EWI [electronic wind instrument], and cosmic poetry, which Anderson backed with bluesy fills and Ra colored with pipings from a cedarwood flute. Nevertheless, the night belonged to Grimes, whose customized space bass boomed beneath his lean, agile fingers. He knew exactly what to do.'[44]

April witnessed an extended tour of Europe with Marc Ribot's quartet Spiritual Unity, followed in May by another European tour, this time in a trio with Marilyn Crispell (piano) and Andrew Cyrille (drums). Back in the United States, Grimes could be heard on June 14 at New York's Vision Festival, where he appeared with his quartet, consisting of himself with Marshall Allen, Andrew Lamb, and Hamid Drake. Maggie Williams, the editor of the now defunct magazine *Double Bassist*, wrote of the concert: 'Grimes sculpts tones from his bass with a sense of time that continually subdivides the pulse into tributaries of counter-comments. As the energy of the performance reaches a natural cadence, Grimes pulls a funky riff from the air that relights fire-crackers under the band. And with his final solo, Grimes' fingers scurry down the fingerboard in some seemingly abstractly choreographed pattern, except that the musical sense of what he plays communicates instantly.'[45]

The festival was accompanied by a book in which the participating musicians wrote about their personal visions. Grimes' contribution shows that, for him, improvisation is a living dialogue and a free expression of will *per se*. Yet his words express gratitude toward all those who had made it possible for him to return to music. He had indeed recovered his voice, and it allowed him to grow with each new day:

> *I have a vision – and a dream. Both things coincide. Each is part and parcel of each other thing.*
>
> *It includes the groove that I love, playing and making a language come over to someone in my audience to communicate what I can only feel, not hold out to the communing. Something readily synchronic as success.*
>
> *Don't get me wrong. I feel successful, very successful. Doing the things that I want to do that find room and time as aesthetic, and as often finding the incidence of my art. It's good that it takes in life and time as they are now, and in and at this time of life. It is my dream to do this. It is my dream of being.*
>
> *I love that groove.*
>
> *The Vision Festival is certainly part with both my dream (or dreams) and my vision (or visions). I am very happy and proud to be and have a part with it. I have grown immensely by being here.*
>
> *Many thanks.*
> *Henry A. Grimes* [46]

On September 17, 2005, Grimes played the violin for the first time in public (as an adult). It happened in the New York club The Stone during a duo concert with William Parker that bore the legend 'Sharing the Torch'. The club's website has this note on the event in its archive:

Henry Grimes and William Parker, both primarily bassists, share a deep brotherhood in the music. When William was a young teenager, he heard and never forgot Henry Grimes playing bass in a bowling alley in the Bronx, as well as on many cherished records. When Henry in his later years was without a bass to play, William sent him one so Henry could return with his musical gifts to us all. Let us rejoice![47]

Three days later, on September 20, Grimes appeared with other leading avant-garde figures, including Amiri Baraka, Andrew Cyrille, Bill Dixon, Hamid Drake, and Charles Gayle, at the Vision Festival benefit for New Orleans, held at New York's Angel Orensanz Center. Shortly before then, Hurricane Katrina had wreaked its path of destruction in New Orleans, and the US government had left the ravaged city and its desperate citizens to fend for themselves, provoking widespread public outrage. On September 21 and 22, Grimes, along with Andrew Cyrille (drums), appeared at the John Coltrane birthday celebration in New York's Birdland, where Grimes was a special guest in the band of tenor saxophonist Joe Lovano.[48]

From late September to mid-October Grimes again undertook a long European tour, beginning with a bass master class at the Darmstadt Jazz Institute in Germany. There followed concerts with his trio, now made up of David Murray and Hamid Drake, with Sunny Murray taking over the drums from Drake in Lille on October 7. Laurent Rigaut, in his review of the latter concert, stressed Grimes' harmonic skills as leader: 'After the first set, [David] Murray sent the smile of Batman's Joker in my direction and, as Sunny Murray sped up the tempo to a point where any return to the theme was unthinkable, Grimes patiently reconstructed the harmonic connections so that the three men could find their way back together. What a boss!!!'[49]

On October 8, Grimes again appeared with Marc Ribot's Spiritual Unity, this time at the Frankfurt Jazz Festival in Germany.[50] There followed two further European concerts with Marilyn Crispell (piano) and Andrew Cyrille (drums). Then, back in New York, Henry played at The Stone with Bill Dixon (trumpet) at the Don Cherry Festival on October 16.

The year 2005 also saw a few recording sessions for albums. Two of the year's numerous concert appearances, many accompanied by interviews,[51] were recorded live and released. On October 22 Henry Grimes and his trusty trio of Andrew Lamb (reeds, flutes) and Newman Taylor Baker (drums, percussion) gave a high-powered concert in Ann Arbor, Michigan, that was released on CD in 2006. The longest improvisation on the CD, with the evocative title *Dancestors*, comes from Grimes, the two others from his fellow trio members.[52] Grimes aficionado Marc Medwin compared Henry's bass playing with that of two great avant-garde guitarists: 'From note one, the disc crackles with an almost unbearable energy as Sir Henry roars in with speed, power and precision; he's almost 'shredding', so to speak, combining the effortless tonal range of a Derek Bailey with the visceralgia and wide timbral pallet of Sonny Sharrock.'[53]

On October 28, Grimes performed at the Madame Walker Theatre in Indianapolis, Indiana, as leader and bassist in a trio with Andrew Lamb (reeds, flute, clarinet) and Avreeayl Ra (drum kit, percussion, bamboo flute, mbira, small instruments), along with

Their last performance together: Amiri Baraka and Henry Grimes at Arika's Episode 4: 'Freedom is a Constant Struggle' at Tramway, Glasgow, April 21, 2013 (© Alex Woodward).

guest artist Aaron Ibn Pori Pitts (spoken word). At the end of the concert they all joined forces with the IsWhat? duo, who had opened the concert. The performance was broadcast by the radio station WFHB of Bloomington (Indiana) and released in a limited edition on CD.[54] Grimes ended this musically active year on December 17 with a studio date in Brooklyn at the invitation of pianist Luis Perdomo.[55]

The years that followed have likewise proved enormously productive. Every year, Grimes tours Europe at least once and appears at the Vision Festival in New York. He has already served as artist-in-residence or held bass workshops and master classes at several renowned universities and institutes of learning. In the United States and Canada these include Bard College (upstate New York), Berklee College of Music (Boston), Buffalo Academy for Visual and Performing Arts (upstate New York), CalArts – hosted by Wadada Leo Smith (Valencia, California), City College of New York, Hamilton College of Performing Arts – with Rashied Ali (upstate New York), Humber College (Toronto), Mills College – hosted by Roscoe Mitchell (Oakland, California), New England Conservatory (Boston, Massachusetts), University of Illinois at Urbana-Champaign (Illinois), the University of Michigan at Ann Arbor, and several more, while in Europe he appeared at the Carlucci School with Andrew Lamb and Newman Taylor Baker (Portugal), Jazz Institute Darmstadt (Germany), Scuole Brusio and Scuole Poschiavo in Switzerland (Uncool Festival), and the University of Gloucestershire (U.K.).[56]

The list of the world's leading musicians and artists Grimes has worked with since 2006, sometimes repeatedly, is long: Pheeroan aKlaff, Rashied Ali, Geri Allen,[57] Marshall Allen,[58] Fred Anderson,[59] Billy Bang, Amiri Baraka (who died in 2014 – Grimes' last date with him was in spring 2013 in Glasgow),[60] Cooper-Moore, Marilyn Crispell,[61] Andrew Cyrille,[62] Dave Douglas, Edward 'Kidd' Jordan, Andrew Lamb, Joe McPhee, Roscoe Mitchell, David Murray, Sunny Murray (in his big-band project and documentary film *Sunny's Time Now*, 2007),[63] Zim Ngqawana, Kresten Osgood, Evan Parker, Profound Sound Trio (Andrew Cyrille, Paul Dunmall, Henry Grimes), Avreeayl Ra, Marc Ribot,[64] Roswell Rudd, Wadada Leo Smith,[65] Tyshawn Sorey, Cecil Taylor, Newman Taylor Baker, John Tchicai, John Zorn, and many others.[66]

A few remarkable way stations in his musical career since 2006 merit special notice. On July 1, 2006, he played in a duo with the California multi-instrumentalist Oluyemi Thomas (bass clarinet, soprano saxophone, musette, gong, flute, percussion) at the Modern Formations Gallery in Pittsburgh. The concert was recorded live and released under the title *The Power of Light* in 2007.[67] Marc Medwin reviewed the album with his usual sensitivity:

> [I]t affirms again the voices of those brave souls, past and present, who dared to make this music what it is, to endow it with such multivalent and beautiful traditions, steeped in the language of victory over oppression. [. . .] This meeting of veterans blends intuition and craft in a way that makes each player sound larger than life. If Thomas creates a world, Henry Grimes is the world beneath, rapping propulsion and rock-solid support into inspired technique. He too draws into what John Coltrane has labeled the reservoir from which all musicians drink, blues celebration pervading the opening of 'Fractured Flow'. Plucked notes produce wondrously shadowy counterparts an octave or more above as the rhythmic solo builds, the point of most tension topped off by a transcendentally humorous rising bit of arco, a crowning gesture of which only the finest musicians are capable. On 'Hidden Mystery', Grimes' arco work sounds as if it's coming from two bassists, so wide are the intervals he's mastered. As Thomas plays bells, Grimes covers the range of a string quartet, interweaving hushed harmonics with deft precision and exquisite taste. 'Hidden Mystery' demonstrates how well the two musicians' approaches mesh; as Grimes lays down a spacious and constantly morphing series of patterns, Thomas responds with contrapuntal flute exhortations, the two becoming benevolent gatekeepers of world culture transmitted through the microtone.[68]

Time and again, music journalists have emphasized Grimes' calm and modest demeanor combined with his charismatic and deeply spiritual personality. Here, for example, is Daniel Graham writing about the concert Henry Grimes gave with David Murray and Sunny Murray at the Haarlem Jazzstad Festival (Netherlands) on August 18, 2006: 'A man of few words, Henry was, however, completely accommodating and grateful – a giant of the music and one helluva nice man. Speaking specifically of the music played, Grimes displayed his trademark sound, deft technique, creativity and authority on the instrument [. . .].'[69]

Rashied Ali and Henry Grimes, WKCR Studios, NYC, March 20, 2007 (© Michael Lowe).

Grimes' appearance in Marc Ribot's Spiritual Unity project, and a brief meeting that followed his performance in London with Evan Parker left the critic similarly impressed:

> Grimes was superb throughout, demonstrating the same commanding technique and large, authoritative tone that dominated his recorded work of the 1960s. [...] Later that night Grimes, Taylor and Campbell were joined onstage at the Pizza Express Jazz Club in Soho by none other than British Jazz Godfather Evan Parker for a brief, ten-minute performance being recorded for a radio broadcast. [...] It was pure gold. An experience that was over so quickly but one that will linger for a long time to come. As an addendum to this piece, a brief conversation with Henry Grimes after the late night gig revealed his feelings about working with musicians such as Cecil Taylor. Grimes recounted that Taylor's standard of musicianship was so high that playing with him automatically lifted your own performance and, as a consequence, that of the entire group. Henry Grimes himself is now that man who inspires greatness by example.[70]

Hardly a year later, Grimes once again had an opportunity to appear on stage with Cecil Taylor. Following this concert at New York's Blue Note, Jonathan Kantor asked him whether his music had changed since the 1960s. He was at no loss for an answer: 'I think it's changed vastly and drastically. The change is in a technical sense, but the philosophy of life really changed the way I play.'[71]

Kantor also asked Grimes whether he was shocked to be playing at the same place where he had appeared thirty-five years earlier. Henry answered with characteristic thoughtfulness:

> Yeah, the same place, except for people like Margaret, William, and others helping me and giving me the support I needed to get to where I am going. They were beautiful. It's hard to explain. Was it fate? Well, I can think of a poem or a sketch that could describe how I feel about it, but poetry wouldn't be the best way to describe things to a material society. If you want to say that it was meant to be, philosophically or something like that, you can go ahead and do that if you want. I just prefer to describe it as something that came to me. Things come to me in many directions and it's just a matter of enlightenment or spirit. I would call it an act of God, in a sense, which is a term I got from one of the European philosophers.[72]

One of Grimes' outstanding recent musical achievements is the duo concert he gave with Rashied Ali (trap drums) at the studio of Columbia University's WKCR radio station on March 20, 2007, released on CD under the title *Going To The Ritual* (2008). Here Grimes plays bass and violin and recites the poem 'Easternal Mysticism, Virtue And Calm' from his début volume of poetry, *Signs Along The Road*. The album takes its title from a line in the poem.[73] The titles of the first piece ('Hidden Forces Aggregate'), the third ('Gone Beyond the Gate'), and the fourth ('This Must Have Always Happened') are also taken from lines in this poem, which lent its title to the second piece. Besides the poem itself, the CD booklet also contains drawings by Grimes entitled 'Musicology', 'Going To The Ritual', and 'Easternal Mysticism.' Revealingly, the drums in these drawings are depicted with wings, as is the bass in 'Easternal Mysticism.' This was Grimes' and Rashied Ali's first musical get-together in forty-two years; in 1965 they had both played on Archie Shepp's album *On This Night*. Marc Medwin, in his liner notes, sheds light on the musical cosmos of the recording:

> When craft and commitment equalize, especially as reflected in this music, born of dawned, dimmed, and dashed hopes and fears of life in our bittersweet country, only then can what you're hearing emerge; only after the prerequisite travail can the burden be laid

down, the journey documented, and some sort of uneasy peace attained. Sticks, bows and strings embrace, enmesh and encircle, simultaneously support and entrapment necessitating raging love, the forceful play of willing and wise men whose growth defies enforced apathy and brutal stagnation – as, with humility and certainty, Henry Grimes and Rashied Ali approach The Ritual. [...] Henry enters, introspection worn lightly on his shoulders, joining Rashied in roots movement, the clicking strings bearing immediate polyrhythmic fruit. Aware of the increase, so absolutely and completely aware, Rashied greets him with pleasure, three bass-drum hits, adorned with cymbal, falling in perfect syncronicity as Henry triton[e]s his way to ... the brief repose of two brothers at the first of many hilltops. Just for a moment, a jeweled instant, time hangs suspended in admiration.[74]

Marc Medwin found Henry Grimes' violin playing especially spellbinding: '[T]he greatest surprise is Henry on violin! Ethereal, gritty, luminously frozen and heatedly static by turn, his violin manifests his poetry; the Easternal is so wonderfully captured in every moment, every microtone, every soft peak and valley along the road issuing forth from wells of infinite calm'[75].

In no small measure, the publication of the first volume of his poetry, *Signs Along The Road*,[76] gave Grimes a boost and helped him to reach these musical heights. The book appeared in early 2007, shortly before the studio recording with Rashied Ali. Since then Grimes has regularly recited his poetry at concert dates. Anyone who reads the poems by themselves may well discover, like David Grundy, that they too raise their voices in the silence: '*Signs Along The Road* seems to read itself aloud inside one's head as one reads. It's a phenomenon that I don't recall ever happening to me with any other kind of poetry – the voice that plays itself out in my head is not that of Henry Grimes, nor is it mine, and perhaps it is not even fully a voice, but it does exist in some capacity.'[77]

The year 2007 held another surprise in store: a tour of Japan and Korea with a group headed by Yoriyuki Harada (piano) and featuring Tobias Delius (tenor saxophone), Tristan Honsinger (cello), Henry Grimes (bass, violin), and Louis Moholo-Moholo (drums). The group played to large crowds in concert halls, arts centers, and museums in Tokyo, Kofu City, Nagoya, and Kyoto, Japan, and in Seoul, South Korea.

Grimes continued to develop his powers of improvisation in the next year, 2008. An email arrived from the Danish drummer and record producer Kresten Osgood on March 8, 2008. It read:

Dear Henry and Margaret,

I am arriving in New York on Monday and I have a proposition for you. Sitting right in front of you at the concert in Copenhagen, Henry, I heard some things that I have never heard before, and I got to thinking that I would really like to hear a solo recording of you so that I could listen even more closely to your melodies. I don't know if such an album has been made, but I would like to offer to record you solo. I don't know if you are interested in doing it or if you have time in your schedule while I am in New York. I imagine something like this: We will find one day between March 13th and 30th. I will book a studio and pay all expenses – car service, food, studio rent, tech, and so on. You come in, do exactly what you feel like for as long as you feel like. [...] I will put the music out on a Danish artist-owned label called ILK music, where I have released most of my own records. Its not big business, but the vibe is right and I like that fact that it's not corporate. You will own all composing rights and receive some cds you can sell (we can figure out together how many).[78]

On March 22 Grimes entered Peter Karl Studios in Brooklyn to make the solo album. The appreciation and respect Kresten Osgood showed him inspired Grimes greatly, and while Osgood thought Grimes would probably play for forty-five minutes or an hour, he began by playing the bass for a while, then switched smoothly to violin, played that for a while and switched back, and when he came to a stop, it was more than two hours later.[79] The result was two-and-a-half hours of continuous improvisation, played alternately on bass and violin, and 'digging deep into his most creative world of sounds'.[80]

Once immersed in this flow of ideas, he keeps the listener transfixed. Marc Medwin: 'Much of the intrigue of his playing comes from the emergence of these movements in his mind. So unpredictable is each motivic and timbral transformation that when Grimes trades bass for violin, you'd never guess that a half-hour has already passed.'[81] It is the spontaneous multi-layered variety that breathes such vitality into this extended solo, whose violin sections sometimes recall Gidon Kremer's readings of the Bach partitas. Mark Urness: 'The music is at turns disjunct and conjunct, atonal and diatonic, non-pitched and melodic, arhythmic and grooving; it is a study in variety and timbral / rhythmic / melodic opportunity.'[82]

Canadian critic Nilan Perera describes the solo double album as 'uninterrupted documents of Grimes flowing from arco to pizzicato, from bass to violin, with blurs of dense complexity folded into the melodic simplicity of nursery rhymes. It's a stream-of-consciousness that's unmarred by affectation, uncertainty or a lack of clarity, and, yes, it has a story (albeit a long one) to tell, with theme and narrative intact. This is a stunning piece of work!'[83]

Mitch Myers finds 'the fearless confidence Grimes exudes on bass [...] most impressive, and his stream-of-consciousness solo work puts him right up there in the pantheon of rare improvisers like his old boss Cecil Taylor. Grimes' technical mastery is sometimes overshadowed by his amazing creativity, but his organic skill with string-driven-things should serve as a clinic for devotees. [...] [H]e's a true model of self-realization through music.'[84]

A good two months after this solo recording, Grimes returned to the studio, again with bass and violin. The invitation had come from Roswell Rudd, who was then recording the album *Trombone Tribe*.[85] The driving force is unmistakably Grimes' bass, especially in 'No End' and the final third of 'Sand In My Slide Shuffle', and his distinctive violin playing adds effectively to the collective performance in 'Slide And The Family Bone'.

On June 14, Grimes made his annual appearance at the Vision Festival, held in 2008 at the Clemente Soto Vélez Cultural Center. A live recording of the concert, in a trio with Andrew Cyrille (drums) and Paul Dunmall (tenor saxophone, bagpipes), was released on CD the following year as *Opus de Life*.[86] The trio met for the first time on this blisteringly hot evening, and a short while later the group's name became the Profound Sound Trio – a name proposed by Margaret Davis Grimes. The trio's beginnings were highly propitious: Henry Grimes and Andrew Cyrille knew each other very well, especially from their intensive work with Cecil Taylor in the 1960s, but also from their recent post-2003 collaboration. Directly after the performance, Cyrille, alluding to Grimes' long musical silence, is recorded as saying, 'He was always in my mind.'[87] The rapport is evident from beginning to end of this roughly fifty-minute live recording, an idiosyncratic blend of 'New Thing', European classical music, folk music, and Caribbean rhythms. Having attended the concert, here are some of this author's impressions:

> The improvisation starts abruptly with 'This Way, Please', which takes up roughly the first fifteen minutes. Here one can find that the three musicians already have much to tell each other while still feeling their way. The trio quickly finds an egalitarian mode of communication. Intensity immediately fills the room, a ceaseless torrent of statements, rejoinders, and new statements, interspersed with new, delicately discerned sound relationships and continuations. Those who heard the concert live (like the present writer) saw Andrew Cyrille, at the very beginning, standing in front of his working equipment with his back to the audience, testing the spatial acoustics with his drumsticks. He deliberately entered the ritual of musical performance art, generating various tapping sounds and showing that from moment to moment, or from place to place, he rediscovers the drumset afresh. It was also Cyrille who gave the album its name, *Opus De Life*. The rattlesnake drumstrokes of this universally trained musician, the pizzicati from Henry Grimes, at first remaining discreetly in the background, only to switch quickly into the foreground with heavy, dark-toned bow-strokes (as if two bass players were on stage), and the cello-like tone from Paul Dunmall's tenor saxophone launch the trio onto its journey, accompanied again and again by cries from the excited audience. The British reedman Paul Dunmall, who combines free jazz with folk elements and for a long time traveled completely different paths with Johnny Guitar Watson, hacks through the dense undergrowth of cymbal sounds and bass pizzicati with low-register blows from his tenor-machete. Then he switches to ballad-like passages, followed by aggressive runs propelled by a wealth of pulsating improvised ideas from Andrew Cyrille. 'Call Paul', the roughly six-minute second section of *Opus De Life*, contains what is probably the strongest folk sequence on the recording: a finely gradated sound-painting of acrobatic freestyle violin, Caribbean bells, and Scottish bagpipes, the latter prolonged with baffling verisimilitude by Henry Grimes on the violin. The third piece, 'Whirligigging', does full credit to its title: Andrew Cyrille's relaxed but gradually accelerating drum rolls, seemingly

directly descended from New Orleans, mingle with cheers of delight from the audience. After three-and-a-half minutes they lead into the seventeen-minute 'Beyonder', introduced by Paul Dunmall's powerful tenor playing. Occasionally we hear a Rollins-like snippet from 'Oleo', a deeper and rougher Ayleresque tone, and judiciously applied Coltrane-like tenor shouts. The whole occurs in interaction with bass runs of orchestral proportions, bowed and plucked in swift alternation. Much as in the 'epic theatre' of Bertolt Brecht, a jolting beat wrenches the audience from what is perhaps the loveliest violin-saxophone sequence of the evening. Here Henry Grimes' extraordinary ear and intuitive sense of timbre (e.g. Paul Dunmall's East Broadway Rundown-like sounds on the saxophone mouthpiece) are heard to special advantage. After the drum beat, Andrew Cyrille continues the piece with a fairly long solo in increasing tempo, accompanied by twitterings from Dunmall's saxophone. Those who listen closely can hear Cyrille panting several times at the end of his solo act. He had almost pressed his face on the drum, remained in this unsettling posture for a good thirty seconds, and finally startled the audience yet again with a sudden beat. Roaring applause. After Lewis Barnes' brief words about the musicians comes a seven-minute encore, 'Futurity', giving another chance to experience the extraordinarily tight-knit communication among these three musicians.[88]

It comes as no surprise that the Profound Sound Trio met with great success in England the following year. As Peter Bacon puts it in his review of their concert in Cheltenham, May 2009: 'This music not only has the elemental sound of human beings, the blood pumping, the synapses snapping, but it has that astronomical scope too, the crackle, shudder of space. All three make sounds that contain multiple layers of timbre, tone and overtone which on the surface might sometimes feel like chaos, but if it is chaos it contains all manner of truths and beauties.'[89]

On March 3, 2009, Henry appeared in Brooklyn's Issue Project Room with the poet Amiri Baraka, a meeting owed not least to the publication of *Signs Along The Road*. Eli Dvorkin attended the musical reading of these two poet-artists and wrote an illuminating report of it:

The frigid wind whipping across Brooklyn's Gowanus Canal rendered Issue Project Room that much more inviting, as a throng of radicals, jazz heads, and literati poured in from the cold last

Tuesday to experience an evening with Amiri Baraka and Henry Grimes. Part of the IPR's Littoral Reading Series, which explores the intersections of music and language, Tuesday's program paired two of America's greatest living talents in a freeform encounter between poetry and jazz. [...] Baraka and Grimes are very different men with intriguing similarities. Baraka exudes a political intensity grounded both in history and in current events, while Grimes' quieter disposition hints at a complex and individualistic spirituality. However, both men remain passionate about their work, channeling powerful waves of artistic energy that belie their years (Grimes is 73; Baraka is 74). While Baraka moves in a slightly stooped shuffle, his voice retains its vitality, sounding like that of a far younger man. Grimes, meanwhile, speaks softly and with a halting cadence, although the raw physicality of his performances would seemingly tire a man half his age. Performing individually and together, the two men took the stage to warm applause. [...] Grimes' solo performance found the bassist spending equal time coaxing unearthly tones from his bass (named 'Olive Oil') and a violin, alternating short bursts of musical experimentation with excerpts from his newly published first collection of poems, *Signs Along The Road*. As Grimes' poetry came into being during his years without a musical instrument, the juxtaposition of his first love with his literary endeavors is a recent development that feels long overdue. His words articulate similar ideas as his music: a heightened spiritual sensitivity, an acute awareness of rhythm and repetition, and an obsession with the patterns behind myth and mythology.'[90]

This reading was yet further compensation for the decades that Grimes spent writing poetry in isolation and anonymity in downtown Los Angeles.

Of special personal importance in the spring and fall of 2009 were Grimes' appearances with tenor saxophonist Fred Anderson in his Chicago club Velvet Lounge. On March 18, 21, and 22, Grimes played there on the occasion of Anderson's eightieth birthday gala celebration concerts; also invited were Hamiet Bluiett, Richard Davis, Hamid Drake, Edward 'Kidd' Jordan, Nicole Mitchell, Avreeayl Ra, Chad Taylor, and the AACM star-studded Great Black Music Ensemble. On September 5 and 6, Grimes made another appearance there and joined Muhal Richard Abrams, Edward 'Kidd' Jordan, and Oliver Lake at the Chicago Jazz Festival after-sets at the Velvet Lounge.

Grimes felt especially close to Anderson both musically and personally. That the feelings were mutual is shown by the release of *Fred Anderson: 21ˢᵗ Century Chase*, on Delmark DVD #1589, with selected film clips from the eightieth birthday gala celebration concerts. In addition to Harrison Bankhead (bass, cello), Edward 'Kidd' Jordan (tenor saxophone), Jeff Parker (guitar), and Chad Taylor (drums), Henry Grimes too is immortalized on bass and violin on this DVD, released after Anderson's death.[91] "'Gone But Not Forgotten", which Jordan belatedly dedicates to Albert Ayler, is a bonus track featuring the once-and-future bassist Henry Grimes': thus Neil Tesser's liner notes to Grimes' contribution on the DVD.[92] Tesser also describes Grimes' almost devout participation in the week-long birthday gala: 'Grimes played three roles during the week marking Anderson's 80th. He performed, leading a band on the opening night of the celebration; he remained on hand as an engrossed fan, sitting front and center all week, lending his quiet authority to the proceedings; and both onstage and off, he provided another living link to the times in which he, Anderson, and Jordan took up the torch and helped propel the jazz revolution of the 60s and 70s.'[93] On "Gone But Not Forgotten", however, Grimes' uniquely agile and daunting gift for improvisation tends to remain in the background; Anderson and Jordan's tenor saxophones have the say. Still, it was the Chicagoan Fred Anderson and his like-minded colleagues who gave Grimes a renewed sense of musical and personal belonging in free music – a feeling he had lacked for decades.

Another large expansion of Grimes' musical cosmos occurred on February 7, 2009, in Gordon Theatre at Rutgers University's Camden Center: his second and, regrettably, last duo recording with Rashied Ali, who died six months later on August 12, 2009. Grimes headed the recording, which was released on CD in 2010 as *Spirits Aloft*.[94] Here, as on *Going To The Ritual*, he plays bass and violin and recites two poems ('Moments' and 'The Arch Stairwells') from *Signs Along The Road*. All the music on the album was composed jointly. It was, Grimes' website claims, 'the culminating recorded achievement of these giants as a duo, since Rashied Ali left this life a few months later. They shared three recordings, five duo concerts, one trio concert, a duo residency, and a lot of love and inspiration.'[95] Marc Medwin calls the get-together 'two brothers in hip conversation'.[96]

In the brief time allotted to these two men, they inspired each other to full flowering. Grimes made this clear in the address he gave at the Rashied Ali memorial celebration in Philadelphia's Clef Club on October 25, 2009: 'I was fortunate enough to share in the last days of brother Rashied Ali. We came out of each other's beings and had the opportunity to work on some music in a short time, and in that time we became friends.'[97] *Spirits Aloft* left the critics astonished: 'When you think of drums and bass you generally think of instruments holding the foundation of a composition together. Solid beats and structured rhythms that begin together and flow through a marching time to end on a solid down beat, however Grimes and Ali have molded a work of sound art, woven with colour, depth and passion.' Thus Paul J. Youngman's summary of the pioneering improvisations of this bass-and-drums duo.[98]

Phil Freeman, too, was amazed at their dense interdisciplinary interplay: 'Improvising in a quietly intense way that forces the listener to wonder who's making what sound.' He also stressed the high level of Grimes' playing: 'With this release, and a few before it, he proves that his chops have returned and he's every bit the player he was in the '60s.'[99]

An event of historic proportions took place the following year: a four-week concert series in which Grimes invited select musicians to the Stone in New York to celebrate his seventy-fifth birthday on November 3, 2010.[100] Gordon Marshall, in his review of this month of concerts, describes Grimes as a star who also makes his fellow musicians shine when he lays out: 'This is just a snapshot of a great, month-long event of historic significance. Other remarkable artists have included Edward 'Kidd' Jordan, Marc Ribot and Matana Roberts – and the trio Harriet Tubman. Grimes is too humble to steal the spotlight every night from his collaborators. That said, his work is so powerful and passionate, and the scope of his mind so amazingly absorbent, he is always felt – especially when he plays; but even when he is laying out, the musicians of his particular choosing still embody and magnify his vision, like light streaming from a star.'[101]

On February 17 of the following year Grimes played bass and violin in a charismatic performance with Roscoe Mitchell (saxophones) in New York, recorded live for an album.[102] Russ Musto attended the concert:

> In a belated celebration of his 70th birthday (Aug. 4th, 2010), Roscoe Mitchell made an all-too-rare New York appearance at Roulette [...] before a packed-to-the-walls audience [...]. Mitchell engaged in two sets that showed why his music is equally enthralling to modern jazz and contemporary classical listeners. [...] a second set of completely improvised music with an imposing quartet featuring Dave Burrell, Henry Grimes and Tani Tab[b]al. That music unfolded naturally from the first notes of Mitchell's alto blending harmoniously with Grimes' bowed bass, with Tab[b]al's brushes establishing a rhythmic context within which Burrell's piano roamed freely, alternately offering reinforcement and counterpoint. The music built in intensity with Mitchell's soprano mining minute tones (mirrored by Grimes' violin) while his alto filled the room with a robust sound that would climax with long amazing circular-breathed lines that pushed physical limits.[103]

Nine days later, on February 26, Grimes recorded several pieces as leader, bassist, and violinist in a concert with Roberto Pettinato (saxophones, piano, effects) and Tyshawn Sorey (drums, piano) at New York's East Side Sound Studio.[104] In this concert, he takes off on improvisatory violin and bass flights that mesh tightly with Pettinato's Ayleresque saxophone playing. Half a year later, on August 13, Grimes enlarged the group into a quartet by adding pianist Dave Burrell and recorded the album *Purity*.[105]

Grimes returned to Chicago on September 4 to play in the Velvet Lounge. Two months earlier, on June 24, his close friend Fred Anderson, the club's legendary operator and a co-founder of the AACM, had died. A live recording captures Grimes' appearance with a riveting violin solo (*Violin Song for Fred Anderson*).[106]

In 2011, Grimes himself was especially moved by his guest appearance in the Charles Mingus Big Band at New York's Jazz Standard on March 14. Here he performed 'Haitian Fight Song' on Mingus' bass, which he had already played in the 1960s in Mingus' band when the leader himself played piano. Equally important to him was his participation in the Velvet Birdhouse Coalition Community Memorial Concert for Fred Anderson, held at Chicago's

Fred Anderson and Henry Grimes, Velvet Lounge, Chicago 2010 (© Lauren Deutsch).

DuSable Museum on March 20, 2011. Also involved were the AACM Great Black Music Ensemble and Tatsu Aoki's Miyumi Project. Lauren Deutsch took a group photograph of the participants, with Grimes sitting front and center.[107] The serenity he exudes in this company reflects what he had lacked during his decades in Los Angeles: a sense of belonging.

Two days later Henry played in another memorial birthday concert for Anderson at Chicago's Jazz Showcase. Here, too, there is a live recording on which Grimes plays a violin solo invocation.[108]

Grimes still remains an intensely busy musician today. At the very beginning of 2012 he traveled with his Sublime Communication Trio to Israel, where he appeared at the Tel Aviv Jazz Festival on February 21 and at the Jerusalem Conservatory Hassadna one day later, giving a workshop with his trio and earning great acclaim and gratitude.[109] He was reluctant to play in Israel because of the Israeli treatment of the Palestinians, but after much thought and discussion, he decided to go ahead with it, believing that his music offers enlightenment and peace.[110]

On February 20, 2012, the album *Monk Mix* was released with remixes and new interpretations by various artists of music by the singer, composer, choreographer, and performance artist Meredith Monk. Here a Henry Grimes remix entitled 'Evening' (track 13) appears alongside tracks by Monk herself as well as Björk, Vijay Iyer, Paul D. Miller (*aka* DJ Spooky), Lee Ranaldo, and many others.[111]

On May 2 the Sublime Communication Trio entered Zurcher Studio in New York for a recording date. Two weeks later, from May 16 to 22, Grimes toured Canada in various formats, playing at the FIMAV Improvised Music Festival (Victoriaville, Quebec), the Quebec City Jazz Festival, and Club L'Envers (Montreal). On June 15 he made his annual visit to the Vision Festival, this time held at Roulette in Brooklyn, where he appeared with Wadada Leo Smith. Further rewarding successes of 2012 included his concerts with the Marc Ribot Trio at New York's Village Vanguard (June 26 – July 1),[112] where he had last played with Albert Ayler in 1966, and a duo concert with pianist Geri Allen at The Stone on July 24.[113] Asked about his renewed appearance at the Village Vanguard, Grimes gave this answer: 'Even though one takes place now and the other happened then, the Vanguard remains the same place for me. And I am the same person, even though I'm not.'[114]

Henry Grimes' importance to today's world of free improvisation is reflected, not only in his many concert appearances all over the world, but also in the media, including the broadcasting corporations NPR, ABC-TV News, and BBC, and such newspapers and magazines as the *New York Times*, *DownBeat*, and *Jazz Times*, all of which have followed him since 2003.[115] He has also received a number of awards and distinctions, including four Meet The Composer grants and a grant from the Acadia Foundation. In June, 2006, the Jazz Journalists Association nominated him for Acoustic Bassist Of The Year award alongside Ron Carter, Charlie Haden, Dave Holland, Christian McBride, and William Parker.[116] Especially moving for Grimes personally were a medal and certificate awarded to him by the mayor of the Hungarian City of Szeged, on November 4, 2011 (one day after his 76th birthday) during an appearance at the Szeged Jazz Days. The award honored him for his contribution to the history and ongoing evolution of jazz music.

9

'Futurity'[1] – Impressions of Henry Grimes

Like John Coltrane, Henry could play all kinds of music. We don't need to validate his existence by mentioning Juilliard (which he attended). What Henry got to on the bass you don't learn at Juilliard. Henry could get the job done with a big tone, a knack for connecting phrases together rhythmically and harmonically, deft technique and feeling whether playing arco (bowing) or pizzicato (plucking). It was all necessary and done brilliantly. When Henry Grimes was called, he could do the job to its ultimate level.

William Parker, 2005[2]

What William Parker finds praiseworthy in his fellow bassist is part of Grimes' carefully phrased self-image: 'I'm a jazz musician. Eventually I'd like to be any kind of musician.'[3] Grimes views his work as a 'challenge to go from one kind of music to another, one design to another, one expression to another. I think that is often the challenge.'[4] It is this ability of Grimes that inspired Sonny Rollins in 1959 and 1963, an ability he values to the present day: 'Whatever I attempted to play, he would never flinch. He was ready to play anything.'[5] To Andrew Cyrille, Henry is 'a quintessential bass player. He composes as he plays, and this is what the music is all about – composing, organizing, varying, then performing spontaneously. That's my definition of improvisation.'[6]

Grimes' musical universe far exceeds mechanical typologies of the sort advanced not long ago by Simon Frith:

As far as bassists are concerned, a similar broad division can be made on the basis of attack or in this case pluck. This distinction is not formally recognized by jazzmen in their argot, but it exists nonetheless, I think, and the opposition will be described here as 'stringy, light, sustained and bass-like' versus 'chunky, heavy, percussive and drum-like'. The former school (e.g., Paul Chambers, Scott LaFaro, Ron Carter, Steve Swallow) plucks higher up on the strings, away from the bridge, usually with the full side of the finger, and the tone 'emerges'. The latter group (e.g., Wilbur Ware, Henry Grimes, Percy Heath, Milt Hinton, Ahmed Abdul Malik, Gene Ramey, Eddie Jones) pluck lower down on the strings, nearer the bridge, usually with the tip of the finger, and the tone 'bursts'.[7]

By elevating musical snapshots or tendencies into 'schools', Frith overlooks the broad improvisational range not only of Henry Grimes, but of these musicians as a whole.

David Borgo comes closer with his classification scheme, though he speaks of an improvisational approach common to major pioneering avant-garde musicians rather than the technical proclivities of leading bassists: 'Despite their many differences, the first generation of African-American free jazz musicians all seemed to share an intense approach to energy, momentum, and rhythmic drive; think of Cecil Taylor, Albert Ayler, John Coltrane, Pharoah Sanders, Henry Grimes, Archie Shepp, and Sunny Murray.'[8]

The musicologist and journalist Marc Medwin, an expert on Henry Grimes, asked him specifically about his multivalent approach to music after a 2010 concert with the Marc Ribot Trio: 'How do you get from one note to the next with so many choices?' Grimes replied, 'You go forward,' and added, after a pause, 'it's very natural.'[9] Grimes' playing style embodies the flow of life, with its ceaseless transformations and unpredictable outcomes, without a prior conceptual frame of reference.[10] Not only is a logical superstructure unnecessary, but it would probably obstruct the process of improvisation.[11]

Still, Henry has a full grasp of musical concepts and musicological insights and knows exactly what he is doing. Both tend to be connected 'rhizomatically',[12] that is, the independent, unpredictable subject tends to make arbitrary use of logical references – and thus memories – at the moment of improvisation rather than constantly subordinating itself to them or 'deriving' the improvisation from them. It is more a matter of a spontaneous interplay between subliminal memory (reservoir of knowledge) and momentary expectation (dialogue with the outside world). George

E. Lewis: 'As the phenomenologists and music theorists tell us, music unfolds in both recollective and expectational time, and that process can take quite a while, extending deep into memory and involving lots of concatenative [*sic*] work.'[13]

Marc Medwin compared Grimes' instantaneously available flux of ideas with water flowing from a faucet that he can turn on or off at will – a method of operation resembling that of James Joyce: 'When you turn on a faucet, the water flows. When you turn it off again, the water stops. There's nothing simpler than that, and it's the first thing that comes to my mind when Grimes begins to play. There's no preamble, no discernable instant of consideration; everything begins, as if the music had been there, a current which Grimes taps at will and out of which he steps to speak, eat and pursue daily activities. [...] He switches between textures with uncanny ease, his narrative a stream of consciousness as rich as Joyce's.'[14]

Grimes himself sees in contemporary jazz music, and thus in his own, something which 'has grown over the years to the extent of being a new cosmic force in the universe, and that's because jazz always had the image and force of power about it, so when you talk about jazz, you talk about art being experienced way out in front of itself. People feel, understand, and speak jazz before they know other languages or things of language.'[15] For him, as for other representatives of free music, this 'something' is *a priori*, comes from the future: 'Music first. The musical idea first and then the other ideas come along later.'[16] For Grimes (and not only for him), the avant-garde principle is part of the essence of improvised music: 'The avant-garde has been with us since the 1920s and must continue to go ahead of the others into future music.'[17] He equates playing the bass with 'the science of invention'.[18]

To the free jazz bassist Michael Bisio and several of his colleagues,[19] Henry Grimes is the personification of the bass avant-garde, 'as forward-thinking as it could possibly be'.[20] The music journalist Ben Young sees in the early Grimes a musician who shocked his era as a youth and was thus far ahead of his time: 'His once rare audacity of note choice is not as shocking as it once was, and the bedrock, pep, and force of his tone while walking are now prized and rare assets.'[21]

Grimes personifies not just the bass avant-garde, but also the close interconnection between music and poetry: 'Actions and desires, truths and falsehoods, all the kinds of things that happen with music happen with poetry also.'[22] One finds deep insights into this in his notebook,[23] where he uses verbal resources to lay bare processes of improvisation (though this was not necessarily his intent). To his way of thinking, the spontaneous creation of music or series of words in poetic form resides in the future, in what one might call the perceptive mode of expecting the unexpected: 'If music is predicted to you from the future, your energy might be something that grows stronger and stronger. [...] Riding yourself to where something is stretched to that point in your imagination, that you might not be using, you know, you might want to stretch beyond the things where they are now. [...] it is a good idea, you know, you're stressing the future and a lot of things, a lot of ideas come and evolve. The whole thing is like a plan.'[24]

Here Grimes is certainly not speaking about the world of physical experience, but of what he calls a 'semantic' level. When he is in the process of finding his 'ID code' (to use his own term), he is beyond the sphere in which he does things by volition.[25] 'Most of the music in the jazz field,' he maintains, 'has a lot to do with people taking a chance, going out there'.[26] One radical advocate is, he feels, Albert Ayler, who, having set out on this path, never returned.[27] Grimes once described this quasi-automatic creative process as 'shoveling aside that aspect: me and praise of the self.'[28] For a free improviser like himself, this also means that he is unconcerned with short-term political statements. He begins at a deeper level, though without being apolitical (he participated with Amiri Baraka and others in the civil-rights and black power movements in the 1960s). He treats political causes as 'a whole other lesson, one that requires study – not just of the forces involved – but of the mythical, the mythic counterpart [to "history"].'[29] As Marc Medwin noted in this context, 'it's the mystical [...] that is the central focus of his art.'[30]

Grimes finds that many people lack the patience necessary to experience music in its totality.[31] Like other musicians who practice free improvisation, he emphasizes that music (or poetry) can never be reached on the rational level conditioned by language. Neither music nor poetry can be logically relativized. When making music, or when writing poetry, it is something 'like a real ghost who tells you, do the work.'[32] As Marc Medwin aptly notes, 'he chooses not to speak of art as creation but as essence.'[33] It is only in this sphere, which Grimes calls 'transcendent', that he makes contact, as he once put it, 'with that emotion, musical emotion. [...] It feeds [...] awareness of another world.'[34] To quote the drummer Clarence Becton, who worked closely with Grimes in 1967, 'He is going where angels fear to tread. But anyway, he has this angelic vibe about him. When I look in his eyes I don't see any malice; I see integrity, humaneness, warmth.'[35]

Henry Grimes sees his instruments – bass and violin – as 'tools I use and people that I know. [...] the violin or the double bass – with that wooden scheme – that wood holds emotions itself, they're built into it by the violin maker. [...] The instrument's voice, in theory, makes contact as a sort of theistic thought.'[36]

In the music he plays today, Grimes sees a further evolution brought about both by technique and, especially, by his life experience.[37] This is recognizable to anyone who listens closely to his recordings of the 1950s and 1960s and his playing of today. To be sure, one can note a stylistic continuity – an 'insistent pulse and skittery arco fields'[38] – but improvisational license has always been paramount, constantly communicating with the here and now and maintaining contact with the future, thereby transcending what he has learned and recalled. Howard Mandel: 'The freedom of Henry Grimes, half a century ago, evidently lent similar confidence to a generation of outward-bound explorers. He taps that same seemingly inexhaustible vein of inner freedom today from his instruments, dependably offering an immediate, unpretentious, generous and genuine response to others' musical expressions, though they may be far out and his specific pitches and note placements anything but predictable.'[39]

Grimes has conspicuously expanded his skills as a soloist with a distinctive orchestral sound, to which he has added another multi-faceted voice with the violin since 2005. His playing today reveals a change that cannot be captured in words, but only becomes manifest when tracked over a longer time span. At least since the early 1960s, his bold improvisatory energy and freedom have made him the musical leader he is today, yet never sought to become. Nowadays critics draw attention to his subtle, even subversive group charisma.[40] For example, Stephen Graham, after hearing him in concert with the Marc Ribot Trio in 2011, praised 'the simpático Grimes who, and it's not unfair to Ribot, carried the gig, presiding over every shift, subtle, obvious, rhythmic, conceptual, or otherwise.'[41]

Grimes once said of himself, 'I don't think I am really an introvert.'[42] He is fundamentally indifferent toward the material world; whenever he has something to say, he begins directly with the practice of his art and becomes virtually the opposite of the taciturn, reserved man he seems on the surface. Marc Medwin, in his interviews, similarly noted that Grimes only begins to relax and step outside himself when asked about his art: 'He does not initiate in the verbal realm; rather, he comments in brief staccato utterances. His answers to even simple questions are confusing, illuminating and touching in turn [...]. Only when he discusses his art, his ever-changing never-changing refuge, does he relax control and allow the melody of his speech to rise and fall.'[43]

Howard Mandel describes Grimes fittingly as at once silent and sound-producing: 'One is confronted with an unusual stillness as well as sound-generating impulse, ostensibly elements in contradiction, wrapped around each other at his core.'[44] Not only does he have trouble with trite tales and anecdotes from everyday life, but he takes no interest in them. Rarely does he speak about people or events. On the other hand, he gladly puts metaphysical thoughts into words. He scarcely remembers the external circumstances of recording sessions or concert tours from the 1950s and 1960s – a disappointment to some people – but when he hears old recordings on which he took part, he can often recall the music note for note.[45] Uncompromisingly, he embodies the close connection between music and a quest for truth.

William Parker touched on something essential by comparing Henry Grimes' mode of perception with that of a shaman: 'The shaman is often living on the border between these two worlds (real and ethereal). In fact, the things that would frighten most people become a source of inspiration for the beautiful ones who live in these border towns. One such person is Henry Grimes. [...] From

Henry's point of view he was never lost. He was always Henry
Grimes. Waiting and ready to fulfil his destiny. A destiny that is
bigger than any logic system.'[46]

Futuristic

> With coming spring and summer thrall
> with her —
> days on end with sound and fury
> we dance atop
> we weather —
> on top of miles musicians always play
> for continuity and futurist rounds
> of inward ways
> and time and beginnings —
> the ways of sound and fury
> on top of chords of Philosophies
> the ways of time and value —
> with her with me
> and — yes, with you.
> On days lived on top of profound years —
> we — and dancing
> from the other side of the avant-garde
> from the magic ways
> the awe of coming days
> from the times of seasons
> on apprehension days
> with all of awe and structure
> charismatic rays
> day and night to love the music.
> We climb to discover
> mind signs these days —
> hear music, magic, deep,
> the sounds before — and now —
> the sounds of life.
> And mind the colors of the reach at hand
> as they rise before
> each climax of the mind,
> the Yin and Yang
> and temples of response
> finding lost music unheard
> from other times untold
> and then the silences

Henry Grimes, 2012

Henry Grimes, artist in residence 2013 (Uncool Festival), Poschiavo, Switzerland, May 2013 (© Cornelia Müller).

Notes

Introduction

1   Henry Grimes' life story also found its way into a cultural study: Sven-Erik
Klinkmann, 'Synch/Unsynch', in Orvar Löfgren and Richard Wilk, eds.:
Off the Edge: Experiments in Cultural Analysis (Copenhagen: Museum
Tusculanum Press, 2006), pp. 84f. Klinkmann categorizes Henry Grimes
as an 'unsung person' – a stereotypical view I do not agree with.

2   He published a selection of his poetry in 2007: Henry Grimes, *Signs Along
The Road. Poems* (Cologne: buddy's knife jazz edition, edited by Renate Da
Rin, 2007).

3   Henry went on to live there for some thirty-six years.

Chapter One

1   Henry Grimes, *Henry Grimes Solo,* ILK Music 151 (2009), double CD set.
Solo on bass and violin.

2   See note 1. And for example, *Going to the Ritual*, Henry Grimes (bs, vln) and
Rashied Ali (dm), 2007; Profound Sound Trio, *Opus De Life*, (Andrew Cyrille
(dm), Henry Grimes (bs, vln), Paul Dunmall (ts, bagpipes)) 2009; *The Tone
of Wonder*, Henry Grimes (bs, vln), Uncool Edition, #2, 2013.

3   Marc Medwin, 'Playing the vibrations', *Signal To Noise* 58 (2010), pp. 12-19,
quote on p. 17.

4   Barbara Frenz, Interviews with Henry Grimes, New York City, December
2006 and January 2007; see also Medwin, 'Playing the vibrations' (see note
3), p. 17, Grimes is more restrained here: 'My parents didn't discourage me,
but they didn't encourage me either'.

5   Jonathan Kantor, 'Interview with Henry Grimes', Blue Note, New York,
May 10, 2007, bluenotenyc.blogspot.com/2007/07/interview- with-henry-
grimes-henry.html.

6   Addendum by M. Davis Grimes, in Michael Fitzgerald, 'Henry Grimes,
Past & Present: A Story in Two Parts. Part 1: A Lost Giant Found',
henrygrimes.com (viewed: January 11, 2015). See also Michael Fitzgerald,
'Into Thin Air', *Signal To Noise* 2003, pp. 40-44; a portrait of Henry Grimes
in *Double Bassist* (Winter 2007).

7   Fred Jung, 'A Fireside Chat with Henry Grimes', allaboutjazz.com/a-fire-
side-chat-with-henry-Grimes-henry-Grimes-by-aaj-staff.php?width=1024

8   M. Davis Grimes in an email, 2010. See also *Double Bassist* (see note 6).

9   Kantor, 'Interview …' (see note 5).

10   Ken Weiss, 'Interview Henry Grimes, (July 12, 2003, New York City), Taken
and transcribed by Ken Weiss', *Cadence* 2004/09, pp. 5-10, quote on p. 6.
Grimes talks about an 'elementary school' here, but probably means the
'junior high school' he attended in Philadelphia as a 12-year-old boy.

11   On the term 'jazz': Art Taylor, *Notes and Tones. Musician-to-Musician Interviews* (Boston: Da Capo Press, (1st edition 1977) 1993); Nicholas Payton , 'An Open Letter To My Dissenters On Why Jazz Isn't Cool Anymore' (2012), nicholaspayton.wordpress.com/2011/12/02/1319/ (viewed: January 3, 2015). Grimes, with his undogmatic way of thinking, convinced me to continue using the term 'jazz' or better 'jazz music'. See his thoughts about it in chapter 4.

12   Christian Broecking, ed., *Sonny Rollins, Improvisation und Protest: Interviews* (Berlin: Broecking, 2010), p. 38, interview with Max Roach in Eisenach, Germany, 1996. See also Ingrid Monson, *Freedom Sounds: Civil Rights Call Out to Jazz and Africa* (New York: Oxford University Press, 2007), pp. 283f.

13   Amiri Baraka, 'Blues, Poetry, and the New Music', in Amiri Baraka (Le Roi Jones) and Amina Baraka, *The Music: Reflections on Jazz and Blues* (New York: Morrow, 1987), p. 263.

14   Frenz, Grimes interviews 2006 and 2007 (see note 4).

15   Fitzgerald, 'Henry Grimes. Past & Present' (see note 6), Part 1.

16   Ibid.

17   Weiss, Interview (see note 10).

18   Felix Contreras, 'A Fresh Start for Jazzman Henry Grimes' (April 21, 2005), npr.org/templates/archives/archive.php?thingId=4607354&startNum=3&pageNum=5 (scroll down; viewed: January 3, 2015).

19   'They call me an introvert. I don't talk a lot. That's what they say.' Weiss, Interview (see note 10).

20   Barbara Frenz, Phone interview with Andrew Cyrille, August 8, 2008.

21   A selection of his poems appears in his volume *Signs Along The Road: Poems* (see introduction, note 2); see p. 151ff below.

Chapter Two

1   Jimmy Garrison was born in Florida and grew up in Philadelphia.

2   When Archie Shepp was about seven years old, his family moved from Fort Lauderdale, Florida, to Philadelphia, where he lived until 1960. LeRoi Jones, 'Voice From The Avant-Garde: Archie Shepp', *DownBeat* (January 14, 1965), pp. 18f. and 36.

3   Ralf Dombrowski, *John Coltrane: Sein Leben, seine Musik, seine Schallplatten* (Waakirchen: Oreos, 2002), pp. 28f.

4   Philadelphia-born trumpeter Wilmer Wise (1936-2015) in an interview with the Jazz Museum in Harlem ('Harlem Speaks', August 9, 2007), jazzmuseuminharlem.org/photos80.html (viewed: 2009).

5   Jones, 'Archie Shepp', (see note 2).

6   Hank Cherry, 'In Heaven with Henry Grimes', *Artvoice* 9, no. 36 (September 9, 2010), pp. 20f.

7   Frenz, Grimes interviews 2006-07 (see chapter 1, note 4). Grimes described

his piano playing with more restraint to Marc Medwin: 'No … My sister did that [i.e. played the piano], but I used to, well, just sort of …' Medwin, 'Playing the vibrations' (see chapter 1, note 3), p. 17.

8   Dombrowski, *Coltrane* (see note 3), p. 14.

9   See p. 7 below.

10 Frenz, Grimes interviews 2006 and 2007 (see chapter 1, note 4).

11 Medwin, 'Playing the vibrations' (see chapter 1, note 3).

12 See also Hans-Jürgen von Osterhausen, 'Die "wundersame Geschichte" des Henry Grimes', *Jazz Podium* (July 2005), pp. 11-13: 'I was told that my father played trumpet and my mother piano, but not in my time.'

13 Frenz, Grimes interviews 2006 and 2007 (see chapter 1, note 4).

14 Gerard Rouy, 'Un Revenant Nommé: Henry Grimes', *Jazz Magazine* 2004/11, pp. 26-29; see also the Henry Grimes biography on henry-grimes.com/biography/.

15 See chapter 7, p. 193ff. – His Muslim name is spelled Hassan Ibn Ali, though it is shown on the front of his one recording with Max Roach as Hasaan. His birth name was William Langford.

16 'His parents … didn't have a record player, so Wise used to go to violinist Henry Grimes' apartment to listen to bebop recordings.' Wise, Interview (see note 4); see also Osterhausen, 'Die "wundersame Geschichte"' (see note 12).

17 Grimes gave me this information personally. Frenz, Grimes interviews 2006 and 2007 (see chapter 1, note 4). However, he lost contact with his sister. See chapter 5, p. 127.

18 Jung, 'Fireside Chat with Henry Grimes' (see chapter 1, note 7).

19 Frenz, Grimes interviews 2006 and 2007 (see chapter 1, note 4).

20 Jung, 'Fireside Chat with Henry Grimes' (see chapter 1, note 7). See also Osterhausen, 'Die "wundersame Geschichte"' (see note 12).

21 Frenz, Grimes interviews 2006 and 2007 (see chapter 1, note 4). See also the addendum by Henry Grimes and M. Davis Grimes (2009) in Fitzgerald, 'Henry Grimes. Past & Present' (see chapter 1, note 6), Part 1.

22 Frenz, Andrew Cyrille phone interview 2008 (see chapter 1, note 20). See also Perry Robinson and Florence Wetzel, *The Traveler* (San José et al.: Writers Club Press, 2002), p. 119. Robinson writes that Grimes' twin brother Leon probably became a 'black nationalist'. Henry does not confirm this.

23 Jones, 'Archie Shepp' (see note 2).

24 Frenz, Grimes interviews 2006 and 2007 (see chapter 1, note 4).

25 Fitzgerald, 'Into Thin Air' (see chapter 1, note 6). See also the Henry Grimes biography on henrygrimes.com/biography/.

26 David H. Rosenthal, *Hard-Bop: Jazz and Black Music. 1955-1965* (Oxford University Press US, 1992), pp. 4f.

27 Barry Davis, 'The prodigal bass player returns', *Jerusalem Post* (February 17, 2012), jpost.com/ArtsAnd Culture/Music/Article.aspx?id=258100

28 Jones, 'Archie Shepp' (see note 2).

29   webgui.phila.k12.pa.us/schools/m/mastbaum (viewed: January 3, 2015); mast-baum.com (viewed: January 3, 2015).

30   Fitzgerald, 'Into Thin Air' (see chapter 1, note 6).

31   Frenz, Grimes interviews 2006 and 2007 (see chapter 1, note 4).

32   Marshall Marrotte, 'Henry Grimes: The *Signal to Noise* Interview', *Signal To Noise* (2003), pp. 43-47. The same interview, slightly abridged, in Marshall Marrotte, 'Surviving Albert Ayler', *The Wire* (January 2003), pp. 42f. See also Fitzgerald, 'Into Thin Air' (see chapter 1, note 6); Jung, 'Fireside Chat with Henry Grimes' (see chapter 1, note 7).

33   Medwin, 'Playing the vibrations' (see chapter 1, note 3), p. 17, where Grimes says, 'I played violin, because I played that before, and I learned bass, tympani, English horn and tuba along with it.'

34   Medwin, 'Playing the vibrations' (see chapter 1, note 3), p. 17.

35   Fitzgerald, 'Into Thin Air' (see chapter 1, note 6). See also the Henry Grimes biography on henrygrimes.com/biography/; Stefano Galvani, Interview with Henry Grimes, French trans. by Guy Reynard, *Jazz Hot* (February 2004), pp. 17f.; Grimes portrait in *Double Bassist* (see chapter 1, note 6); Jung, 'Fireside Chat with Henry Grimes' (see chapter 1, note 7).

36   For example Burton Greene; see p. 117 below.

37   Frenz, Grimes interviews 2006 and 2007 (see chapter 1, note 4).

38   Rouy, 'Un Revenant Nommé' (see note 14). In an interview with Ken Weiss Grimes said: 'By the time I got out of high school […] I got used to bass and thought I was more for the bass than other instruments.' Weiss, Interview (see chapter 1, note 10).

39   Frenz, Grimes interviews 2006 and 2007 (see chapter 1, note 4).

40   Jung, 'Fireside Chat with Henry Grimes' (see chapter 1, note 7).

41   Ibid.

42   Davis, 'Prodigal bass player' (see note 27).

43   Rosenthal, *Hard Bop* (see note 26), pp. 4f.

44   Wilmer Wise, Interview (see note 4).

45   *Coda* 1964/08, p. 27.

46   Dombrowski, *Coltrane* (see note 3), p. 36.

47   Galvani, Interview (see note 35); see also Rosenthal, Hard Bop (see note 26), p. 5 (Lee Morgan and Henry Grimes).

48   Weiss, Interview (see chapter 1, note 10).

49   Rosenthal, Hard-Bop (see note 26), pp. 4f.

50   Jones, 'Archie Shepp' (see note 2).

51   Frenz, Grimes interviews 2006 and 2007 (see chapter 1, note 4).

52   Thierry Pérémarti, 'At Home With Henry Grimes', *Jazzman* (June 2003), p. 20.

53   'When I got to Juilliard, I took up bass and stopped playing the violin.', Kantor, 'Interview…' (see chapter 1, note 5). See also Rouy, 'Un Revenant Nommé' (see note 14).

54   Profile Henry Grimes (2005), allaboutjazz.com/php/musician.php?id=1284 (viewed: 2009).

55   Kantor, 'Interview…' (see chapter 1, note 5); see also von Osterhausen, 'Die "wundersame Geschichte"' (see note 12).

56   Weiss, Interview (see chapter 1, note 10).

57   Lynell George, 'A jazz mystery unravels: Henry Grimes, the Juilliard-trained bassist who quietly walked away decades ago, is slowly reemerging', *Los Angeles Times* (March 21, 2003).

58   Ibid.

59   Frenz, Grimes interviews 2006 and 2007 (see chapter 1, note 4).

60   Ibid.

61   Marrotte, '*Signal to Noise* Interview' (see note 32).

62   Jung, 'Fireside Chat with Henry Grimes' (see chapter 1, note 7).

63   Fitzgerald, 'Henry Grimes: Past & Present' (see chapter 1, note 6), Part 1.

64   Davis, 'Prodigal bass player' (see note 27).

65   Frenz, Grimes interviews 2006 and 2007 (see chapter 1, note 4).

66   Marrotte, '*Signal to Noise* Interview' (see note 32); Frenz, Grimes interviews 2006 and 2007 (see chapter 1, note 4).

67   Galvani, Interview (see note 35).

68   Neil Strauss, 'Silent 30 Years, a Jazzman Resurfaces', *New York Times* (May 26, 2003), query.nytimes.com/gst/fullpage.html?res=9C04EFD81231F935 A15756C0A9659C8B63; also on ejazznews.com/modules.php?op=mod-load&name=News&file=article&sid=1340.

69   Frenz, Grimes interviews 2006 and 2007 (see chapter 1, note 4).

70   Kantor, 'Interview…' (see chapter 1, note 5).

71   Jung, 'Fireside Chat with Henry Grimes' (see chapter 1, note 7); see also Marrotte, '*Signal to Noise* Interview' (see note 32);

72   Marrotte, '*Signal to Noise* Interview' (see note 32).

73   Frenz, Grimes interviews 2006 and 2007 (see chapter 1, note 4).

74   Email from M. Davis Grimes to Chloé Cutts, editor of the now discontinued magazine *Double Bassist* (2007), referring to Grimes' memories.

75   Frenz, Andrew Cyrille phone interview 2008 (see chapter 1, note 20).

Chapter Three

1   Stefano Galvani, Interview (see chapter 2, note 35).

2   On Clifford Brown, Max Roach, and Sonny Rollins as an avant-garde group of the 1950s see Amiri Baraka (Le Roi Jones), 'The Phenomenon of *Soul* in African-American Music', in *The Music* (see chapter 1, note 13), p. 273.

3   Barbara Frenz, Phone interview with Sonny Rollins, January 9, 2007.

4   Pérémarti, 'At Home With Henry Grimes' (see chapter 2, note 52).

5   Frenz, Grimes interviews 2006 and 2007 (see chapter 1, note 4).

6   Peter Niklas Wilson, *Sonny Rollins: The Definitive Musical Guide* (Berkeley, 2001), p. 16; see also Nick Catalano, *Clifford Brown: the life and art of the legendary jazz trumpeter* (Oxford University Press NY, 2000), pp. 184f. (fatal car accident); Eric Nisenson, *Open Sky: Sonny Rollins and his World of Improvisation* (New York: Da Capo, 2000), pp. 186-90.

7   See p. 21 and p. 24 below.

8   See p. 52ff and p. 94ff.

9   Perry Robinson and Florence Wetzel, *The Traveler* (see chapter 2, note 22), p. 119.

10   Frenz, Phone interview with Andrew Cyrille (see chapter 1, note 20).

11   Frenz, Grimes interviews 2006 and 2007 (see chapter 1, note 4); Michael Fitzgerald, Henry Grimes Discography, 2015 (first published November 1994), jazzdiscography.com/Artists/Grimes/hg-disc.htm (viewed: May 1, 2015).

12   Michael Fitzgerald, 'Into Thin Air' (see chapter 1, note 6).

13   Frenz, Grimes interviews 2006 and 2007 (see chapter 1, note 4).

14   Ibid.

15   Ibid.

16   Ibid.

17   Weiss, 'Interview Henry Grimes' (see chapter 1, note 10); see also Medwin, 'Playing the vibrations' (see chapter 1, note 3), esp. p. 17.

18   Marrotte, '*Signal to Noise* Interview' (see chapter 2, note 32); von Oster-hausen, 'Die "wundersame Geschichte" des Henry Grimes' (see chapter 2, note 12).

19   Wilson, *Rollins* (see note 6), p. 56.

20   Frenz, Grimes interviews 2006 and 2007 (see chapter 1, note 4).

21   Ibid.

22   See also Medwin, 'Playing the vibrations' (see chapter 1, note 3), p. 17.

23   Robinson and Wetzel, *Traveler* (see chapter 2, note 22), p. 119.

24   Marrotte, '*Signal to Noise* Interview' (see chapter 2, note 32), p. 47.

25   Ibid.

26   Weiss, 'Interview' (see chapter 1, note 10).

27   Frenz, Grimes interviews 2006 and 2007 (see chapter 1, note 4).

28   Quoted from George, 'A jazz mystery unravels' (see chapter 2, note 57).

29   Fitzgerald, Grimes Discography (see note 11).

30   Shafi Hadi played the soundtrack to John Cassavetes' *Shadows* with Mingus in 1960, see Wolf Kampmann, ed., *Reclams Jazzlexikon*, (Stuttgart, 2004), p. 217.

31   Fitzgerald, Grimes Discography (see note 11).

32   *DownBeat* (September 4, 1958), pp. 28f. A mixed review of Mulligan's *Songbook* album appeared in *Jazz Hot* 136 (October 1958), p. 25, which does not mention the rhythm section.

33   *DownBeat* (September 4, 1958), pp. 29f.; Vladimir Bogdanov, Chris Wood-
     stra, and Stephen Thomas Erlewine, eds., *All Music Guide: The Definite
     Guide to Popular Music* (San Francisco: Backbeat Books, 2001), p. 1340:
     'With expert backings by bassist Henry Grimes and drummer Dave Bailey,
     these 13 selections [...] should please fans of both Mulligan and Baker.'

34   Fitzgerald, Grimes Discography (see note 11). The TV film from April 30,
     1958, was unavailable for this book.

35   Eric T. Vogel, 'Newport-Rückblick', *Jazz Podium* (August 9, 1958), pp. 181f.
     Fitzgerald, Grimes Discography (see note 11), does not list Grimes'
     Newport appearance with Gerry Mulligan, though it is mentioned in
     Vogel's review. See p. 23 below.

36   Kantor, 'Interview...' (see chapter 1, note 5).

37   Rouy, 'Un Revenant Nommé' (see chapter 2, note 14).

38   Frenz, Grimes interviews 2006 and 2007 (see chapter 1, note 4). See also
     Kantor, 'Interview...' (see chapter 1, note 5).

39   Rouy, 'Un Revenant Nommé' (see chapter 2, note 14).

40   Weiss, 'Interview' (see chapter 1, note 10).

41   Fitzgerald, Grimes Discography (see note 11).

42   Contreras, 'A Fresh Start ...', npr.org/templates/archives/archive.php?thing
     Id=4607354&startNum=3&pageNum=5 chapter 1, note 18); see also Fitzger-
     ald, 'Into Thin Air' (see chapter 1, note 6).

43   Ibid.

44   Pérémarti, 'At Home' (see chapter 2, note 52). Addendum by M. Davis
     Grimes to Michael Fitzgerald, 'Henry Grimes, Past & Present' (see chapter
     1, note 6) Part 1.

45   Christian Broecking, 'Community Talk 23. Special: Miles Today', *Jazz
     Thing*, no. 64 (June-August 2006), p. 20.

46   Weiss, 'Interview' (see chapter 1, note 10).

47   John Goldsby and Ron Carter, *The Jazz Bass Book: Technique and Tradition*
     (San Francisco: Backbeat Books, 2002), p. 124.

48   Scott Yanow, *Jazz on Record: The First Sixty Years* (San Francisco: Backbeat
     Books, 2003), pp. 557f.

49   Vogel, 'Newport-Rückblick' (see note 35).

50   Fitzgerald, Grimes Discography (see note 11).

51   Fitzgerald, 'Into Thin Air' (see chapter 1, note 6).

52   Frenz, Grimes interviews 2006 and 2007 (see chapter 1, note 4).

53   Michael Jackson, 'Backstage with ... Henry Grimes', *DownBeat* (July 2005),
     p. 14.

54   Fitzgerald, Grimes Discography (see note 11).

55   All tunes on the *Giants of Jazz* LP GoJLP 1011; see Fitzgerald, Grimes
     Discography (see note 11).

56   Weiss, 'Interview' (see chapter 1, note 10).

57   Denise Jokinen, 'Débauche de musique aussi à Newport: Soixante Mille Spectateurs Au 'Veteran' Des Grandes Festivals', *Jazz Hot* 135 (September 1958), pp. 13-15 and 35.

58   Eric T. Vogel, 'Die Sensation von Newport: Das Jazzfestival 1958 – 60.000 Besucher – Vom Duke bis Satchmo – Fergusons Wunderband: Sonderbericht unseres USA-Korrespondenten ETV', *Jazz Podium* 8, no. 7 (1958), pp. 157-60.

59   Vogel, 'Newport-Rückblick' (see note 35), p. 181.

60   *DownBeat* (August 7, 1958). The critic's name is given as '-dom'; 'Butterfield' is probably the trumpeter Billy Butterfield.

61   Jokinen, 'Débauche' (see note 57), p. 35.

62   Vogel, 'Sensation von Newport' (see note 58), p. 158; see also Whitney Balliett, *The Sound of Surprise: 46 Pieces on Jazz* (Dutton, 1959), S. 124.

63   Fitzgerald, Grimes Discography (see note 11).

64   Fitzgerald, Grimes Discography (see note 11). It is uncertain whether these tunes were released.

65   Vogel, 'Sensation von Newport' (see note 58), p. 158.

66   Jokinen, 'Débauche' (see note 57), p. 15; see also Don Gold and Dom Cerulli, 'Newport Jazz 1958', *DownBeat* (August 7, 1958), pp. 14-20 and 32f.

67   All tunes released on Philology CD W 65-2, *Newport To Nice* (1992); Fitzgerald, Grimes Discography (see note 11).

68   Jokinen 'Débauche' (see note 57), p. 35.

69   Gold/Cerulli, 'Newport Jazz' (see note 66).

70   The tune 'I Want To Be Happy', released on *Newport Jazz 1958-59* (FDC 1024). Fitzgerald, Grimes Discography (see note 11). The same tune was reissued as bonus track 1 on Sonny Rollins – Don Cherry Quartet, *Complete 1963 Stuttgart Concert*, RLR Records 2009 (the mentioned recording date of July 7, 1958, is incorrect).

71   Jokinen, 'Débauche' (see note 57), p. 35.

72   Gold/Cerulli, 'Newport Jazz' (see note 66).

73   Wilson, *Rollins* (see note 6), p. 157.

74   *Jazz On A Summer's Day (Newport Festival 1958)* by Bert Stern. Charly Films Release 2001, DVD; see Rebecca D. Clear, *Jazz on Film and Video in the Library of Congress* (Washington, DC: Library of Congress, 1993), p. 74.

75   Kantor, 'Interview...' (see chapter 1, note 5).

76   The tune 'Just You, Just Me' is released on *Newport Jazz Festival* (FDC LP 12": 1025). Fitzgerald, Grimes Discography (see note 11); the four tunes on Thelonious Monk, Trio & Quartet, *Unissued Live At Newport 1958-59 + 3 Bonus Tracks* (In Crowd Records, 2013).

77   Jokinen, 'Débauche' (see note 57), p. 35.

78   Vogel, 'Newport-Rückblick' (see note 35), p. 158.

79   Gold/Cerulli, 'Newport Jazz' (see note 66).

80 Thelonious Monk, *Thelonious Monk Trio* (Prestige CD, P-7027), 'Blue Monk' recorded Sept 22, 1954.

81 *Jazz On A Summer's Day* (see note 74). See also Vogel, 'Newport-Rückblick' (see note 35), p. 158; Burt Goldblatt, *Newport Jazz Festival: The Illustrated History* (New York: Dial Press, 1977), p. 55.

82 At the recording sessions for Thelonious Monk, *Brilliant Corners* (Riverside CD 1987, RLP 12-226), from December. See Robin D. G. Kelley, *Thelonious Monk: The Life and Times of an American Original* (New York: Free Press, 2009), pp. 211f.

83 Weiss, 'Interview' (see chapter 1, note 10).

84 Ibid.

85 Kantor, 'Interview…' (see chapter 1, note 5).

86 Rouy, 'Un Revenant Nommé' (see chapter 2, note 14).

87 *Sonny Rollins And The Big Brass* (Verve 1958), reissued on *Sonny Rollins Brass / Trio* (Polygram 1983). See also Fitzgerald, Grimes Discography (see note 11).

88 Fitzgerald, Grimes Discography (see note 11).

89 Demètre Joakimidis, *Jazz Hot* 152 (March 1960), p. 60.

90 Ibid.

91 Wilson, *Rollins* (see note 6), p. 157; see also *The Jazz Review* (1960), p. 33f.

92 See p. 12 above.

93 Frenz, Sonny Rollins interview 2007 (see note 3).

94 Fitzgerald, Grimes Discography (see note 11).

95 See p. 20 above.

96 Frenz, Grimes interviews 2006 and 2007 (see chapter 1, note 4). See also Fitzgerald, Grimes Discography (see note 11) and 'Into Thin Air' (see chapter 1, note 6).

97 Email by pianist Larry Vuckovich from December 22, 2014. See the photo on: larryvuckovich.com/photo_gallery-san_fran-fifties_sixties.htm (viewed: January 11, 2015).

98 'Interview – Don Menza (tenor saxophonist, *1936)', *Jazz Improv Magazine* 8, no. 2 (2006).

99 Patti Jones, *One Man's Blues: The Life And Music Of Mose Allison* (London: Quartet, 1995), pp. 59-61; see also Gordon Jack, *Fifties Jazz Talk: An Oral Retrospective* (Oxford: Scarecrow Press, 2004), p. 19.

100 Fitzgerald, 'Into Thin Air' (see chapter 1, note 6).

101 Weiss, 'Interview' (see chapter 1, note 10).

102 Dom Cerulli, 'Theodore Walter Rollins: Sonny Believes He Can Accomplish Much More Than He Has To Date', *DownBeat* (July 10, 1958), pp. 16f.

103 Jackson, 'Backstage' (see note 53), p. 14.

104 Bret Primack, Phone interview with Henry Grimes about his work with Sonny Rollins (2005), sonnyrollins.com (viewed: 2005). See also Rouy, 'Un Revenant Nommé' (see chapter 2, note 14).

105 Wilson, *Rollins* (see note 6), pp. 164-169; idem, *Sonny Rollins: Sein Leben, seine Musik, seine Schallplatten* (Schaftlach: Oreos, 1991), pp. 162-166.

106 'Clarke, Kenny', *Reclams Jazzlexikon* (see chapter 3, note 30), pp. 102f.

107 Frenz, Grimes interviews 2006 and 2007 (see chapter 1, note 4). See also p. 28f above.

108 Frenz, Grimes interviews 2006 and 2007 (see chapter 1, note 4).

109 Weiss, 'Interview' (see chapter 1, note 10).

110 Jung, 'A Fireside Chat with Henry Grimes' (see chapter 1, note 7).

111 Fitzgerald, 'Into Thin Air' (see chapter 1, note 6).

112 Frenz, Sonny Rollins interview 2007 (see note 3).

113 *Jazz Podium* 2, no. 8 (February 1959), p. 31.

114 Sonny Rollins, *1959 Aix-en-Provence*, CD (Royal Jazz, 1989). See also Fitzgerald, Grimes Discography (see note 11). Fitzgerald does not list the concerts in San Remo, Paris, and Stuttgart (February 21; February 23-28 and March 8; March 6). The South German Broadcasting Company (Süddeutscher Rundfunk) probably has a recording of the Stuttgart concert, but it is currently unavailable.

115 Coleridge Goode and Roger Cotterrell, *Bass Lines: A Life in Jazz* (London: Northway, 2002), p. 123. See also Jacob Larsen's liner notes for the CD Sonny Rollins, *1959 Aix en Provence* (Jeal Records, Denmark, 1989).

116 Goode/Cotterrell (see note 115), pp. 123f.

117 Frenz, Grimes interviews 2006 and 2007 (see chapter 1, note 4).

118 Goode/Cotterrell (see note 115), p. 123, and Larsen, Liner notes (see note 115).

119 Ibid.

120 Lars Westin, Liner notes for the CD *St. Thomas: Sonny Rollins Trio in Stockholm 1959* (Dragon Records, 1993). – The video clips of 'It Don't Mean a Thing', 'Paul's Pal', and 'Love Letters' on sonnyrollins.com/videolibrary/ (viewed: January 3, 2015).

121 *St. Thomas: Sonny Rollins Trio* (see note 120), reissued on Sonny Rollins Trio. *Live in Europe 1959: Complete Recordings*, two CDs (Solar Records, 2011), CD 1: tracks 1-7, CD 2: tracks 8-11.

122 Wilson, *Rollins* (see note 6), pp. 166-68. Also see the the video clip of 'It Don't Mean a Thing' on www.eyeneer.com/video/jazz/sonny-rollins/it-dont-mean-a-thing.

123 Wilson, *Rollins* (see note 6), p. 167.

124 Ibid.

125 Ibid.

126 Sonny Rollins Trio, *Live in Europe 1959* (see note 121), CD 1: tracks 8-12.

127 Dieter Zimmerle, 'Alleingang und Team: Rollins und die Silver-Truppe', *Jazz-Podium* 4, no 8 (1959), p. 86.

128 'Pour ou Contre: Le trio Sonny Rollins', *Jazz Hot* 142 (April 1959), p. 32 (Gérard Brémond) and p. 33 (Aris Destombes); quote from Brémond on p. 32.

129 Review by Aris Destombes (see note 128).

130 Frenz, Grimes interviews 2006 and 2007 (see chapter 1, note 4).

131 Fitzgerald, Grimes Discography (see note 11).

132 The 4 tunes of the Frankfurt concert were issued for the first time on Sonny Rollins Trio, *Live in Europe 1959* (see note 121), CD 2, tracks 4-7.

133 The dates for this booking conflict; see footnote 134 below.

134 sonnyrollins.com/videolibrary/ (viewed: January 3, 2015); youtube.com/watch?v=szUmFrzHbCA&playnext=1&list=PL2D4oC92437FD71A5&index =21 (viewed: January 3, 2015); Fitzgerald's presumed date of February 21 for Laren is unlikely, for the trio was in distant San Remo on that day, *Grimes Discography* (see note 11). The new CD release Sonny Rollins Trio, *Live in Europe 1959* (see note 121), tracks 1-3 on CD 2, gives the date as March 7. This is unlikely, for the trio is known to have appeared twice in Paris on that day. See p. 34f above.

135 Three tunes of the Laren concert ('I've Told Every Little Star', 'I Want To Be Happy', 'A Weaver Of Dreams') have been reissued on the 3-CD-set Sonny Rollins Trio, *Live in Europe 1959* (see note 121), CD 2, tracks 1-3.

136 Old issue: Sonny Rollins, *Aix En Provence, 1959* (CD, Royal Jazz, 1989); reissued on Sonny Rollins Trio, *Live in Europe 1959* (see note 121), CD 3, tracks 1-3.

137 Frenz, Grimes interviews 2006 and 2007 (see chapter 1, note 4).

138 Larsen, Liner notes (see note 115).

139 Wilson, *Rollins* (see note 6), p. 168.

140 Ibid., p. 169.

141 Larsen, Liner notes (see note 115). Actually, Pete La Roca was replaced after the concert in Laren (Holland) (probably) on March 9.

142 Ibid.

143 See note 136.

144 Rouy, 'Un Revenant Nommé' (see chapter 2, note 14).

145 Frenz, Grimes interviews 2006 and 2007 (see chapter 1, note 4).

146 Ibid.

Chapter Four

1 A. Philip Randolph, quoted from the original liner notes by Nat Hentoff for *We Insist! Max Roach and Oscar Brown, Jr.'s Freedom Now Suite* (Candid, 1960).

2 Charles Eric Lincoln, *The Black Muslims in America*, Grand Rapids, MI: Wm. B. Eerdmans; Trenton, NJ: Africa World Press, 1961, 31994), p. 91.

3   LeRoi Jones (Amiri Baraka), *Blues People* (New York: William Morrow, 1963); idem, 'The Changing Same (R&B and New Black Music)', in idem, *Black Music* (New York: William Morrow, 1968; repr. New York: Da Capo, 1998), pp. 180-211; idem, 'Greenwich Village and African-American Music', in idem and Amina Baraka, *The Music* (see chapter 1, note 13), pp. 184f.; A.B. Spellman, *Four Lives in the Bebop Business* (New York: Pantheon, 1966); Frank Kofsky, *Black Nationalism and the Revolution in Music* (New York: Pathfinder, 1970); Val Wilmer, *As Serious As Your Life* (London: Pluto Press (first edition 1977), 1987); Monson, *Freedom Sounds* (see chapter 1, note 12); Ekkehard Jost, *Free Jazz* (New York: Da Capo, 1994), pp. 8-16; Christian Broecking, *Respekt!* (Berlin, 2004); idem, *Black Codes* (Berlin: Verbrecher-Verlag, 2005).

4   Baraka, 'Greenwich Village' (see note 3), p. 186.

5   See p. 40 below (Grimes as part of the evolving New Music) and p. 97 (Grimes' letter of December 2006).

6   Sam Stephenson, ed., *The Jazz Loft Project* (New York: Knopf, 2009), p. 140.

7   See chapter 3.

8   Marrotte, 'Henry Grimes' (see chapter 2, n. 32).

9   Galvani, Interview with Henry Grimes (see chapter 2, note 35).

10   Medwin, 'Playing the vibrations' (see chapter 1, note 3), p. 17.

11   Mike Hobart, 'A jazz bassist is back in action' (December 5, 2009), ft.com /cms/s/2/1e010160-e05a-11de-8494-00144feab49a.html (with registration).

12   Baraka, 'Blues, Poetry, and the New Music', (see chapter 1, note 13), p. 266. See also idem, 'The Phenomenon of *Soul* in African-American Music', ibid., p. 274.

13   David Keenan, 'Henry Grimes & William Parker: Philadelphia University of Pennsylvania, USA', *The Wire* 4 (2004), pp. 90f., quote on p. 91. On the various terms used to explain jazz music since the 1960s (avant-garde, free jazz, New Black Music, New Thing, New Music) see Monson, *Freedom Sounds* (see chapter 1, note 12), p. 261.

14   See chapter 7.

15   Marrotte, 'Henry Grimes' (see chapter 2, note 32), p. 47.

16   George, 'A jazz mystery unravels: Henry Grimes' (see chapter 2, note 57).

17   Jung, 'A Fireside Chat with Henry Grimes' (see chapter 1, note 7).

18   Weiss, 'Interview Henry Grimes' (see chapter 1, note 10).

19   Ibid.

20   von Osterhausen, 'Die "wundersame Geschichte"' (see chapter 2, note 12).

21   Kantor, 'Interview...' (see chapter 1, note 5).

22   Ibid.

23   Ibid.

24   Frenz, Grimes interviews 2006 and 2007 (see chapter 1, note 4).

25   Ibid.

26   Baraka, 'Greenwich Village' (see note 3), p. 187.

27   Stephenson, ed., *The Jazz Loft Project* (see note 6). Also: jazzloftproject.org/

index.php. Audio material on Grimes playing in that loft at Smith Archive (tapes #22, #87, #88, #95, #121, #633) at the Center for Creative Photography at the University of Arizona, creativephotography.org/collections/research-archives. Further material of the Jazz Loft Project at Rubenstein Library (box 2 Folder 19), part of Duke University Library, library.duke.edu/rubenstein/findingaids/jazzloftproject/#ref2647 (links viewed: May 5, 2015). The author is grateful to Sam Stephenson for sharing information about his Jazz Loft Project and its archives, and to Rubenstein Library for sharing Stephenson's Grimes-interview from 2003. Also see Fitzgerald, Grimes Discography (see chapter 3, note 11), on four of the above mentioned audio tapes.

28   Ibid., blurb and p. 3ff.

29   Ibid., p. 28.

30   Fitzgerald, *Grimes Discography* (see chapter 3, note 11).

31   Ibid.

32   Stephenson, ed., *Jazz Loft Project* (see note 6); also Fitzgerald, *Grimes Discography* (see chapter 3, note 11).

33   Fitzgerald, *Grimes Discography* (see chapter 3, note 11).

34   Further details about Grimes' 1960 recording dates in Fitzgerald, *Grimes Discography* (see chapter 3, note 11).

35   See p. 20 above; Contreras, 'A Fresh Start …' (see chapter 1, note 18).

36   'Ted Panken Interviews – Sam Rivers' (WKCR-FM New York, September 25, 1997), pubd. 1999 on jazzhouse.org. In 1964 Blue Note issued the album *Fuchsia Swing Song* that Rivers recorded with Jaki Byard, Ron Carter, and Tony Williams. Presumably he had therefore recorded the music once before with Hal Galper and Henry Grimes, but never released the recording.

37   *DownBeat*, November 4, 1965, p. 14.

38   Perhaps proceeding from this information: '[…] Neidlinger eventually being replaced by Henry Grimes who was to play intermittently with the pianist until leaving New York in 1966.' Wilmer, *As Serious as Your Life* (see note 3), p. 57.

39   'Buell Neidlinger: Interview', taken by Bob Rusch, transcribed by Kea D. Rusch, *Cadence* 12, no. 6, pp. 5-21 and 66; see also Leonard Lyons, *The 101 Best Jazz Albums: A History of Jazz on Records* (New York: W. Morrow, 1980), p. 395: 'Sunny Murray […] joined him [Cecil Taylor] along with Henry Grimes, a more driving bassist than Buell Neidlinger.'

40   All titles of the October 10 session are on the Impulse! albums (issued under the name of sponsor Gil Evans) *Into The Hot* (1962), *Into The Hot* (1988), and *Mixed* (1998), for further details see Fitzgerald, *Grimes Discography* (see chapter 3, note 11). Also Wilmer, *As Serious as Your Life* (see note 3), p. 161.

41   See p. 101ff below.

42   Marian McPartland, 'Caught in The Act: John Bunch, Hickory House, New York City, Personnel: Bunch, piano; Henry Grimes, bass', *DownBeat* (January 5, 1961), p. 44.

43   *The New Yorker*, 1960, Nov. 12, Nov. 19, Nov. 26, and Dec. 3, respectively p. 8.

44   Fitzgerald, Grimes Discography (see chapter 3, note 11).

45   *Metronome* 11, 1961, p. 5.

46   *Metronome* 08, 1961, p. 4.

47   Fitzgerald, Grimes Discography (see chapter 3, note 11).

48   Ibid. – Ben Young gave Grimes a copy of the recording, asking him to confirm that he was the bassist on it (email by M. Davis Grimes, December 2013).

49   Michael Cuscuna, Liner notes to *Roy Haynes: Out Of The Afternoon*, 1962 (Blue Note, 1995), in reference to Henry Grimes.

50   Kantor, 'Interview...' (see chapter 1, note 5).

51   All the Birdland recordings are available on CD: *In Concert*, released by Jazzman (Italy), and *Charles Mingus*, released by Tempi di Jazz (Italy). See Todd S. Jenkins, Sy Johnson, *I Know What I Know: The Music of Charles Mingus* (Westport, CT: Praeger, 2006), p. 90, and Fitzgerald, Grimes Discography (see chapter 3, note 11).

52   Jenkins/Johnson, *Mingus* (see note 51), p. 90; also Brian Priestley, *Mingus: A Critical Biography* (New York: Da Capo Press, 1984), p. 273.

53   Ibid.; Fitzgerald, Grimes Discography (see chapter 3, note 11).

54   Kantor, 'Interview...' (see chapter 1, note 5).

55   Weiss, 'Interview' (see chapter 1, note 10).

56   Fitzgerald, Grimes Discography (see chapter 3, note 11).

57   Cuscuna, Liner notes (see note 49); see also Compton Mackenzie and Christopher Stone, *The Gramophone* (1963), p. 43 ('admirable group').

58   Kevin Amos, Interview with Henry Grimes, Pittsburgh, 2012. The author is grateful to M. Davis Grimes for alerting her to this quote.

59   *The New Yorker*, 1962, April 28, p. 11.

60   *Coda*, Vol. 5, No. 1, August 1962, p. 15, 16.

61   Fitzgerald, Grimes Discography (see chapter 3, note 11).

62   Dan Morgenstern, Liner notes to McCoy Tyner, *Reaching Fourth*, 1962 (Blue Note, 1998).

63   LeRoi Jones (Amiri Baraka), 'Review: McCoy Tyner, Reaching Fourth (Blue Note, 1962)', *Kulchur* (1962), pp. 96f; see also Charles Fox, 'Review: McCoy Tyner, Reaching Fourth (Blue Note, 1962)', *The Gramophone* 1964, 01, Vol. 41, No. 488, p. 346.

64   *Coda*, June 1966, p. 22.

65   *Coda*, Vol. 5, No. 5, December 1962, p. 17.

66   *DownBeat* 1963, January 31, p. 43/4.

67   Fitzgerald, Grimes Discography (see chapter 3, note 11).

68 Howard Mandel, Liner notes (1987) to *The Perry Robinson 4*, 1962, CD release 1987.

69 Ibid.

70 Robinson and Wetzel, *Perry Robinson* (see chapter 2, note 22), p. 92. See also Yanow, *Jazz on Record* (see chapter 3, note 48), p. 564.

71 Yanow, *Jazz on Record* (see chapter 3, note 48), p. 564.

72 Fitzgerald, 'Into Thin Air' (see chapter 1, note 6).

73 Ibid.

74 See p. 94ff below. At the time (1962) Henry Grimes had further studio dates in New York with Roy Burns, Philip Guilbeau, and Jerome Richardson. Fitzgerald, Grimes Discography (see chapter 3, note 11).

75 Pérémarti, 'At Home With Henry Grimes' (see chapter 2, note 52).

76 Frenz, Sonny Rollins interview 2007 (see chapter 3, note 3). Rollins' statement is also quoted in Henry Grimes, *Signs Along The Road: Poems* (Cologne: Buddy's Knife, 2007), p. 6, and on henrygrimes.com/press/.

77 Grimes again toured America with Rollins at the beginning of the 1960s, as is proved by several photographs of a concert they gave in New Orleans with Don Cherry and Billy Higgins (photographs only temporarily accessible in the internet).

78 Andy Hamilton, *Lee Konitz: Conversations on the Improviser's Art* (Ann Arbor: University of Michigan Press, 2007), p. 92.

79 Frenz, Sonny Rollins interview 2007 (see chapter 3, note 3).

80 Primack, Phone interview with Henry Grimes (see chapter 3, note 104).

81 Ibid.

82 Ibid.

83 Rouy, 'Un Revenant Nommé: Henry Grimes' (see chapter 2, note 14).

84 Jost, *Free Jazz* (see note 3), p. 139.

85 E.g. Fitzgerald, 'Into Thin Air' (see chapter 1, note 6), p. 43: 'The influence of Ornette Coleman was strong [...].'

86 Jost, *Free Jazz* (see note 3), p. 139.

87 Frenz, Sonny Rollins interview 2007 (see chapter 3, note 3). In a 2006 interview with Victor L. Schermer, Rollins expressed himself very clearly on Coleman's much-touted influence: 'Well, first of all, Ornette didn't just influence me – I was a big influence on him as well. It was mutual. [...] I met Ornette on the West Coast [1957]. We used to go out and practice together. [...]'. Quoted from the CD booklet for *Sonny Rollins and Don Cherry Quartet, New York 1962 / Stockholm 1963* (RLR Records, 2009).

88 Jost, *Free Jazz* (see note 3), p. 140.

89 Reissued on a double CD in 2009 as Sonny Rollins / Don Cherry Quartet, *The Complete Copenhagen Concert* (Jazz Lips Music, 2009). CD 1 contains 52nd Street Theme, On Green Dolphin Street, and an improvised medley quoting The Bridge, You Don't Know What Love Is, and Sly Mongoose; CD 2 contains Without A Song and Oleo.

90 *Live Mid-6os* (Landscape CD LS2-915, 1992): Without A Song, Valse Hot, 52nd Street Theme. Fitzgerald, Grimes Discography (see chapter 3, note 11). Reissued and technically remastered on a double CD in 2009 (see preceding note). Wilmer, *As Serious as Your Life* (see note 3), reports that Albert Ayler, who was in Stockholm at the time, visited the band backstage after the concert (p. 101).

91 Reissued on CD by Gambit Records (2008): Solitude, On Green Dolphin Street, Announcement by Sonny Rollins, Without A Song, Sonnymoon For Two, Everything Happens To Me, 52nd Street Theme. Liner notes by Lawrence Steele: 'This CD contains the complete second concert by the group at the celebrated Olympia Theatre in Paris, France, on January 19, 1963. Portions of this long unavailable performance were sometimes issued with inferior sound quality on difficult to find LPs. This is considered the second concert because Rollins and Cherry performed two concerts at the Olympia on January 19. [...]' The liner notes of the earlier CD release (Sonny Rollins Quartet, *In Europe 1963, Vol. 1, Featuring Don Cherry*, Moon Records, 1994) indicate that practically all the recordings on the CD stem from the Paris concert of the European tour (venue wrongly given as Salle Pleyel). However, some of the pieces are taken from the Copenhagen Concert (see note 89).

92 sonnyrollins.com/videolibrary/ (viewed: January 3, 2015) (1960s, '52nd Street Theme'); youtube.com/watch?v=9_UoyHKavno (viewed: January 3, 2015) (52nd Street Theme). Fitzgerald, Grimes Discography (see chapter 3, note 11), lists '52nd Street Theme' and 'Doxy' for the Rome concert.

93 Fitzgerald, Grimes Discography (see chapter 3, note 11). The Stuttgart concert is now reissued on CD: Sonny Rollins–Don Cherry Quartet, *Complete 1963 Stuttgart Concert* (RLR Records, 2009): 52nd Street Theme, On Green Dolphin Street, Sonnymoon For Two, and Oleo. Liner notes by Matias Rinar: 'This CD contains all known existing recordings from the January 29, 1963 Stuttgart concert. These are private recordings [...].'

94 The Milan photo from 1963: bopandbeyond.wordpress.com/2007/10/ (viewed: January 11, 2015).

95 Announcement by Sonny Rollins (see note 91).

96 Jef Gilson and Claude Lénissois, 'Jazz Actualités: Free Jazz à l'Olympia avec Sonny Rollins', *Jazz Hot* (February 1963), pp. 6f.

97 Dieter Zimmerle, 'Der neue alte Rollins', *Jazz Podium* 2, no. 12 (1963), p. 29.

98 Wilson, *Rollins* (chapter 3, note 105), pp. 171ff. The English edition says nothing about these bootleg recordings of 1963. See also note 91 above.

99 Wilson is referring to the live recording from the Village Gate, which appeared as the album *Our Man in Jazz* on the RCA label in 1963.

100 Wilson, *Rollins* (chapter 3, note 105), pp. 171ff.

101 Ibid.

102 Ibid., p. 172.

103 See the internet links in note 92. The tune is now available as a bonus track on the CD Sonny Rollins–Don Cherry Quartet, *New York 1962/Stockholm 1963* (RLR Records, 2009).

104 Wilson, *Rollins* (see chapter 3, note 105), pp. 171ff.

105 Fitzgerald, Grimes Discography (see chapter 3, note 11). These tunes are now available as bonus tracks on the CD reissues of *Our Man in Jazz* (2002) and *Sonny Meets Hawk* (1999).

106 Jackson, 'Backstage with…Henry Grimes' (see chapter 3, note 53).

107 H.P., *DownBeat* (April 9, 1964), p. 29.

108 *DownBeat* (June 1964), reissued in *DownBeat* (December 1991), p. 69.

109 Wilson, *Rollins* (see chapter 3, note 6), p. 178.

110 In summer of 1963 'Sonny Rollins played Birdland accompanied by bassist Henry Grimes and drummer Clarence [Charles?] Moffett', see *DownBeat* 1963, June 06, p. 10; a few weeks later 'Sonny Rollins' new group includes pianist Paul Bley, bassist Henry Grimes, and drummer Roy McCurdy' (*DownBeat* 1963, July 04, p. 43), a group which toured Japan the following September.

111 Marrotte, '*Signal to Noise* Interview' (see chapter 2, note 32).

112 Fitzgerald, Grimes Discography (see chapter 3, note 11).

113 youtube.com/watch?v=omjpIXnaqRw (viewed: January 3, 2015).

114 Ira Gitler, 'Report From Newport', *DownBeat* (August 15, 1963), pp. 13-17, quote on p. 13.

115 Sonny Rollins and Coleman Hawkins, *Sonny Meets Hawk!* (Hawkins (ts), Rollins (ts), Paul Bley (p), Bob Cranshaw (1,2,5), and Henry Grimes (3,4,6) (b), Roy McCurdy (dr)), Tunes: 1 Yesterdays, 2 All The Things You Are, 3 Summertime, 4 Just Friends, 5 Lover Man, 6 At McKies. RCA 1963, reissued on CD in 2000.

116 Rouy, 'Un Revenant Nommé' (see chapter 2, note 14).

117 Goldsby and Carter: *The Jazz Bass Book* (see chapter 3, note 47), p. 124.

118 Wilson, *Rollins* (see chapter 3, note 6), p. 180.

119 Medwin, 'Playing the vibrations' (see chapter 1, note 3), p. 15.

120 '[Miles] Davis' engagement [at the Village Vanguard] was followed with a one-weeker by Sonny Rollins.' Rollins' quartet 'included pianist Paul Bley, drummer Roy McCurdy, and bassist Bob Cranshaw, subbing for Henry Grimes, who was ill.' (*DownBeat* 1963, August 29, p. 43).

121 'Sonny Rollins and his regular group (Paul Bley (p), Henry Grimes (b), Roy McCurdy (dr)) were joined by Clark Terry, Coleman Hawkins, and Ben Webster for an RCA Victor date.' (*DownBeat* 1963, September 12, p. 43).

122 'Al Cohn and Zoot Sims played three weeks at the Half Note recently. Roger Kellaway split the piano chores with Jaki Byard; Henry Grimes was on bass for a week and was later replaced by Wyatt Ruther; Mousey Alexander was the drummer.' (*DownBeat* 1963, September 26, p. 44).

123 Fitzgerald, Grimes Discography (see chapter 3, note 11); see also William R. Bauer, *Open the Door: The Life and Music of Betty Carter* (Ann Arbor: University of Michigan Press, 2002), pp. 91f.; 'Sonny Rollins Meets the Japanese Press', *DownBeat* (December 19, 1963), p. 16.

124 Sonny Rollins Quintet, *Tokyo 1963*, issued for the first time on CD by RLR Records in 2008: 'Moritat (Mack The Knife)', 'The Way You Look Tonight', 'When I Fall In Love', 'Oleo'.

125 Barbara Frenz, Interviews with Henry Grimes, New York City, December 2009 and January 2010.

126 'Sonny Rollins Meets the Japanese Press' (see note 123).

127 Ibid.

128 Jean French: 'Taping the Artists. Sonny Rollins', in: *Abundant Sounds*, 2/3 (Jul.1964), p. 10-13 (I). See also Matias Rinar's liner notes for Sonny Rollins Quintet, *Tokyo 1963* (RLR Records, 2008).

129 Frenz, Grimes interviews 2009 and 2010 (see note 125).

130 Paul Bley, David Lee, *Stopping Time: Paul Bley and the Transformation of Jazz* (Montreal, Quebec: Vehicle Press, 1999), p. 80, 82.

131 Frenz, Sonny Rollins interview 2007 (see chapter 3, note 3), p. 80, 82.

132 Ibid.

133 See p. 30 above.

134 Frenz, Sonny Rollins interview 2007 (see chapter 3, note 3).

135 Ibid.

136 'Although Rollins and Henry Grimes played together often (their first recordings date back to 1958), no further collaborations between the two musicians are known to exist after this Tokyo performance.' Rinar, Liner notes (see note 128).

137 Frenz, Grimes interviews 2009 and 2010 (see note 125).

138 See p. 30.

139 Peter Kostakis, Liner notes (1993) for the CD Steve Lacy, *School Days: Live at Phase Two Coffee House, New York City, March 1963* (Hat Hut, 1994).

140 Jean-Paul Ricard, 'Interview: Denis Charles, Last Words of an Outlaw', *Jazz Magazine* no. 481 (Paris, May 1998), www.denischarles.com/Jazz Magazine.html.

141 Jason Weiss, *Steve Lacy: Conversations*, (Middletown, CT: Wesleyan University Press, 2006), p. 37; see also Fitzgerald, Grimes Discography (see chapter 3, note 11). Also Wilmer, *As Serious as Your Life* (see note 3), p. 54.

142 Bye-Ya, Brilliant Corners, Monk's Dream, Monk's Mood, Ba-Lue Bolivar Ba-Lues-Are, Skippy, Pannonica.

143 Kostakis, Liner notes (see note 139).

144 Ibid.

145 Ibid.

146 Steven L. Isoardi, 'The Return of Henry Grimes: A Memoir', *Current Research in Jazz* 2 (2010, Chicago 15th ed.). Also available at www.crj-online.org/v2/CRJ-HenryGrimes.php.

147 Bill Barron, *West Side Story Bossa Nova* (Dauntless CD, DC 6004, 2002); Walt Dickerson Quartet, *Jazz Impressions Of Lawrence Of Arabia*, reissued on CD as Walt Dickerson, *Vibes In Motion* (Fresh Sound Records, 2006), tracks 3-10. Fitzgerald, Grimes Discography (see chapter 3, note 11).

148 See p. 101ff below.

149 Liner notes for *Vibes In Motion* (see note 147). Also Wilmer, *As Serious as Your Life* (see note 3), pp. 176 and 266 on Walt Dickerson.

150 Ibid., p. 57; Gene Santoro, *Dancing in Your Head: Jazz, Blues, Rock, and Beyond* (New York: Oxford University Press, 1994), p. 239 (Cecil Taylor quote).

151 Ibid.

152 Dan Warburton, Interview with Sunny Murray, November 3, 2000, paristransatlantic.com/magazine/interviews/murray.html (viewed: 2009).

153 Marrotte, '*Signal to Noise* Interview' (see chapter 2, note 32); see also Strauss, 'Silent 30 Years' (see chapter 2, n. 69); Larry Blumenfeld, 'The Ballad of Henry Grimes (and other recent visions)', *Jazziz* no. 11 (2003), pp. 34f.; Pérémarti, 'At Home With Henry Grimes' (see chapter 2, note 52), p. 20; Robinson and Wetzel, *The Traveler* (see chapter 2, note 22), p. 119.

154 Fitzgerald, Grimes Discography (see chapter 3, note 11). See also: jdisc.col umbia.edu/session/cecil-taylor-december-31-1963 (viewed: January 3, 2015).

155 See p. 101ff below.

156 Dr. Martin Luther King, Jr., 'On the Importance of Jazz: Opening Address to the 1964 Berlin Jazz Festival'. Full text: hartford-hwp.com/archives/45a/626.html (viewed: January 3, 2015)

157 Quoted in an email by M. Davis Grimes, 2012.

158 *DownBeat* (April 11, 1963), pp. 16-21. Also Monson, *Freedom Sounds* (see chapter 1, note 12), pp. 238ff., and Broecking, *Black Codes* (see note 3), pp. 63ff. (Oscar Brown Jr.).

159 James Farmer, *Lay Bare the Heart: An Autobiography of the Civil Rights Movement* (New York: Arbor House, 1985).

160 Also see p. 74. These historical documents also on henrygrimes.com/biogra phy/#HistoricalP1 (scroll down; viewed: January 3, 2015).

161 Sincere thanks to M. Davis Grimes for sending me this statement by Henry Grimes via email, January 14, 2014. – Also see in this context Babatunde Olatunji, *The Beat Of My Drum: An Autobiography* (Philadelphia: Temple University Press 2005), p. 163-192.

162 iipdigital.usembassy.gov/st/english/article/2008/02/20080211124919liamer uoyo.4420282.html#axzz3OYFpsniX (viewed: January 11, 2015).

163 Wayne Enstice and Janice Stockhouse, *Jazzwomen: Conversations with Twenty-One Musicians* (Bloomington: Indiana University Press, 2004), p. 261.

164 See p. 55f above.

165 Marrotte, '*Signal to Noise* Interview' (see chapter 2, note 32), p. 45.

166 Ibid.

167 Christian Broecking came to the same conclusion in, 'Zurück am Bass nach dreißig Jahren', *Berliner Zeitung* (August 26, 2005).

168 Henry Grimes, June 1, 2003. See the CD booklet for Albert Ayler, *Holy Ghost, Rare & Unissued Recordings (1962-70)*, 9 CD Spirit Box, ed. Ben Young (Revenantrecords, 2004), p. 126.

169 John Kruth, 'The Healing Force of the Universe: Albert Ayler's Life and Legacy (34 Years Hence)', *Signal to Noise* (winter 2005).

170 Nat Hentoff, 'The Truth is Marching In', *DownBeat* (November 17 1966), pp. 16-19 and 40.

171 Gudrun Endress, 'Albert Ayler: We Play Peace!', *Jazz Podium* 10, no. 15 (1966), pp. 254-57, quote on p. 254.

172 Henry Woodfin, 'Whither Albert Ayler?', *DownBeat* (November 17, 1966), p. 19.

173 See p. 12 above. Ayler's rhythm and blues-experiences are discussed in Peter Niklas Wilson, *Spirits Rejoice! Albert Ayler und seine Botschaft* (Hofheim: Wolke, 1966), p. 50. On Ayler's music in general see ibid., pp. 115-47, and *Holy Ghost* (see note 168), with taped interviews from 1964 and 1970 and a booklet containing musicians' statements and articles about Albert Ayler and his music.

174 Marrotte, '*Signal to Noise* Interview' (see chapter 2, note 32), p. 47.

175 Daniel Caux, 'The Road To Freedom', interview conducted with Albert Ayler in Saint Paul de Vence, France, July 28, 1970, one day after his concert at Fondation Maeght and four days before his death; published in *The Wire* 1 (2003), pp. 39-41, quote on p. 41 (with partly incorrect transcriptions). Also released on disc 8, track 13, of *Holy Ghost* (see note 168).

176 Wilson, *Spirits Rejoice!* (see note 173), p. 45.

177 Caux, 'The Road To Freedom' (see note 175). Also Endress, 'Albert Ayler', (see note 171).

178 Wilson, *Spirits Rejoice!* (see note 1673), p. 57.

179 Hentoff, 'The Truth' (see note 170).

180 *DownBeat* editor Dan Morgenstern. Kruth, 'Healing Force' (see note 169), and Jost, *Free Jazz* (see note 3), p. 121 ('thoughtless attacks', 'crude insults').

181 Endress, 'Albert Ayler', (see note 171), p. 155.

182 Ibid., p. 156. See also the musicological analysis of Ayler's music in Jost, *Free Jazz* (see note 3), pp. 124-32.

183 Galvani, Interview (see chapter 2, note 35).

184 A facsimile of Ayler's *Cricket* article ('To Mr. Jones – I Had A Vision') appears in the *Holy Ghost* booklet (see note 168).

185 John Litweiler, *The Freedom Principle: Jazz after 1958* (New York: William Morrow, 1990), p. 165, referring to interviews with Albert Ayler.

186 Hentoff, 'The Truth' (see note 170).

187 Kruth, 'Healing Force' (see note 169).

188 Rouy, 'Un Revenant Nommé' (see chapter 2, note 14).

189 Weiss, 'Interview' (see chapter 1, note 10).

190 Ibid.

191 Kruth, 'Healing Force' (see note 169).

192 Ibid.

193 Ibid.

194 Fitzgerald, Grimes Discography (see chapter 3, note 11).

195 Jost, *Free Jazz* (see note 3), p. 122; Wilson, *Spirits Rejoice!* (see note 173), p. 167.

196 CD release as *Witches And Devils* (Black Lion and da music, 2000), with Albert Ayler (ts), Norman Howard (tp), Henry Grimes (b) on tunes 2 and 4 ('Spirits' and 'Saints'), Earle Henderson (b) on tunes 1 and 3, and Sunny Murray (dr). Wilmer, *As Serious as Your Life* (see note 3), p. 108; Wilson, *Spirits Rejoice!* (see note 173), p. 47.

197 CD release as *Goin' Home* (Black Lion and da music, 1994), with Albert Ayler (ts, ss), Call Cobbs Jr. (p), Henry Grimes (b), and Sunny Murray (dr).

198 Wilson, *Spirits Rejoice!* (see note 173), pp. 48-50.

199 Ibid., p. 155; Wilmer, *As Serious as Your Life* (see note 3), p. 108.

200 Wilson, *Spirits Rejoice!* (see note 173), p. 50.

201 François Postif, 'Albert Ayler – Le Magicien', *Jazz Hot* 213, no. 10 (1965), pp. 20-22, quote on p. 21.

202 Wilson, *Spirits Rejoice!* (see note 173), p. 154.

203 Jones, 'Apple Cores #1' [1964], in idem, *Black Music* (New York, 1968; repr. New York: Da Capo, 1998), p. 117.

204 Ibid., p. 155.

205 Barry McRae, Liner notes for CD reissue of *Goin' Home* (see note 197).

206 Wilson, *Spirits Rejoice!* (see note 173), p. 155.

207 McRae, Liner notes (see note 205).

208 Paul Olson, 'Interview with Marc Ribot: That's the Way I View It From New York', allaboutjazz.com/marc-ribot-thats-the-way-i-view-it-from-new-york-marc-ribot-by-paul-olson.php?width=1024 (published March 27, 2006; viewed: January 3, 2015).

209 Quoted from Larry Blumenfeld, 'Communion At The Temple', review of the Marc Ribot Trio with Henry Grimes and Chad Taylor at the Village Vanguard, New York, June 26 to July 1, 2012, at jazziz.com/pageflip/bobwilloughbyfall2012/files/42.html.

210 Wilmer, As *Serious as Your Life* (see note 3), p. 105.

211 Fred Jung and Rex Butters, Liner notes for the CD reissue (ESP 2006). Also Jost, *Free Jazz* (see note 3), p. 130.

212 Jung/Butters, Liner notes (see note 211), and Jost, *Free Jazz* (see note 3), p. 130. Also *DownBeat*, November 18, 1965, p. 48: 'ESP Records held an open-house afternoon record date at Judson Hall Sept. 23. [...].'

213 Wilson, *Spirits Rejoice!* (see note 173), p. 72.

214 Guy Kopelovicz, Liner notes for CD issue of *Spirits Rejoice!* (ESP, 2006). Whether Sunny Murray ever shared an apartment with Henry Grimes is not verified, except by himself. Grimes does not remember anything about it (see also below on p. 93f).

215 Wilmer, *As Serious as Your Life* (see note 3), p. 107.

216 Ibid.

217 Max Harrison, Liner notes for CD issue of 2006, originally pubd. in *Jazz Monthly* (January 1967); Don Nelsen, Review of *Spirits Rejoice* (ESP 1020), *DownBeat* (September 8, 1966), no. 1, p. 28 (3.5 stars).

218 Fitzgerald, 'Into Thin Air' (see chapter 1, note 6).

219 Fitzgerald, Grimes Discography (see chapter 3, note 1).

220 Albert Ayler, *Live In Greenwich Village: The Complete Impulse Recordings* (CD, 1998). The tunes with Henry Grimes are tracks 2-5 on CD 1. The Impulse! double album was first released in 1978 (Impulse AS 9155). See also Pete Welding, Review of Albert Ayler, *In Greenwich Village*, *DownBeat* (1968, July 11), p. 28 (5 stars), and Michel Le Bris, Review of Albert Ayler, *In Greenwich Village*, *Jazz Hot* 245, no. 12 (1968), p. 45 (5 stars).

221 Jeff Schwartz, *Albert Ayler: His Life and Music*, chapter 4, www.reocities. com/jeff_l_schwartz/chpt4.html. The author is grateful to M. Davis Grimes for alerting her to this quote.

222 Wilson, *Spirits Rejoice!* (see note 173), p. 167.

223 Endress, 'Albert Ayler', (see note 171), p. 155.

224 Hentoff, 'The Truth' (see note 170).

225 Wilson, *Spirits Rejoice!* (see note 173), p. 167. Also Wilmer, *As Serious as Your Life* (see note 3), p. 109.

226 Broecking, 'Zurück am Bass' (see note 167).

227 Kruth, 'Healing Force' (see note 169). On the ESP label in general see Jason Weiss, *Always in Trouble: An Oral History of ESP-Disk, the Most Outrageous Record Label in America* (Middletown, CT: Wesleyan University Press, 2012).

228 Kruth, 'Healing Force' (see note 169).

229 Wilson, *Spirits Rejoice!* (see note 173), p. 52.

230 Hentoff, 'The Truth' (see note 170).

231 Wilson, *Spirits Rejoice!* (see note 173), p. 86.

232 Wilmer, *As Serious as Your Life* (see note 3), pp. 92-111 (Albert Ayler).

233 Don Heckman, 'Roots, Culture & Economics: An Interview with Avant-Garde Pianist-Composer Andrew Hill', *DownBeat* (May 5, 1966), pp. 19-21.

234 Pannonica de Koenigswarter, *Three Wishes: An Intimate Look at Jazz Greats* (New York: Abrams, 2008), pp. 195 and 25. The 'three wishes' questions and answers date from somewhere between 1961 and 1966.

235 LeRoi Jones, 'New York City's lofts and coffee houses have become havens for the new thing', *DownBeat* (May 9, 1963), pp. 13 and 42.

236 Ibid.

237 Warburton, Sunny Murray interview (see note 152).

238 Spellman, *Four Lives* (see note 3), pp. 18f.

239 Ibid., pp. 19f. and 23f.

240 Gus Matzorkis, 'Down Where We All Live: Today's Avant-Garde Revolution As Seen In Light Of Jazz' Long History Of Internal Strife, Part II', *DownBeat* (April 21, 1966), pp. 17f.

241 See p. 88 above.

242 Interview with Peter Kowald on *Rising Tones Cross: A Jazz Film by Ebba Jahn, NYC 1984* (DVD 2005), spoken in German with English subtitles.

243 On the exploitative and racist working conditions of jazz musicians see also Wilmer, *As Serious as Your Life* (see note 3), pp. 129ff., and Monson, *Freedom Sounds* (see chapter 1, note 12), pp. 267ff.

244 Heckman, 'Roots' (see note 233).

245 Wilmer, *As Serious as Your Life* (see note 3), p. 105.

246 Heckman, 'Roots' (see note 233).

247 Ibid.

248 'Qui êtes-vous, Bernard Stollman?, Interview', *Jazz Hot* 230, no. 4 (1967), pp. 13-17, quote on p. 16.

249 Ibid., p. 17. Also Wilmer, *As Serious as Your Life* (see note 3), pp. 231-33; Weiss, *Always in Trouble* (see note 227).

250 Wilmer, *As Serious as Your Life* (see note 3).

251 Frenz, Grimes interviews 2006 and 2007 (see chapter 1, note 4).

252 Marrotte, '*Signal to Noise* Interview' (see note 32), p. 47.

253 See the photo on p. 92 below.

254 LeRoi Jones, 'Voice From The Avant-Garde' (see chapter 2, note 2).

255 Fitzgerald, 'Into Thin Air' (see chapter 1, note 6).

256 Caroline Barbier de Reulle, who is working on a thesis about the relationship between the visual and sound generously shared this information in an email, April 30 2015, referring to *DownBeat*, April 21, 1966, p. 15; email from M. Davis Grimes, January 27 2015.

257 Robinson and Wetzel, *The Traveler* (see chapter 2, note 22), p. 120. Also p. 94ff below ('*The Call*').

258 'Autumn in New York: Voyage au Coeur de la New Thing: Un reportage de Guy Kopelowicz', *Jazz Hot* 214, no. 11 (1965), pp. 28-31.

259 'Autumn in New York' (see note 258), p. 29. See also Kopelowicz's above report on Albert Ayler's recording date for *Spirits Rejoice*, where Grimes was on bass (pp. 82f).

260 Warburton, Sunny Murray interview (see note 152).

261 Henry Grimes Trio, *The Call*, LP 12" (ESP 1026), CD (ESP 1020-2). Fitzgerald, Grimes Discography (see chapter 3, note 11).

262 See p. 120 below.

263 *The Call* (see note 261).

264 Frenz, Grimes interviews 2006 and 2007 (see chapter 1, note 4).

265 Ibid.

266 Ibid.

267 Ibid.

268 Robinson and Wetzel, *The Traveler* (see chapter 2, note 22), p. 121. See also p. 52ff above.

269 Frenz, Grimes interviews 2006 and 2007 (see chapter 1, note 4).

270 Robinson and Wetzel, *The Traveler* (see chapter 2, note 22), p. 121.

271 Frenz, Grimes interviews 2006 and 2007 (see chapter 1, note 4).

272 Ibid.

273 Henry Grimes, letter of December 30, 2006.

274 Frenz, Grimes interviews 2006 and 2007 (see chapter 1, note 4).

275 Monson, *Freedom Sounds* (see chapter 1, note 12), p. 307.

276 Rouy, 'Un Revenant Nommé' (see chapter 2, note 14).

277 Medjuck, organissimo.org/forum/index.php?showtopic=44978 (posted: July 18, 2008).

278 Max Harrison, *A Jazz Retrospect* (Boston: Crescendo, 1976), pp. 112f.

279 Philippe Nahman, Review of Henry Grimes' *The Call*, *Jazz Hot* 228, no. 2 (1967), p. 32.

280 Ibid.

281 Ibid.

282 Daniel Berger, Review of Henry Grimes' *The Call*, *Jazz Hot* 228, no. 2 (1967), p. 32.

283 See p. 174ff below.

284 Jung, 'Fireside Chat with Henry Grimes' (see chapter 1, note 7).

285 Nat Hentoff, 'The Persistent Challenge Of Cecil Taylor', *DownBeat* (February 25, 1965), pp. 17f. and 40.

286 See pp. 47f above for the years 1961 and 1963.

287 Warburton, Sunny Murray interview (see note 152).

288 Wilmer, *As Serious as Your Life* (see note 3), p. 46.

289 Spellman, *Four Lives* (see note 3), pp. 11f.

290 Ibid., p. 14.

291 Jost, *Free Jazz* (see note 3), p. 77.

292 Ibid.

293 Ibid., p. 83.

294 Gudrun Endress, 'Cecil Taylor: Musik macht Freude', *Jazz Podium* 7, no. 15 (1966), pp. 176-79, quote on p. 177.

295 Ibid.

296 Ibid., p. 178.

297 Ibid., p. 179.

298 Hentoff, 'Persistent Challenge' (see note 285).

299 See also p. 47f above.

300 Fitzgerald, 'Into Thin Air' (see chapter 1, note 6).

301 Jung, 'Fireside Chat with Henry Grimes' (see chapter 1, note 7); Galvani, Interview (see chapter 2, note 35).

302 Medwin, 'Playing the vibrations' (see chapter 1, note 3), p. 17.

303 Marrotte, '*Signal to Noise* Interview'(see chapter 2, note 32).

304 'Joachim E. Berendt berichtet vom Newport Jazz Festival', *Jazz Podium* 8, XIV 1965, August 1965, p. 196-198, p. 196/7; Dan Morgenstern, Newport Report, *DownBeat*, August 12, 1965, p. 22-25, p. 24/25; see also concertvault.com/cecil-taylor-quintet/newport-jazz-festival-july-02-1965.html with audio files of the three tunes and liner notes by Bill Milkovski (viewed: January 11, 2015). A 'Cecil Taylor Group' also is listed in an advertising of the *DownBeat* Jazz Festival, "a musical event of first importance", in Chicago, August 13-15, 1965, showing a photo of Henry Grimes (without saying that it's him) by Lars Swanberg, see *DownBeat* July 15, 1965, on the inside back cover. See also Fitzgerald, Grimes Discography (see chapter 3, note 11).

305 'Pianist Cecil Taylor made his first appearance since 1963 at a major New York jazz club when he opened at the Village Vanguard July 20. With Taylor were Grimes, bass, and Andrew Cyrille, drums. [...]' (*DownBeat*, August 26 1965, p. 16); also Endress, 'Musik macht Freude' (see note 294), p. 177; Kofsky, *Black Nationalism* (see note 3), p. 145; Cecil Tayor sessionography on webmutations.com.

306 Jost, *Free Jazz* (see note 3), p. 68; Spellman, *Four Lives* (see note 3), p. 8.

307 Fitzgerald, Grimes Discography (see chapter 3, note 11).

308 Cecil Taylor, *Piano Solo At Town Hall 1971*, Free Factory 062 (CD 2009).

309 Endress, 'Musik macht Freude' (see note 294), p. 177.

310 Dan Morgenstern, 'Caught In The Act: Cecil Taylor, Town Hall, NYC', *DownBeat* (July 28, 1966), p. 24.

311 Musicological analysis of *Unit Structures* in Jost, *Free Jazz* (see note 3), pp. 77-83.

312 Cecil Taylor, *Unit Structures*, 1987 (Blue Note CD: CDP 7 84237 2). Also Fitzgerald, Grimes Discography (see chapter 3, note 11).

313 Cecil Taylor, Liner notes for *Unit Structures* (see note 312).

314 Medwin, 'Playing the vibrations' (see chapter 1, note 3), p. 17.

315 Frenz, Andrew Cyrille phone interview 2008 (see chapter 1, note 20).

316 Jost, *Free Jazz* (see note 3), p. 77.

317 A.C., Review of Cecil Taylor's *Unit Structures*, *Jazz Hot* 231 (May 1967), p. 7.

318 Bill Mathieu, 'Review: Cecil Taylor, *Unit Structures* – Blue Note 4237', *DownBeat* (February 23, 1967), p. 31.

319 See also Jost, *Free Jazz* (see note 3), p. 78; Max Harrison, *Modern Jazz, The Essential Records: A Critical Selection* (Aquarius Books, 1975), p. 117 ('*Unit Structures*'); Elisabeth van der Mei, Coda 1966/06, p. 23.

320 Cecil Taylor, *Conquistador!*, Blue Note CD: 7243 5 90840 2 2 (2004).

321   Shortly after Grimes' reappearance in 2002-03, *Conquistador!* was reissued on CD. Inside the jewel case there is a recording-session photograph of Grimes playing bass by Francis Wolff.

322   Nat Hentoff, Original liner notes, *Conquistador!* (see note 320).

323   Ibid.

324   Bob Blumenthal, Liner notes (2003) for *Cecil Taylor: Conquistador!*, Blue Note CD: 7243 5 90840 2 2 (2004).

325   Bill Quinn, 'Four Modernists', *DownBeat* (June 13, 1968), pp. 28f.

326   Wilmer, *As Serious as Your Life* (see note 3), pp. 57f.

327   Litweiler, *Freedom Principle* (see note 185), pp. 210f.

328   Barbara Frenz, Interview with Andrew Cyrille, New York City, June 14, 2008 (at the Vision Festival), and Frenz, Andrew Cyrille phone interview 2008 (see chapter 1, note 20).

329   Wilmer, *As Serious as Your Life* (see note 3), p. 48.

330   Frenz, Andrew Cyrille interviews (see note 328 and chapter 1, note 21).

331   Fitzgerald, 'Into Thin Air' (see chapter 1, note 6).

332   Frenz, Andrew Cyrille phone interview 2008 (see chapter 1, note 20).

333   Ibid.

334   Ibid. Some accounts, e.g. Medwin, 'Playing the vibrations' (see chapter 1, note 3), p. 15, incorrectly give the year 1967 for the meeting at the airport at which Grimes failed to appear. In fact, the meeting occurred in 1966, when Taylor's European tour actually took place.

335   Pérémarti, 'At Home With Henry Grimes' (see chapter 2, note 52), p. 20.

336   Frenz, Andrew Cyrille phone interview 2008 (see chapter 1, note 20).

337   Marrotte, '*Signal to Noise* Interview' (see chapter 2, note 32).

338   Rouy, 'Un Revenant Nommé' (see chapter 2, note 14).

339   See p. 49 above.

340   See p. 54ff above.

341   Jost, *Free Jazz* (see note 3), pp. 133-62 (Don Cherry's music).

342   Don Cherry, *Complete Communion*, Blue Note CD 7243 5 22673 2 3 (2000). Fitzgerald, *Henry Grimes Discography* (see chapter 3, note 11).

343   Fitzgerald, Grimes Discography (see chapter 3, note 11).

344   Jost, *Free Jazz* (see note 3), p. 141.

345   Nat Hentoff, Original Liner notes (1965) to Don Cherry, *Complete Communion* (see note 331).

346   See p. 91 above.

347   Hentoff, Original Liner notes (1965) to Don Cherry, *Complete Communion* (see note 331).

348   'Bassist Henry Grimes has fast fingers. He is, however, a clumsy improviser (most bass players, it must be admitted, are unable to develop a first-rate melodic line). And his arco playing is dull and lifeless.' William Russo, 'Review: Don Cherry, Complete Communion − Blue Note 4226', *DownBeat* (July 28, 1966), p. 27.

349 'It is very nice to encounter Don Cherry as we like to hear him, in this case together with Ed Blackwell – a complexity that has existed for six or seven years – and with Henry Grimes, whom we remember well (with Rollins and Higgins in the Olympia). […],' Daniel Berger, Review of Don Cherry's *Complete Communion*, *Jazz Hot* 224 (October 1966), p. 32. See also Max Harrison, *Modern Jazz* (see note 319), p. 116 ('Complete Communion'), and Dean Tuder, Nancy Tuder, *Jazz* (Littleton, CO: Libraries Unlimited, 1979), p. 179: 'The latter [Grimes] promoted discipline and organizational skill, so much so that the bass and percussion were at the front line with the melody'.

350 Don Cherry, *Symphony For Improvisers*, Blue Note CD 7243 5 63823 2 9 (2005). Fitzgerald, Grimes Discography (see chapter 3, note 11).

351 Bob Blumenthal, Liner notes for *Symphony For Improvisers* (see note 350).

352 Jost, *Free Jazz* (see note 3), p. 147.

353 A.B. Spellman, Original liner notes for *Symphony For Improvisers* (see note 350).

354 Ibid.

355 E.C.L., Review of Don Cherry's *Symphony For Improvisers*, *Jazz Hot* 240 (April 1968), p. 31.

356 Ira Gitler, Review of Don Cherry's *Symphony For Improvisers*, *DownBeat* (1967), p. 28.

357 Jost, *Free Jazz* (see note 3), p. 141.

358 Ibid., p. 141; Jost analyzes Don Cherry's formal conception in greater detail for *Complete Communion*, see pp. 142ff.

359 Ibid., p. 144.

360 Ibid.

361 Ibid., p. 146.

362 Ibid., pp. 146f.

363 Ibid., p. 147.

364 Fitzgerald, Grimes Discography (see chapter 3, note 11).

365 Don Cherry, *Where Is Brooklyn?* Blue Note CD 0946 3 11435 2 6 (2005). Fitzgerald, *Henry Grimes Discography* (see chapter 3, note 11).

366 Ornette Coleman, Original liner notes (1967) for Don Cherry, *Where Is Brooklyn?* (see note 365).

367 Archie Shepp, *On This Night*, GRP/Impulse! CD GRD 125 (1993). Fitzgerald, Grimes Discography (see chapter 3, note 11). Jost, *Free Jazz* (see note 3), p. 114, gives the recording date as August 1968. The correct date is August 12, 1965.

368 Also Wilmer, *As Serious as Your Life* (see note 3), p. 28f.

369 The 1993 CD issue of *On This Night* additionally contains an alternative version of 'The Mac Man' plus five further tracks recorded at an earlier date (March 9, 1965) with David Izenzon (bs) and J. C. Moses (dm).

370 Musicological analysis of Shepp's album *On This Night* in Jost, *Free Jazz* (see note 3), pp. 114 and 117f.

371   Ibid., p. 114.

372   Nat Hentoff, Original liner notes (1966) for Archie Shepp, *On This Night*, Impulse! (1966).

373   Wilmer, *As Serious as Your Life* (see note 3), p. 29, translates 'Mac Man' as 'pimp.' This conflicts with Shepp's own information about the meaning of 'Mac Man', quoted in Nat Hentoff's original liner notes.

374   Hentoff, Liner notes for *On This Night* (see note 372); Wilmer, *As Serious as Your Life* (see note 3), p. 29.

375   Harvey Pekar, 'Review: Archie Shepp, On This Night – Impulse! 97', *Down-Beat* (July 1966), p. 32.

376   Sunny Murray spelled his name 'Sonny' at this time.

377   Fitzgerald, Grimes Discography (see chapter 3, note 11); Wilson, *Spirits Rejoice!* (see note 173), pp. 162f., says the album was recorded at 'LeRoi Jones' Spirit House in Newark [...], which he founded after the Harlem BART had collapsed.'

378   Sonny Murray, *Sonny's Time Now*, DIW CD DIW 355 (n.d.). Fitzgerald, Grimes Discography (see chapter 3, note 11).

379   Wilson, *Spirits Rejoice!* (see note 173), pp. 162f.

380   Wilmer, *As Serious as Your Life* (see note 3), p. 162.

381   Ibid.

382   Ibid., p. 159.

383   Wilson, *Spirits Rejoice!* (see note 173), pp. 162f.

384   Ibid.

385   'Black Art – by Amiri Baraka', Dudley Randall, ed.: *The Black Poets: A New Anthology* (New York: Bantam, n.d.), pp. 223f. – The spoken version from Sunny Murray's album *Sonny's Time Now*: www.youtube.com/watch?v=Dh2P-tlEH_w (viewed March 8, 2015).

386   Wilson, *Spirits Rejoice!* (see note 173), pp. 162f.

387   See also Weusi, Original LP liner notes (1966) for *Sonny Murray: Sonny's Time Now* (see note 367).

388   Brief interview with Sunny Murray before his concert in Dudelange (Luxembourg) in November 2007, where Grimes played bass and violin. Parts of the concert can be seen on the DVD documentary *Sunny's Time Now* (2008).

389   Bill Quinn, review 'Sunny Murray, *Sunny's Time Now* – Jihad 663', *DownBeat* (March 23, 1967), p. 33. – Grimes also performed with Sunny Murray in and around New York, see Stu Broomer's review of the Sunny Murray Orchestra at the University of Buffalo, March 12, 1966, with Grachan Moncur III and Henry Grimes: 'Henry has one of the biggest sounds I've heard' (*Coda* 1966/04, p. 28/9), and John Norris' review of Marion Brown, Grahan Moncur III, Grimes, and Murray at the Cellar Jazz Club, March 13, 1966 (*Coda* 1966/04, p. 29-31). In summer of 1966 Grimes played with Murray's Turn Of The Century group (Brown (as), Bennie Maupin (ts), Alan Shorter (tp), Moncur III (tb), Perry Robinson (cl), Joel Freedman (cello) at the Five Spot

- a benefit for Murray's son who had passed away shortly before; with the same group Grimes also performed in Canada (*Coda* 1966/06, p. 22).

390 Burton Greene, *Bloom In The Commune* ESP-Disk 4038 (2007) [interview-track 1].

391 Burton Greene, quoted from henrygrimes.com/biography/ (viewed: January 3, 2015)

392 Ibid.

393 Ibid.

394 Dan Warburton, Interview with Burton Greene, Amsterdam, December 22, 2003, paristransatlantic.com/magazine/interviews/greene.html (viewed April 30, 2015).

395 *Bloom In The Commune* (see note 390).

396 Bill Mathieu, 'Review: Burton Greene, Quartet – ESP Disk 1024', *Down-Beat* (March 1967), p. 40, sums up Henry Grimes' contribution: 'Grimes plays with usual sensitivity.'

397 *Cullen Knight Music* CD CKM-319/320: *The Life And Times Of Cullen Knight*, vol. 1 (1962-86), vol. 2 (1965-99). Fitzgerald, Grimes Discography (see chapter 3, note 11).

398 Fitzgerald, Grimes Discography (see chapter 3, note 11).

399 ESP-LP, *Frank Wright Trio*, ESP-Disk CD 4007, *The Complete ESP-Disk Recordings*, 2 CDs (2005), CD 1, tracks 1-3. Fitzgerald, Grimes Discography (see chapter 3, note 11).

400 See p. 94ff above.

401 *Charles Tyler Ensemble*, ESP-Disk CD ESP 1029-2. Fitzgerald, Grimes Discography (see chapter 3, note 11): 'Incorrectly listed as from Indianapolis in some sources, but Henry Grimes recalls this as being in New York City.'

402 See p. 101ff above.

403 See p. 109ff above.

404 See p. 75ff above.

405 Pharoah Sanders, *Tauhid*, GRP/Impulse! CD GRD-129 (1993). Fitzgerald, Grimes Discography (see chapter 3, note 11).

406 Rouy, 'Un Revenant Nommé' (see chapter 2, note 14).

407 Quinn, 'Four Modernists' (see note 325). Here Quinn reviewed albums by Archie Shepp, Pharoah Sanders, Bill Taylor, and Albert Ayler, awarding four stars to Sanders' *Tauhid*.

408 Nat Hentoff, Original liner notes (1967) for *Tauhid* (see note 405). Also Fitzgerald, Grimes Discography (see chapter 3, note 11).

409 Karl Berger, *From Now On*, ESP-Disk LP 12": ESP 1041. Fitzgerald, Grimes Discography (see chapter 3, note 11).

410 *Marzette Watts And Company*, ESP-Disk LP 12": ESP 1044. Fitzgerald, Grimes Discography (see chapter 3, note 11).

411 Fitzgerald, Grimes Discography (see chapter 3, note 11).

412 Albert Ayler, *Live In Greenwich Village: The Complete Impulse Recordings*, 1966, 2 CDs (Impulse, 1998); for more details see p. 83f above.

413 *Liberator* 6, no. 6 (June 1966). The author is grateful to M. Davis Grimes for this information.

414 See the Sunny Murray DVD documentary *Sunny's Time Now* (2008) and the statement by Albert Ayler quoted above on p. 85f. Also Wilmer, *As Serious as Your Life* (see note 3), pp. 129ff. and 213ff., on the precarious lives of many musicians she interviewed.

Chapter Five

1   Wilmer, *As Serious as Your Life* (see chapter 4, note 3), p. 58.

2   *Reclams Jazzlexikon* (see chapter 3, note 30), p. 97.

3   Frenz, Sonny Rollins interview 2007 (see chapter 3, note 3).

4   Burton Greene, 'Commentary on the new music', Burton Greene, *Bloom in the Commune*, ESP Disk 4038 (2007) [liner notes].

5   Sonny Rollins, at the end of 'In A Sentimental Mood', on Sonny Rollins, *Road Shows Vol. 2*, Doxy Records (2011), track 2.

6   Miles Davis and Quincy Troupe, *Miles: The Autobiography* (New York: Simon & Schuster Paperbacks (1st edition 1989), 2005), pp. 271ff.

7   Frenz, Sonny Rollins interview 2007 (see chapter 3, note 3).

8   Wilson, *Sonny Rollins* (chapter 3, note 6), p. 27.

9   Nisenson, *Open Sky* (see chapter 3, note 6), pp. 186-90.

10   Frenz, Sonny Rollins interview 2007 (see chapter 3, note 3).

11   Medwin, 'Playing the vibrations' (see chapter 1, note 3), p. 20.

12   Strauss, 'Silent 30 Years' (see chapter 2, note 68).

13   Blumenfeld, 'The Ballad of Henry Grimes' (see chapter 4, note 153), pp. 34f. Being asked 'in previous interviews, you have admitted to having [...] depression. Did that affect your decisions?', Grimes responded differently, 'No, not at that time. Not at the time I left New York. That was before [...].' Weiss, 'Interview' (see chapter 1, note 10).

14   George, 'A Jazz Mystery Unravels' (see chapter 2, note 57).

15   Blumenfeld, 'Ballad of Henry Grimes' (see chapter 4, note 153).

16   Ibid.

17   Galvani, Interview with Henry Grimes (see chapter 2, note 35).

18   Marrotte, '*Signal to Noise* Interview' (see chapter 2, note 32), pp. 43-47.

19   Galvani, Interview with Henry Grimes (see chapter 2, note 35).

20   Weiss, 'Interview' (see chapter 1, note 10).

21   Jackson, 'Backstage with ...Henry Grimes' (see chapter 3, note 53), p. 14.

22   Strauss, 'Silent 30 Years' (see chapter 2, note 68).

23   Ssirus W. Pakzad (2005), jazzthing.de/issues/60/henry-grimes.shtml (viewed: 2009).

24   Ssirus W. Pakzad, 'Wiederauferstehung: Der Bassist Henry Grimes', jazz zeitung.de/jazz/2005/06/portrait-grimes.shtml (viewed: 2009).

25   Frenz, Grimes interviews 2009 und 2010 (see chapter 4, note 125).

26   Kantor, 'Interview with Henry Grimes', (see chapter 1, note 5).

27   Ibid.

28   Frenz, Andrew Cyrille phone interview 2008 (see chapter 1, note 20).

29   Wu Ming 1, 'The Old New Thing Is Newer Than Ever', liner notes for *The Old New Thing: A Free Jazz Anthology*, Abraxas/Esp-Disk (2007). Grimes' story can also be found in a small publication about 'vanishing': Marc Tyler Nobleman, *Vanished: True Stories of the Missing* (New York: Scholastic, 2010). See also Klinkmann, 'Synch/Unsynch', (see introduction, note 1).

30   Email by M. Davis Grimes, December 2013.

31   In an interview from 2003 Grimes gives this information: 'I moved to San Francisco first and played some music there. I worked with a group of young guys called Lambert, Hendricks and Ross. [...].' Marrotte, *'Signal to Noise* Interview' (see chapter 2, note 32), p. 46. The vocal trio Lambert, Hendricks & Ross disbanded in 1964, and Lambert died in an automobile accident in 1966. Thereafter Hendricks continued to work with Annie Ross, but it is unlikely that Ross joined Hendricks' tour at the time. Clarence Becton knows nothing about it.

32   Weiss, 'Interview' (see chapter 1, note 10).

33   Barbara Frenz, Interview with Clarence Becton, Amsterdam, October 14, 2007.

34   The following account is mainly based on Clarence Becton's recollections simply because they are more detailed than Henry Grimes' on this point.

35   armandocairo.com/biographys/clarence/biography_clarence.html (viewed: January 4, 2015). Frenz, Becton interview (see note 33). Selected discography of Becton at discogs.com/artist/Clarence+Becton (viewed: January 4, 2015). de.wikipedia.org/wiki/Clarence_Becton (viewed: May 16, 2015).

36   Frenz, Becton interview (see note 33).

37   Email by Larry Vuckovich from December 22, 2014.

38   Frenz, Becton interview (see note 33); email by M. Davis Grimes, December 2013 (about Grimes' memories of Jon Hendrick's car).

39   Marrotte, *'Signal to Noise* Interview' (see chapter 2, note 32); Kantor 'Interview...', (see chapter 1, note 5); Barbara Frenz, *'Signs Along The Road*, or Conversing with Silent Powers: The legendary bass player Henry Grimes publishes his first volume of poems', jazzitalia.net/viscomunicatoemb.asp?EN=1&ID=3320 (published: April 28, 2007); Arne Reimer, `Henry Grimes, Eine völlig neue Musikwelt', *American Jazz Heroes. Besuche bei 50 Jazz-Legenden* (Cologne: Jazz Thing Verlag Axel Stinshoff, 2013), pp. 138-41.

40   Email by Larry Vuckovich from December 22, 2014.

41   Frenz, Becton interview (see note 33).

42   Ibid.

43   Ibid.

44   Ibid.

45   Frenz, Grimes interviews 2006 and 2007 (see chapter 1, note 4).

46   Ibid.

47   See Osterhausen, 'Die "wundersame Geschichte"' (see chapter 2, note 12).

48   Frenz, Becton interview (see note 33).

49   Email by M. Davis Grimes, March 2014.

50   On the Trident: Endress, 'Jon Hendricks Interview' (see note 36), p. 62.

51   Frenz, Becton interview (see note 33).

52   Weiss, 'Interview' (see chapter 1, note 10).

53   'Cecil Taylor knows about this story too', Email by M. Davis Grimes, December 2013.

54   Frenz, Becton interview (see note 33).

55   Ibid.

56   Ibid.

57   Ibid.

58   Rouy, 'Un Revenant Nommé: Henry Grimes' (see chapter 2, note 14); Weiss, 'Interview' (see chapter 1, note 10); henrygrimes.com/biography.

59   Warburton, Interview Sunny Murray (see chapter 4, note 152).

60   Blumenfeld, 'Ballad of Henry Grimes' (see chapter 4, note 153).

61   Marrotte, '*Signal to Noise* Interview' (see chapter 2, note 32).

62   Frenz, Becton interview (see note 33).

63   Weiss, 'Interview' (see chapter 1, note 10).

64   Ibid. Lyrics by E.Y. Harburg from *The Wizard of Oz* ('Follow the Yellow Brick Road').

65   Pakzad, 'Wiederauferstehung' (see note 24).

66   Strauss, 'Silent 30 Years' (see chapter 2, note 68).

67   Rouy, 'Un Revenant Nommé' (see chapter 2, note 14); henrygrimes.com/biography.

68   George, 'A Jazz Mystery Unravels' (see chapter 2, note 57).

69   Kantor, 'Interview …', (see chapter 1, note 5); Fitzgerald, 'Into Thin Air' (see chapter 1, note 6); henrygrimes.com/biography.

70   Jung, 'Fireside Chat with Henry Grimes' (see chapter 1, note 7). In Kantor's interview of 2007 (see chapter 1, note 5) Grimes said that the cost of the repairs was $500. He thus sold his bass for the original repair price of $500. Grimes gives inconsistent years for his move to L.A., varying between 1968 (Jung interview, ibid.) and 1969 (Marrotte interview, see chapter 2, note 32). Proceeding from Clarence Becton's recollections, it is most likely that Grimes lived in Los Angeles no later than early 1968.

71   Jung, 'Fireside Chat with Henry Grimes' (see chapter 1, note 7).

72   Strauss, 'Silent 30 Years' (see chapter 2, note 68).

73   Frenz, Becton interview (see note 33).

74   Frenz, Grimes interviews 2006 and 2007 (see chapter 1, note 4).

NOTES CHAPTER SIX

267

75 Pakzad, 'Wiederauferstehung' (see note 24).

76 Kantor, 'Interview…' (see chapter 1, note 5).

77 Frenz, Becton interview (see note 33).

78 Ibid.

79 Ibid.

80 Ibid.

81 Ibid.

Chapter Six

1   Frenz, Grimes interviews 2006 and 2007 (see chapter 1, note 4).

2   Frenz, Sonny Rollins interview 2007 (see chapter 3, note 3).

3   'Interview – Don Menza (tenor saxophonist, b. 1936)' (see chapter 3, note 98).

4   'Ted Panken Interviews Sam Rivers' (see chapter 4, note 36).

5   See p. 47 above.

6   Rusch, 'Buell Neidlinger: Interview' (see chapter 4, note 39), p. 5.

7   Frenz, Becton interview (see chapter 5, note 33).

8   Weiss, 'Interview Henry Grimes' (see chapter 1, note 10).

9   Frenz, Andrew Cyrille interview (see chapter 1, note 20).

10 George, 'A jazz mystery unravels: Henry Grimes' (see chapter 2, note 57). The year 1972 is surely wrong, for by then Henry had already sold his bass (probably in 1969), after which he stopped playing altogether.

11 Cherry, 'In heaven with Henry Grimes' (see chapter 2, note 6).

12 Blumenfeld, 'The Ballad of Henry Grimes' (see chapter 4, note 153).

13 Jung, 'Fireside Chat with Henry Grimes' (see chapter 1, note 7); Howard Mandel, 'Out Of The Woodwork', *The Wire* (April 2008), pp. 26-29.

14 Weiss, 'Interview' (see chapter 1, note 10).

15 Rouy, 'Un Revenant Nommé: Henry Grimes' (see chapter 2, note 14).

16 Marc Ribot, 'still things – that / move: The Poetry of Henry Grimes', Preface to Henry Grimes, *Signs Along The Road* (see introduction, note 2), p. 15 (on the poem 'Peace').

17 Grimes, *Signs Along The Road* (see introduction, note 2), pp. 98f.

18 See p. 126 above.

19 See p. 127 above.

20 Pérémarti, 'At Home With Henry Grimes' (see chapter 2, note 52). On Grimes' family see also chapter 2.

21 Marrotte, 'Henry Grimes' (see chapter 2, note 32).

22 Weiss, 'Interview Henry Grimes' (see chapter 1, note 10).

23 Rouy, 'Un Revenant Nommé' (see chapter 2, note 14).

24 Contreras, 'A Fresh Start…' (see chapter 1, note 18).

25 Grimes, *Signs Along The Road* (see introduction, note 2), p. 99 (from the poem *Peace*). See p. 140f above.

26 Frenz, Grimes interviews 2006 and 2007 (see chapter 1, note 4).

27 Strauss, 'Silent 30 Years' (see chapter 2, note 68). M. Davis Grimes (email, December 2013): 'Except for very short periods after Henry first arrived in Los Angeles, he was never homeless. Homelessness was his biggest dread, and he made sure to hold onto his apartment no matter what.'

28 Marrotte, '*Signal to Noise* Interview' (see chapter 2, note 32).

29 Ibid.

30 Frenz, Grimes interviews 2006 and 2007 (see chapter 1, note 4). See also Marrotte, '*Signal to Noise* Interview' (see chapter 2, note 32); George, 'A jazz mystery unravels' (see chapter 2, note 57).

31 The author is grateful to Henry Grimes and M. Davis Grimes for kindly providing photocopies of the form.

32 Frenz, Grimes interviews 2006 and 2007 (see chapter 1, note 4).

33 Marrotte, '*Signal to Noise* Interview' (see chapter 2, note 32).

34 Pérémarti, 'At Home' (see chapter 2, note 52), p. 20.

35 Also Jung, 'Fireside Chat with Henry Grimes' (see chapter 1, note 7).

36 George, 'A jazz mystery unravels' (see chapter 2, note 57).

37 Isoardi, 'The Return of Henry Grimes...' (see chapter 4, note 146).

38 See p. 71 above.

39 *Cadence* (March 1984), p. 93.

40 Marrotte, '*Signal to Noise* Interview' (see chapter 2, note 32); Fitzgerald, 'Henry Grimes, Past & Present' (see chapter 1, note 6); Profile Henry Grimes, 2005 (see chapter 2, note 54).

41 Isoardi, 'The Return of Henry Grimes...' (see chapter 4, note 146).

42 Frenz, Grimes interviews 2006 and 2007 (see chapter 1, note 4).

43 Ibid.

44 Ibid.

45 Ibid.

46 Pérémarti, 'At Home' (see chapter 2, note 52). The hotel was renovated in 2011. See Ryan Vaillancourt [staff writer of *Los Angeles Downtown News*], 'From Blight to Bright: Remaking the Huntington Hotel', ladowntown-news.com/news/from-blight-to-bright-remaking-the-huntington-hotel/article_97b9d020-00e9-11e1-a1dc-001cc4c03286.html (posted October 28, 2011).

47 Frenz, Grimes interviews 2009-10 (see chapter 4, note 125).

48 Pérémarti, 'At Home' (see chapter 2, note 52).

49 Strauss, 'Silent 30 Years' (see chapter 2, note 68).

50 Frenz, Grimes interviews 2006 and 2007 (see chapter 1, note 4).

51 Osterhausen, 'Die "wundersame Geschichte"' (see chapter 2, note 12).

52 Marrotte, '*Signal to Noise* Interview' (see chapter 2, note 32).

53 Frenz, Grimes interviews 2006 and 2007 (see chapter 1, note 4).

54 Osterhausen, 'Die "wundersame Geschichte"' (see chapter 2, note 12).

55 Frenz, Grimes interviews 2006 and 2007 (see chapter 1, note 4).

56 Ibid.

57 Ibid.

58 Frenz, Grimes interviews 2006 and 2007 (see chapter 1, note 4).

59 Ibid.

60 Ashante Infantry, 'Jazz Master Henry Grimes Makes Up for Lost Time', *Toronto Star* (September 11, 2010).

61 Isoardi, 'The Return' (see chapter 4, note 146) writes that Heather Evans had told Nick Rosen 'she had traveled to the west coast with him [Grimes] in 1968 and had last seen him in 1970.' This information is inaccurate, as is the given year 1968. Heather Evans traveled separately and met Grimes there, as M. Davis Grimes later verified with both Henry and Heather Evans.

62 Grimes, *Signs Along The Road* (see introduction, note 2), p. 23.

63 Frenz, Grimes interviews 2006 and 2007 (see chapter 1, note 4).

64 Ibid.

65 Ibid.

66 Ibid.

67 Ibid.

68 Ibid.

69 Ibid. A 2009 interview mentions a radio that Grimes owned in Los Angeles. See Eli Dvorkin, 'Exclusive: Henry Grimes' emotional explosions', flavorwire.com/13361/exclusive-henry-grimes-emotional-explosions (published March 10, 2009; viewed: January 3, 2015).

70 Dvorkin, 'Exclusive: Henry Grimes' emotional explosions' (see note 69).

71 Weiss, 'Interview Henry Grimes' (see chapter 1, note 10).

72 Kantor, 'Interview …' (see chapter 1, note 5).

73 Frenz, Grimes interviews 2006 and 2007 (see chapter 1, note 4).

74 Medwin, 'Playing the vibrations' (see chapter 1, note 3).

75 Frenz, Grimes interviews 2006 and 2007 (see chapter 1, note 4); Jackson, 'Backstage with …Henry Grimes' (see chapter 3, note 53), p. 14.; Kantor, 'Interview …' (see chapter 1, note 5).

76 Rouy, 'Un Revenant Nommé' (see chapter 2, note 14).

77 Frenz, Grimes interviews 2006 and 2007 (see chapter 1, note 4).

78 George, 'Jazz Mystery' (see chapter 2, note 57).

79 Frenz, Grimes interviews 2006 and 2007 (see chapter 1, note 4).

80 Mizar5, Interview with Henry Grimes (2005), writingaffairs.com/mizar5/hg.html (viewed: January 3, 2015).

81 Line from the poem *Coasts* (probably early 1980s) in Grimes, *Signs Along The Road* (see introduction, note 2), p. 68.

82 Frenz, Grimes interviews 2006 and 2007 (see chapter 1, note 4).

83   Grimes, *Signs Along The Road* (see introduction, note 2). See Frenz, '*Signs Along The Road*, or Conversing with Silent Powers' (see chapter 5, note 39); Edwin Pouncey, '*Signs Along The Road*: *Poems*: Henry Grimes – *Who Owns Music?* William Parker', *The Wire* (August 2007), p. 71; Hans-Jürgen von Osterhausen, 'Signs Along The Road von Henry Grimes, Who Owns Music von William Parker', *Jazz Podium* (May 2007), p. 62.

84   Dvorkin, 'Exclusive: Henry Grimes' emotional explosions' (see note 69).

85   Kantor, 'Interview …' (see chapter 1, note 5).

86   Dvorkin, 'Exclusive: Henry Grimes' emotional explosions' (see note 69).

87   Amiri Baraka (LeRoi Jones), 'New Music / New Poetry', in idem and Amina Baraka, *The Music* (see chapter 4, note 3), p. 243.

88   Ribot, 'still things – that / move' (see note 16), p. 18.

89   Frenz, '*Signs Along The Road*, or Conversing with Silent Powers' (see chapter 5, note 39).

90   Grimes, *Signs Along The Road* (see introduction, note 2), p. 60.

91   Ribot, 'still things – that / move' (see note 16), p. 18.

92   Frenz, '*Signs Along The Road*, or Conversing with Silent Powers' (see chapter 5, note 39).

93   Grimes, *Signs Along The Road* (see introduction, note 2), pp. 43 and 47.

94   Ibid., p. 72.

95   Dvorkin, 'Exclusive: Henry Grimes' emotional explosions' (see note 69).

96   Grimes, *Signs Along The Road* (see introduction, note 2), pp. 90f.

97   Ibid., pp. 110f.

98   Reviews of *Signs Along The Road* include David Francis, 'Metaphysical Free: The Poetry of Henry Grimes', cosmoetica.com/B813-DF1.htm (published May 28, 209), and Carol Pearce Bjorlie, Review of *Signs Along The Road* in *Bass World: Magazine of the International Society of Bassists* (summer 2009).

99   Among others Kenneth Burke, *The Philosophy of Literary Form: Studies in Symbolic Action* (Baton Rouge: Louisiana State University Press, 1967), and John William Draper, *History of the Intellectual Development of Europe* (New York: Harper & Brothers, 1863).

100 Ribot, 'still things – that / move' (see note 16), p. 18. Also Frenz, '*Signs Along the Road*, or Conversing with Silent Powers' (see chapter 5, note 39).

101 Cecil Taylor, Liner notes for *Unit Structures*.

102 Here the Grimesean neologisms are viewed outside the original context of his notebook. To analyze their meaning within that context would go beyond the scope of this biography.

103 In the age of the internet, it is easy to recognize which of these neologisms were also developed or employed independently by other people ('artitude', 'pragmagic', 'proantagonist', 'con/tra-gedy'). Nonetheless, Henry Grimes invented them himself long before the internet was publicly accessible.

104 Henry Grimes, Notebook (dating roughly from 1979 to 1981), p. 27.

105 See note p. 153 above

106 Medwin, 'Playing the vibrations' (see chapter 1, note 3), p. 17.

107 Dvorkin, 'Exclusive: Henry Grimes' emotional explosions' (see note 69).

108 Grimes, Notebook (see note 104), p. 34.

109 This is not to be confused with the technique of onomatopoeia, which plays a subordinate role in Grimes' poetry.

110 Grimes, Notebook (see note 104), p. 49.

111 Ribot, 'still things – that / move' (see note 16), pp. 18f.; 'Monk Music', Grimes, *Signs Along The Road* (see introduction, note 2), pp. 102f.

112 They appear in the Notebook as follow: Tense -3-1 / Faro – Faro! / A Pall / Perspectives diaanimisms / Pina Colada / Lover-IS / Land – that rests on kind illusions: / The OCEAN from – above – beyond: / Distinguishes / The Pigeonhole / Symbol / The emotions above are / O – moonlit cove / Ganymed / (App-) as a Poeticus mentus / (Epi) / Self Knowledge / A lit mis-en scene / Heteronym / Points.

113 The text entitled '(App-) as a Poeticus mentus' is signed '(H. A. Grimes) written 2.12.80' at the bottom. The text 'Heteronym' is signed 'H. A. Grimes' followed on a new line by 'Los Angeles 1.13.81.'

114 Bjorlie, Review of *Signs Along The Road* (see note 98), writes 'the sound of words, sometimes more important than the meaning.'

115 Grimes, Notebook (see note 104), p. 58 (signed 'Henry Grimes').

116 Ibid., p. 66 (signed 'Henry Grimes').

117 Ibid., pp. 67f. (signed 'H. A. Grimes').

118 Ibid., p. 75f. (signed 'H. A. Grimes').

119 Ibid., p. 92. The colon at the end of the poem is followed by a blank line and the signature 'H. A. Grimes.'

120 Ibid., pp. 168f. Signed 'H. A. Grimes' above 'Los Angeles 1.13.81', the whole encircled.

121 The text is given in excerpt below.

122 Ibid., pp. 101-06. The colon at the end of the poem is followed by a blank line and the signature '(H. A. Grimes)'.

123 Ibid., pp. 172-209.

124 Sheet 3.

125 Sheets 5-6.

126 If so, Grimes cannot have written down the story before 1983, when Lessing's novel appeared in print.

127 Beverly Blvd. 'begins off Santa Monica Boulevard in Beverly Hills and ends on the Lucas Avenue overpass near Downtown Los Angeles to become 1st Street' (en.m.wikipedia.org/wiki/Beverly_Boulevard - viewed: January 4, 2015) There is also a 'Flower St.' in downtown Los Angeles.

128 See p. 150 above.

129 Valentine, Jean. Excerpt from 'Anesthesia' from *Door in the Mountain* © 2004 by Jean Valentine. Reprinted with permission of Wesleyan University Press.

130 From the poem 'At Melville's Tomb', in *The Complete Poems of Hart Crane*, edited by Marc Simon, New York: Liveright, 1993, c1986.

131 The word 'gauge' is preceded by 'gaughe', heavily underlined.

Chapter Seven

1   Frenz, Grimes interviews 2006 and 2007 (see chapter 1, note 4)

2   See pp. 149 and 93 above.

3   Frenz, Sonny Rollins interview 2007 (see chapter 3, note 3).

4   Frenz, Andrew Cyrille interview 2008 (see chapter 4, note 328).

5   Instances of Henry Grimes' presence in the memory of the jazz world can be found in: *Cadence* 1, no. 3 (1976), p. 73 ('It leads off with a jaunty run through of Henry Grimes' Farmer Alfalfa'); *Cadence* 20, no. 7 (1994), p. 98 ('[William] Parker plays Henry Grimes and [Hamid] Drake plays Sunny Murray'); Ian Carr, *Keith Jarrett: The Man and His Music* (New York: Da Capo, 1992), p. 23: 'At the Dom, Jarrett also played [...] with bassist Henry Grimes, of whom he says: 'I thought he was great – even though his bass was a piece of shit – and he knew it!'"); Abraham Chapman, *New Black Voices: An Anthology of Contemporary Afro-American Literature* (New York: New American Library, 1972), p. 31 ('[...] Milford Graves, Cecil Taylor, Ornette Coleman, Henry Grimes. The one thing they all have in common is work'); W. Royal Stokes, *The Jazz Scene: An Informal History from New Orleans to 1990* (New York: Oxford University Press, 1993), p. 111 ('One night early on in our stay at the Five Spot I [Charlie Haden] was unpacking my bass and getting ready to play the first set and I looked out and standing at the bar was Charles Mingus, Wilbur Ware, Paul Chambers, Ron Carter, Richard Davis, Percy Heath, Henry Grimes, I mean every great bass player in jazz was standing at the bar [...]'); Addison Gayle, *The Black Aesthetic* (New York: Doubleday, 1972), p. 145 ('[...] bass and drums became soloists in a collective performance. Mingus influenced the new bassists, and blacks Henry Grimes and Richard Davis emerged with an indestructible foundation for rhythm [...]'); *Jazz Times* 31 (2001), p. 88 ('Bisio also plays tribute to a major bass influence on Grimes, Henry Grimes').

6   tinyurl.com/6dkn2w (viewed: January 4, 2015). M. Davis Grimes kindly shared this information about the court hearing (email, June 26, 2009).

7   Ribot, 'still things – that / move' (see chapter 6, note 16), pp. 16f.

8   Marrotte, '*Signal to Noise* Interview' (see chapter 2, note 32), p. 45.

9   Ibid.

10   Ibid.

11   George, 'A jazz mystery unravels' (see chapter 2, note 57).

12   Marrotte, '*Signal to Noise* Interview' (see chapter 2, note 32), p. 45.

13   Marrotte, 'Surviving Albert Ayler' (see chapter 2, note 32), p. 43. Also see Marshall Marrotte's statement in the video documentary by Henry Cherry, *The Resurrection of Henry Grimes*, n.d., vimeo.com/69922806 (go to 3:30).

14 Hobart, 'A jazz bassist is back in action' (see chapter 4, note 11).

15 Ibid.

16 Cherry, 'In heaven with Henry Grimes' (see chapter 2, note 6).

17 Hobart, 'A jazz bassist is back in action' (see chapter 4, note 11).

18 Frenz, Grimes interviews 2006 and 2007 (see chapter 1, note 4).

19 Marrotte, 'Surviving Albert Ayler' (see chapter 2, note 32), p. 43.

20 Marrotte, '*Signal to Noise* Interview' (see chapter 2, note 32), p. 45.

21 Ibid., p. 47.

22 Ibid.

23 Ibid.

24 Ibid.

25 Ibid.

26 Strauss, 'Silent 30 Years, a Jazzman Resurfaces' (see chapter 2, note 68).

27 Marrotte, '*Signal to Noise* Interview' (see chapter 2, note 32), p. 47.

28 Ibid.

29 Ibid.

30 See p. 135 above.

31 Marrotte, '*Signal to Noise* Interview' (see chapter 2, note 32), p. 47.

32 Jung, 'Fireside Chat with Henry Grimes' (see chapter 1, note 7).

33 Marrotte, '*Signal to Noise* Interview' (see chapter 2, note 32), p. 47.

34 Ibid.

35 George, 'A jazz mystery unravels' (see chapter 2, note 57).

36 Blumenfeld, 'The Ballad of Henry Grimes' (see chapter 4, note 153).

37 Pakzad (2005) (see chapter 5, note 23).

38 Marrotte, '*Signal to Noise* Interview' (see chapter 2, note 32), p. 47.

39 Ibid.

40 Davis was her family name then. Since 2007 she has been married to Henry Grimes and her family name is now Davis Grimes.

41 M. Davis Grimes, 'Henry Grimes & Olive Oil' (as of August 2003), henry-grimes.com/biography.

42 Ibid. She also reports this in the interview she gave with Hans-Jürgen von Osterhausen in 2005: 'I began to work for Henry and asked many people for help […] to get him a new bass. Henry, I should point out, is not a man to ask for help. He doesn't have the nerve.' Osterhausen, 'Die "wundersame Geschichte"' (see chapter 2, note 12).

43 Davis Grimes, 'Olive Oil' (see note 41).

44 Ibid.

45 Fred Jung, 'A fireside chat with William Parker', allaboutjazz.com/a-fire-side-chat-with-william-parker-william-parker-by-aaj-staff.php?width=1024 (published: May 16, 2003; viewed: January 3, 2015).

46 Email from William Parker to M. Davis, November 29, 2002. Permission to publish kindly granted by William Parker.

47   Email from M. Davis to Marshall Marrotte, December 4, 2002.

48   Davis Grimes, 'Olive Oil' (see note 41); entry by M. Davis on jazznewyork. org (*ca.* 2002-03).

49   Jung, 'Fireside chat with William Parker' (see note 45).

50   Email from Marshall Marrotte to M. Davis, December 9, 2012. Permission to publish kindly granted by Marshall Marrotte.

51   Frenz, Grimes interviews 2006 and 2007 (see chapter 1, note 4).

52   Email from M. Davis to Marshall Marrotte, December 13, 2002.

53   Davis Grimes, 'Olive Oil' (see note 41); Frenz, Grimes interviews 2006 and 2007 (see chapter 1, note 4).

54   Frenz, Grimes interviews 2009 and 2010 (see chapter 4, note 125).

55   Ibid.

56   Ibid.

57   Ibid.

58   M. Davis Grimes, 'Olive Oil' (see note 41); Frenz, Grimes interviews 2006 and 2007 (see chapter 1, note 4).

59   Cherry, 'In heaven with Henry Grimes' (see chapter 2, note 6).

60   Frenz, Grimes interviews 2006 and 2007 (see chapter 1, note 4); Jackson, 'Backstage with…Henry Grimes' (see chapter 3, note 53).

61   Jung, 'Fireside chat with Henry Grimes' (see chapter 1, note 7).

62   Andrey Henkin, 'Henry Grimes', *All About Jazz* 7 (2003), p. 16.

63   George, 'A jazz mystery unravels' (see chapter 2, note 57).

64   Email from M. Davis to Wendy Oxenhorn, December 16, 2002.

65   Frenz, Grimes interviews 2006 and 2007 (see chapter 1, note 4).

66   Entry by M. Davis on jazznewyork.org (ca. 2002-03).

67   Ibid.

68   Ibid.

69   Email from M. Davis to Marshall Marrotte, April 9, 2003, sent just after she had spoken by phone with Sonny Rollins.

70   Marrotte, '*Signal to Noise* Interview' (see chapter 2, note 32); George, 'A Jazz Mystery Unravels' (see chapter 2, note 57); Strauss, 'Silent 30 Years' (see chapter 2, note 68); 'Bassist Henry Grimes, Alive', *Jazztimes* (April 2003), p. 24; Blumenfeld, 'Ballad' (see chapter 4, note 153); 'Noticias: El Regreso de Henry Grimes', *Cuadernos De Jazz* (2003), no. 7, p. 18; and a radio feature by Felix Contreras for NPR in 2003.

71   Pakzad, 'Wiederauferstehung: Der Bassist Henry Grimes' (see chapter 5, note 24).

72   Kantor, 'Interview …' (see chapter 1, note 5).

73   Frenz, Grimes interviews 2009 and 2010 (see chapter 4, note 125).

74   Val Wilmer, Letter to the editor, *The Wire* 228 (February 2003), p. 6.

75   outerspaceways.info/forum/saturn/23727 (viewed: 2009).

76   Email from Marshall Marrotte to M. Davis and others, February 5, 2003. Permission to publish kindly granted by Marshall Marrotte.

77   Davis Grimes, 'Henry Grimes & Olive Oil' (see chapter 7, note 41).

78   Isoardi, 'The Return of Henry Grimes...' (see chapter 4, note 146).

79   Ibid.; and email by Steven L. Isoardi from April 26, 2015.

80   Ibid. There exists a private recording of this session; see Fitzgerald, Grimes Discography (see chapter 3, note 11).

81   Isoardi, 'The Return of Henry Grimes...' (see chapter 4, note 146).

82   George, 'A jazz mystery unravels' (see chapter 2, note 57). However, in all likelihood Grimes sold his bass, not in 1972, but in 1969, after which date he says that he no longer played bass at all; see p. 135f above.

83   George, 'A jazz mystery unravels' (see chapter 2, note 57).

84   Ibid.

85   Ibid.

86   M. Davis Grimes, 'The Miraculous Return of the Great Henry Grimes!', henrygrimes.com/biography.

87   email by M. Davis Grimes, January 2014; Isoardi, 'The Return of Henry Grimes...' (see chapter 4, note 146).

88   There exists a private recording of this concert; Fitzgerald, Grimes Discography (see chapter 3, note 11). Fitzgerald gives the date of the concert as March 21, 2003; Isoardi knows of two concerts on March 21 and 22, 2003.

89   Isoardi, 'The Return of Henry Grimes...' (see chapter 4, note 146), names reed-master Charles Owens; Fitzgerald, Grimes Discography (see chapter 3, note 11), gives the tenor saxophonist of this concert as George Harper. There exists a private recording of this concert (Fitzgerald, ibid.) as well as a report on the second set of the second concert (March 22) in the forum on forums.allaboutjazz.com/archive/index.php/t-713.html (viewed: January 4, 2015), where it is said that Owens (at least at this set) did not appear and Harper is not listed among the ensemble members.

90   George, 'A jazz mystery unravels' (see chapter 2, note 57); Isoardi, 'The Return of Henry Grimes...' (see chapter 4, note 146).

91   George, 'A jazz mystery unravels' (see chapter 2, note 57).

92   Ibid.

93   Isoardi, 'The Return of Henry Grimes...' (see chapter 4, note 146).

94   Chris Abani, Kalakuta Republic (London: Saqi, 2000); idem, Daphne's Lot (Granada Hills, CA: Red Hen, 2003); Isoardi, 'The Return of Henry Grimes...' (see chapter 4, note 146).

95   Isoardi, 'The Return of Henry Grimes...' (see chapter 4, note 146).

96   Ibid.

97   Greg Burk, 'Henry Grimes Ensemble at the World Stage', *LA Weekly* (March 21, 2003), p. 44; also Isoardi, 'The Return of Henry Grimes...' (see chapter 4, note 146).

98   Greg Burk, 'Jazz Pick of the Week: Henry Grimes and Friends', *LA Weekly* (September 5-11, 2003), p. 127; also Isoardi, 'The Return of Henry Grimes...' (see chapter 4, note 146).

99   Forum entry by 'Adam' on forums.allaboutjazz.com/archive/index. php/t-713.html (viewed: January 4, 2015).

100   Isoardi, 'The Return of Henry Grimes...' (see chapter 4, note 146).

101   Copy of the concert announcement ('Howling Monk News') kindly supplied by M. Davis Grimes; also Isoardi, 'The Return of Henry Grimes...' (see chapter 4, note 146). There is no known recording of this concert; neither of these two concert dates is listed in Fitzgerald, Grimes Discography (see chapter 3, note 11).

102   Personal email from Alex Cline to Steven L. Isoardi, April 22, 2003, Isoardi, 'The Return of Henry Grimes...' (see chapter 4, note 146).

103   Nels Cline, 'New Spiel for Spring 2003' (May 1, 2003), nelscline.com; quotation from Isoardi, 'The Return of Henry Grimes...' (see chapter 4, note 146).

104   Email from M. Davis to Marshall Marrotte, February 25, 2002.

105   Jung, 'Fireside chat with William Parker' (see note 45).

106   Email from M. Davis Grimes, May 7, 2012.

107   Isoardi, 'The Return of Henry Grimes...' (see chapter 4, note 146).

108   Email from Dave Holland to M. Davis, May 28, 2003, quoted on henrygrimes.com/press/ (viewed: January 11, 2015).

109   Strauss, 'Silent 30 Years' (see chapter 2, note 68).

110   Ibid. Grimes left New York City in 1967, not in 1968; see p. 129ff above.

111   Strauss, 'Silent 30 Years' (see chapter 2, note 68).

112   Frenz, Grimes interviews 2009 and 2010 (see chapter 4, note 125).

113   Dvorkin, 'Exclusive: Henry Grimes' emotional explosions' (see chapter 6, note 69).

114   M. Davis Grimes, 'Henry Grimes & Olive Oil' (see note 41).

115   Email from M. Davis Grimes, May 7, 2012; artsforart.org/events/archive/schedule/vision8 (viewed: January 4, 2015); Fitzgerald, Grimes Discography (see chapter 3, note 11). See also henrygrimes.com/biography.

116   Blumenfeld, 'The Ballad of Henry Grimes' (see chapter 4, note 153).

117   youtube.com/watch?v=9l-vY7tN5i8 (viewed: January 4, 2015).

118   These musicians are mentioned by name in the Vision Festival flyer as ensemble members of the Jeanne Lee project of May 26, 2003; information kindly supplied by M. Davis Grimes. See also artsforart.org/events/archive/schedule/vision8 (viewed: January 4, 2015) and the concert video on youtube.com/watch?v=hOnXEJjNQfA (viewed: January 4, 2015). There is also a cd/dvd set with audio and video recordings of the concert (*Vision* Vol. 3, released 2005); henrygrimes.com/biography; Isoardi, 'The Return of Henry Grimes...' (see chapter 4, note 146); Fitzgerald, Grimes Discography (see chapter 3, note 11), with different names of some ensemble members.

119 Gary Giddins, *Village Voice*; see also Gary Giddins, *Jazz Times* (quoted on henrygrimes.com/press/) and Laurence Donohue-Greene (managing editor), *All About Jazz / New York* (quoted on henrygrimes.com/press/).

120 Jim Eigo, 'Top 10 for 2003'; quoted from henrygrimes.com/press/.

121 M. Davis, Liner notes to Henry Grimes, *More Call: Solo acoustic bass played on the air at WKCR 89.9 FM Sunday June 1, 2003,* Mastered by Jeff Willems (CD 2004, available through henrygrimes.com). May 28 – June 1: Henry Grimes Radio Festival, WKCR-FM, 89.9 on the dial, NYC. See Davis Grimes, 'The Miraculous Return of the Great Henry Grimes!' (see note 86). Fitzgerald, Grimes Discography (see chapter 3, note 11), only mentions the recorded broadcasts from May 31 and June 1 for this radio festival.

122 Frenz, Grimes interviews 2006 and 2007 (see chapter 1, note 4). See below pp. 200.

123 Fitzgerald, Grimes Discography (see chapter 3, note 11).

124 Davis, Liner notes (see note 121); Fitzgerald, Grimes Discography (see chapter 3, note 11).

125 Davis, Liner notes (see note 121). The usual spelling of the legendary pianist's name is Hasaan Ibn Ali.

126 'Hassan Ibn Ali wanted Henry to play that line on Hassan's first, and sadly, as things turned out, his only album, *The Max Roach Trio featuring the Legendary Hassan*. Henry was to be the bassist on that recording but was not able to make the recording date, so Art Davis can now be heard playing that bass line.' Email from M. Davis Grimes, January 2014.

127 Davis Grimes, 'The Miraculous Return of the Great Henry Grimes!' (see note 86).

128 Blumenfeld, 'The Ballad of Henry Grimes' (see chapter 4, note 153).

129 There exists a private recording of this session; Fitzgerald, Grimes Discography (see chapter 3, note 11).

130 Osterhausen, 'Die "wundersame Geschichte"' (see chapter 2, note 12).

131 Henkin, 'Henry Grimes' (see note 62). It was a workshop and not a benefit concert (information kindly supplied by M. Davis Grimes).

132 Davis Grimes, 'Henry Grimes & Olive Oil' (see note 41).

133 Ibid.

134 Isoardi, 'The Return of Henry Grimes...' (see chapter 4, note 146). Rex Butters, 'Henry Grimes Quartet at The Jazz Bakery 6.10.03', All About Jazz (2003), no. 7, p. 16.

135 Jung, 'Fireside chat with Henry Grimes' (see chapter 1, note 7).

136 Ibid.

137 Ibid. See also henrygrimes.com/press/ with further press statements about Grimes' return to the music world in 2003 (by Scott Yanow, Ken Frankling, and others).

Chapter Eight

1   Blumenfeld, 'The Ballad of Henry Grimes' (see chapter 4, note 153).

2   David Adler, *All About Jazz / New York*; Kelvin Leander Williams, *Time Out New York*; both quoted on henrygrimes.com/press/.

3   All the information below on Grimes' concerts, gigs, and awards is taken from the 'Henry Grimes Sessionography' (2003-), kindly placed at the author's disposal by M. Davis Grimes.

4   Dvorkin, 'Exclusive: Henry Grimes' emotional explosions' (see chapter 6, note 69).

5   A transcript of the letter can be found on henrygrimes.com/press/. On Lindberg's letter see Corey Kilgannon, 'An Unlikely Duo, Bound By Jazz', *New York Times: City Room* (April 16, 2009).

6   Isoardi, 'The Return of Henry Grimes…' (see chapter 4, note 146).

7   Grimes experienced the same in 2010 in the Angel City Jazz Festival and 'said it did trouble him, but he wanted to play so badly that he didn't dare object.' (email by M. Davis Grimes, January 2014).

8   Frenz, Grimes interviews 2009 and 2010 (see chapter 4, note 125).

9   Isoardi, 'The Return of Henry Grimes…' (see chapter 4, note 146).

10 Ibid.

11 Frenz, Grimes interviews 2009 and 2010 (see chapter 4, note 125).

12 Email from M. Davis Grimes, September 26, 2012.

13 Frenz, Grimes interviews 2006 and 2007 (see chapter 1, note 4).

14 Frenz, Grimes interviews 2009 and 2010 (see chapter 4, note 125).

15 Ibid.

16 Ibid.

17 Email by M. Davis Grimes, January 2014.

18 Grimes, *Signs Along The Road* (see introduction, note 2). Taken from the poem 'moments', which also is the first track (spoken by Henry Grimes) on the album Henry Grimes and Rashied Ali, *Spirits Aloft*, Porter Records PRCD-4049 (2010).

19 Isoardi, 'The Return of Henry Grimes…' (see chapter 4, note 146); Burk, 'Jazz Pick of the Week: Henry Grimes and Friends' (see chapter 7, note 98).

20 Dennis Gonzalez, *Nile River Suite*, Daagnim CD 9 (2004), temporarily out of stock. See henrygrimes.com/store/; Fitzgerald, Grimes Discography (see chapter 3, note 11).

21 Quoted from henrygrimes.com/press/.

22 Email correspondence between M. Davis Grimes and Chloe Cutts, a former writer for the now defunct magazine *Double Bassist*. The winter 2007 issue carried Henry Grimes on the cover.

23 allaboutjazz.com/php/news.php?id=14367 (posted July 17, 2007; viewed: January 4, 2015); Davis, 'Henry Grimes & Olive Oil' (see chapter 7, note 41).

24 Weiss, 'Interview Henry Grimes' (see chapter 1, note 10).

25 Pheralyn Dove, 'Whatever happened to Henry Grimes?', *Philadelphia*

Tribune (February 2009), tinyurl.com/ccqzjt (viewed: 2009).

26   *Sublime Communication*. All titles on JazzNewYork Productions (2004), temporarily out of stock.

27   Quoted from the CD booklet to Henry Grimes Trio featuring Andrew Lamb and Newman Tylor Baker, *Sublime Communication. Live at WKCR Studios* July 16, 2004 (temporarily out of stock).

28   Quoted from henrygrimes.com/press/.

29   *Live At The Kerava Jazz Festival* (2004), Ayler Records CD #AYL-CD-028 (2005).

30   Liner notes by William Parker and Ben Young for Henry Grimes Trio, *Live At The Kerava Jazz Festival* (Henry Grimes, Hamid Drake, David Murray), Ayler Records (2005). See also the review by Andrey Henkin at allaboutjazz.com/php/article.php?id=17465.

31   See also Charles L. Latimer, 'Improv The Grimy Way', metrotimes.com/blog/musicblahg.asp?month=11&year=2006 (viewed: 2009).

32   Glenn Astarita, 'Henry Grimes Trio, Live At the Kerava Jazz Festival / Marc Ribot, Spiritual Unity', *DownBeat* (September 2005), p. 77. Further reviews at *All About Jazz, Los Angeles* (by Fred Jung, chief editor), downtownmusicgallery.com (by Bruce Lee Gallanter), paristransatlantic.com (by Dan Warburton, chief editor), and *All About Jazz* (by Rex Butters). Quotes from these reviews at henrygrimes.com/press/. These and further reviews (full text) at ayler.com/henry-grimes-kerava-jazz-festival.html (viewed: January 4, 2015).

33   Marc Medwin, bagatellen.com (2005).

34   Dominique Queillée, Grimes, Le Revenant, liberation.fr/cahier-special/2004/06/05/grimes-le-revenant_482071 (viewed: April 13, 2015).

35   Bill Shoemaker, 'Henry Grimes Trio: Open Windows – Music with a View, Vienna 25 September 2004', *Jazz Review* (October 2004), p. 7.

36   Grimes also played with Charles Gayle on May 22, 2004: Henry Grimes with William Parker & Charles Gayle, Victoriaville Festival, Colisee des Bois-Francs, Quebec, Canada (email by M. Davis Grimes, January 2014).

37   Rouy, 'Un Revenant Nommé: Henry Grimes' (see chapter 2, note 14).

38   William Parker, *Requiem*, Splasc(H) World #H885 (2006). See also Fitzgerald, Grimes Discography (see chapter 3, note 11).

39   Daniel Graham, Review of Marc Ribot Trio: London, October 28, 2011, allaboutjazz.com/php/article.php?id=40897 (published November 26, 2011).

40   Marc Ribot, Roy Campbell, Jr., Henry Grimes, and Chad Taylor, *Spiritual Unity*, Pi Recordings CD #15 (2005). Also Astarita, 'Live at the Kerava Jazz Festival' (see note 32).

41   See Marc Ribot's liner notes to *Spiritual Unity* (see note 40).

42   Olson, 'Interview with Marc Ribot ...' (see chapter 4, note 208).

43   Medwin, 'Playing the vibrations' (see chapter 1, note 3).

44   Jackson, 'Backstage with ... Henry Grimes' (see chapter 3, note 53). Further reviews by John Litweiler (*Chicago Sun-Times*), Matthew Lurie (*Time Out, Chicago*), Maggie Williams (*Double Bassist*), and Howard Reich (*Chicago Tribune*). Quotes from these reviews on henrygrimes.com/press/; Aaron Ibn Pori Pitts wrote down his thoughts about this concert in a note published on this website.

45   Maggie Williams, *Double Bassist*, quoted from henrygrimes.com/press/.

46   Patricia Parker, ed., *Vision Festival: Peace*, (2005).

47   thestonenyc.com/calendar.php?month=-112 (viewed: January 4, 2015).

48   On September 23 and 24 Lonnie Plaxico played bass, since Grimes was committed to a concert in Chicago. The club is not the historic Birdland named after Charlie Parker, located at 52nd Street and Broadway from 1949 to 1965.

49   Laurent Rigaut, 'Henry Grimes Trio, Salle Charcot, Marcq en Baroeul, 7 Octobre 2005: Une belle date', *Impro Jazz* (November-December 2005), p. 26.

50   This was the first time I met Henry Grimes in person.

51   For example Pakzad (see chapter 5, notes 23 and 24); Osterhausen, 'Die "wundersame Geschichte"' (see chapter 2, note 12); Rigaut, 'Henry Grimes Trio' (see note 49), who erroneously gives Grimes' absence from the music world as twenty years instead of *ca.* thirty-five; Broecking, 'Zurück am Bass nach dreissig Jahren' (see chapter 4, note 167); and Mizar5, Interview with Henry Grimes (see chapter 6, note 80).

52   Henry Grimes Trio, *Sublime Communication 2: Live at Edgefest* (JazzNewYork Productions, 2006). See also henrygrimes.com/store.

53   Marc Medwin, *dustedmagazine.com* (quoted from henrygrimes.com/press/). Another review by Will Stewart, *Ann Arbor News* (see the quote on henrygrimes.com/press/).

54   The CD is available only from Aaron Ibn Pori Pitts' family (see information at henrygrimes.com/store/). Aaron Ibn Pori Pitts dedicated several poems to Grimes, of which two are published on henrygrimes.com and another is heard on the concert CD *For Ibn Pori*, recorded at WFHB in 2005.

55   Luis Perdomo, *Awareness*, RKM Music #1123 (2006).

56   henrygrimes.com/biography/.

57   Duo concert at The Stone, New York, on July 24, 2012.

58   March 2006: Spaceship On The Highway tour with Marshall Allen. Review by Sean Westergaard, *All Music Guide* (see the quote from this review at henrygrimes.com/press/).

59   On March 22 Grimes played in Chicago's Velvet Lounge on the occasion of Fred Anderson's eightieth birthday. His appearances, along with those of the other guests, were recorded live and released on DVD as Fred Anderson, *21st Century Chase* DVD, featuring Fred Anderson, Harrison Bankhead, Henry Grimes, Edward 'Kidd' Jordan, Jeff Parker, and Chad Taylor (delmark DVD-1589).

60   ARIKA symposium, 'Freedom Is a Constant Struggle', Glasgow, Scotland, April 21 2013: *WordMusic* by Amiri Baraka and Henry Grimes. See Grimes' statement about his history with Amiri Baraka in chapter 4, p. 73f.

61   Frank Rubolino, *All About Jazz 2004* (a quote from this review at henry grimes.com/press/).

62   Ibid.

63   Live recordings of the concert in Dudelange (Luxembourg), November 2007, can be found on *Sunny's Time Now* (DVD 2008).

64   In this context a portrait of Henry Grimes appeared in the *Financial Times*; see Hobart, 'A jazz bassist is back in action' (see chapter 4, note 11). Also worth reading is Marc Medwin's review of the concert by the Marc Ribot Trio with Henry Grimes and Chad Taylor, 2010, at Brooklyn's Rose Live Music Club in New York, in Medwin, 'Playing The vibrations' (see chapter 1, note 3), p. 20. Video clip of *I'll Get By As Long As I Have You* from this concert on henrygrimes.com/videos/ (viewed: January 4, 2015). See also the reviews by Daniel Graham, 'Marc Ribot Trio: London, England, October 28, 2011' (see note 39), and Stephen Graham, 'Jazz breaking news: Marc Ribot Calls Upon The Holy Ghost', jazzwisemagazine.com/news-main-menu-139/68-2011/12104-jazz-breaking-news-marc-ribot-trio-calls-upon-the-holy-ghost-at-city-sessions (published October 31, 2011; viewed: 2011). A bluesy sequence from the London concert of 2011 on henrygrimes. com/videos/. Further reviews with quotations at henrygrimes.com/press/.

65   See the review by Larry Blumenfeld, 'Intimate Encounters at June's Jazz Fests', *Village Voice* (July 18, 2012), villagevoice.com/2012-07-18/music/intimate-encounters-at-june-s-jazz-fests (viewed: January 4, 2015).

66   Further reviews of Grimes' concert appearances since 2003 can be found at henrygrimes.com/press/, which also contains a collection of relevant video clips. The copy deadline for this book was December 31, 2012 (with a few exceptions after this date). Readers interested in Grimes' artistic activities after this date are referred to his website.

67   Henry Grimes and Oluyemi Thomas, *The Power of Light*, NotTwo Records #MW 787-2 (2007).

68   Marc Medwin, Review to Henry Grimes and Oluyemi Thomas (see note 67), dustedmagazine.com/reviews/3899 (published October 19, 2007). See also the review by John Sharpe, 'Henry Grimes Twofer: The Power Of Light & Going To The Ritual', allaboutjazz.com/php/article.php?d=29412 (published June 8, 2008).

69   Daniel Graham, 'Henry Grimes, Sunny Murray and David Murray at the Haarlem Jazzstad', allaboutjazz.com/php/article.php?id=22859 (published August 27, 2006).

70   Daniel Graham, 'Henry Grimes at the London Jazz Festival 2006', allaboutjazz.com/php/article.php?id=23775 (published November 14, 2006).

71   Kantor, 'Interview …' (see chapter 1, note 5).

72   Ibid.

73   Henry Grimes and Rashied Ali, *Going to the Ritual* (Porter Records #PRCD

4005, 2008).

74   Marc Medwin, Liner notes for ibid. Selected reviews: Glenn Astarita, allaboutjazz.com/php/article.php?id=31710 (published January 27, 2009); Dove, 'Whatever happened to Henry Grimes?' (see note 25); John Sharpe, Henry Grimes Twofer (see note 68); Jeph Jerman, Henry Grimes & Rashied Ali, *Going To The Ritual*, squidsear.com/cgi-bin/news/newsView.cgi?newsID=1112 (published February 2, 2010).

75   Medwin, Liner notes (see note 74). Selected reviews by Astarita, Dove, Jerman, and Sharpe all ibid.

76   Henry Grimes, *Signs Along The Road* (see introduction, note 2).

77   David Grundy, Cambridge University (UK), editor of *Eartrip* magazine (quoted after henrygrimes.com/press/). Further reviews of *Signs Along The Road* by Pearce Bjorlie ('Henry's making wordmusic', see chapter 6, note 98), Pouncey (see chapter 6, note 83), Carina Prange in *Jazz Dimensions*, Francis (see chapter 6, note 98), and Frenz (see chapter 5, note 39). Quotes at henrygrimes.com/press/. See also chapter 6 of this book.

78   M. Davis Grimes forwarded this email to the author in 2012. Permission to publish it kindly granted by Kresten Osgood.

79   *Henry Grimes Solo*, ILK Music 151 (2009), double CD set.

80   Review by Bruce Lee Gallanter of Downtown Music Gallery (quoted from henrygrimes.com/press/).

81   Marc Medwin in *dustedmagazine.com* (quoted from henrygrimes.com/press/). See also Wolfram Knauer, Review of *Henry Grimes Solo*, ILK Music 151 CD (2009), *Jazz Podium* 2009/02, p. 62. Further reviews of this album with quotations at henrygrimes.com/press/. See also Cherry, 'In heaven with Henry Grimes' (see chapter 2, note 6).

82   Mark Urness, *Bass World*, quoted from henrygrimes.com/press/.

83   Nilan Perera, Review of *Henry Grimes Solo*, exclaim.ca/Music/article/henry_grimes-solo (published: July 21, 2009).

84   Mitch Myers, Review of *Henry Grimes Solo*, jazztimes.com/articles/24423-solo-henry-grimes (published: April 2009).

85   Roswell Rudd, *Trombone Tribe*, Sunnyside SSC 1207 (2009), with Henry Grimes on tracks 2, 5, 7, 8 and 9. Review by Raul d'Gama Rose at allaboutjazz.com/php/article.php?id=32682 (published May 1, 2009).

86   Profound Sound Trio, *Opus de Life* (Andrew Cyrille (dm), Paul Dunmall (ts, bagpipes), and Henry Grimes (bs, vln)), Porter Records PRCD-4032 (2009).

87   Frenz, Andrew Cyrille interview 2008 (see chapter 4, note 328).

88   Barbara Frenz, Review of Profound Sound Trio, *Opus de Life* (see note 86) in *Jazz Podium* (2009), no. 58, p. 72. Further reviews by John Sharpe in *All About Jazz* (August 2008), Glenn Astarita in *EJazz News*, and Ed Hazell in *Signal To Noise* no. 55 (Fall 2009). Quotes from these reviews at henrygrimes.com/press/.

89   Peter Bacon, Review 'From Cheltenham: The Profound Sound Trio', the-jazzbreakfast.com/2009/05/02/from-cheltenham-the-profound-sound-trio/ (published May 2, 2009): 'His [Grimes'] famous beat and strong sense of forward momentum rang clearly throughout. [...] This was a listening band above all as evidenced by the varying tempi, identifiable but constantly shifting tonal centres, sense of dynamics, complete instrumental virtuosity and the need to communicate. This is the way forward for the music. [...].' Daniel Graham, Review of The Profound Sound Trio At The Vortex Jazz Club, London, November 23 2009, allaboutjazz.com/php/article.php?id =34872 &width=1024#.UwjN4sFxt3s (published December 11, 2009): 'But while the individual parts are top notch, it is the quality of their interactions which sets the Profound Sound Trio apart. [...].' John Sharpe, Review of The Profound Sound Trio At The Vortex, London, November 23 2009, allaboutjazz.com/php/article.php?id=34875&width=1024#.UwjPt8Fxt3s (published December 12, 2009); Peter Bacon, Concert review, Profound Sound Trio: CBSO Centre Birmingham, UK, November 28, 2009, the-jazzbreakfast.com/2009/11/29/concert-review-profound-sound-trio (published November 29, 2009); Derek Briggs, report from the Cheltenham Jazz Festival, 2009 (quotation from this review at henrygrimes.com/press/).

90   flavorwire.com/category/music; Dvorkin, 'Exclusive: Amiri Baraka and Henry Grimes' Idea of Rhythm' (see chapter 6, note 69). Audio recording: soundcloud.com/issueprojectroom/play-that-amiri-baraka-henry (viewed: January 4, 2015).

91   Fred Anderson, *21st Century Chase: 80th Birthday Bash, Live at the Velvet Lounge,* Delmark DVD 1589 (2009).

92   Neil Tesser, 'Two tenors, a rhythm section, an enthusiastic audience – the essential ingredients of a jazz tradition', liner notes for ibid.

93   Ibid.

94   Henry Grimes and Rashied Ali, *Spirits Aloft* (see note 18), with drawings by Henry Grimes inside the CD case.

95   See henrygrimes.com/store/.

96   Marc Medwin, Liner notes for *Spirits Aloft* (see note 18).

97   The full wording of Grimes' funeral address is printed in the CD booklet for *Spirits Aloft* (see note 18).

98   Paul J. Youngman, jazzreview.com/cd-reviews/free-jazz-avante-garde-cd-reviews/spirits-aloft.html (published September 8, 2011; viewed: January 3, 2015).

99   Phil Freeman, allmusic.com/album/spirits-aloft-mw0002029550 (without date of publication). Concert announcement in Dove, 'Whatever happened to Henry Grimes?' (see note 25). Another review in Marc Medwin, 'Playing the vibrations' (see chapter 1, note 3), p. 20.

100 The following musicians contributed to this event: Marshall Allen, Charles Burnham, Connie Crothers, Andrew Cyrille, Mark Dresser, Melanie Dyer, Richard Fairfax, Ken Filiano, Craig Harris, Max Johnson, Edward 'Kidd' Jordan, J.T. Lewis, Marc Medwin, Mixashawn (Lee Rozie), Zim Ngqawana,

Kevin Norton, Pat O'Leary, Marc Ribot, Scott Robinson, Tyshawn Sorey, Carmen Staaf, Sublime Communication Trio (with Andrew Lamb and Newman Taylor Baker), Edwin Torres, Salim Washington, and Jeff 'Tain' Watts. Two video recordings from November 3 and 30 – *Let My People Go* together with Kidd Jordan and *Stone Communion* together with Zim Ngqawana and Andrew Cyrille – can be found at henrygrimes.com/videos/.

101 Gordon Marshall, 'Henry Grimes at The Stone: Alive at 75', allaboutjazz. com/php/article.php?id=38198&pg=1&&page=1 (published January 1, 2010).

102 This album had not been released at the time of editing this book (May 17, 2015).

103 Russ Musto, Concert review of February 17, 2011 @ Roulette: Roscoe Mitchell 70th Birthday Celebration, interpretations.info/reviews/#12.

104 This album had not been released at the time of editing this book (May 17, 2015).

105 *Purity*, Sony Music Argentina 8872 542082 2 (2012) with Henry Grimes (ldr, bs, vln), Roberto Pettinato (saxes), Dave Burrell (p), and Tyshawn Sorey (dm, percussion).

106 henrygrimes.com/videos/.

107 Not all the participating AACM musicians appear in the photograph. The photograph can be seen on Henry Grimes' facebook page, facebook.com/ HenryGrimes?fref=ts (viewed: May 17, 2015).

108 henrygrimes.com/videos/.

109 A letter sent to M. Davis Grimes by Ronit Berman, the conservatory's artistic director, expressing his thanks for the trio's inspiration and commitment, can be found at henrygrimes.com/press/.

110 Email by M. Davis Grimes, February 2014.

111 *Monk Mix* (House Foundation for the Arts, 2012). See also meredithmonk. org/media/monkmix-1.html (viewed: January 4, 2015).

112 Marc Ribot Trio, *Live At The Village Vanguard* (Henry Grimes, Marc Ribot, Chad Taylor) Pi Recordings, 2014; backstage photos can be found at npr. org/event/music/155441977/marc-ribot-trio-live-at-the-village-vanguard (viewed: January 4, 2015). See also Blumenfeld, 'Communion At The Temple' (see chapter 4, note 209).

113 All of Grimes' musical and poetic activities after December 31, 2012, can be followed at his website henrygrimes.com.

114 Blumenfeld, 'Communion At The Temple' (see chapter 4, note 209).

115 See henrygrimes.com/press/.

116 Further honors: Jez Nelson of BBC Radio ('Jazz on 3') chose the appearance of the Henry Grimes Quartet at the 2005 Vision Festival as one of the twelve best live broadcasts of the year; the duo concert of June 2, 2005, with Henry Grimes and Ted Curson was chosen as one of the best concerts of the year; *All About Jazz / New York* chose Marc Ribot's *Spiritual Unity* with Henry Grimes on bass as one of the best recordings of 2005; *Time Out Chicago* nominated Henry Grimes' *Spaceship on the Highway* Quartet with Marshall Allen, Fred Anderson, and Avreeayl Ra as one of the best

concerts of the year; in August 2006 Grimes reached twelfth place of the bassist category in the *Downbeat* Critics' Poll; in late 2006 *All About Jazz* placed the Cecil Taylor Trio with Henry Grimes and Pheeroan akLaff among the ten best concerts of the year, as did *Time Out New York* in late 2007. Further information about Henry Grimes' honors at henrygrimes. com

Chapter Nine

1   'Futurity' is the title of a collective improvisation from the live album Profound Sound Trio, *Opus de Life* (see chapter 8, note 6). Grimes gave the name to the tune the Trio played as an encore at the Vision Festival concert of 2008.

2   Parker, Liner notes for Henry Grimes Trio, *Live at the Kerava Jazz Festival* (see chapter 8, note 30).

3   Frenz, Grimes interviews 2006 and 2007 (see chapter 1, note 4).

4   Weiss, 'Interview Henry Grimes' (see chapter 1, note 10).

5   Frenz, Sonny Rollins interview 2007 (see chapter 3, note 3).

6   Frenz, Andrew Cyrille interview 2008 (see chapter 4, note 328). Music journalists characterize Henry Grimes in similar terms: 'consummate virtuosity and astounding musicianship in all styles, in and out from bop to free' (Dan Warburton, chief editor, *paristransatlantic.com*, 2005); 'Henry Grimes is a rare virtuoso without ostentation, an ideal ensemble player of countermelodies and aggressive rhythms, with a big, true sound' (John Litweiler, *Chicago Sun-Times*, 2005). Both quoted from henrygrimes.com/press/.

7   Simon Frith, ed., *Popular Music* (London: Routledge, 2004), p. 126. See also Thomas Kochman, *Rappin' and Stylin' out: Communication in Urban Black America*, (Univ. Illinois Press, 1972), p. 93.

8   David Borgo, *Sync or Swarm: Improvising Music in a Complex Age* (London: Continuum, 2005), p. 20.

9   Marc Medwin, 'Playing the vibrations' (see chapter 1, note 3).

10   See also Harrison, *A Jazz Retrospect* (see chapter 4, note 278), p. 112, relating to Ornette Coleman's violin improvisations.

11   When asked what he is thinking about when improvising, Sonny Rollins commonly replies, 'my mind is blank when I'm improvising.' See Victor L. Schermer, 'Sonny Rollins: Hardy Perennial', at allaboutjazz.com/php/article.php?id=23853#.UGCRNq64pIg (published November 28, 2006).

12   See Gilles Deleuze and Félix Guattari, *Capitalisme et Schizophrénie*, 2 vols. (Paris, 1972-1980); Eng. trans. as *Capitalism and Schizophrenia* (London and New York, 1977-87).

13   George E. Lewis, 'When improvisers speak, where do their words go?', foreword to Renate Da Rin, ed., *Silent Solos – Improvisers Speak* (Cologne, 2010), p. 11. See also Daniel Fischlin and Ajay Heble, eds., *The Other Side Of Nowhere: Jazz, improvisation, and communities in dialogue* (Middletown, CT:

Wesleyan University Press, 2004); Wolfram Knauer, ed., *Improvisieren...*, Darmstädter Beiträge zur Jazzforschung 8 (Hofheim: Wolke, 2004).

14   Medwin, 'Playing the vibrations' (see chapter 1, note 3), p. 20.

15   Mizar5, Interview with Henry Grimes (2005) (see chapter 6, note 80).

16   Frenz, Grimes interviews 2006 and 2007 (see chapter 1, note 4).

17   Quoted from Barry Davis, 'The prodigal bass player returns' (see chapter 2, note 27).

18   Quoted from Mandel, 'Out Of The Woodwork'(see chapter 6, note 13).

19   See p. 173f above on Marc Ribot's musical experiences with and thoughts about Grimes.

20   Frank Tafuri, Interview with Michael Bisio, omnitone.com/undulations/bisio-interview.htm (2011).

21   Young, Liner notes for *Live at the Kerava Jazz Festival* (see chapter 8, note 30).

22   Henry Grimes, quoted from Mandel, 'Out Of The Woodwork' (see chapter 6, note 13).

23   See chapter 151ff above.

24   Frenz, Grimes interviews 2006 and 2007 (see chapter 1, note 4). Manfred Miller, in his New Thing analysis of 1966, adds: 'Up to now music has been perceived through anticipation. The listener approached the music from the pattern of particular expectations. [...] Departures from those expectations were seen as personal expression. [...] This manner of listening is impossible in the New Thing. There is no longer any pattern that makes anticipation possible. The listener must spontaneously and completely grasp what is happening in the music.' Manfred Miller, 'Free Jazz: Eine New Thing Analyse', *Jazz Podium* 15 (July 1966), pp. 182-84, quote on p. 184 (originally in German).

25   Frenz, Grimes interviews 2006 and 2007 (see chapter 1, note 4).

26   Ibid.

27   Ibid.

28   Ibid.

29   Dvorkin, 'Exclusive: Henry Grimes' emotional explosions' (see chapter 6, note 69).

30   Medwin, 'Playing the vibrations' (see chapter 1, note 3).

31   Frenz, Grimes interviews 2006 and 2007 (see chapter 1, note 4).

32   Ibid.

33   Medwin, 'Playing the vibrations' (see chapter 1, note 3).

34   Dvorkin, 'Exclusive: Henry Grimes' emotional explosions' (see chapter 6, note 69).

35   Frenz, Becton interview (see chapter 5, note 33).

36   Dvorkin, 'Exclusive: Henry Grimes' emotional explosions' (see chapter 6, note 69).

37   See chapter 214f above.

38   Mandel, 'Out Of The Woodwork' (see chapter 6, note 13).

39   Ibid.

40   See p. 223 above.

41   Graham, 'Marc Ribot Calls Upon The Holy Ghost' (see chapter 8, note 64).

42   Jung, 'Fireside Chat with Henry Grimes' (see chapter 1, note 7).

43   Medwin, 'Playing the vibrations' (see chapter 1, note 3).

44   Mandel, 'Out Of The Woodwork' (see chapter 6, note 13).

45   See p. 18 above.

46   Parker, Liner note for *Live at the Kerava Jazz Festival* (see chapter 8, note 30)

Back cover

For sources of quotes on the back cover, see henrygrimes.com/press/; Strauss, *Silent 30 Years* (see chapter 2, note 68); Frenz, Sonny Rollins interview 2007 (see chapter 3 note 3).

References

Unpublished

Barbara Frenz, *Interviews with Henry Grimes*, (New York City, December 2006 and January 2007)

Phone interview with Sonny Rollins, (January 9, 2007)

–, *Interview with Clarence Becton*, (Amsterdam, October 14, 2007)

–, *Interview with Andrew Cyrille*, (New York City, June 14, 2008, at the Vision Festival)

–, *Phone interview with Andrew Cyrille*, (August 8, 2008)

–, *Interviews with Henry Grimes*, New York City, (December 2009 and January 2010)

Henry Grimes, *Notebook* (dating roughly from 1979 to 1981)

Published

Audio, Video

Henry Cherry, *The Resurrection of Henry Grimes*, vimeo.com/69922806 (viewed: January 3, 2015) (video documentary)

Burton Greene: Bloom In The Commune ESP-Disk 4038 (2007) [interview-track 1]

Interview with Peter Kowald on *Rising Tones Cross: A Jazz Film* by Ebba Jahn, NYC 1984 (DVD 2005)

Jazz On A Summer's Day (Newport Festival 1958) by Bert Stern. Charly Films Release 2001, DVD

Print

Chris Abani, *Kalakuta Republic (London: Saqi, 2000)*

–, *Daphne's Lot* (Granada Hills, CA: Red Hen, 2003)

Glenn Astarita, 'Henry Grimes Trio, Live At the Kerava Jazz Festival / Marc Ribot, Spiritual Unity', *DownBeat* (September 2005), p. 77

Whitney Balliett, *The Sound of Surprise: 46 Pieces on Jazz*, (New York: E. P. Dutton, 1959)

Amiri Baraka (LeRoi Jones), 'Blues, Poetry, and the New Music', in idem and Amina Baraka, *The Music: Reflections on Jazz and Blues* (New York: Morrow, 1987), p. 262-267

– , 'Greenwich Village and African-American Music', in ibid., p.181-189

–, 'New Music / New Poetry', in ibid., p. 243-245

–, 'The Phenomenon of *Soul* in African-American Music', in ibid., p. 268-276

William R. Bauer, *Open The Door: The Life and Music of Betty Carter* (Ann Arbor, MI: University of Michigan Press, 2003)

Joachim E. Berendt berichtet vom Newport Jazz Festival, *Jazz Podium* 8, XIV 1965, p. 196-198

Daniel Berger, Review of Don Cherry's *Complete Communion*, *Jazz Hot* 224 (1966), p. 32

–, Review of Henry Grimes' *The Call*, *Jazz Hot* 228 (1967), p. 32

Paul Bley, David Lee, *Stopping Time: Paul Bley and the Transformation of Jazz*, (Montreal, Quebec: Vehicule Press, 1999)

Larry Blumenfeld, 'The Ballad of Henry Grimes (and other recent visions)', *Jazziz* 2003, 11, p. 34f.

Bob Blumenthal, Liner notes (2003) for Cecil Taylor: *Conquistador!*, Blue Note CD: 7243 5 90840 2 2 (2004)

Vladimir Bogdanov, Chris Woodstra, Stephen Thomas Erlewine, *All Music Guide: The Definite Guide to Popular Music*, (Backbeat Books, 2001)

David Borgo, *Sync or Swarm: Improvising Music in a Complex Age* (London: Continuum, 2005)

Gerard Bremond, 'Pour ou Contre: Le trio Sonny Rollins', *Jazz Hot* 142 (April 1959), p. 32

Christian Broecking, *Respekt!* (Berlin: Verbrecher Verlag, 2004)

–, 'Zurück am Bass nach dreißig Jahren', *Berliner Zeitung* (August 26, 2005)

–, *Black Codes* (Berlin: Verbrecher Verlag, 2005)

–, 'Community Talk 23. Special: Miles Today', *Jazz Thing* 64 (June-August 2006), p. 20

–, *Sonny Rollins, Improvisation und Protest: Interviews* (Berlin: Broecking, 2010)

Greg Burk, 'Henry Grimes Ensemble at the World Stage', *LA Weekly* (March 21, 2003), p. 44

–, 'Jazz Pick of the Week: Henry Grimes and Friends', *LA Weekly* (September 5-11, 2003), p. 127

Rex Butters, 'Henry Grimes Quartet at The Jazz Bakery 6.10.03', *All About Jazz* (July 2003), p. 16

–, 'Rob Brown/Henry Grimes Trio @ line space line 8.4.03', *All About Jazz* (September 2003), p. 13

–, 'Henry Grimes Band @ Rocco 8.9.03', *All About Jazz* (September 2003), p. 14

–, (see Fred Jung)

A.C., Review of Cecil Taylor's *Unit Structures*, *Jazz Hot* 23 1967/05, p. 7

Ian Carr, *Keith Jarrett. The Man and His Music* (Boston, MA: Da Capo Press, 1992)

Ron Carter (see John Goldsby)

Nick Catalano, *Clifford Brown: the life and art of the legendary jazz trumpeter* (Oxford University Press NY, 2000)

Daniel Caux, 'The Road To Freedom', interview conducted with Albert Ayler in Saint Paul de Vence, France, July 28, 1970, *The Wire* 1 (2003), pp. 39 41

Dom Cerulli, 'Theodore Walter Rollins: Sonny Believes He Can Accomplish Much More Than He Has To Date', *DownBeat* (July 10, 1958), pp. 16f

– (see Don Gold)

Abraham Chapman, *New Black Voices: An Anthology of Contemporary Afro-American Literature*, (New York: New American Library, 1972)

Hank Cherry, 'In heaven with Henry Grimes', *Artvoice* 9, no. 36 (September 9, 2010), pp. 20f. (download from: artvoice.com/issues/v9n36/issue_print)

Rebecca A. Clear, *Jazz on Film and Video in the Library of Congress*, (Darby, PA: Diane Publishing Co., 1993)

Ornette Coleman, Original Liner notes (1967) for *Don Cherry: Where Is Brooklyn?*, Blue Note CD 0946 3 11435 2 6 (2005)

Roger Cotterrell (see Coleridge Goode)

Noticias: 'El Regreso de Henry Grimes', *Cuadernos De Jazz* 2003, 07, p. 18

Michael Cuscuna, Liner notes for *Roy Haynes: Out Of The Afternoon*, 1962 (Blue Note, 1995)

Miles Davis and Quincy Troupe, *Miles: The Autobiography* (New York: Simon & Schuster Paperbacks, 2005, 1989)

Margaret Davis, Liner notes for *Henry Grimes, More Call*, Solo acoustic bass played on the air at WKCR 89.9 FM Sunday June 1, 2003, Mastered by Jeff Willems

Gilles Deleuze and Félix Guattari: *Capitalisme et Schizophrénie*, 2 vols. (Paris, 1972-1980); Eng. trans. as *Capitalism and Schizophrenia* (London and New York, 1977-87)

Aris Destombes, 'Pour ou Contre: Le trio Sonny Rollins', *Jazz Hot* 142 (April 1959), p. 33

Ralf Dombrowski, *John Coltrane: Sein Leben, seine Musik, seine Schallplatten* (Waakirchen: Oreos, 2002)

Henry Grimes in *Double Bassist* (Winter 2007)

'Sonny Rollins meets the Japanese Press', *DownBeat* (December 9, 1963), p. 16

Gudrun Endress, 'Cecil Taylor: Musik macht Freude', *Jazz Podium* 7, no. 15 (1966), pp. 176-79

–, Albert Ayler: We Play Peace!', *Jazz Podium* 10, no. 15 (1966), pp. 254 57

Wayne Enstice and Janice Stockhouse, *Jazzwomen: Conversations with Twenty-One Musicians* (Bloomington: Indiana University Pres, 2004)

James Farmer, *Lay Bare the Heart: An Autobiography of the Civil Rights Movement* (New York: Arbor House, 1985)

Daniel Fischlin and Ajay Heble, eds., *The Other Side Of Nowhere: Jazz, improvisation, and communities in dialogue* (Middletown, CT: Wesleyan University Press, 2004)

Michael Fitzgerald, 'Into Thin Air', *Signal To Noise* (winter 2003), pp. 40-44

Charles Fox, 'Review: McCoy Tyner, *Reaching Fourth* (Blue Note 1962)', *The Gramophone* 1964, 01, Vol. 41, no. 488, p. 346

Jean French, 'Taping the Artists. Sonny Rollins', *Abundant Sounds*, 2/3 (Jul.1964), p. 10-13 (I)

Barbara Frenz, Review of Andrew Cyrille (d), Paul Dunmall (ts, bagpipes), and Henry Grimes (b, vn), *Opus de Life*, Profound Sound Trio (Porter Records PRCD-4032, 2009), *Jazz Podium*, no. 58 (2009), p. 72

Simon Frith (ed.), *Popular Music: Critical Concepts in Media and Cultural Studies* (London: Routledge, 2004)

Stefano Galvani, 'Interview with Henry Grimes, French trans. by Guy Reynard', *Jazz Hot* (February 2004), pp. 17f.

Addison Gayle, *The Black Aesthetic* (New York: Doubleday, 1972)

Lynell George, 'A jazz mystery unravels: Henry Grimes, the Juilliard trained bassist who quietly walked away decades ago, is slowly reemerging', *Los Angeles Times* (March 21, 2003)

Jef Gilson and Claude Lénissois, 'Jazz Actualités: Free Jazz à l'Olympia avec Sonny Rollins', *Jazz Hot* (February 1963), pp. 6f.

Ira Gitler, 'Report From Newport', *DownBeat* (August 15, 1963), pp. 13-17

–, Review of Don Cherry's *Symphony For Improvisers*, *DownBeat* (November 30, 1967), p. 28

Don Gold and Dom Cerulli: 'Newport Jazz 1958', *DownBeat* (August 7, 1958), pp. 14-20 and 32f.

Burt Goldblatt, *Newport Jazz Festival: The Illustrated History* (New York: Dial Press, 1977)

John Goldsby and Ron Carter: *The Jazz Bass Book: Technique and Tradition* (San Francisco: Backbeat Books, 2002)

Coleridge Goode and Roger Cotterrell, *Bass Lines: A Life in Jazz* (London: Northway, 2002)

Burton Greene, 'Commentary on the new music', *Burton Greene: Bloom in the commune*, ESP Disk 4038 (2007) [liner notes]

– (see Dan Warburton)

Henry Grimes, *Signs Along The Road. Poems* (Cologne: buddy's knife jazz edition, edited by Renate Da Rin, 2007)

Félix Guattari (see Gilles Deleuze)

Andy Hamilton, *Lee Konitz: Conversations on the Improviser's Art* (Ann Arbor, MI: University of Michigan Press, 2007)

Max Harrison, Liner notes for Albert Ayler, *Spirits Rejoice!* (CD issue of 2006), originally pubd. in *Jazz Monthly* (January 1967)

–, *Modern Jazz. The Essential Records. A Critical Selection* (Aquarius Books, 1975)

–, *A Jazz Retrospect* (Boston: Crescendo, 1976)

Ajay Heble (see Daniel Fischlin)

Don Heckman, 'Roots, Culture & Economics: An Interview with Avant Garde Pianist Composer Andrew Hill', *DownBeat* (May 5, 1966), pp. 19 21

Andrey Henkin, 'Henry Grimes', *All About Jazz* 7 (2003), p. 16

Nat Hentoff, Original liner notes to *We Insist! Max Roach and Oscar Brown, Jr.'s Freedom Now Suite* (Candid, 1960)

–, Original Liner notes (1965) for *Don Cherry: Complete Communion*, Blue Note CD 7243 5 22673 2 3 (2000)

–, 'The Persistent Challenge Of Cecil Taylor', *DownBeat* (February 25, 1965), pp. 17f. and 40

–, Original liner notes (1966) for Cecil Taylor: *Conquistador*, Blue Note CD: 7243 5 90840 2 2 (2004)

–, 'The Truth is Marching In', *DownBeat* (November 17 1966), pp. 16 19 and 40

–, Original liner notes for *Archie Shepp: On This Night*, Impulse! (1966)

–, Original liner notes (1967) for Pharoah Sanders: *Tauhid* GRP/Impulse! CD GRD-129 (1993)

Ashante Infantry, 'Jazz Master Henry Grimes Makes Up for Lost Time', *Toronto Star* (September 11, 2010)

Steven L. Isoardi, 'The Return of Henry Grimes: A Memoir, *Current Research in Jazz* 2 (2010, Chicago 15th ed.). Also available at www.crjonline.org/v2/CRJ HenryGrimes.php (viewed: January 3, 2015)

Gordon Jack, *Fifties Jazz Talk: An Oral Retrospective*, (Lanham, MD: Scarecrow Press, 2004)

Michael Jackson, 'Backstage with ...Henry Grimes', *DownBeat* (July, 2005), p. 14

'Qui êtes vous, Bernard Stollman?, Interview', *Jazz Hot* 230, no. 4 (1967), pp. 13 17

'Interview – Don Menza (tenor saxophonist, *1936)', *Jazz Improv Magazine* 8, no. 2 (2006)

Bassist Henry Grimes, Alive, *Jazz Times* (April 2003), p. 24

Grimes' Time. *Jazz Times* (January 2004), p. 62

Todd S. Jenkins, Sy Johnson, *I Know What I Know: The Music of Charles Mingus* (Westport, CT: Praeger, 2006)

Demètre Joakimidis, *Jazz Hot* 152 (March 1960), p. 60

Denise Jokinen, 'Débauche de musique aussi à Newport: Soixante Mille Spectateurs Au "Veteran" Des Grandes Festivals', *Jazz Hot* 135 (September 1958), pp. 13 15 and 35

LeRoi Jones (Amiri Baraka), 'Review: *McCoy Tyner, Reaching Fourth* (Blue Note, 1962)', *Kulchur* (1962), pp. 96f.

–, *Blues People* (New York: Morrow & Co., 1963)

–, 'New York City's lofts and coffee houses have become havens for the new thing', *DownBeat* (May 9, 1963), pp. 13 and 42

–, 'Voice From The Avant-Garde: Archie Shepp', *DownBeat* (January 14, 1965), pp. 18f. and 36

–, 'Apple Cores #1' [1964], in idem, *Black Music* (New York, 1968; repr. New York: Da Capo, 1998), p. 113-120

–, 'The Changing Same (R&B and New Black Music)', in ibid, p. 180-211

Patti Jones, *One Man's Blues: The Life And Music Of Mose Allison* (London: Quartet, 1995)

Ekkehard Jost, *Free Jazz* (New York: Da Capo Press, 1981, 1974)

Fred Jung and Rex Butters, Liner notes for the CD reissue of Albert Ayler, *Spirits Rejoice!* (ESP 2006)

Reclams Jazzlexikon, ed. Wolf Kampmann (Stuttgart: Reclam, 2004), p. 217

Robin D. G. Kelley, *Thelonious Monk, The Life and Times of an American Original* (New York: Free Press, 2009)

David Keenan, 'Henry Grimes & William Parker. Philadelphia University of Pennsylvania, USA', *The Wire* 04/2004, p. 90/1

Corey Kilgannon, 'An Unlikely Duo, Bound By Jazz', *New York Times: City Room* (April 16, 2009)

Sven-Erik Klinkmann, 'Synch/Unsync', in Orvar Löfgren and Richard Wilk (eds.), *Off The Edge. Experimants in Cultural Analysis* (Copenhagen: Museum Tusculanum Press, 2006), pp. 81-87

Wolfram Knauer, ed., *Improvisieren…*, *Darmstädter Beiträge zur Jazzforschung* 8 (Hofheim: Wolke, 2004)

–, Review of *Henry Grimes Solo*, ILK Music 151 CD (2009), *Jazz Podium* 2009/02, p. 62

Thomas Kochman, *Rappin' and Stylin' out: Communication in urban Black America* (Urbana, IL: University of Illinois Press, 1972)

Pannonica de Koenigswarter, *Three Wishes: An Intimate Look at Jazz Greats* (New York: Abrams, 2008)

Frank Kofsky, *Black Nationalism and the Revolution in Music* (New York: Pathfinder Press, 1970) [later retitled *John Coltrane and the Jazz Revolution of the 60s*]

Guy Kopelowicz, 'Autumn in New York: Voyage au Coeur de la New Thing: Un reportage de Guy Kopelowicz', *Jazz Hot* 214, no. 11 (1965), pp. 28-31

–, Liner notes for CD issue of Albert Ayler's *Spirits Rejoice!* (ESP, 2006)

Peter Kostakis, Liner notes (1993) for the CD *Steve Lacy: School Days: Live at Phase Two Coffee House, New York City, March 1963* (Hat Hut, 1994)

John Kruth, 'The Healing Force of the Universe: Albert Ayler's Life and Legacy (34 Years Hence)', *Signal To Noise* (winter 2005), also on: www.johnkruth.com/ayler.html

–, E.C.L., Review of Don Cherry's *Symphony For Improvisers*, *Jazz Hot* 240 (April 1968), p. 31

Jacob Larsen, Liner notes for *Sonny Rollins: 1959 Aix en Provence* (Jeal Records, Denmark, 1989)

Michel Le Bris, Review of Albert Ayler: In Greenwich Village, *Jazz Hot* 245, no. 12 (1968), p. 45

David Lee (see Paul Bley)

Claude Lénissois (see Jef Gilson)

George E. Lewis, 'When improvisers speak, where do their words go?', foreword to *Silent Solos – Improvisers Speak*, ed. Renate Da Rin (Cologne: buddy's knife jazz edition, ed. Renate Da Rin, 2010)

Charles Eric Lincoln, *The Black Muslims in America* (Trenton, New Jersey: Wm. B. Eerdmans Publishing Co., Grand Rapids, Michigan / Africa World Press Inc., 1994, 1961)

John Litweiler, *The Freedom Principle: Jazz after 1958* (New York: Morrow, 1990)

Leonard Lyons, *The 101 Best Jazz Albums: A History of Jazz on Records* (New York: Morrow, 1980)

Compton Mackenzie, Christopher Stone, *The Gramophone* (1963), p. 43

Howard Mandel, Liner notes (1987) for *The Perry Robinson 4*, 1962, CD release 1987

–, 'Out Of The Woodwork', *The Wire* (April 2008), pp. 26-29

Marshall Marrotte, 'Henry Grimes: The Signal To Noise Interview', *Signal To Noise* (2003), pp. 43-47 (the same interview, slightly abridged, appears in 'Surviving Albert Ayler', *The Wire* (January 2003), pp. 42f.)

Bill Mathieu, 'Review: Cecil Taylor, *Unit Structures* – Blue Note 4237', *DownBeat* (February 23, 1967), p. 31

–, 'Review: *Burton Greene, Quartet* – ESP Disk 1024', *DownBeat* (March, 1967), p. 40

Gus Matzorkis, 'Down Where We All Live: Today's Avant Garde Revolution As Seen In Light Of Jazz' Long History Of Internal Strife, Part II', *DownBeat* (April 21, 1966), pp. 17f.

Marian McPartland, 'Caught in The Act: John Bunch, Hickory House, New York City, Personnel: Bunch, piano; Henry Grimes, bass', *DownBeat* (January 5, 1961), p. 44

Barry McRae, Liner notes for CD reissue of *Goin' Home* (Black Lion and da music, 1994)

Marc Medwin, Liner notes for: Henry Grimes and Rashied Ali: *Going to the Ritual* (Porter Records #PRCD 4005, 2008

–, 'Playing the vibrations', *Signal To Noise* 58 (2010), pp. 12-19

Manfred Miller, 'Free Jazz: Eine New Thing Analyse', *Jazz Podium* 15 (July 1966), pp. 182-84

Ingrid Monson, *Freedom Sounds: Civil Rights Call Out to Jazz and Africa* (New York: Oxford University Press, 2007)

Dan Morgenstern, Liner notes for McCoy Tyner: *Reaching Fourth*, 1962 (Blue Note, 1998)

–, 'Caught In The Act: Cecil Taylor, Town Hall, NYC', *DownBeat* (July 28, 1966), p. 24

Sunny Murray (see Dan Warburton)

Philippe Nahman, Review of Henry Grimes' *The Call*, *Jazz Hot* 228, no. 2 (1967), p. 32

Don Nelsen, Review of Spirits Rejoice (ESP 1020), *DownBeat* (September 8, 1966), p. 28

Eric Nisenson, *Open Sky. Sonny Rollins and His World of Improvisation* (New York: Da Capo Press 2000)

Babatunde Olatunji, *The Beat Of My Drum. An Autobiography* (Philadelphia: Temple University Press 2005)

Adam Olschewski, *Frankfurter Rundschau*, May 03 2005 (column 'Times Mager' on Henry Grimes)

Hans-Jürgen von Osterhausen, 'Die ,wundersame Geschichte' des Henry Grimes', *Jazz Podium* (July 2005), pp. 11-13

–, '*Signs Along The Road* von Henry Grimes, *Who Owns Music* von William Parker', *Jazz Podium* (May 2007), p. 62

H.P., *DownBeat* (April 9, 1964), p. 29

Patricia Parker, ed., *Vision Festival: Peace* (2005)

Liner notes by William Parker and Ben Young for H*enry Grimes Trio: Henry Grimes, Hamid Drake, David Murray: Live At The Kerava Jazz Festival* (Ayler Records 2005)

Carol Pearce Bjorlie, Review of *Signs Along The Road* in *Bass World: Magazine of the International Society of Bassists* (summer 2009)

Harvey Pekar, Review of Archie Shepp, *On This Night* – Impulse! 97, *DownBeat* (July, 1966), p. 32

Thierry Pérémarti, 'At Home with Henry Grimes', *Jazzman* (2003), no. 6, p. 20

François Postif, 'Albert Ayler – Le Magicien', *Jazz Hot* 213, no. 10 (1965), pp. 20-22

Edwin Pouncey, '*Signs Along The Road: Poems*: Henry Grimes – *Who Owns Music?* William Parker', *The Wire* (August 2007), p. 71

Brian Priestley, *Mingus. A Critical Biography* (New York: Da Capo Press, 1984), p. 273

Bill Quinn, Review of 'Sunny Murray, *Sunny's Time Now* – Jihad 66', *DownBeat* (March 23, 1967), p. 33

–, 'Four Modernists', *DownBeat* (June 13, 1968), pp. 28f.

Dudley Randall, ed., *The Black Poets: A New Anthology* (New York: Bantam, n.d.)

Arne Reimer, 'Henry Grimes, Eine völlig neue Musikwelt', *American Jazz Heroes. Besuche bei 50 Jazz-Legenden* (Cologne: Jazz Thing Verlag Axel Stinshoff, 2013), pp. 138-141

Marc Ribot, Liner notes for Marc Ribot, Roy Campbell, Jr., Henry Grimes, Chad Taylor: *Spiritual Unity* (Pi Recordings CD #15, 2005)

–, 'still things – that / move: The Poetry of Henry Grimes', Preface to Henry Grimes, *Signs Along The road: Poems* (Cologne: Buddy's Knife Jazz Edition, ed. Renate Da Rin, 2007), pp. 15-21

Laurent Rigaut, 'Henry Grimes Trio, Salle Charcot, Marcq en Baroeul, 7 Octobre 2005: Une belle date', *Impro Jazz* (November-December 2005), p. 26

Matias Rinar, Liner notes for *Sonny Rollins Quintet: Tokyo 1963* (RLR Records, 2008)

Perry Robinson (see Florence Wetzel)

David H. Rosenthal, *Hard Bop: Jazz and Black Music. 1955 –1965* (Oxford University Press, 1992)

Gerard Rouy, 'Un Revenant Nommé: Henry Grimes', *Jazz Magazine* 2004/11, pp. 26-29

W. Royal Stokes, *The Jazz Scene: An Informal History from New Orleans to 1990*, (Oxford University Press, 1993)

Bob Rusch, 'Buell Neidlinger: Interview', *Cadence* (June 1986), pp. 5-21 and 66

William Russo, 'Review: Don Cherry, Complete Communion – Blue Note 4226', *DownBeat* (July 28, 1966), p. 27

Gene Santoro, *Dancing in Your Head: Jazz, Blues, Rock, and Beyond* (Oxford Univ. Press, 1994), p. 239

Bill Shoemaker, 'Henry Grimes Trio. Open Windows – Music with a View, Vienna 25 September 2004', *Jazz Review* (October 2004), p. 7

A.B. Spellman, *Four Lives in the Bebop Business* (New York: Pantheon Books, 1966) [later retitled *Black Music: Four Lives*]

Sam Stephenson, ed., *The Jazz Loft Project* (New York: Knopf, 2009)

Janice Stockhouse (see Wayne Enstice)

Cecil Taylor, Liner notes for *Unit Structures: Cecil Taylor*, 1966 (Blue Note CD: CDP 7 84237 2, 1987)

Neil Tesser, 'Two tenors, a rhythm section, an enthusiastic audience – the essential ingredients of a jazz tradition', liner notes for Fred Anderson, *21st Century Chase: 80th Birthday Bash, Live at the Velvet Lounge* (Delmark DVD 1589, 2009)

Dean Tuder, Nancy Tuder, *Jazz* (Littleton, Colorado: Libraries Unlimited, 1979)

John A. Tynan, *DownBeat* (September 4, 1958), pp. 28f. and 29f.

Elisabeth van der Mei, *Coda* 1966/06, p. 23

Eric T. Vogel, 'Newport Rückblick', *Jazz Podium* (August 9, 1958), pp. 181f.

–, 'Die Sensation von Newport: Das Jazzfestival 1958 – 60.000 Besucher – Vom Duke bis Satchmo – Fergusons Wunderband: Sonderbericht unseres USA-Korrespondenten ETV', *Jazz Podium* (August 1958), pp. 157 60

Jason Weiss, *Steve Lacy: Conversations* (Durham, NC: Duke University Press, 2006)

–, *Always in Trouble: An Oral History of ESP-Disk', the Most Outrageous Record Label in America* (Middletown, CT: Wesleyan University Press, 2012)

Ken Weiss, 'Interview Henry Grimes (July 12, 2003, New York City), *Cadence* 2004/09, pp. 5-10

Pete Welding, Review of Albert Ayler: In Greenwich Village, *DownBeat* (July 11, 1968), p. 28

Lars Westin, Liner notes for the CD *St. Thomas: Sonny Rollins Trio in Stockholm 1959* (Dragon Records, 1993)

Perry Robinson and Florence Wetzel, *The Traveller* (San José et al.: Writers Club Press, 2002)

Weusi, Original LP liner notes (1966) for *Sonny Murray: Sonny's Time Now*, DIW CD DIW 355

Val Wilmer, *As Serious As Your Life. The Story of The New Jazz* (London: Pluto Press, 1977, 2nd edition 1987)

–, Letter to the editor, *The Wire* 228 (February 2003), p. 6

Peter Niklas Wilson, *Sonny Rollins: Sein Leben, seine Musik, seine Schallplatten* (Schaftlach: Oreos, 1991)

–, *Spirits Rejoice! Albert Ayler und seine Botschaft* (Hofheim: Wolke, 1996)

–, *Sonny Rollins: The Definitive Musical Guide* (Berkeley, CA: Berkeley Hills Books, 2001)

Henry Woodfin, 'Whither Albert Ayler?', *DownBeat* (November 17, 1966), p. 19

Wu Ming 1, 'The Old New Thing Is Newer Than Ever', liner notes for *The Old New Thing: A Free Jazz Anthology*, Abraxas/Esp-Disk (2007)

Scott Yanow, *Jazz on Record: The First Sixty Years* (San Francisco: Backbeat Books, 2003), pp. 557f.

Ben Young, Liner notes for *Live at the Kerava Jazz Festival* (see William Parker)

– (ed.), *Albert Ayler: Holy Ghost, Rare & Unissued Recordings (1962 70)*, 9 CD Spirit Box including booklet (Revenantrecords, 2004)

Dieter Zimmerle, 'Alleingang und Team: Rollins und die Silver Truppe', *Jazz Podium* 4, no 8 (1959), p. 86

–, 'Der neue alte Rollins', *Jazz Podium* 2, no. 12 (1963), p. 29

Web

Glenn Astarita, Review of Henry Grimes and Rashied Ali: *Going to the Ritual* (Porter Records #PRCD 4005, 2008), www.allaboutjazz.com/php/article.php?id=31710 (published January 27, 2009; viewed: January 3, 2015)

Profile Henry Grimes (2005), www.allaboutjazz.com/php/musician.php?id =1284 (viewed: 2009)

Peter Bacon, Review From Cheltenham: The Profound Sound Trio, thejazzbreakfast.com/2009/05/02/from-cheltenham-the-profound-sound-trio/ (published May 2, 2009; viewed: January 3, 2015)

–, Concert Review: *Profound Sound Trio, CBSO Centre Birmingham, UK, November 28 2009*, thejazzbreakfast.com/2009/11/29/concert-review-profound-sound-trio (published November 29, 2009; viewed: January 3, 2015)

Larry Blumenfeld, 'Communion At The Temple', review of the Marc Ribot Trio with Henry Grimes and Chad Taylor at the Village Vanguard, New York, June 26 to July 1, 2012, www.jazziz.com/pageflip/bobwillough-byfall2012/files/42.html (viewed: January 3, 2015)

–, 'Intimate Encounters at June's Jazz Fests', Village Voice (July 18, 2012), www.villagevoice.com/2012-07-18/music/intimate-encounters-at-june-s-jazz-fests (viewed: January 3, 2015)

Felix Contreras, 'A Fresh Start for Jazzman Henry Grimes' (April 21, 2005), www.npr.org/templates/archives/archive.php?thingId=4607354&startNum=3&pageNum=5 (scroll down; viewed: January 3, 2015)

Barry Davis, 'The prodigal bass player returns', *Jerusalem Post* (February 17, 2012), www.jpost.com/ArtsAndCulture/Music/Article.aspx?id=258100 (viewed: January 3, 2015)

Margaret Davis Grimes, 'Henry Grimes & Olive Oil' (as of August 2003), henryGrimes.com/biography/ (scroll down; viewed: January 3, 2015)

–, 'The Miraculous Return of the Great Henry Grimes!' henryGrimes. com/biography/ (scroll down; viewed: January 3, 2015)

Raul d'Gama Rose, Review of Roswell Rudd, *Trombone Tribe* (Sunnyside SSC 1207, 2009), www.allaboutjazz.com/php/article.php?id=32682 (published May 1, 2009; viewed: January 3, 2015)

Pheralyn Dove, 'Whatever happened to Henry Grimes?', *Philadelphia Tribune* (February 2009), tinyurl.com/ccqzjt (viewed: 2009)

Eli Dvorkin, 'Exclusive: Henry Grimes' emotional explosions', flavorwire.com/13361/exclusive-henry-Grimes-emotional-explosions (published March 10, 2009; viewed: January 3, 2015)

Michael Fitzgerald, Henry Grimes Discography, 2015, first pubd. November 1994,www.jazzdiscography.com/Artists/Grimes/hg-disc.htm (viewed: January 3, 2015)

–, 'Henry Grimes, Past & Present: A story in two parts. Part 1: A Lost Giant Found', henryGrimes.com/biography/ (published 2003; scroll down; viewed: January 3, 2015)

David Francis, 'Metaphysical Free: The Poetry of Henry Grimes', www.cosmoetica.com/B813-DF1.htm (published May 28, 2009; viewed: January 3, 2015)

Phil Freeman, Review: Henry Grimes and Rashied Ali, *Spirits Aloft* (Porter Records PRCD-4049, 2010), www.allmusic.com/album/spirits-aloft-mw0002029550 (viewed: January 3, 2015)

Barbara Frenz, 'Signs Along The Road, or Conversing with Silent Powers. The legendary bass player Henry Grimes publishes his first volume of poems', www.jazzitalia.net/viscomunicatoemb.asp?EN=1&ID=3320 (published 2007; viewed: January 3, 2015)

Daniel Graham, 'Henry Grimes, Sunny Murray and David Murray at the Haarlem Jazzstad', www.allaboutjazz.com/php/article.php?id=22859 (published August 27, 2006; viewed: January 3, 2015)

–, 'Henry Grimes at the London Jazz Festival 2006', www.allaboutjazz. com/php/article.php?id=23775 (published November 14, 2006; viewed: January 3, 2015)

–, Review of The Profound Sound Trio At The Vortex Jazz Club, London, November 23 2009,www.allaboutjazz.com/php/article.php?id=34872&width=1024#.UwjN4sFxt3s (published December 11, 2009; viewed: January 3, 2015)

–, Review of Marc Ribot Trio: London, England, October 28 2011, www.allaboutjazz.com/php/article.php?id=40897 (published November 26, 2011; viewed: January 3, 2015)

Stephen Graham, 'Jazz breaking news: Marc Ribot Calls Upon The Holy Ghost', jazzwisemagazine.com/news-mainmenu-139/68-2011/12104-jazz-breaking-news-marc-ribot-trio-calls-upon-the-holy-ghost-at-city-sessions (published October 31, 2011; viewed: 2011)

Biography Henry Grimes, henryGrimes.com/biography/ (viewed: January 3, 2015)

Andrey Henkin, Review of Henry Grimes Trio: Henry Grimes, Hamid Drake, David Murray: Live At The Kerava Jazz Festival (Ayler Records, 2005), viewed: January 3, 2015)

Mike Hobart, 'A jazz bassist is back in action' (December 5, 2009), www.ft.com/cms/s/2/1e010160-e05a-11de-8494-00144feab49a.html (with registration; viewed: January 3, 2015; printout kindly supplied by Margaret Davis Grimes)

Jeph Jerman, Review of Henry Grimes and Rashied Ali: *Going to the Ritual* (Porter Records #PRCD 4005, 2008), www.squidsear.com/cgi-bin/news/newsView.cgi?newsID=1112 (published February 2, 2010; viewed: January 3, 2015)

Fred Jung, 'A fireside chat with William Parker', www.allaboutjazz.com/a-fireside-chat-with-william-parker-william-parker-by-aaj-staff.php?width=1024 (published: May 16, 2003; viewed: January 3, 2015)

–, 'A Fireside Chat with Henry Grimes',www.allaboutjazz.com/a-fireside-chat-with-henry-Grimes-henry-Grimes-by-aaj-staff.php?width=1024 (published: November 13, 2003; viewed: January 3, 2015)

Jonathan Kantor, 'Interview with Henry Grimes', Blue Note, New York, May 10, 2007, bluenotenyc.blogspot.com/2007/07/interview-with-henry-grimes-henry.html (viewed: January 3, 2015)

Dr. Martin Luther King, Jr., 'On the Importance of Jazz: Opening Address to the 1964 Berlin Jazz Festival'. Full text: www.hartford-hwp.com/archives/45a/626.html (viewed: January 3, 2015)

Charles L. Latimer, 'Improv The Grimy Way', metrotimes.com/blog/musicblahg.asp?month=11&year=2006 (published 2006; viewed: 2009)

Gordon Marshall, 'Henry Grimes at The Stone: Alive at 75', www.allaboutjazz.com/php/article.php?id=38198&pg=1&&page=1 (published January 1, 2010; viewed: January 3, 2015)

Medjuck, www.organissimo.org/forum/index.php?showtopic=44978 (posted 18 July 2008; viewed: January 3, 2015)

Marc Medwin, Review of Henry Grimes and Oluyemi Thomas, *The Power of Light* (NotTwo Records #MW 787-2, 2007), www.dustedmagazine.com/reviews/3899 (published October 19, 2007; viewed: January 3, 2015)

Mizar5, Interview with Henry Grimes (2005), www.writingaffairs.com/mizar5/hg.html (viewed: January 3, 2015)

Russ Musto, Concert review of: February 17, 2011 @ Roulette: Roscoe Mitchell 70th Birthday Celebration, www.interpretations.info/reviews/#12 (viewed: January 3, 2015)

Mitch Myers, Henry Grimes Solo, jazztimes.com/articles/24423-solo-henry-Grimes (published: April 2009; viewed. January 3, 2015)

Paul Olson, 'Interview with Marc Ribot: That's the Way I View It From New York', www.allaboutjazz.com/marc-ribot-thats-the-way-i-view-it-from-new-york-marc-ribot-by-paul-olson.php?width=1024 (published March 27, 2006; viewed: January 3, 2015)

Ssirus W. Pakzad, www.jazzthing.de/issues/60/henry-Grimes.shtml (published: 2005; viewed: 2009)

–, 'Wiederauferstehung: Der Bassist Henry Grimes', www.jazzzeitung.de/jazz/2005/06/portrait-Grimes.shtml (published: 2005; viewed: January 3, 2015)

'Ted Panken Interviews Sam Rivers (WKCR-FM New York, September 25, 1997)', www.jazzhouse.org/library/?read=panken20 (published: 1999; viewed: January 3, 2015)

Nicholas Payton, 'An Open Letter To My Dissenters on Why Jazz Isn't Cool Anymore', nicholaspayton.wordpress.com/2011/12/02/1319/ (viewed: January 3, 2015)

Nilan Perera, Review of *Henry Grimes Solo*, exclaim.ca/Reviews/ImprovAndAvantGarde/henry_Grimes-solo (published: July 21, 2009; viewed: January 3, 2015)

Bret Primack, Phone interview with Henry Grimes (audio file, 2005, downloaded in 2005 from sonnyrollins.com)

Dominique Queillée, Grimes, Le Revenant, www.liberation.fr/cahier-special/2004/06/05/grimes-le-revenant_482071 (viewed: April 13, 2015)

Jean Paul Ricard, 'Interview: Denis Charles, Last Words of an Outlaw', *Jazz Magazine* no. 481 (Paris, May 1998), www.denischarles.com/JazzMagazine.html (viewed: January 3, 2015)

Victor L. Schermer, 'Sonny Rollins: Hardy Perennial', at www.allaboutjazz.com/php/article.php?id=23853#.UGCRNq64pIg (published November 28, 2006; viewed: January 3, 2015)

Jeff Schwartz, Albert Ayler: His Life and Music, www.reocities.com/jeff_l_schwartz/ayler.html (viewed: January 3, 2015)

John Sharpe, Henry Grimes Twofer: The Power Of Light & Going To The Ritual,www.allaboutjazz.com/php/article.php?id=29412 (published June 8, 2008; viewed: January 3, 2015)

–, Review of Henry Grimes, Paul Dunmall & Andrew Cyrille: The Profound Sound Trio At The Vortex, London, November 23 2009, www.allaboutjazz.com/php/article.php?id=34875&width=1024#.UwjPt8Fxt3s (published December 12, 2009; viewed: January 3, 2015)

Neil Strauss, 'Silent 30 Years, a Jazzman Resurfaces', *New York Times* (May 26, 2003), query.nytimes.com/gst/fullpage.html?res=9C04EFD812 31F935 A15756C0A9659C8B63 (viewed: January 3, 2015)

Frank Tafuri, Interview with Michael Bisio, www.omnitone.com/undulations/bisio-interview.htm (published 2011; viewed: January 3, 2015)

Ryan Vaillancourt [staff writer of *Los Angeles Downtown News*], 'From Blight to Bright: Remaking the Huntington Hotel', www.ladowntownnews.com/news/from-blight-to-bright-remaking-the-huntington-hotel/article_97b9d020-00e9-11e1-a1dc-001cc4c03286.html (published: October 28, 2011; viewed: January 3, 2015)

Dan Warburton, Interview with Sunny Murray, Paris, November 3, 2000, www.paristransatlantic.com/magazine/interviews/murray.html (viewed: 2009)

–, Interview with Burton Greene, Amsterdam, December 22, 2003, www.paristransatlantic.com/magazine/interviews/greene.html (viewed: January 3, 2015)

Wilmer Wise, Interview with the Jazz Museum in Harlem ('Harlem Speaks', August 9, 2007), www.jazzmuseuminharlem.org/photos80.html (viewed: 2009)

Paul J. Youngman, Review of Henry Grimes and Rashied Ali, *Spirits Aloft* (Porter Records PRCD-4049, 2010), www.jazzreview.com/cd-reviews/free-jazz-avante-garde-cd-reviews/spirits-aloft.html (published September 8, 2011; viewed: January 3, 2015)

Index

Other books by Barbara Frenz

Poems:

Als sie so vor ihm stand in ihrer grünen Cordjacke. Gedichte. Mit
Zeichnungen von Thomas Rösch. (Passagen Verlag, Wien 2010).

Am blauschwarzen Rand des Tages. Gedichte. (Deutscher Lyrik
Verlag, Imprint Karin Fischer Verlag, Aachen 2006).

History:

Frieden, Rechtsbruch und Sanktion in deutschen Städten vor
1300: Mit einer tabellarischen Quellenübersicht nach Delikten
und Deliktgruppen. Mit einem Vorwort von Gerhard Dilcher.
(Konflikt, Verbrechen und Sanktion in der Gesellschaft
Alteuropas, ed. Klaus Lüderssen, Klaus Schreiner, Rolf Sprandel,
Dietmar Willoweit. Symposien und Synthesen 8) Böhlau-Verlag,
Köln/Weimar/Wien 2003.

Gleichheitsdenken in deutschen Städten des 12. bis 15. Jahrhun-
derts. Geistesgeschichte, Quellensprache, Gesellschaftsfunktion.
(Städteforschung. Veröffentlichungen des Instituts für
vergleichende Städtegeschichte in Münster, ed. Peter Johanek,
Reihe A: Darstellungen, Bd. 52) Böhlau-Verlag,
Köln/Weimar/Wien 2000.

See also *www.barbara-frenz.com*

Jazz books from Northway

Available from

www.northwaybooks.com

or http://inpressbooks.co.uk/

distributed by www.centralbooks.com

Jazz books from Northway

Graham Collier,
The Jazz Composer – Moving Music off the Paper

Derek Ansell,
Workout: The Music of Hank Mobley

Derek Ansell,
Sugar Free Saxophone: The Life and Music of Jackie McLean

Coleridge Goode and Roger Cotterrell,
Bass Lines: A Life in Jazz

Mike Hennessey,
The Little Giant – The Story of Johnny Griffin

Alan Robertson,
Joe Harriott – Fire in His Soul

Ian Carr,
Music Outside: Contemporary Jazz in Britain

Peter Vacher,
Soloists and Sidemen: American Jazz Stories

Jim Godbolt,
A History of Jazz in Britain 1919–50

Ronnie Scott with Mike Hennessey,

Some of My Best Friends Are Blues

Chris Searle,

Forward Groove:

Jazz and the Real World from Louis Armstrong to Gilad Atzmon.

Alan Plater,

Doggin' Around

Leslie Thompson with Jeffrey Green,

Swing from a Small Island

Jim Godbolt,

All This and Many a Dog

John Chilton,

Hot Jazz, Warm Feet

Vic Ash,

I Blew It My Way: Bebop, Big Bands and Sinatra

Digby Fairweather,

Notes from a Jazz Life

Ron Brown with Digby Fairweather,

Nat Gonella – A Life in Jazz

www.northwaybooks.com